MASTERPIECES OF T W9-ADI-889

A NINE VOLUME SET EDITED BY ROBERT W. CORRIGAN

CENTRAL EUROPEAN THEATRE / *The Game of Love* and
La Ronde Schnitzler / *Electra* Hofmannsthal / *R.U.R.* Čapek /
The Play's the Thing Molnár

ENGLISH THEATRE / *The Importance of Being Earnest* Wilde /
Major Barbara Shaw / *Loyalties* Galsworthy / *Dear Brutus* Barrie /
Enter Solly Gold Kops

FRENCH THEATRE / *The Parisian Woman* Becque / *Christo-
pher Columbus* de Ghelderode / *Electra* Giraudoux / *Eurydice
(Legend of Lovers)* Anouilh / *Queen After Death* Montherlant /
Improvisation or The Shepherd's Chameleon Ionesco

GERMAN THEATRE / *Woyzeck* Buechner / *Maria Magdalena*
Hebbel / *The Weavers* Hauptmann / *The Marquis of Keith*
Wedekind / *The Caucasian Chalk Circle* Brecht

IRISH THEATRE / *The Countess Cathleen* Yeats / *The Playboy
of the Western World* and *Riders to the Sea* Synge / *The Silver
Tassie* and *Cock-a-Doodle Dandy* O'Casey

ITALIAN THEATRE / *Six Characters in Search of an Author*
and *The Pleasure of Honesty* Pirandello / *Crime on Goat Island*
Betti / *Filumena Marturano* Filippo / *The Academy* and *The
Return* Fratti

RUSSIAN THEATRE / *A Month in the Country* Turgenev /
Uncle Vanya and *The Cherry Orchard* Chekhov / *The Lower
Depths* Gorky / *The Bedbug* Mayakovsky

SCANDINAVIAN THEATRE / *Hedda Gabler* Ibsen / *Miss
Julie* and *The Ghost Sonata* Strindberg / *The Difficult Hour*
Lagerkvist / *The Defeat* Grieg / *Anna Sophie Hedvig* Abell

SPANISH THEATRE / *The Witches' Sabbath* Benavente / *The
Cradle Song* Martínez-Sierra / *The Love of Don Perlimplín and
Belisa in the Garden* Lorca / *The Dream Weaver* Buero Vallejo /
Death Thrust Sastre

MASTERPIECES OF THE MODERN FRENCH THEATRE

Edited by ROBERT W. CORRIGAN

SIX PLAYS

THE PARISIAN WOMAN

CHRISTOPHER COLUMBUS

ELECTRA

EURYDICE (LEGEND OF LOVERS)

QUEEN AFTER DEATH

IMPROVISATION or THE SHEPHERD'S CHAMELEON

COLLIER BOOKS, *NEW YORK*

CONTENTS

CONTENTS

AVANT-GARDISM IN THE CLASSICAL EMBRACE

by Robert W. Corrigan

IF the German and Scandinavian dramatists (Kleist, Buechner, Hebbel, Ibsen, Strindberg, Hauptmann, and Wedekind)
were the major innovators during the nineteenth century, certainly the French have produced the most consistently avant-
garde theatre of the twentieth. Beginning with "*merde*," the
tradition-shattering opening line of Alfred Jarry's *Ubu Roi*
(1896), the playwrights of France have been stretching the
frontiers of theatrical expression ever since. After Jarry came
the symbolist experiments of Paul Fort and Lugné-Poe at the
Théâtre d'Art and the *Théâtre de l'Oeuvre;* in 1917 Apollinaire's *Les Mamelles de Tirésias,* a play so daring that the
hysterical ravings of the German expressionists seem dully
middle-class by comparison, was produced; in the 1920's both
Jean-Jacques Bernard's "Theatre of Silence" and Jean Cocteau
emerged as major influences; in the 'thirties it was Giraudoux
and Antonin Artaud; as the Second World War was coming
to a close and the theatre came up from the underground, it
was Sartre and Camus who led the way; when disillusionment
and despair set in, Beckett, Ionesco, and Adamov created the
"Theatre of the Absurd," only to be followed by the more
apocalyptic writers, Genet and Ghelderode (who had written
earlier in Belgium, but was first recognized in France in 1949
with the production of his *Chronicles of Hell*); and now
today, in the mid-1960's, the epic–symbolistic techniques of
Georges Schehadé, François Billetdoux, and David Guerdon
seem to be setting the theatre's newest trend. This catalogue,
albeit sketchy and oversimplified, is ample evidence that artists
of the French Theatre have been among the most significant
pioneers of the twentieth-century Theatre.

However—and almost paradoxically—the vitality and daring of these men is in large measure due not so much to a

[7]

spirit of rebellion as it is to the strong sense of tradition which
has dominated the French Theatre since the days of Louis
XIV. There has always been an "establishment" in the French
Theatre (the *Comédie Française*), and a strong sense that
the past must be kept alive in the present—hence the policy
of alternating classical and modern productions in most of the
major theatres. But the hand of tradition in the French
Theatre has not, for the most part, been a heavy one. Because
the French believe that tradition—the passing on of values
and past achievements—is as much a matter of the future as
it is of the past, they are convinced that the great masterpieces of the seventeenth and eighteenth centuries must be
blended with the most significant accomplishments of contemporary artists. For this reason the establishment gradually,
but inevitably, subsumes or incorporates all avant-garde movements. This process, while it may destroy the rebelliousness
of the individual playwright, also makes the spirit of revolt
a continuing necessity and tends to keep it alive.

There is another reason why this deeply embedded sense
of tradition has been a source of continuing vitality in the
French Theatre. This theatre is unique—at least in our century—in that it encourages major writers of every form to
write for it. Most of the major French novelists have written
successful plays; the same is true of many of the poets. The
reverse is equally true of playwrights. One need only mention
a dozen names—Apollinaire, Gide, Cocteau, Romains, Giraudoux, Claudel, Sartre, Camus, Montherlant, Beckett, Genet,
and Julien Green—to see how apparent this fact is. This
phenomenon has tended to keep the theatre in the center of
French artistic life, with the result that it has never ceased
to continue growing.

Finally, the tradition has been responsible for maintaining
the steady stream of great directors and actors who have kept
the theatre alive (even when it was in the doldrums) and who
have also provided a climate of stimulation which has
prompted writers to new heights through new dramatic forms.
Antonine, the already-mentioned Fort and Lugné-Poe, were
the first of such men. Then came Jacques Copeau, who at
his *Vieux Colombier* set the esthetic and production standards
which still dominate the French "new" theatre. In the 1920's,
the Grand Cartel of Four was established. Composed of
Charles Dullin, Louis Jouvet, Gaston Baty, and Georges
Pitoëff, the Cartel controlled the French Theatre for more

than twenty-five years. And now, today, we have Jean Vilar, Roger Blin, and Roger Planchon who are encouraging the new rebels. And through all the years there have been the great actors who have not only made the theatre exciting, but have also maintained a well-trained audience which is both willing and able to accept the wildest kind of theatrical experience.

However, the most significant characteristic of the French Theatre is that it is, and always has been, essentially a classic theatre. Even its most extreme avant-garde playwrights have classic aims. Ionesco, who led the avant-garde in the decade of the 'fifties, describes this urge with provocative clarity. He writes:

In the end I realized I did not really want to write "anti-theatre" but "theatre." I hope I have rediscovered intuitively in my own mind the permanent basic outlines of drama. In the long run I am all for classicism: that is what the "avant-garde" is. The discovery of forgotten archetypes, changeless but expressed in a new way: Any true creative artist is classical. . . . The *petit bourgeois* is the person who has forgotten the archetype and is absorbed in the stereotype. The archetype is always young.

The implications of this statement for the theatre are tremendous. Classicism is essentially sacramental in nature; it implies that the outward and visible is expressive of that which is inward and spiritual. The classic writer agrees with W. H. Auden that a "man's face is what he is." On the same grounds, he would reject Oscar Wilde's *The Picture of Dorian Grey,* although he would acknowledge the possibility of a temporary split between our inner and outer realities. Classicism also involves mystery and transcendence. Classic writers have always reached back to the beginnings of things, and in so doing they see that while social values keep shifting, there are certain human values which always have existed and will continue to do so. These values may be submerged or even atrophied, but eventually they always reassert themselves. It cannot be too strongly emphasized that classicism is not something which can be defined in terms of form. The forms of art are constantly changing, and the reason we think of writers, who in their forms are as diverse as Sophocles and Shakespeare, Molière and Ibsen, or Corneille and Ionesco, as classical is the fact that in their works there is an affirmation that man is essentially a metaphysical and poetic being who can never be fully defined, and who certainly cannot be explained by his psychology and his material and social environment. The modernist sees the reality of man in relation to his milieu; the classicist always sees his reality in terms of universals.

The genius of the French Theatre, then, lies in its classicism —the fact that it has always used its past to create its future. Today we find ourselves looking to the French for the new directions the theatre will take. The great advances in the French film movement—and I am convinced that in our time and henceforth the theatre will take its cues from the film— tend to substantiate this trust. As all of the arts tend to become increasingly contextual (that is, when art is based more on the tensions of context than on those of sequence), it seems likely that the French, with their open and classical spirit, will continue to lead us—just as they have for most of the twentieth century.

MASTERS OF THE MODERN THEATRE

by Robert W. Corrigan

AFTER VISITING the United States in 1835, Alexis de Tocqueville described the kind of literature he believed an industrialized democratic society would produce. "I am persuaded," he wrote in *Democracy in America*, "that in the end democracy diverts the imagination from all that is external to man and fixes it on man alone. . . . It may be foreseen in like manner that poets living in democratic times will prefer the delineation of passions and ideas to that of persons and achievements. The language, the dress, and the daily actions of men in democracies are repugnant to conceptions of the ideal. . . . This forces the poet constantly to search below the external surface which is palpable to the senses, in order to read the inner soul. . . . The destinies of mankind, man himself taken aloof from his country, and his age, and standing in the presence of Nature and of God, with his passions, his doubts, his rare prosperities and inconceivable wretchedness, will become the chief, if not the sole theme of poetry." Any examination of the arts of the past century would seem to indicate that Tocqueville's prophecy has been fulfilled, and it is certainly clear that the theatre's general pattern of development during this time can be best described as a gradual but steady shift away from universal philosophical and social concerns toward the crises and conflicts of man's inner and private life. It is possible to discover foreshadowings of this change in direction and emphasis in the plays of the early nineteenth-century romantics—Buechner, Hebbel, Kleist, Gogol, Musset—but it was not until Ibsen that the theatre's revolutionary break with the past became clearly discernible. In fact, Ibsen's career as a playwright to a large extent parallels both in form and in theme the modern drama's increasing tendency to be concerned more with the conflicts of the individual's interior world than with the significance of his public deeds.

The causes of any revolution are always as difficult to untangle as its consequences are to assess, and any attempt on the part of the critic to describe them will inevitably result in oversimplification. But it is possible to discover certain basic changes in attitude which had been evolving in Europe since the time of Luther and which had begun to crystallize in Continental thought by the second half of the nineteenth century. And the works of the revolutionary playwrights—Ibsen, Strindberg, Chekhov, Shaw, and Hauptmann —were the first to express in the theatre certain of these radical shifts in the way man had come to think of nature, society, and himself. What follows is an attempt to set forth briefly some of the more important aspects of this revolution in the drama which Ibsen referred to as "a war to the knife with the past."

One of the dominant ideas of the modern *Weltanschauung* is the belief that it is impossible to know what the world is really like. Beginning with Luther's refusal to accept that there was any intelligible relationship between faith and works, the sacramental view of experience gradually disappeared. In rejecting the phenomenal world as an outward and visible manifestation of man's spiritual condition, Luther began a revolution in thought which, because of the achievements of science and technology in the past two hundred years, now makes it impossible for man to attach any objective value to the observations of his senses. This insistence on such a clear-cut division between the physical and the spiritual aspects of reality had a profound effect on the modern dramatist. Inevitably, it made him increasingly distrustful of his sensory responses to the "outside" world, and at the same time it tended to negate whatever belief he might have had in the objective validity of his subjective feelings and sensations. The modern artist no longer holds a mirror up to nature, at least not with any confidence; he can only stare at his own image. He becomes a voyeur to his own existence.

Probably no force in the nineteenth century did more to destroy man's belief in an established norm of human nature, and hence begin this process of internalization in the theatre, than the advent of psychology as a systematized field of study. In his book *"Modernism" in The Modern Drama*, Joseph Wood Krutch argued that the basic issue confronting all the dramatists of the past hundred years was the problem of "modernism." Briefly, modernism involves both the conviction and the practice that to be modern is to be, in many important ways, different from anyone who lived before. This does not mean that man has changed; human nature is the same, but man's way of looking at himself has changed significantly. It is this new view of man that creates the problem for the dramatist.

Good examples of this changed perception can be found in Ibsen's *Hedda Gabler* (1890) and Strindberg's *Miss Julie* (1888). Hedda and Julie have the distinction of being the first fully and consciously developed neurotic heroines in dramatic literature. By neurotic we mean that they are neither logical nor insane (in the sense of being random and unaccountable) but that the aims and motives of each has a secret personal logic of their own. The significant thing about both characters is that they are motivated by the premise that there is a secret, and sometimes unconscious, world of aims and methods, a secret system of values which is more important in human experience than rational ones. This approach to character is not, however, the same as the Romantic attitude which affirms the superior validity of the nonrational. We need only read Strindberg's famous Preface to *Miss Julie* or Ibsen's working notes for *Hedda Gabler* to discover that they did not believe, as did the nineteenth-century Romantic poets, that the irrational was a supernatural and unknowable force; rather, in giving detailed account of why their heroines behaved as they did, Ibsen and Strindberg insisted that neurotic behavior and mysterious events are always explainable in terms of natural causes. The significant difference is that neither of these characters can be explained or judged by a common standard; the actions of each character (and by extension, of each human being) are explicable only in terms of that peculiar combination of forces, frustrations, and desires which is unique to himself.

For us living in the middle of the twentieth century there is nothing very new in these psychological ideas; but, coming when they did, they were quite revolutionary, and they have created problems for the playwright which have not yet been solved. By convincingly demonstrating that normal people are not as rational as they seem, and that abnormal people

do not act in a random and unintelligible way, psychology
has made it difficult, if not impossible, for the dramatist to
present his characters in a direct way. In earlier times when
it was believed that there was a sharp distinction between
the sane and the insane, the irrational "aberrations" of human
behavior were dramatically significant because they could be
defined in terms of a commonly accepted standard of sane
conduct. It seems clear, for instance, that Shakespeare believed
Lear on the heath to be insane, while it is equally clear that
Macbeth at the witches' cauldron was not. But for the modern
dramatist deeds do not necessarily mean what they appear to
mean, and in themselves they are not directly revelatory of the
characters who commit them. Miss Julie, Hedda Gabler, and
Kostya Treplev of Chekhov's *The Sea Gull* are all suicides;
but, unlike Othello's suicide, the meaning of each of their
deaths cannot be clearly ascertained from the actions that pre-
ceded it. The plight of the modern dramatist in this regard
becomes apparent when we realize that without Strindberg's
Preface or Ibsen's Notebook we could never know for certain
what the significance of each heroine's death really was. And
the ambiguity of almost every interpretation of *The Sea Gull*
is largely due to the fact that Chekhov never made the meaning of Treplev's suicide explicit.

All drama of the past is based upon the axiom "By their
deeds shall ye know them." The significance of the dramatic
hero was revealed by his deeds, and there was a direct relationship between the hero's overt acts and his inner spiritual
condition. The significance of Oedipus, for instance, is revealed by his deeds, not by some explanation that he is
suffering from an Oedipus complex; and there is a direct
relationship between the act of tearing out his own eyes
and his solving the riddle of the Sphinx. Even when a character commits a dissembling deed, it is to deceive the other
characters in the play, not the spectators. Certainly one of the
chief functions of the soliloquy in Elizabethan drama was to
keep the audience informed as to what was going on. Hamlet
may put on an antic disposition, but not before he tells the
audience he is going to do so. However, beginning in the nineteenth century, the drama began to reflect man's growing distrust in the ability of his senses to comprehend the true nature
of reality. Appearances are no longer believed to be direct
reflections of ideal reality, like the shadows on the wall of
Plato's cave; rather they are thought of as a mask which hides

or distorts reality. And by the time of Pirandello, particularly in such plays as *Right You Are, If You Think You Are* (1916), *Six Characters in Search of an Author* (1921), and *The Mock Emperor* (*Enrico IV*) (1922), appearances not only do not express reality, they contradict it, and the meaning of these plays is not to be found in appearance or reality but in the contradiction itself.

One of the great achievements of the Elizabethan dramatic form was its ability to express several levels of experience simultaneously. The world of Hamlet is both public and private, a world in which personal and familial relationships, fantasy and mystery, and political and psychological conflict co-exist in a state of constant dramatic tension. One of the main reasons why the Elizabethan dramatic form works so successfully is that appearances can be taken at face value. But when the dramatist begins to distrust the validity of his sensory perceptions, it becomes difficult, if not impossible, for him to dramatize the complex totality of experience in a single form. Reality must be broken down into its component parts, and each part can be expressed only in a form peculiar to itself. Admitting individual differences in the works of each dramatist's writing of any given period, it is nonetheless possible to describe with some accuracy the dramatic form employed by the playwrights of the fifth-century Greek theatre, the Elizabethan and Restoration theatres of England, and the French neo-classic theatre of the seventeenth century. But in discussing the modern theatre we must always speak of forms, for there is no single, dominant form in the serious theatre of the past hundred years. It is for this reason that the evolution of the drama since the time of Shakespeare has been so aptly described as a process of fragmentation.

It is likely that every serious dramatist believes it his artistic duty to be true to his presuppositions about the real nature of the world in which he lives. However, once a playwright believes that the meaning of every human action is relative and intelligible only in terms of a unique and subsurface combination of forces, the dramatic events of the plot cease to have meaning in themselves, and they take on significance only as the secret motivations of the characters who participate in them are revealed. (The technique of earlier drama is just the reverse: the motivations of the characters are revealed by the events of the plot.) But how does the dramatist objectify the hidden and unconscious, and what happens to the theatre when he feels obligated to explain and probe into his characters' hidden lives? Explanation is always a dangerous business in the theatre (since the time of the ancient Greeks, exposition has always been the dramatist's most difficult problem), but the moment a playwright assumes that if he explains his characters he has written a play, that danger becomes mortal. All too often the writers of the modern theatre have forgotten that a dramatic situation requires not that we *understand* a character but simply that we *believe* in him. Dramatic action always leads to a judgment; it requires that something shall happen to and through the characters; something that is embodied in the events of which the characters are a part. Whenever the personality of the character, rather than the action of which the character should be a part, becomes the playwright's chief concern, dramatic process dissolves into explanation, and when that occurs, the range of the theatre is drastically reduced, if not unalterably damaged.

One has only to compare the plays of the mid-twentieth century to those of Ibsen, Shaw, or Strindberg to realize just how much the scope of the theatre has been narrowed. However, early evidence of the gradual loss of belief in dramatic heroes, who needed no explaining, can be found in the sentimental bourgeois drama of the eighteenth century. For the first time a character was no longer noble, responsible, or morally significant, and therefore dramatically interesting just because of his birth, position, power, or wealth. As a result, the dramatist was obliged to justify both his choice of characters and the situations in which they are engaged. The Romantic drama of the eighteenth and nineteenth centuries resisted a break with the past and attempted unsuccessfully to perpetuate the forms and figures of earlier times. Certainly the revolt of Ibsen and his contemporaries in the last quarter of the nineteenth century was in some measure due to their conviction that the dramatic conflicts of the Romantic drama were inflated and without significance, and that the nobility of its characters was artificial and contrived. In rejecting the artificialities of Romanticism, the modernists changed the theatre in many ways; but for all their dissatisfaction with their predecessors they were unable to forestall disbelief in the possibility of heroic characters who needed no explaining.

This was largely because as a literary movement nineteenth-century naturalism was so closely related to nineteenth-century biology. Darwin's theories of evolution (*Ori-*

gin of Species, 1859) and the discovery of new genetic laws had convinced many writers that man's existence, including his personality, was a phenomenon that could be explained in terms of scientific laws. As a result, increasingly, man's complex biological needs rather than his capacity to make moral choices were thought to be his most significant characteristic. Once such a view was accepted, however, the exceptional man, who because of his position and power had the greatest freedom of choice, ceased to be the fullest embodiment, and therefore the best representative, of those conflicts and choices that most clearly define the human condition. Instead, the lives of the poor—where the role of natural necessity is most readily observable—became the playwright's most suitable subjects. The drama of the common man, then, did not happen by accident, nor did it evolve because some dramatist or group of dramatists wanted it to. Given the problem of creating in a world in which all human actions tend to be explained in terms of psychological or sociological cause and effect, a world in which the possibility of deliberative and moral choice is doubted if not rejected outright, it is difficult, if not impossible, for the playwright to fashion a character of traditional heroic stature.

There is an old saw about no man being a hero to his valet. Neither is he one to his psychoanalyst. Nor can he be one to a playwright who views his actions as behavioral phenomena explicable in terms of some kind of laws—scientific or otherwise. Oedipus, for example, remains a hero of great stature so long as he is not suffering from an Oedipus complex. But once we learn to explain him in terms of repressed hopes and fears, traumatic childhood experience, or a vitamin deficiency in infancy, although he may remain interesting—in fact he may gain a new kind of interest, as Cocteau's *The Infernal Machine* attests—he loses stature. Even if we are able, temporarily to accept the Elizabethan attitude toward heroes, which of us can understand a Hamlet or a Lear? And which of us can forgive an Othello or a Macbeth? But it is precisely because they seem mysteriously beyond our powers of understanding that they remain heroes for us. And it is a belief in a mysterious, unknowable quality in men that substantiates man's sense of his own importance in the universe. However, if a playwright comes to believe that all human actions are in reality predictable behavioral responses, and his moral judgments of these actions can be dissolved by psychological understanding, how can he pattern a tragedy or create characters with stature? If there can be no possibility for an appraisal of personality as such, why should Hamlet's death be any more significant than that of Rosencrantz and Guildenstern?

But the problem does not end here. For once the dramatist dismisses the possibility of passing moral judgments on his characters' actions, he comes face to face with an even more frightening spectre—guilt that has no form of expiation and thus turns into anxiety. It has long been known that art must ultimately fail in its attempt to come to grips with the facts of death. Perhaps this is also true of anxiety. How can there be drama in an Age of Anxiety? What kind of play will be produced when the central conflict is between something and nothing? Many of the arts may be able to express the condition of anxiety; but the theatre, because of the objective reality and irremovable presence of the living actor, and because the drama is essentially an embodiment of the conflict between at least two opposing recognizable and nameable forces, is incapable of dealing with anxiety, or it does so to its own great peril. Beginning with the Watchman in the opening scene of the *Orestia* right on through the ghosts of Elsinore and the tormented heroes of Schiller and Kleist, the theatre has always found a way to transform anxiety into fear; that is, give it a definite object. But when we come to such plays as Ibsen's *Ghosts* and *The Master Builder* and Strindberg's *There Are Crimes and Crimes*, and *The Ghost Sonata*, we discover that although this process of objectification is attempted, it is not totally successful. And when the transformation does not take place, the form and content of drama begin to change in uncontrollable ways, as some of the plays of Beckett and Ionesco, Pinter and Albee will attest. It is difficult enough to find a meaning for man in a world that views a return to nothingness as the ultimate reality, but it is next to impossible to create a dramatic "action" which can encompass the terror of being on the edge of the abyss. Kierkegaard, and more recently Paul Tillich, have declared that this threat of nothingness is the central anxiety of modern man. Many modern playwrights have sought to overcome the despair of this situation by maintaining that the only meaning of life is to be found in that death which is inevitable. But this is not an assertion that gives meaning to any of the particularities of life; in fact, it drains them of meaning. At best, it is a method of redeeming existence from meaningless anarchy by showing that the pattern of life is simple and imperturbable. But such a pattern, though it may appear to conquer chaos, is too abstract to live successfully in the theatre.

In life as we experience it, we are conscious of our physical natures, our social situation, and our unique psychic existence; and we live on all three of these levels simultaneously. For this reason it is impossible for us to act or make a choice without some element of human behavior—what we do out of physical necessity or because of social habit—playing a significant role in our decision. At the same time, because of the simultaneity of our being, it is impossible for us to understand completely the individuality of our actions. But in the theatre we see life as pure deed, that is, life in which the arbitrariness of human behavior has been eliminated and in which the mysterious transformations of individuality have been fixed. Thus, in contrast to a person in life, who is recognized by the continuity of his being and finally can only be known through intuition, a character in a play is an identity who is defined by the coherence of his acts. For this reason the deeds of a dramatic action are always public, and the characters best suited to drama are men and women who, either by fate or choice, lead a public life and whose deeds are of public concern. This explains why kings, princes, and nobility have traditionally been the most suitable subjects for drama. But as the increasing dominance of the machine in modern life has gradually destroyed the direct relation between a man's intention and his deeds, public figures have ceased to be our most appropriate heroes because, as W. H. Auden points out, "the good and evil they do depends less upon their characters and intentions than upon the quantity of impersonal force at their disposal."

Our world, it would seem, has become almost too big for the playwright. Power is too impersonal, great deeds are collective achievements, and the great man is one who is capable of withstanding some of the pressures of a mass society and manages, somehow, to maintain a face and stance more or less his own. Compare, for example, the achievement of a Lindbergh (our last "lone" hero) to that of a Colonel Glenn, who was interchangeable with five other astronauts. Or, how can the power of a Napoleon be envisioned today? In our times power is so enormous that it is barely visible and those who govern are little more than incidental and easily replaceable expressions of that power. Power is like an iceberg; the largest part is submerged—in abstraction, anonymity, and bureaucracy. Government, like modern physics, has lost its physical reality and can be expressed only in statistics and formulae. Indeed, the true men of action in our time, those who transform the world, are not the statesmen and politicians but the scientists. Unfortunately, their most significant actions are not suitable subjects for the theatre, because their deeds are concerned with things, not people, and are, therefore, speechless.

But what are the implications of this for the theatre? Who are the true representatives of a world whose heroes are nameless? As the Swiss playwright Duerrenmatt put it: "Any small-time crook, petty government official, or policeman better represents our world than a senator or president. Today art can only embrace victims if it can reach men at all; it can no longer come close to the mighty. Creon's secretaries close Antigone's case."

That there has been a shift in attitude toward the heroic is easily seen when we examine any one of the many modern adaptations of the Greek tragedies. For example, today most people find Anouilh's *Antigone* much more a reflection of their attitudes and thus more immediately interesting than Sophocles' tragic working of the theme. The characters and the dilemma of their situation seem more human. Antigone is not a hard and almost inhuman girl, with such a monomaniacal fixity of purpose that she rejects all other feelings and desires. In the modern version she is, humanly, both weak and strong. She has a lover in Haemon, whom she rejects; but she is also a helpless little girl who runs to "Nanny" for comfort and strength; as she approaches death, she is afraid and seeks the consolations of even the most callous of guards. Creon is not a blind and power-mad tyrant; he is a businessman king who is caught in the complex web of compromise and expediency which will not allow abstract moral principles to upset the business of government.

However, what the play gains in humanity it loses in tragic force. The sense of Antigone's aloneness and Creon's moral blindness, and of the inevitable destruction implicit in their conflict, has been softened. Anouilh's Antigone is not alone and unloved, and his Creon is not blind. We pity their situation because they are two quite attractive people caught up in a situation which neither of them likes but which they cannot control. They are victims in a disordered world which they have not created and which they have no moral obligation to correct. As the play ends, we are left with an ambiguity that allows for no reconciliation.

One of the most important functions of the hero, both in art and life, is to supply those images, values, and ethical standards which people aspire to and which they would like, if possible, to incorporate into their own lives. It would seem, however, that increasingly our modern industrialized society not only does not need heroes, but it actually suppresses or perverts our need of them. In their important book *Industrialism and Industrial Man,* Kerr, Dunlop, Harbison, and Myers convincingly demonstrate that "like ideologies, the great personality—the one great figure around whom historians so frequently weave their story—began to seem less important. Instead of ideologies and dominant personalities, we became increasingly attentive to the inherent nature of the particular industrializing system and the basic strategy and forces at work within it." Only the system, then, is important, and it fills men's remaining need for heroes by promoting celebrities, those heroes of the surface who play well their constantly shifting roles.

Furthermore, specialization—the key operative principle of an industrial society—produces not only pluralism in our economic system but also a pluralistic deviation of heroic types. However, when there are and can be so many heroic types—one cannot even begin to count all the heroes of the popular imagination—you begin to get a leveling; and with that leveling not only is the stature of heroism diminished, but the individual's sense of his own identity is actually invalidated.

Traditionally, the hero is always best described in terms of those forces that urge him to spiritual redemption. Maxwell Anderson once wrote that "from the point of view of the playwright, the essence of a tragedy, or even a serious play, is the spiritual awakening, or regeneration, of his hero." But the one thing that characterizes the hero of surfaces—and this is certainly in large measure due to industrialization and bureaucracy—is precisely the fact that he lacks the dimensions of spiritual awareness, personal morality, and social responsibility. Paul Tillich wrote in his *The Religious*

Situation that "the fundamental value in ethics of a capitalistic society is economic efficiency—developed to the utmost degree of ruthless activity." Such an ethical standard is hardly conducive to the creation of great heroes in the drama.

That we live in an antiheroic age is a commonplace. Carlyle proclaimed its coming in the nineteenth century when he said: "We shall either learn to know a hero . . . when we see him, or else go on to be forever governed by the unheroic." This transformation has occurred; we have accepted it; we are even used to it. Whatever nostalgia we may still occasionally feel is more than adequately taken care of by television. In the place of the hero we have the celebrity, that triumph of the ordinary. In our time, hero worship has become horizontal; indeed, we even look down to a "man like myself."

While the advent of psychology as a systematized field of study may have been the most powerful single force to shape the modern theatre, actually the process of internalization had begun much earlier. For instance, it is clear from Hebbel's essays on the drama that the despair of old Anton's "I don't understand the world any more" in the final scene of *Maria Magdalena* is much more than an expression of the age-old frustration of the parent who does not understand the behavior of his children. It also reflects his dimly understood but tremendously painful realization that it is no longer possible for him to comprehend what the world has become or to imagine what the future will be like. Until the Industrial Revolution, patterns of life were passed on from father to son with the confidence that these patterns would satisfy the needs and desires of each new generation. Such confidence was justified, for life changed so gradually and imperceptibly that when changes did occur they were easily assimilated into the shared life of the community. But by the middle of the nineteenth century the effects of the Industrial Revolution had begun to be felt on all levels of society. Technology, with its ever increasing capacity to transform man's way of living, not only made the future so unpredictable that it soon became impossible for him to imagine what his life would be like twenty years hence, but in its singular concern with the individual's functional qualities technology tended to isolate him from his fellows and invalidate his spiritual values and metaphysical concerns. At the same time, the discoveries of the nineteenth-century archeologists, and the ensuing interest in anthropology, tended to break down provincial and absolutist attitudes concerning human nature. Early anthropologists like Mannhardt, Robertson-Smith, Tylor, and the great James Frazer made it clear that human nature was not something fixed and unchanging but only that kind of behavior exhibited in each culture. In fact, as early as 1860 scholars were demonstrating that human nature is so plastic that it can, as Frazer was later to point out in the Preface to the first edition of *The Golden Bough* (1890), "exhibit varieties of behavior which, in the animal kingdom could only be exhibited by different species." Furthermore, by the middle of the century, democracy was finally beginning to be established both as a way of life and as a form of government. Today we tend to forget what a revolutionary idea democracy is and the shattering effects that it had upon the values of eighteenth- and nineteenth-century Europe. Alexis de Tocqueville told us long ago: "Not only does democracy make every man forget his ancestors, but it hides his descendants and separates his contemporaries from him, it throws him back forever upon himself alone and threatens in the end to confine him entirely within the solitude of his own heart." In short, by the middle of the nineteenth century every established view of God, human nature, social organization, and the physical universe was beginning to be seriously challenged if not invalidated. And this revolutionary climate had a profound effect on the theatre.

Of all the arts, theatre is the only art that has always concerned itself with human destinies. Dramatic action is historical in the sense that the perpetual present of each moment on the stage is created out of past events and is directed toward a definite, if yet unknown, future. In previous ages the destiny of any dramatic action was significant because the ever-changing events in the lives of dramatic heroes could be meaningfully related to eternity, that is, to some permanent value or idea such as Fate, the Gods, or Heaven and Hell, which transcends the human condition and which is believed in by the dramatist and/or his audience.

In the plays of Buechner and Hebbel we discover the first indications in the theatre of that sense of alienation from both God and Society which underscores the fact that man's belief in eternity had been shaken. And one of the most significant aspects of Ibsen's work (at least after *Peer Gynt,* 1867) is the fact that the realm of ultimate value has either disappeared or has become so mysterious that it has ceased to have dramatic relevance. In its place we find instead a belief in some form of social ideal or societal structure; first, as the agent of some unknown Destiny, and then as Destiny itself. But when society begins to assume the role of Destiny, that is, is thought of as the determining force for good or evil in the lives of men, man cannot help but feel eventually that the meaning of his Destiny has been drastically reduced. For Society, as Robert Bolt writes in the Preface to his *A Man for All Seasons,* "can only have as much idea as we have what we are about, for it has only our brains to think with. And the individual who tries to plot his position by reference to our society finds no fixed points, but only the vaunted absence of them, 'freedom' and 'opportunity'; freedom for what, opportunity to do what, is nowhere indicated. The only positive he is given is 'get and spend' . . . and he did not need society to tell him that. In other words we are thrown back by our society upon ourselves, which of course sends us flying back to society with all the force of rebound."

Any mind capable of spiritual aspiration seeks in the actions of the dramatic hero that which affirms the vitality of the free will in any given situation. Man's free will may be defeated by the forces of Destiny—in fact, the great plays have always testified that the destroying forces of Destiny are as much a part of the hero's character as his free will; it may be paralyzed and thus incapable of action; it may be submerged by the battle in such a way as to become part of that Destiny; it may even turn out to be an illusion; but it must always be an active force if we are to believe that we are partaking in human greatness. Such a Destiny must be greater than an aggregate of human beings or an expression of social patterns.

Ironically, the revolt of Ibsen and Shaw against the conventional nineteenth-century drama was motivated by a desire to enlarge the range of Destiny in the theatre. In their attempts to present men in his total historical and social setting, they were rebelling against the narrow and private worlds that had been dominating the stage since the Restoration. But in spite of their efforts, nothing could change the fact that in the two hundred years since Shakespeare the world of the spirit had greatly diminished. The Ekdals' attic and Mrs. Warren's drawing room were not—and never could be—the same as Elsinore or Cleopatra's barge.

Nonetheless, the pioneers of the modern drama had revitalized the theatre precisely because they believed that significant social issues should be dealt with in the theatre. Thus for nearly three decades the theatre had a vitality of spirit and a forcefulness of manner which it had lacked for more than a century for the very reason that its context had been reduced. To the playwright writing at that time the human and social problems, which were the source materials of the naturalistic play, appeared capable of solution if only man and society would learn to use their common sense; which usually meant one of two things—the acceptance of a less rigid standard of social morality or the espousal of some form of socialism. But with the collapse of the established social order in the first World War, the validity of these too-easy solutions was impugned, and beginning with the plays of the early German Expressionists (written 1912-1916) the positive optimism of the Edwardian era gave way to a sense of bewilderment, exasperation, and defeatism, only occasionally tempered by the slim hope that the war had brought man to the threshold of a "New Age." The theatre reflects these changes from confidence to doubting and despair, from complacent faith in cherished values to an anxious questioning, from a rigorous but rigid morality to the mystic evangelism, the fanatical polemics, and the frivolous apathy of a disintegrating world. These changes are most apparent in the Jekyll and Hyde theatre of the German Expressionists whose nerve-shattered playwrights alternated between a militant idealism and grotesque nightmares. But one need only compare Shaw's *Heartbreak House* to *Major Barbara*, Pirandello's *Right You Are, If You Think You Are* to *Liolá*, or Hauptmann's *Winter Ballad* to *The Weavers* to realize that the effects of the collapse of the old order were widespread and were reflected in the works of established writers as well as those of the new generation. Immediately after the war the theatre on the continent was dominated by attitudes of emotionalism and cynicism, but these gradually gave way to feelings of frustration, futility, and despair, and by the middle of the 1920's the serious drama of Europe had become almost totally introspective and psychological in its orientation.[1]

Obviously, this tendency toward paralyzing introspection has by no means been accepted by everyone writing for the theatre. In fact, a large segment of the modern theatre might be best described as a reaction against the despair and dehumanizing implications of the modernist position. These "resistance movements" have sought to discover the means, both formal and substantive, whereby the possibility and validity of selfhood and human integrity, personal responsibility, and morally significant judgments could be reasserted in the theatre. Some playwrights—especially Eliot, Fry, Betti, and Claudel—have turned to orthodox Christian belief to provide a metaphysical structure for their drama. Others, like Lorca and Synge, have written out of the traditions and value systems of premodern hieratic societies. Probably the largest group of all is composed of those dramatists who have sought to escape the deadly strictures of modernism by turning to classical mythology.

All of these writers shared one common and fundamental attitude: each of them was in some way rebelling against the conditions of the modern world. They were not only conscious of that lack of a sense of community which inevitably occurs in an increasingly democratic society; more important, they were aware of man's growing sense of his own isolation. The modern world, with its growing collectivism, paradoxically tends to throw man back upon himself, while at the same time it increasingly tends to destroy the individual's sense of his own selfhood. This creates an im-

---

[1] Because they were essentially isolated from the main currents of European history in the first two decades of the century, the Irish and American theatres were not immediately effected by the spreading paralysis which was transforming the rest of modern drama. But it is clear from O'Casey's *The Plow and the Stars* (1926) and *The Silver Tassie* (1927) that the Abbey Theatre could not withstand for long the theatre's introspective tendencies, and there was no serious American drama until O'Neill's plays were first produced right after the war. In the twenty years between O'Neill's *Beyond the Horizon* (1920) and *The Iceman Cometh* (1941) the American theatre repeated the Continental cycle in its own terms, and by the beginning of the Second World War all of the Western theatre had reached that No Man's Land between comedy and tragedy, between pathetic aspirations and ridiculous bewilderment, between never-beginning action and never-ending talk.

passe which the modern dramatist, for the most part, has been unable to overcome.

Joseph Warren Beach, in analyzing the problems of modern fiction, describes the reaction of many writers to this condition in this way: "One of the hardest things for man to bear is spiritual isolation. The sense that he stands alone in the universe goes terribly against his gregarious instincts. He has an over-powering impulse to construct a system which will enable him to feel that he does not stand alone but is intimately associated with some force or group infinitely more powerful and significant than himself." It is clearly evident in the work of all those playwrights who have rebelled against modernism that they too are seeking to construct a system that will restore meaning to life and validity to art. In the end, however, they have not been completely successful, because they have all too often had to deny the realities of the modern world in the process. Furthermore, they have not accepted the wisdom of Brecht's statement that "when one sees that our world of today no longer fits into the drama, then it is merely that the drama no longer fits into the world." By insisting upon values that we may once have cherished but which no longer in actuality exist, the playwrights of the resistance have not been able to revitalize the theatre or its audiences. And most important, they have not succeeded in stretching the imaginations of men in order that they might conquer that sense of isolation and despair that pervades the modern world. And this brings us to the playwrights of the mid-twentieth century.

In an age dominated by space orbits and telestars, the fear of nuclear war, the tension of cold war diplomacy, and the insecurity of a defense economy, our greatest uncertainty is whether or not in the midst of epochal disorder man has any good chance, to borrow Faulkner's phrase, of prevailing; and if he does, what kind of man will prevail?

This uncertainty has had a profound effect on our theatre, and if there is one thing that characterizes the work of almost all of our serious playwrights of the last two decades it is that their plays express the contemporary theatre's tremendous concern to find a metaphor for universal modern man as he lives on the brink of disaster—a metaphor that expresses the inalienable part of every man, that irreducible part of each of us that exists after all the differences have been stripped away and which is beyond and beneath all that is social, political, economic, religious, and ideological. In short, they are searching for a metaphor of man left face to face with himself.

Such an idea of the theatre has tremendous implications for the drama, and we are just now becoming aware of them. First of all, it abolishes the traditional linear plot because our contemporary playwrights are not interested in presenting an action in any Aristotelian sense but are, rather, dramatizing a condition. Whenever one asks what the central action of a Beckett, Ionesco, or Pinter play is, he comes a cropper; "action" for the contemporary playwright is an artificial concept. He is concerned with showing life as it is, and in life there is no central action, there are only people, and the only thing that is basic to each individual is the ontological solitude of his being. The dramatist's only concern is to create in his plays a situation which will reveal the private drama that each man has inside himself and which is enacted every day in the random, apparently meaningless, and undramatic events of our common routine. "History," said James Joyce's Stephen Daedalus, "is a nightmare from which I must awake." The rapidity of historical change and the apparent powerlessness of the individual to affect Collective History has led in the theatre to a retreat from history. Instead of tracing the history of an individual who is born, grows old, and dies, many modern playwrights have devoted their attention to the timeless passionate moments of life, to states of being. They want to express the paradox, the contradiction, and the incompleteness of experience. They are attempting to suggest the raggedness, the confusion, the complexity of motivation, the "discontinuous continuity," and the basic ambiguity of all human behavior. They are, in short, pursuing the premises of modernism to their fullest and most logical conclusions. The writers of the contemporary theatre are facing the "facts of life." If the dramatic meaning of their plays is that drama is no longer possible, they would contend that any other meaning would be artificial, illusory, false; if the dialogue in their plays consists of meaningless clichés and stereotyped phrases, they would insist that this is the way we talk; if their characters are constantly changing their personalities, these playwrights would point out that no one today is really consistent or truly integrated. If the people in their plays seem to be helpless puppets without any will of their own, they would argue that we are all passively at the mercy of blind fate and meaningless circumstance. They call their theatre "Anti-Theatre," and this they insist is the true theatre of our times. If they are correct, so be it! Then history has again followed its own inexorable laws. The very forces that gave life and strength to the modern theatre have caused its decline and death.

But the theatre is always dying, and with equal regularity, like the phoenix, it is resurrected. No one can say with certainty what its new form will be, but that there will be a future seems certain. First, largely because of the development of college and university theatre programs in this country and the large increase in the number of professional repertory theatres here and abroad, there are more people who have experienced good theatre than ever before. And this enlarged audience wants and needs theatre, and it will not be satisfied for long with the maimed rites of psychological and moral cliché, or impassioned jeremiads from prophets of doom, or the meandering contemplations of writers who are morbidly consumed in introspection and self-analysis. Fortunately, there are audiences who want and need the theatre, and they go to the theatre in the hopeful anticipation that the stage will be capable of accommodating all of the terrible-wonderful emotions and insoluble dilemmas of our shared life together. This insistence by audiences on a drama that deals with the significant issues and concerns of our public life will, I believe, force our playwrights to open up new frontiers in the drama and thus extend the boundaries of the theatre. The second great hope of the theatre is that, in spite of the overriding temper of despair and the dominance of antitheatricality in current drama, our playwrights still find human action significant, still find it necessary to write plays, and, in the very act of writing, attest to the miracle of life. We live in one of the most dramatic ages in the history of mankind, and if the past is any kind of reliable guide to what the future of the theatre will be, we have good reason to believe that the theatre of tomorrow can be as dramatic as the world in which we live today.

MASTERPIECES OF THE
MODERN FRENCH THEATRE

HENRY BECQUE

1837–1899

HENRY BECQUE was, in fact, the father of naturalism in the modern French Theatre. While Zola—the man most often referred to as the patriarch of the movement—thundered away in the name of naturalism in the theatre, his attempts and those of his followers—the De Goncourts, Daudet—remained largely novelistic, moralistic, and even a little sentimental. It was Becque who first broke through the seemingly endless morass of inane comedies and sentimental melodramas which dominated the Parisian theatre of the 1890's.

Becque's notion of drama was to present a slice of life on the stage with as much impartiality as he could muster. Aware of the need for social criticism, Becque nonetheless knew that this was an impossible endeavor for the theatre without true-to-life characters. The most important accomplishment of his dramaturgy was the incorporation of his ideas into the very personalities of these characters.

Becque purged his drama of the common comic complications and diversionary dialogue. Simplicity and directness, not without ironies but clear of trifling clichés, is the natural language of his characters. This is particularly apparent in *The Parisian Woman*, the play of this volume. The characters are amusing in the seriousness with which they live in obvious contradiction to their "values"; meanwhile, they indict themselves and their audience, not in speech form, but in the hypocrisy lurking between the lines of their compact, everyday dialogue. It was Becque's ability to achieve such a dramatic integration as this that finally brought the French Theatre into the stream of naturalism begun by Ibsen.

Becque was not a prolific writer, and only *The Parisian Woman* and *The Vultures* are important to us today. Becque had to expend altogether too much energy in seeing to the proper production of his work. Had he not insisted relentlessly on direct delivery and simplicity of style for his new naturalism, his plays might well have been corrupted by the silly vultures of the nineteenth-century Parisian Theatre. Indeed, in pursuing production reform in Antoine's *Théâtre Libre,* he made a contribution to the modern French Theatre that has turned out to be as important as the plays themselves.

ON THE THEATRE[1]

By Henry Becque

Let us love each other just because of the diversity of our talents. . . . Let us laugh with some and weep with others. Let verse be the friend of prose and let prose give homage to verse. No preferences. Above all, no theories. From the time of Aristotle, who had instituted, as is known, immutable rules, to that poor Scribe, whose ridiculous maxims are still dinned into our ears, we have not been lacking in professors of dramatic art. What have they created? Nothing. What have they prevented? Again, nothing. . . . One single truth seems definitive today; there is no measure for talent, there are no conventions that originality cannot destroy or replace. . . . The history of art is nothing but a struggle between original talents and routinary minds.

*****

A dramatist may have two ends in view, one to please the public, the other to satisfy only himself. I have chosen to satisfy myself.

*****

The drama is the art of elimination.

*****

There is in me a sentimental revolutionist. I imagine at times that some of my troubles come from that source.

*****

For the nearly fifteen years that I have been writing for the stage, and it will soon be ten that I have been a member of

[1] From *Antoine and the Théâtrelibre* by S. M. Waxman, published by the Harvard University Press. By permission of the publishers.

the *Commission des Auteurs*, I have fought everywhere for unknown authors. A useless and mediocre undertaking, in which one is likely to make more enemies than to do any real service. Kindly disposed friends have advised me to drop that sort of thing and not bother my head with common interests, but to stick to my own work. I feel that I should reproach myself if I abandoned my fellow artists who are still struggling with difficulties from which I myself have scarcely escaped. I must plead their cause. I should be very happy if their talent should prove me to be in the right and should triumph over so much ill will. Others will come after us who ought to be happier than we, who cannot be condemned in advance to discouragement, sadness, and sterility. If there is to be a renaissance of dramatic art, it will certainly not come from the dead and from the dying. Let us encourage production as much as we can. Let us insist constantly for an outlet and support for this production. Let us demand from our theatre directors more decision and more ability. Let us insist that they be men of artistic imagination rather than men with business preoccupations.

*****

"For the guidance of the municipal officials of the city of Paris"

1. There shall be created a theatre extraordinary for the making and remaking of dramatic authors.

2. This theatre will be situated in the center of Paris. In construction, name, make-up of the company, etc., it will resemble the other theatres. Everything that might cause it to be maligned by the public will be carefully avoided.

3. A competition will be held for the position of director. People out of employment or who have failed in other walks of life must, when presenting themselves as candidates, give proof of one indispensable quality: austerity.

4. The director will perform his duties without pay, but will receive a fixed amount for each new play.

5. If, during a crisis in his management, the director should be forced to make the following decision, "Entrance to the theatre is forbidden to all those not connected with the personnel," authors cannot possibly be included in that category.

6. Every play produced at this theatre shall run for three weeks, giving just enough time to prepare another one.

7. The revival of an ancient or modern play is rigorously prohibited.

8. The gratuity known by the name of "curtain raiser" is suppressed.

9. The properties of the theatre should not contain more than four settings: a temple, a forest, a street, and a drawing room. In case a fifth setting should seem necessary by way of exception, the matter will be referred to the *Commission Supérieure des Théâtres*, which has never met since its establishment.

10. In questions concerning gowns to be paid for by the theatre, the director will make a difference between actresses who live with their families and those who live in a hotel. This distinction should favor the first category and not the second, as the director might possibly think.

11. A government official will be attached to the theatre with new duties: he will undertake to defend authors against the directors, which is contrary to the procedure heretofore in practice.

12. There will be introduced in his contract a special clause in accordance with which the director will be held to fulfill all the other clauses.

Translated by S. M. Waxman

THE PARISIAN WOMAN

by HENRY BECQUE

1885

THE PARISIAN WOMAN[1]
Comedy in Three Acts

Translated by Eric Vaughn

CHARACTERS

CLOTILDE
LAFONT
DU MESNIL
ADELE
SIMPSON

The scene takes place in Paris, during the 1880s.

[1] *The Parisian Woman,* by Henry Becque, translated by Eric Vaughn, is reprinted here by permission of Chandler Publishing Company. Copyright © 1963 by Chandler Publishing Company. All rights reserved: no public or private performance of the play, professional or amateur, may be given, no film, radio or television use or public reading, without authorization from Chandler Publishing Company, 124 Spear Street, San Francisco 5, California.

ACT ONE

[*The setting represents an elegant drawing room. Upstage center, a pair of folding doors; upstage, to the left, a second pair of folding doors; to the right, a window. Side doors, the one on the right, in the middle, folding; the one on the left, ordinary, single and downstage. To the right, against the wall, a light writing desk. On stage, to the left, a small round table, and, on the table, a blotting pad. Various pieces of furniture, mirrors, flowers, etc.*]

Scene 1

[*As the curtain rises, the stage is empty.* CLOTILDE, *in street dress, gloved, wearing a hat, enters hurriedly upstage center. She holds a letter in her hand, goes to the table, raises the blotter, and hides the letter underneath. She reaches the desk while taking a bunch of keys from her pocket.* LAFONT *appears at that moment, sees her there. She pretends to triple-lock the desk.* LAFONT *takes off his hat and advances toward her, very disturbed, controlling himself with difficulty.*]

LAFONT. Open the desk and give me that letter.
CLOTILDE. No.

[*Pause.*]

LAFONT. Open the desk and give me that letter.
CLOTILDE. I don't wish to.

[*Another pause, longer than the first.*]

LAFONT. Where have you been?
CLOTILDE. Ah! That's something else now.
LAFONT. Yes, that's something else. I'm asking you where you've been.

CLOTILDE. I will tell you. I wish that you could look at your-self at this moment to see the figure that you present to me. You're not attractive, my dear. You please me more in your usual humor. My god, what are we coming to if you lose all restraint over a silly note which almost anyone may have addressed to me?

LAFONT. Open the desk and give me that letter.

CLOTILDE. You shall have it. You ought to consider that scenes like this, if often repeated, would soon alienate me from you. I warn you, I cannot submit to a cross-examina-tion every time I set foot outside the house.

LAFONT. Where have you been?

CLOTILDE. I suggest that you at least try to be logical. It is not likely that I would leave someone, and, on returning home, find a note from him.

LAFONT. Open the desk and give me that letter.

CLOTILDE. You're joking, aren't you?

LAFONT. I don't appear to be.

CLOTILDE. You suspect me, then?

LAFONT. That's more likely. [*He motions her toward the desk with his hand.*]

CLOTILDE. You really wish it? You insist on it? You com-mand it? Very well. [*Slowly, with affectation, she searches the pocket of her dress; first she takes out a handkerchief, then a notebook and the keys. She replaces the notebook and the handkerchief, tossing the keys aside at random.*] Open it yourself. [*She turns her back. He remains motion-less, undecided, clenching his teeth.*] Go on, pick them up and open it. Once you've begun something, see it through to the end. Show that you're a man.

[*He decides, moves toward the keys, and stoops, touching them.*]

Take care in what you're about to do. If you touch those keys with so much as your fingertips . . . your fingertips . . . I won't be the one to regret it; you will.

LAFONT [*hesitates, picks up the keys, and gives them to her*]. Take back your keys.

[*Pause, while* CLOTILDE *takes off her hat and gloves, making herself at home.*]

CLOTILDE. It's getting worse, you know.

LAFONT. What's getting worse?

CLOTILDE. I warn you, the disease is gaining.

LAFONT. What disease?

CLOTILDE. I had already noticed that you were keeping me under surveillance, and I laughed at the trouble you were taking . . . so fruitlessly. But, till now, there was nothing to say. It was jealousy, but a pleasant jealousy, which flatters the vanity of a woman and amuses her. Now you've come to that other, stupid, crude, brutal jealousy which wounds us deeply, and which we never forgive twice. Will you start it again?

LAFONT. Clotilde?

CLOTILDE. Will you start it again?

LAFONT. No.

CLOTILDE. Good.

LAFONT. Clotilde?

CLOTILDE. What, my dear?

LAFONT. Do you love me?

CLOTILDE. Less than yesterday.

LAFONT. Do you want me to be happy?

CLOTILDE. I've shown it often enough, I think.

LAFONT. I'm worried about all the young men you chance to meet, who turn about you so.

CLOTILDE. You're quite wrong. I chat with this one and that one; our backs turned, I no longer know who has spoken to me.

LAFONT. You don't recall anyone you might have encouraged, inadvertently, who would have felt entitled to write to you?

CLOTILDE. No one.

LAFONT [*piteously*]. Open the desk and give me that letter.

CLOTILDE. Again! That letter is from my friend, Madame Doyen-Beaulieu,

[LAFONT *starts.*]

the most virtuous of women—under her flighty appearance. I know what Pauline has written me, and I shall be the first to tell you, whenever you stop asking me.

LAFONT. Clotilde?

CLOTILDE. What now?

LAFONT. Are you quite rational?

CLOTILDE. More than ever.

LAFONT. Your head is cool?

CLOTILDE. My head is cool, and my heart, as well.

LAFONT. Think of me, Clotilde, and think of yourself. Consider that an indiscretion is all too quickly committed, and that it's never made up. Don't let yourself give in to that taste for adventures, which claims so many victims nowadays. Resist, Clotilde, resist! By remaining faithful to me, you remain respectable and honorable; the day when you deceive me . . .

[*She stops him, takes several steps toward the door upstage left, and returns.*]

CLOTILDE. Take care, here comes my husband.

Scene 2

[*Enter* DU MESNIL.]

DU MESNIL. I thought sure it was Lafont that I heard! You sit, you talk, you gossip when you're together; a cloudburst wouldn't stop you!

CLOTILDE [*going to* DU MESNIL, *sotto voce*]. Then you'd returned?

DU MESNIL. Yes, I'd returned.

CLOTILDE. Long ago?

DU MESNIL. Some time ago.

CLOTILDE. It seems to me that when one of your friends is here, you might show yourself and welcome him.

DU MESNIL. I was finishing something.

CLOTILDE. What did your uncle tell you?

DU MESNIL. I didn't find him in.

CLOTILDE. One doesn't find him easily.

DU MESNIL. He left me word to come again today.

CLOTILDE. Do you want me to go with you?

DU MESNIL. You'd get in our way.

CLOTILDE. Thanks.

DU MESNIL [*going to* LAFONT *and giving him his hand*]. How are you?

LAFONT. Not bad. And you?

DU MESNIL. Anh! I'm not very lively at the moment.

LAFONT. What's the matter with you?

DU MESNIL. I work a great deal and my health suffers for it.

LAFONT. Then take a rest.

DU MESNIL. It takes time and money to take a rest.

LAFONT. As for money, you earn it.

DU MESNIL. I get it with one hand and I give it with the other.

LAFONT. Well, it's amusing.

DU MESNIL. It's amusing . . . when one's a bachelor.

CLOTILDE. You'll soon be finished complaining, won't you? You think that you interest Monsieur Lafont and that you please me? Why all these lamentations? You eat well; you sleep well; I know of no husband who is pampered like you. You work! No doubt you do work! Everyone works! If I were in your place, I'd do four times more work and say forty times less about it.

DU MESNIL. She's superb, my wife! You don't know, my dear friend, how it is in a household like mine, where the costs increase every year and the tastes become more expensive every day.

CLOTILDE. You continue?

DU MESNIL. Let me talk a bit. I didn't disturb you a while ago. Sit down and take up your work, if you're so industrious. Take a look at your children's pants; it won't do any harm; the poor little things always have their bottoms in a draft.

CLOTILDE. I spoil them too much.

DU MESNIL. But you don't mend them enough.

CLOTILDE. That's what the maid is for.

DU MESNIL. We're lodged as modestly as possible; I pay very dearly to live in a prison. The servants today are no longer content with wages; it's salaries that they demand. We dine out often, it's true—almost every day; but my wife, naturally, wishes to dress like all the ladies, and what we save on one hand, we waste on the other. We dine better; that's the advantage.

CLOTILDE. You're receptive to that.

DU MESNIL. I don't deny it. I prefer having a good dinner out to a bad one at home.

CLOTILDE [going to him]. Do stop, I beg you, and let's talk about more agreeable things.

DU MESNIL. You're celibate, my dear Lafont; well, believe me, stay that way.

LAFONT. Is that your advice, Madame?

CLOTILDE. Marry or don't marry; it concerns you alone. [She moves away.]

DU MESNIL. Will you be more amiable than my wife, and listen to what I'm about to tell you?

LAFONT. Very gladly.

DU MESNIL. At the moment, effective measures are being taken in my behalf, measures worth the trouble.

LAFONT. Tell me about it.

DU MESNIL. It's my uncle, my uncle Jean-Baptiste, the member of the Institute, who, for a long time, has not been satisfied with my position. He wishes me to return to the Ministry of Finance. He has friends there, most of whom know me; these gentlemen have jointly taken action to find me a particular receiver's office.

LAFONT. That's the position which would suit you, which you could occupy with ease, and where you'd no longer have need of anyone.

DU MESNIL. I'm not progressing badly at the moment. I'm very much appreciated by my Societies now; there's not one figure written down which doesn't pass before my eyes. My collaboration is much sought for the *Monitor of Agricultural Interests*, in which I explode a bomb from time to time; it spreads my name. I accept everything that comes my way. But my uncle turns a deaf ear to that. He feels that, at my age, with a wife and children, one ought to have his place made somewhere.

LAFONT. He's right.

DU MESNIL. Perhaps he is right. I'm not a mathematician; I'm not an economist; I'm something else. I'll tell you, between ourselves, that my little work, my *Moral Considerations on the Budget*, has been much sought after. Such books are addressed only to a discriminating public and don't come out like novels. Nevertheless, they've sold, by this time, one hundred and nineteen copies of my *Considerations*. Or one hundred and eighteen. There's one copy which hasn't found its way back again. It may have been stolen. I see an entirely new field for me there, a gold mine to exploit.

LAFONT. Get the receiver's office first; it's more certain; afterwards, you can do what you wish. I'll try, from my side, to give you a leg up.

DU MESNIL. Keep it down. My uncle has pushed ahead in this campaign, and he wishes to be left alone with his friends to finish it. It seems to me that when a member of the Academy of Moral and Political Sciences consents to solicit, when he solicits for his nephew, when that nephew . . . is something important, the government has only to agree. Is that your opinion?

LAFONT. Positions are not always at his disposal.

DU MESNIL. I know of one that will be very soon.

LAFONT. Tell me. Is it definite that they've promised you a receiver's office in Paris?

DU MESNIL. In Paris, of course. My wife could not endure the country.

[CLOTILDE, *during this exchange, has come to sit near the table; she has withdrawn her letter from under the blotter, and has profited from the fact that her husband has turned his back in order to show it to* LAFONT *several times with a gesture which signifies*: "*Yoo-hoo, here it is!*" *This business should be calculated in such a way that the last words of* DU MESNIL *coincide with it.*]

CLOTILDE. Adolph, read this letter.

DU MESNIL [*turning around*]. What does it say, this letter?

CLOTILDE. Open it and you'll see. [*Rising and giving him the letter.*] It's Pauline who's written me.

DU MESNIL [*reading*]. "My dear, you are about to receive, if you have not already done so, an invitation from Madame Simpson for her grand ball on the 25th. Your self-respect was in good hands and has not had to suffer. I've broached your name; they've caught it on the wing, saying that they were well acquainted with you, that you were a very attractive person, and that they would be charmed to have you at their soirees. You're one of the family there. I'm quite sure that my friend will please you, and that you'll get along together very well. Oh, it's true, she's no longer in her youth. You will tell me the age you think her, and I shall tell you the age she is. That's no obstacle, though, for, at the ball, in décolletée, with all her diamonds, the ex-beauty, Madame Simpson, still creates an illusion. With her arms! With her eyes! A way of smiling that I have never seen except with her! And what indulgence! She is not shocked by anything; she understands every weakness; there is no folly, however great it may be, which does not seem to her either interesting or excusable; she is truly a great lady." [DU MESNIL, *disturbed and shocked, turns his eyes toward* LAFONT. *The latter, even more affected, is anticipating his glance; they exchange their troubled feelings by shaking their heads several times.*]

DU MESNIL [*returning to the letter*]. "And what indulgence!" [*He looks at* LAFONT; *same business.*] "She is not shocked by anything!" [*Same business.*] "She understands every weakness!" [*Same business.*] "There is no folly, however great it may be. . . ." [*Going to* CLOTILDE, *who finds herself placed between the two men,* DU MESNIL *at her right.*] I don't very much like this letter from Pauline.

LAFONT [*at her left*]. Your friend, Madame, is very irresponsible.

DU MESNIL. Look at that, now, look! I know her, that Madame Simpson; they're spreading strange stories about her.

LAFONT. Madame Simpson has a deplorable reputation.

DU MESNIL. Listen to that, now, listen! I do not wish to take you into a compromising house.

LAFONT. Your place is not, I assure you, in the company of such disreputable women.

DU MESNIL. Well? It ought to impress you to see that Lafont and I think in exactly the same way.

CLOTILDE. Very well. We'll do as you wish. [*Looking at* LAFONT.] If we don't go to Madame Simpson's, we'll go elsewhere, that's all. But, in the future, you should wait to discuss certain matters until we're alone. I'm not in the habit of taking advice from strangers. [*She leaves them abruptly.*]

DU MESNIL. What's that you say? Lafont! A stranger! [*To* LAFONT.] Then there's been a disagreement with Clotilde?

LAFONT. It's you, since you've been here, who irritate her uselessly.

DU MESNIL [*going to* CLOTILDE]. I'm leaving.

CLOTILDE [*dryly*]. *Bon voyage!*

DU MESNIL. What are you doing today?

CLOTILDE. Whatever pleases me.

DU MESNIL. Where are we dining this evening?

CLOTILDE. I know nothing of that.

DU MESNIL. How you answer me!

CLOTILDE. I continue to put myself out for a quarrelsome and disagreeable man.

DU MESNIL. So you want very much to go to this ball.

CLOTILDE. It has nothing to do with the ball. I'd already forgotten it. I'm no longer twenty, I'm sure, to worry about one ball more or less. You complain! You shout! You abuse your wife without the least regard for her! If someone were to overhear you, he would have a very sad idea and a very false idea of our homelife.

DU MESNIL. I'm joking, stupid, so don't be angry. You'll find much of it with husbands like me. I growl for three seconds, and, when you've decided something, it always has to happen your way. Who is it that's master here?

[*She smiles.*]

I think a great deal about that receiver's office, which would be a big affair for us, and ought to interest you more. Come, Clotilde, very seriously, you think that I might succeed?

CLOTILDE. We'll see.

DU MESNIL. I have the qualifications, haven't I?

CLOTILDE. The qualifications! They don't count.

DU MESNIL. I'm backed by competent men.

CLOTILDE. They have no influence.

DU MESNIL. And the strong support of the Institute wouldn't seem to you decisive?

CLOTILDE. You don't wish me to get involved in it; perhaps you're wrong.

DU MESNIL. What would you do?

CLOTILDE. A thousand things, which cost a woman nothing, and which she can occupy herself with as she makes her rounds. I'd put all my friends in the field—Pauline first. She admires you very much; Pauline does! She would prefer that her husband were like you! Pauline, who is very close to Madame Simpson, would have interested her in our situation. You make me laugh when you don't wish to visit Madame Simpson. Indeed, she scoffs at us. She receives all the best people in Paris. She has two or three cabinet ministers at her table every day. She would have asked you to dine with them, quietly, as an equal, while you smoked those large cigars that you're so fond of; and, the day when your competent men came to tell you, "We're very angry; the position was promised," you'd have replied, "I'm well aware of that; I have my appointment in my pocket." That's how I understand affairs.

DU MESNIL. Perhaps you're right. Listen. Let's not rush anything. If I see for a moment that things are turning out badly and that my connections aren't enough, then we'll try to make use of yours.

CLOTILDE. Whenever you wish. [*He turns to go; she overtakes him.*] You know that's my motto with you.

[*They laugh.*]

DU MESNIL. I'm going to see my uncle. Do I take Lafont away or do you prefer to keep him?

CLOTILDE. I'll keep him. He irritates me, but he amuses me. His nose always makes me laugh.

[*They laugh.*]

DU MESNIL. You treat him badly—this poor Lafont, who's so amiable and obliging.

CLOTILDE [*in her husband's ear*]. I wouldn't want a man to embrace me with a nose like that.

[*They laugh.*]

DU MESNIL [*going to* LAFONT]. Well, I'll see you later. Don't come with me; stay, if I'm as disagreeable as my wife says. You, you don't know how it is with a wife and children. You love them very much; you think of nothing but them; you'd find yourself completely lost without them; but that does not prevent you, at times, from wishing them all to the devil.

[*Exit.*]

Scene 3

CLOTILDE. You get an inkling of how much caution one must take; had my husband come in one minute sooner, I was lost.

[*Pause.*]

LAFONT. You were making fun of me.
CLOTILDE. How is that?
LAFONT. With that letter!

[*She laughs.*]

It would have been so simple to show it to me right at first.

CLOTILDE. I thought that it wouldn't please you; I was not mistaken. And, besides, it was a trap I'd set for you. I wanted to know if you would stop in time.

LAFONT. For another occasion.

CLOTILDE. For another occasion, precisely. You are stupid, my dear, and unlucky in your suppositions. Look here, I'm quite willing to do something for you, though you hardly deserve it. My husband opens all my letters—all, without exception; I've preferred it so; you may rest assured on that point. Sit down and let's chat a bit, please. Let's chat without getting angry, shall we? My husband on one hand, you on the other, it's perhaps too much in the same day. Do you wish to tell me what bug has bitten you, and what's meant by this jealousy, which could become alarming? It seized you all at once, without giving warning, around January 15th. [*He looks at her; she smiles.*] I have a reason for recalling that date.

LAFONT. What reason?

CLOTILDE. I have one, that's enough. Now you're not going to dwell on every word. Go on, talk a bit; I'm listening to you.

LAFONT [*after having hesitated*]. Where have you been?

CLOTILDE [*laughing*]. That's right. I beg your pardon, my dear. I forgot that you'd asked me that question several times, and that I still hadn't answered it. I had an appointment—don't flare up—with my milliner, where one encounters very few gentlemen, I assure you. You allow me to go to my milliner from time to time. Now, do as I wish and answer me. Unless I knew what my offenses toward you were, I should always have great difficulty in finding them for myself.

LAFONT. I no longer see you.

CLOTILDE. Pooh! And what, then, are you doing at this moment? Am I not here? So much the worse for you, if you waste, in disputes and quarrels, that time which we might spend more agreeably.

LAFONT. I've waited for you all this week . . . last week, too . . . even the week before . . . .

CLOTILDE. What nonsense! Why not for a year? And if that were so, if I had broken my word to you, not once, but a hundred times, fine reason suddenly to imagine such horrid things. Do I always do with myself as I wish? Don't I depend on everyone here? [*Touching his arm.*] I'm married; you don't appear to be aware of it. There's something else. I wish that you'd tell me what it is.

LAFONT. It seems to me that our relationship no longer interests you . . . that you desire novelty and that perhaps you've run across it . . . that we're at that inevitable stage when the lies, the shabby tricks . . . the petty indignities begin.

CLOTILDE. I don't quite know, my dear, at what stage all those pretty things begin; you are more informed of them than I. I'm asking you for facts, something distinct, precise, and positive, that I can annihilate with a single word. As for what happens in your imagination, what could you expect that I'd reply? It doesn't seem to me very cheerful, your imagination, or filled with rosy memories!

LAFONT. That date . . . January 15th . . . which you've remembered so precisely . . . .

CLOTILDE [more attentively]. Well? That date?

LAFONT. It's struck me, too.

CLOTILDE. Admit that it hasn't, that it hasn't struck you at all. I was stupid to have troubled you with that date, which signifies something to me and means nothing to you.

LAFONT. I've taken note of many things since.

CLOTILDE. What?

LAFONT. Many observations.

CLOTILDE. What observations?

LAFONT. Oh! It's nothing; they're nuances. But nuances! One must not trifle with nuances!

CLOTILDE. Let's look at them a bit, these nuances.

LAFONT. You've changed very much, my dear Clotilde, without giving an account of yourself. First, you mock me; that's unkind. I find you absent-minded very often, and very often embarrassed, too. I see that you hide from me what you're doing; then I'm afraid to question you. It sometimes happens that you contradict yourself.

CLOTILDE. That surprises me.

LAFONT. You tell me about people of an entirely different world from yours, whom you know by heart overnight; how do you do it? Now it's you who recount all the scandals to me; till now, I've had the pleasure of telling them to you. Your political opinions are no longer the same!

CLOTILDE. What a big baby you are! And here I am, listening

to you seriously. My political opinions! You mean to say
that I'm a reactionary. I have not changed. Oh! As to that,
yes, you're right; I am a good reactionary. I love order,
peace, well-established principles. I want the churches to
be open, if the mood takes me to make the rounds. I want
the shops to be open, too, and full of pretty things which
I have the pleasure of seeing, if I lack the means to buy
them. But, admitting that my political opinions have been
altered, it seems to me that you less than anyone should
complain of it. You don't turn up your nose at everything new. You're democratic; it's a fashion today which
doesn't bind you to anything; it's in all the parties. You're
a free thinker! I do believe that you could very pleasantly
come to terms with a mistress who had no religion; how
dreadful! What was it that my husband happened to talk
to you about, if I may ask?

LAFONT. He spoke to me about a position that he wishes to
obtain, and which, perhaps, they will give him.

CLOTILDE. That didn't interest you?

LAFONT. Very much.

CLOTILDE. You say "very much" just as you would say "not at
all." How did you find my husband?

LAFONT. Well.

CLOTILDE. He didn't appear to you anxious and tired?

LAFONT. No.

CLOTILDE. Let's leave that. I don't know why I talk to you
about Adolph, for all the affection that you bear him. That
doesn't matter. This is the point I wished to come to. Now,
you know that my husband expects a position; he expects
it from the government—that goes without saying. Whatever government it may be, when someone desires a position, it is clearly to it that he must address himself. And do
you believe that I would criticize the government at the
very moment when it concerns itself with us? A man
would do that. He is always so talkative, a man, so blun-
dering and so ungrateful! Women, never! You wish me to
tell you, my dear? You've yielded to a very nasty scheme.
You've thought, perhaps, that by going ahead you might
discover something; but you don't know anything, and you
won't know anything . . . because there isn't anything to
know. This is a lesson which will not be lost on me. In the
meantime, listen carefully to this: it is necessary that you
be prudent, patient, confident; that you content yourself

with what you're given, without demanding the impossible. You ought to remind yourself that I'm not free, that I have a household to manage, and correspondence to maintain; the game of love comes only after that. Bear in mind, too, that the slightest indiscretion on your part may compromise me, and, if my husband learned something, hurl me I don't know where. I do not wish, understand me clearly, I do not wish to find you a second time, as I did today, planted in front of my door, gesticulating and ready to devour everyone, when I'm quite peacefully returning from my dressmaker's.

[LAFONT, *who has listened to all of this speech with head bowed, raises it suddenly.*]

Well? What is it that's seized you now?

LAFONT. Where have you been?

CLOTILDE. I've just told you.

LAFONT. Is it to your milliner's or to your dressmaker's that you've gone?

CLOTILDE. Why?

LAFONT. Answer. Is it to your milliner's or to your dressmaker's that you've gone?

CLOTILDE. I've been to both; there, are you satisfied? Now, you must get up and be on your way.

LAFONT. No.

CLOTILDE. Yes.

LAFONT. Later.

CLOTILDE. Immediately.

LAFONT. What affair presses you?

CLOTILDE. No one. Nothing presses me.

LAFONT. Then let me stay.

CLOTILDE. That's not possible. If my husband came back and found you still here, he might be seriously disturbed. Come, be reasonable and say good-by. You'll talk less another time.

LAFONT. Clotilde!

CLOTILDE. What is it now?

LAFONT. I'm going home.

CLOTILDE. Go home, my dear; I am not detaining you.

LAFONT. You know the time?

CLOTILDE. Approximately.

LAFONT. The day's not ended yet.

CLOTILDE. It's no longer beginning.

LAFONT. You have only to put on your hat; that's not much of anything.

CLOTILDE. I saw that coming. I would have been quite surprised if all your fuss had ended otherwise.

LAFONT. Put on your hat, will you?

CLOTILDE. Agreed. It's the one good idea that you've had; it's only right that I should profit from it. Be on your way.

LAFONT. You'll follow me?

CLOTILDE. I'll follow you.

LAFONT. Instantly?

CLOTILDE. Instantly. But, now, be off.

LAFONT. Till then?

CLOTILDE. Till then.

[*Exit* LAFONT. CLOTILDE *crosses to ring.*]

ADELE [*entering*]. Madame rang for me?

CLOTILDE. Adele, bring me my dressing gown and my slippers; I'm not going out again.

ACT TWO

Same decor.

Scene 1

CLOTILDE [*who is in street dress, ready to go out, takes a last glance at her attire*]. Do I look all right, Adele?

ADELE. Yes, Madame.

CLOTILDE. Just right?

ADELE. Just right, Madame.

CLOTILDE. Tell me the time.

ADELE. Almost three, Madame.

CLOTILDE. Do I have everything I need on the table?

ADELE. Everything that Madame usually takes. Her keys, her notebook, her box of face powder.

CLOTILDE. Give them to me.

ADELE [*with a knowing air*]. Madame will not return today.

CLOTILDE. It's possible.

ADELE [*same tone*]. It's probable.

CLOTILDE. Why?

ADELE. I believe that Monsieur has his dinner with the economists; he wouldn't miss it for the world.

CLOTILDE. Well?

ADELE. I've noticed that Madame spends that day at the home of a schoolmate, whom Madame's husband never sees.

CLOTILDE. Then you listen to what we say?

ADELE. I don't listen, no, Madame; I hear only a few words in passing. . . . I've informed Madame that my brother . . .

CLOTILDE. Your brother, I know him! You wish to go out; very well, go.

ADELE. Thank you, Madame. [CLOTILDE *moves toward the door upstage center.*] Madame has no further instructions for me?

[57]

CLOTILDE. No. Tell the cook not to leave, so that Monsieur
may have her at his disposal when he returns to dress.

ADELE. Yes, Madame. Madame doesn't wish me to find her
a carriage?

CLOTILDE. It's unnecessary. I'll find one on my way.

ADELE [*following* CLOTILDE]. See you later, Madame. Have
a good time.

[*When they have reached the door upstage, a bell rings,
stopping them abruptly; pause.*]

ADELE. Someone rang, Madame.

CLOTILDE. I'm quite aware of that. [*Returning onstage.*]
Three o'clock! He hasn't come for a very long time! He
knows that the economists' dinner is today! I should expect
some fit of ill temper from him!

[*A second ring of the bell.*]

ADELE. What has Madame decided?

CLOTILDE. Go to the door, Adele; I'm not at home to anyone.

ADELE. If it were Monsieur Lafont, Madame?

CLOTILDE. I've told you, not to anyone. I do not receive
Monsieur Lafont sooner than any other.

ADELE. Very well, Madame.

CLOTILDE. Leave the doors open so that I can hear what they
say to you. If it should be some business for my husband,
admit them and I'll come in.

ADELE. That's understood, Madame.

[*A third ring of the bell.*]

There's impatience for you, and how useless! [*Exit.*]

Scene 2

CLOTILDE [*alone*]. I've been wrong not to hurry. I should
have been gone by this time and no one could have bothered me. [*Going to the door upstage, which she holds
ajar.*] It's him all right! He couldn't miss such a fine opportunity. . . . Talk, my friend, talk. . . . Question the
servant. . . . I do believe that he's asking Adele where I
am. . . . He insists. . . . What's this? Adele's letting him
in . . . ! [*Returning onstage, step by step.*] He's coming
in, really, he's coming in. Is he going to set up camp here?

Ah! Men! When we no longer love them, this is how they behave toward us! [*Exit quickly to the right.*]

Scene 3

LAFONT [*entering*]. It's all right, Mademoiselle, it's all right.

ADELE [*without seeing* CLOTILDE *hiding behind the door*]. Why won't Monsieur listen to me? Monsieur sees very well that there's no one here.

LAFONT. I'll wait.

ADELE. Wait for what? Monsieur and Madame have just gone out.

LAFONT [*after having hesitated*]. Together?

ADELE. No, Monsieur, not together. Monsieur has gone his way, and Madame hers.

LAFONT. Did Monsieur say what time he would be home again?

ADELE. I know only that Madame will not return. She's dining out.

LAFONT [*after having hesitated*]. With Monsieur?

ADELE. Without Monsieur. Monsieur has his plans for dinner, and Madame hers.

LAFONT. Go on with your work, Mademoiselle. I see there's something to write with here; I'll leave a little note.

ADELE. As Monsieur wishes. It's not for me to give instructions here; I can't show Monsieur the door. [*Exit.*]

Scene 4

LAFONT [*alone, while* CLOTILDE *is still hiding behind the door*]. I've come in; I don't know why I've come in; it's another blunder I've committed. . . . I must calm down and resign myself to a necessary separation. . . . In Paris, one can't keep a mistress who's even a bit proper; it's not possible. The more proper she is, the less one can keep her. . . . I'll have a reckoning with Clotilde, a bloody reckoning! . . . It'll be noble on my part, and I'll definitely give her up. I fret, I run, I try to keep track of her on the right, while she eludes me on the left—to what end? What would I learn, besides . . . ? She's the mistress of that Monsieur Mercier; it's as clear as day. Since when? What advantage would I have in knowing that? Why? Ah! Why?

I'd be very embarrassed to say why. Perhaps she doesn't love him; that's one consolation. . . . What shall I do? If Adolph were only here, we could have ended the day together. It's true. When I've lost heart and Clotilde has turned me upside down, it's with her husband that I feel better once again. I feel less alone. Adolph's position consoles me a little for my own; his is not as good, it certainly is not as good. If Clotilde owes me nothing, after all, she's been very much in the wrong toward her husband. . . . I'm certainly inclined to judge her conduct strictly when I put myself in her husband's place. . . . Such desolation! I suddenly find that I'm completely isolated, without a tie, sick at heart, in a situation of the most vulgar sort, where I shall sink indefinitely! Well, men are hardly ever happy; celibates or cuckolds, there's very little choice.

CLOTILDE [*behind the door*]. It can't be helped; I'll show myself. At least I'll find out what he wants of me. [*Enter.*]

Scene 5

LAFONT. What! You're at home?

CLOTILDE. Well! Why is it so strange that I should be at home? The strange thing is that you find yourself here, you, when I'm not at home to visitors, and when you're told so in every way. That's how you thank me for my indulgence! You know nothing more than contriving to displease me, and every time I weaken enough to forgive you.

LAFONT. It's your fault!

CLOTILDE. Oh! Let's not begin again, I beg you. No scenes today, no scenes! Besides, I shouldn't give in to them. Had you a reason at least, a pretext, some terrible discovery which you couldn't keep to yourself any longer?

LAFONT. I feared, I confess it to you, whether you might not be ill.

CLOTILDE. That's very gracious of you. You've seen me, you're reassured, [*She motions him to the door, imitating the flight of a bird with her hand.*] fly away.

[*Pause.*]

LAFONT. You're going out?

CLOTILDE. It seems to me that I am going out. I don't make a habit of promenading with a hat on in my apartment.

LAFONT. You're pressed?

CLOTILDE. I'm late.

LAFONT. We're not deciding anything.

CLOTILDE. What's that meant to imply?

LAFONT. I thought that we would dine together, if I'm still your schoolmate.

CLOTILDE. There's no longer any schoolmate, neither for you nor for anyone. I've come to the conclusion that these escapades in restaurants have all sorts of disadvantages. They lead me into falsehoods which revolt me and which I do not wish to continue. Am I not right?

LAFONT. Don't ask me what I think.

CLOTILDE. You hold it against me?

LAFONT. I expect anything now.

CLOTILDE. That's always the wisest; in that way, one has no disappointments.

[*Pause.*]

LAFONT [*going to her*]. Do be good enough to sit down, and let's chat together affectionately.

CLOTILDE. I have no time . . . to chat. Another day, tomorrow, if you wish.

LAFONT. I'll wait for you tomorrow and there will be something else again, at the last moment, which will keep you from coming.

CLOTILDE. You refuse tomorrow . . . ? As you wish. That suits me perfectly. I'm never in a hurry to find myself with discontented and disagreeable people.

LAFONT. It's love which makes me so.

CLOTILDE [*contemptuously*]. *Love?* It's tiresome!

LAFONT. Complain, I urge you to do so, complain. It's easy to see that you're not in my place. I'm in despair, and here I dance attendance on one side, while you gallop on the other.

CLOTILDE. I gallop! What sort of expression is that? Let's admit that it's possible that I've become a little cool toward you; you believe that you can win back a woman by acting as you have done, by perpetually tormenting her. It's exactly the opposite which happens; you exhaust her, you make her impatient, and you give her ideas which were a thousand miles from her mind. [*Approaching him again with a tender expression which deceives him.*] Go take a little trip.

[*One move by* LAFONT.]

Yes, take a little trip. Go away . . . six months, that's not
a long time. A separation just now would be very pleasant
for you, and you'd be that much more agreeable on your
return. Don't fear anything on my account. I'm not a
woman who forgets easily. You'll find me exactly the
same. Will you? No, you won't. You can't go away for six
months, when your mistress asks it of you and when she
would regard it, on your part, as a real token of affection.

[*Pause.*]

LAFONT. Where are you going?

CLOTILDE. Is that all that you can find to say to me?

LAFONT. Where are you going?

CLOTILDE. I was so sure that you'd ask me that question;
since you're here, I expect it.

LAFONT. Does it embarrass you?

CLOTILDE. Not at all. You'll be much the wiser, won't you,
when you know where I'm going? And what would prevent me from telling you, "I'm going here," when I'm
going elsewhere?

LAFONT. I'll follow you.

CLOTILDE. Follow me, I urge you to do so; you've succeeded
brilliantly that way up till now. Take care. I'm very partial
to you, very partial. I take account of everything, the
state I see you in, and the moments that we've passed
together; but don't presume the right to take advantage of
it. [*Accentuating each word.*] I do whatever pleases me,
and that concerns no one but my husband.

LAFONT. You're deceiving me!

CLOTILDE. Me . . . ! With whom . . . ? Whom . . . ? Whom
. . . ? Whom . . . ? Whom . . . ? Understand that suspicions
are not enough, and that, in order to accuse a woman, you
must have the proof in your hands. When that proof exists,
when the woman is truly guilty, a man of honor knows
what's left for him to do; he leaves her . . . or he holds his
tongue.

LAFONT. Clotilde!

CLOTILDE. Whom . . . ? Then tell me his name, if you only
know who it is! I'd be delighted to know him, this Don
Juan, whom I perhaps weary with my pursuits, and who

hardly suspects his good fortune! You force me to tell you
that which I would always have wished to conceal from
you. I've made a great mistake! I had a husband, children,
an adorable home; I've wished for more, I've wished for
everything. I've dreamt, like all women, of a unique existence, where my duties would be fulfilled without my
heart being sacrificed—earth and heaven! You've taken it
upon yourself to demonstrate to me that it's impossible. I
don't know what would have happened with another; nothing worse could happen to me. What's done is done; I
don't hold it against you, but this has been the first and
the last time. [*She takes out her handkerchief and puts it
to her eyes with a delicate touch.*]

LAFONT. Are you ill?

CLOTILDE [*reaching a seat*]. It's nothing, it will pass.

LAFONT. I've been wrong.

CLOTILDE [*profoundly*]. Very wrong.

LAFONT. I'm leaving.

CLOTILDE. It's the best thing for you to do.

[*He withdraws and returns.*]

LAFONT. Forget the one word I shouldn't have spoken. It
means nothing. I don't believe that you were deceiving me.
You're too good and too sincere; you appreciate, at the
bottom of your heart, the tenderness I feel for you. I
presumed that you were waiting for me, and that our
usual little holiday still held; rage seized me when you told
me no. Where are you going? Paying visits, meeting one
of your friends again? Is it a very great pleasure, or an
absolute necessity? Make an excuse, if you must. Write
that your husband is ill and that you are staying close by
him; it's very simple. Do what I ask. Give me this day
which has belonged to me for a very long time, and which
you have reserved for me till now.

CLOTILDE. I would if I could, but I can't.

LAFONT. Why?

CLOTILDE. They're coming for me in a carriage, and driving
me to the park.

LAFONT. You were about to go out.

CLOTILDE. That's a mistake. I was waiting.

LAFONT. Madame Simpson?

CLOTILDE. Madame Simpson, exactly . . . I'm dining at her

house. [*Rising again.*] What a strange man you are! You take everything amiss, even that which ought to reassure you.

LAFONT. Madame Simpson!

CLOTILDE. That's right. I forgot that Madame Simpson is not among your friends, and that you wished to forbid me her house. A charming house, superbly furnished and irreproachable! Perhaps there are some trifling love affairs; I can't say; they're almost everywhere.

LAFONT. Madame Simpson, you know it very well, has the blackest reputation.

CLOTILDE. So much the worse for those who've made it for her! When a man has beheld a woman, even a bit of her chemise, that woman is sacred to him, sacred! Hold to that principle and it will serve you on occasion. I'm terrified, I admit it to you. I ask myself where we're going, and what more you're preparing for me. The most grievous offense that could come to a woman, you've come to commit against me today. What next? What's left for you now? I see nothing but violence! I hope that you'll be master of yourself, and that you'll stop short of violence! Consider, my dear; it would be better for us to separate immediately, if you must come to violence! Come now, I'm sending you away again, this time very much in earnest. You're calm now, aren't you? Whatever abhorrence you may feel for Madame Simpson, you'd still prefer me to be acquainted with *her*. We'll return to this idea of a voyage, and I'll bring you around to it, I hope, the next time that I see you.

LAFONT [*piteously*]. Tomorrow?

CLOTILDE. Ah! Tomorrow. Then it's changed now? You really do wish to wait for me tomorrow? So be it! I've only one thing to say. But be well on your guard. You're calm enough at the moment, and quite convinced; don't proceed to change on the other side of the door. You have that fatal flight of stairs, I warn you. If, before tomorrow, you call on me, if I encounter you . . . in the park or elsewhere, if I catch sight of the tip of your pretty nose anywhere, you won't see me again for the rest of your life.

LAFONT. Till tomorrow?

CLOTILDE. Till tomorrow.

[*Exit* LAFONT *quickly.*]

Scene 6

CLOTILDE [*alone*]. Well, that was nothing to speak of. He's been reasonable. When he's angry, it's pleasant, but I always dread seeing him weep. [*Going to the window.*] Let's be sure, before going down, that I won't have him behind me. He's leaving, sadly, his head bowed. Poor boy! Oh! Certainly, I'll pay him a little visit tomorrow. What's seized him now? He's stopping. He's coming right back. He's entering the house across the street. Oh, the monster! He means to lie in wait for me and keep me here till he drops from fatigue. I'm going to show him that I've seen him; it's the only way to make him go away.

[DU MESNIL *enters upstage; his attitude is that of a discontented and discouraged man; he throws his hat on a piece of furniture and comes down to sit near the table, which he shakes with anger.*]

Scene 7

CLOTILDE [*returning and seeing her husband*]. The other one now! [*Regarding him more closely.*] Adolph? Adolph? What are you doing here? [*Going to him.*] Adolph? Answer me, I tell you!

DU MESNIL [*harshly*]. Leave me alone a bit, I beg you.

CLOTILDE. What's happened to you? What an expression to come home with! I've never seen you like this before!

DU MESNIL. Don't annoy me any further. I'm not in the mood to laugh and listen to your childish nonsense.

[*Pause.*]

CLOTILDE [*disturbed, changing her tone*]. What's the matter?

DU MESNIL. You'll know what it is, you'll know it all too soon.

CLOTILDE. Then it's serious?

DU MESNIL. Very serious.

CLOTILDE. You're angry?

DU MESNIL. I would be for less.

CLOTILDE. You're angry . . . with me.

DU MESNIL. It doesn't concern you. You were about to go out, go. Go!

[*She takes one step toward the door.*]

But, first, where are you going?

CLOTILDE [*returning*]. To the Louvre.

DU MESNIL. Go to the Louvre, go. Buy some trinkets; the moment's well chosen.

CLOTILDE. You're beginning to annoy me now. I will not budge before you've told me. [*She takes her hat off abruptly.*] I'm not going out when my husband has some trouble and I don't know what that trouble is. [*Sitting down.*] If he waits to tell me about it, very well; I, too, shall wait to be informed.

DU MESNIL [*rising and going to her*]. You're very kind.

CLOTILDE. Then tell me, stupid!

DU MESNIL. We're done for!

CLOTILDE. In what way?

DU MESNIL. In what way? For the receiver's office.

CLOTILDE [*rising again*]. So it's that! Indeed! You, a man, you put yourself into such a state, and start a revolt to upset me as a counter-blow in a campaign which hasn't gone through. It hasn't gone through, that's all. It's always the same with these campaigns. One fails, the other succeeds; one profits from the good and forgets the bad. You thought perhaps that I would complain and reproach you —never, my dearest, never. Come now, pull yourself together, and don't keep that desolate look. Whatever would become of you with a real misfortune? If you lost me, for example! Which of us two is right? Ha! Your uncle, a fine patron we have there! He doesn't think well of anything, neither your position, nor your writings, nor your wife; and, finally, when he does occupy himself with something, one may be certain that it will be a fiasco. I wonder how he was able to get into the Institute? If he weren't a bachelor, it would certainly make me laugh. Explain to me just a bit of what's happened. You've told me everything, but I don't know anything.

DU MESNIL. I don't know anything else.

CLOTILDE. It's settled, isn't it; everything's been settled?

DU MESNIL. Nearly so.

CLOTILDE. Only nearly so? What does that mean, nearly so? The receiver's office has been filled, yes or no?

DU MESNIL. It hasn't been filled yet.

CLOTILDE. They've done nothing about it, then?

DU MESNIL. The receiver's office is to be filled, and they've given me to understand that it would not be by me.

CLOTILDE. That's good. At last, some information. And whom have they chosen in your place?

DU MESNIL [*after having thrown his hands in the air*]. A man . . . very ordinary!

CLOTILDE. I thought as much. Married?

DU MESNIL. What interest have you in that?

CLOTILDE. Answer all the same.

DU MESNIL. Married, yes.

CLOTILDE. His wife is young?

DU MESNIL. About your age.

CLOTILDE. Pretty?

DU MESNIL. Pleasant.

CLOTILDE [*more softly*]. Obliging?

DU MESNIL. So they say.

CLOTILDE. Ah! The slut!

DU MESNIL. I understand you.

CLOTILDE. It's about time.

DU MESNIL. You're mistaken. Such things are never done in Finance.

CLOTILDE. In short, no one's been appointed yet, neither you nor anyone else, and you've despaired of it too soon; that's your habit.

DU MESNIL. So be it! I'll look at it from your side! What's to be done?

CLOTILDE [*after having considered*]. Get out of the way. [*She passes in front of him brusquely, sits down at the table, and begins to write.*]

DU MESNIL. Tell me just a bit. . . .

CLOTILDE. Don't bother me.

DU MESNIL. Let's consult first.

CLOTILDE. That's useless. . . . I'm writing to Lolotte, and I'm asking her for an appointment; she'll understand that it's a matter of serious affairs.

DU MESNIL. Lolotte! Whoever is *she*, this Lolotte?

CLOTILDE. Lolotte is Madame Simpson. We call her Lolotte in private, since she played that role in *Chaumont*; it pleases her.

DU MESNIL. Very well. Write to Lolotte. You'll say whatever you wish. If Lolotte succeeds where a member of the Institute has failed, I, for my part, shall be delighted, but I shall feel sorry for France.

CLOTILDE. Then leave France alone. She doesn't trouble herself about you; don't you trouble yourself about her. [*Rising again.*] Have you anything to do at the moment?

DU MESNIL. My intention is to stay at home and lock myself up for a week.

CLOTILDE. I don't want that. I have no desire for you to make yourself sick over a campaign which may still turn out very well. You'll take this letter and deliver it to Madame Simpson's; it'll give you some exercise. After that, you'll go to see your uncle.

DU MESNIL. Why? A man who's good for nothing; you told me so yourself. I'll write my uncle that I've had enough of his advice, and that he can keep his influence.

CLOTILDE. I don't want that. Everyone knows that your uncle has occupied himself with a position for us; whoever may be the one to get it for us, understand, it will always be to *him* that we owe it. Don't do anything which would let them say that Madame Simpson patronizes you, and that we carry favors away thanks to her or her circle.

DU MESNIL. That's quite true. I'll deliver your letter, and then I'll go to see my uncle. But the economists will have to do without me this time.

CLOTILDE. I don't want that. Why change any of our habits? It's not a chore for you, this dinner. You usually come home very late, lightheaded enough, with stories which give me a slight idea of your conversation. You're among men, you say silly things, you're right. Don't deprive yourself of a pleasure, then; there aren't so many of them in this world. You'll meet those gentlemen, the sort who entertain you, and I, my little friend who would be grieved not to see me.

DU MESNIL. Very well. I don't insist. But, today, when I'm in a very bad humor, I would have preferred to stay with you.

CLOTILDE. Thanks, but I'm sorry, I can't. Don't regret it; go out. Come now, we'll find time again.

DU MESNIL. Well, I'll see you later; I'm going to deliver your letter.

CLOTILDE. That's it.

[*He moves upstage, piteously.*]

Let's keep our chins up, shall we, and a bit of cheerfulness, if it's possible. Let's not take others into our confidence over our troubles; it'll come to nothing.

DU MESNIL [*returning*]. What shall I say to my uncle?

CLOTILDE. Whatever you wish.

DU MENSIL. Well, then, it's all decided; you're sending me off to this dinner. You're sending me there in an atrocious frame of mind.

CLOTILDE. It'll pass . . . when you're at the table.

DU MESNIL. I'm going to gorge myself until it does. [*Exit.*]

Scene 8

CLOTILDE [*alone*]. Bovary! Oh, of course, talk about virtue and discretion in a woman. "Let her stay at home and her home will thrive." I tell you that's a laugh. What would he have done, that husband of mine, if he hadn't had me? Not to mention that honest people are lucky and that everyone is well disposed toward them! Always, always, when there's something to be given, a position, a decoration, a favor, large or small, and when two candidates are facing each other, on one side, a worthy man, not very strong, but modest and deserving, and, on the other, some humbug who has nothing to recommend him but his *savoir-faire;* always, it's the humbug who carries it off and the good man who gets blackballed! Perhaps I'll end up going out today! I hope that Monsieur Lafont will have tired of waiting for me. He won't complain this time if I get some distance ahead of him. Here goes! [*She moves upstage quickly; the door opens slowly and timidly;* LAFONT *appears, with hesitation.*] Oh! This is too much! [*She returns onstage hurriedly, furious, with a concentrated wrath, a woman resolved not to open her lips.*]

Scene 9

LAFONT. You're angry with me for having returned . . . ? This is what happened. I was going away, I assure you. I didn't want to think about you any more until tomorrow. I caught sight of your husband, who was coming back; what was I to do . . . ? I should have been very happy to shake hands with him, but you, perhaps, would prefer that he were ignorant of my visit; it was more prudent, then, not to show myself. . . . You always tell me that I take nothing into account, when I spend my life in an effort to spare misunderstandings with Adolph. . . . I turned back quickly,

since your husband hadn't seen me, and went into a carriage entrance in order to let him pass. He really did come
back, didn't he? You must have seen him? I'm not inventing anything . . . ? After that, it's true, I was weak, it
wasn't necessary for me to stay there. I told myself:
"Clotilde's waiting a long time for Madame Simpson, who
doesn't appear to be coming at all; if her projects no
longer detain her, perhaps she'll be very glad to see me
again." You can't reproach me for a thought so tender
and so modest . . . ? Your husband has gone out again; that
hasn't changed things; it was beyond all expectations. . . . I
looked once more to see if Madame Simpson's carriage
was approaching; I didn't see anything coming; I came up
again. Oh! I came up again—trembling, I assure you, and
perhaps I would have gone down again [*laughing*] if it
hadn't been for one of those little accidents which are
always so curious: your husband had left the door open.
Look, Clotilde, all of this is so simple, so natural; no one
gets angry over such a little thing. . . . Say one word. You
don't wish to answer me? One word? Only one. . . . [*withdrawing.*] Very well. I'll leave you. You actually prefer to
have this day to yourself. Till tomorrow. [*Returning.*] Till
tomorrow? [*Impatiently.*] Say one word. You don't wish
to say one word to me? [*Withdrawing.*] I'm quite hurt,
I tell you. You've been treating me for some time too
lightly and without any consideration for the past. [*Returning.*] You're quite determined not to answer me?
[*Withdrawing.*] Very well, as you wish; let's call it quits.
You no longer love me; I embarrass you; I no longer have
many great joys with you, while I could be happy elsewhere; let's separate. [*Returning to her and taking her
hand.*] Let's separate like intelligent people . . . ! You
wish me to tell you? You're not waiting for anyone. You're
going to meet your lover again, and it's with him that
you're dining; then you don't deny it . . . ? I know who it
is. I didn't wish to mention his name to you at the moment.
It's . . . Monsieur . . . Ernest Mercier.

CLOTILDE. Alfred Mercier.

LAFONT. Alfred?

CLOTILDE. Alfred Mercier.

LAFONT. Rue de la Madeleine, 28.

CLOTILDE. Boulevard de Madeleine, 28.

LAFONT [*troubled*]. Clotilde? Is this a jest on your part, or really the truth that you're confessing . . . ? It's really the truth, isn't it? [*Weeping.*] Ah! Clotilde! Clotilde! What have you come to? You ought to have deceived me delicately, without letting me see it, and without telling me about it. It's really the end, this time, it's really the end! Good-by . . . . [*Stopping.*] Good-by . . . ? Good-by! [*Exit.*]

Scene 10

CLOTILDE [*alone*]. That's enough of that. I've really wanted to be obliging and to give an account of myself on occasion; but every day, twice a day, no. Ah! Indeed, one would have it pleasant with passions like that, which don't leave you time to breathe. Not to mention that one's always on the brink of catastrophe. It's true. I'm no longer at peace unless my husband's here.

ACT THREE

[*Same decor. The folding doors on the right are open; the table has been placed in the center of the stage in order to serve the coffee there.*]

Scene 1

CLOTILDE [*who is near the table*]. Monsieur Simpson?

SIMPSON [*who is sitting and finishing a cup of coffee*]. Madame?

CLOTILDE. Do act here just as you would at your mother's, won't you, and serve yourself?

SIMPSON. Yes, Madame.

CLOTILDE [*giving a cup to* ADELE]. Take this cup to Monsieur, and leave us.

ADELE. Madame will need me no longer?

CLOTILDE. No.

ADELE. I've informed Madame that my brother . . .

CLOTILDE. Go, you can tell me about that later.

ADELE [*sourly*]. Very well, Madame. [*Exit by the doors to the right, carrying the cup.*]

Scene 2

CLOTILDE [*approaching* SIMPSON *slowly; sotto voce*]. It's really true, then, you're definitely leaving Paris?

SIMPSON. Definitely.

CLOTILDE. This very day?

SIMPSON. I'm taking the seven o'clock train which will get me home at midnight.

CLOTILDE. Your trunks are packed?

SIMPSON. My servant's finishing them at this moment.

CLOTILDE. You've nothing to ask of me?

SIMPSON. There's really so little time left me that I hesitate to disturb you.

CLOTILDE. As you wish. [*She leaves him; he rises and goes to put his cup on the table.*] What does your mother think of this sudden decision?

SIMPSON. My mother's delighted to see me go. It's a little on her account that I'm leaving sooner than usual. She's asked me to inspect her property from top to bottom, and supervise the repairs which will be necessary. I hope that my mother won't recognize Parvenu Hall when she comes to settle there.

CLOTILDE. If your mother's on your side, I have nothing more to say.

SIMPSON. You love Paris too much; you won't admit that one may fare badly here and that one can live elsewhere.

CLOTILDE. I don't think that. I find only that, at your age and in your position, a man does not abandon Paris willingly, especially if he's held here by the slightest attachment. Winter's barely ended; the weather's frightful; no one dreams of leaving Paris yet, except you; you must have a reason.

SIMPSON. Rather, I should need one to stay.

CLOTILDE. Then why are you going away?

SIMPSON. I'm bored. I'm irritated and humiliated. I look like a pauper in your Paris. What sort of place is that miserable mezzanine where I lodge? I'm ashamed to live in it; it's even worse when people do me the courtesy of coming to see me. My mother always refuses to set me up in quarters such as I desire. She prefers that I travel. I spend a great deal of money, gaining from it neither pleasure nor respect. Down there, at Parvenu Hall, the scene changes. I lead a great life. I count in the country; they really bow low to me when I pass. I have close at hand everything that I miss here: my horses, my dogs . . . my guns. You know that I have a magnificent collection of guns, which I'm always a bit anxious to see in good condition again. Obviously, Paris is agreeable; perhaps I'd enjoy it here as much as anywhere, if I had the conditions here which would satisfy my self-respect.

CLOTILDE. That's my fault. I haven't known how to console you and keep you. To part as we are doing, so light of heart, after only four months; the time will not have seemed long to you, I hope.

SIMPSON. *Five* months.

CLOTILDE. You think so?

SIMPSON. Let's count: January 15th, February 15th, March 15th . . .

CLOTILDE. That's quite right. Let's leave it at five months and say no more about it.

[*Pause.*]

SIMPSON [*approaching her*]. You ought to come to Parvenu Hall this year, when my mother will be there with a party of her friends.

CLOTILDE. Don't count on me. My husband can't get away so easily.

SIMPSON. You could leave him here.

CLOTILDE. He doesn't like that.

SIMPSON. You'd meet your friend, Madame Beaulieu, again, since such difficulties don't stop her.

CLOTILDE. Oh, Pauline, that's different. First, she has a fortune, which permits her to do whatever she wishes. Furthermore, her husband has committed grave wrongs against her; she profits from it, and she has good reason.

SIMPSON. She enjoys herself, Madame Beaulieu?

CLOTILDE. I know nothing of that. Pauline and I are very intimate, very intimate; but we don't tell each other everything.

SIMPSON. It was she, nevertheless, who put you in touch with my mother.

CLOTILDE. Pauline has never known why I desired it. What is it which makes you imply that Madame Beaulieu does not conduct herself properly; has someone told you something about her?

SIMPSON. I'm aware of her strong infatuation for one of my friends.

CLOTILDE. You recall his name?

SIMPSON. Hector de Godefroy.

CLOTILDE. That's a lie.

SIMPSON. Hardly a secret.

CLOTILDE. Madame Beaulieu, you can't be unaware of it, has lived for years with a charming young man, who adores her and never leaves her.

SIMPSON. What's his name?

CLOTILDE [*after having hesitated; with a smile*]. Alfred Mercier.

SIMPSON. Yes, but Madame Beaulieu is enamored of my friend, Hector, I wonder why, and she no longer spends a day without seeing him.

CLOTILDE. Whom do you have that from?

SIMPSON. From Madame Beaulieu herself, who doesn't shrink from confidences of that sort.

CLOTILDE. What a child that Pauline is! She couldn't keep such things to herself!

SIMPSON [*going away from her*]. That's what I appreciate even more in leaving Paris; one buries a stack of stories which aren't very savory.

CLOTILDE. Is it because of my friend that you form that phrase?

SIMPSON. I think that she may take her share in it.

CLOTILDE. Pauline has suffered much, remember.

SIMPSON. It would hardly seem so today.

CLOTILDE. You've perhaps made love to her.

SIMPSON. The thought would never have occurred to me.

CLOTILDE. But Madame Beaulieu is simply adorable.

SIMPSON. I'd rather not be included with all the others.

CLOTILDE. Still, you surely must expect it just a bit.

SIMPSON. The ladies wouldn't be pleased if they heard you.

CLOTILDE. What does that prove? That we're weak, fickle, guilty, if you will; that we always let ourselves be carried away; that we meet either clumsy oafs who don't love us as we'd like, or ingrates, they're so much the worse, who have admiration and affection only for themselves! Nevertheless, you're right. The wisest thing would be to have nothing to do with either one or the other; to close one's eyes; to stop one's ears; to say courageously: "Your place is there; stay there." Life wouldn't be very amusing or very thrilling, perhaps, but one would avoid many worries, many deceptions and many regrets.

SIMPSON. What's the matter?

CLOTILDE. Forget it.

SIMPSON. You're crying?

CLOTILDE. And quite sincerely, I assure you.

SIMPSON. Why are you crying, my dear?

CLOTILDE. Does anyone know? There's a bit of everything in a woman's tears.

SIMPSON. I'd be grieved if my departure . . .

CLOTILDE. No. Don't make yourself out more blameworthy than you are. We meet, we please each other, we separate

—that's our story every time. But you gentlemen, you're very accommodating in order to obtain our good graces, and very severe once we've granted them to you. Come! I must call my husband, who, with his kind trust and his sublime ignorance of all our follies, would leave us together until tomorrow. [*Holding out her hand to him.*] Say good-by. Keep these five months a fond memory, that's all I ask. Keep them only for yourself, as you should, and as I can expect on your part. It's to you that we're obliged for having succeeded in that which we desired, but the assistance came only after the misbehavior, and wasn't required. If, some day, in passing, you wish to shake my hand, now you know the home where you have done everything that is necessary to be welcome.

SIMPSON. You are charming.

CLOTILDE. I know it. [*Leaving him, and going to the door on the right.*] Come, Adolph, you've smoked enough. You can finish your newspapers another time. Adolph, listen to me. Monsieur Simpson is putting on his hat; get up immediately if you wish to go down with him. [*Returning.*] My husband's coming.

Scene 3

DU MESNIL [*entering*]. I've behaved like a peasant toward you; I've abandoned you.

SIMPSON. It makes no difference.

DU MESNIL. I've acquired the habit of resting a moment after lunch; it's the only time when I really feel at home.

SIMPSON. You're ready?

DU MESNIL. Whenever you wish.

SIMPSON. Let's go, then.

DU MESNIL. Permit me to have a word with my wife.

SIMPSON. Certainly.

DU MESNIL [*going to* CLOTILDE; *softly*]. Is it necessary that I thank this young man?

CLOTILDE. No. We've invited him to lunch, that's enough.

DU MESNIL. We owe a great deal to his friend in the Ministry.

CLOTILDE. It's his mother who's done everything . . . since I wrote her that note in front of you, remember?

DU MESNIL. I didn't know that Madame Simpson had a son of his age; how do you find him?

CLOTILDE. Distinguished.

DU MESNIL. Lots of grand airs, eh?

CLOTILDE. That doesn't displease me.

DU MESNIL. What did he say to you?

CLOTILDE. That I was perfect.

DU MESNIL. Morally.

CLOTILDE. Physically, too.

DU MESNIL. I'm a great one for having left you together.

CLOTILDE. He leaves this evening.

DU MESNIL. He can come back, too.

CLOTILDE [*into her husband's ear*]. Still, he's not the one who'd make me forget my duties. [*She leaves him.*]

SIMPSON [*going to* CLOTILDE]. You'll be good enough to excuse me, Madame, for leaving so quickly.

CLOTILDE. I know that your time is taken up; you've told me, and I don't dare to detain you.

SIMPSON. I regret Paris already, before having left it.

CLOTILDE. You'll forget it very easily.

SIMPSON. My mother will see you soon, no doubt, and she'll give me news of you.

CLOTILDE. We shall ask her about you, too.

SIMPSON. Remember that you're expected at Parvenu Hall.

CLOTILDE. It isn't likely that you'll see me there.

SIMPSON. I don't consider myself defeated. If an occasion presents itself for me to come to Paris, and I'll create one, if need be, I'll try again to persuade you.

CLOTILDE. Come, not to invite me, but to see me.

SIMPSON. Good-by for now, then.

CLOTILDE. Good-by for now!

[*Exit* SIMPSON.]

DU MESNIL. What did I say to you?

CLOTILDE. What did I reply? Don't concern yourself with that, and get on with your campaigns.

[*Exit* DU MESNIL.]

Scene 4

CLOTILDE [*alone*]. Silly adventure! None of the young men today are worth the trouble one take with them. They're dry, full of pretensions; they believe in nothing; they love to pose, and that's all. I thought that Monsieur Simpson, raised by his mother, could be seriously attached to a woman. I've no reason to complain of him, though. He's always been extremely proper and very obliging. . . . He's a bit silly about his guns. . . . It's been good for me. I've had what I needed, an excellent friend—a second husband, one might say. I've mistreated him in every way; he's had enough of it, that's apparent. Who knows? Perhaps he thinks me more angry with him than I am; men understand us so little. We're very weak, it's true, with those who please us, but we always come back to those who love us.

[*The bell rings.*]

Scene 5

ADELE [*entering*]. Monsieur Lafont, Madame.

CLOTILDE. Well? Why do you take that astonished air to announce Monsieur Lafont?

ADELE. Then Madame intends to receive him?

CLOTILDE. Certainly.

ADELE. Very well, Madame.

CLOTILDE. You may leave now, Adele, if you need to go out.

ADELE. Thank you, Madame. [*She shows in* LAFONT.]

Scene 6

LAFONT [*affected; slowly*]. Good afternoon.

CLOTILDE [*with a calculated tone*]. Good afternoon, my dear.

LAFONT. How are you?

CLOTILDE. So so. Just so so. And you?

LAFONT. Bad. Very bad. Am I disturbing you?

CLOTILDE. Not in the least.

LAFONT. You were about to go out, perhaps?

CLOTILDE. No, really. I rarely go out now. Where would I go?

LAFONT. You've had guests for lunch?

CLOTILDE. *Guests*, no, one person.

LAFONT. A friend?

CLOTILDE. A passer-by.

LAFONT. You know his name?

CLOTILDE. My husband told me, but I no longer recall it.

LAFONT. I chanced to see them leave together.

CLOTILDE. Really? You were there, under my windows? If I'd known it, I would have shown myself for a moment. It's very gracious on your part. At least you haven't forgotten me right away.

LAFONT. Who was that gentleman?

CLOTILDE. A passer-by, I repeat, his first visit. It's not possible that you take umbrage at that. My husband introduced him to me this morning, and this evening he'll be gone.

LAFONT. You're telling me the truth?

CLOTILDE. Why should I lie to you now? You, you don't change; that's one thing to your credit. Come here, to this armchair, and stay there, if it's possible. Don't let me see you pace, fidget, and upset yourself as before. You've left me with better memories.

LAFONT. Clotilde!

CLOTILDE. There's no more of Clotilde.

LAFONT. My dear!

CLOTILDE. Let's be a bit calm, shall we, and not lose ourselves so quickly.

LAFONT. I've regretted very much, you may be sure, that ridiculous scene, which you could have prevented so easily. Look at me. Monsieur Alfred Mercier! [*She laughs.*] What could you expect? I'd been jealous of that Monsieur Mercier for a long time; all my suspicions pointed to him. Madame Beaulieu will not complain of your discretion.

CLOTILDE. That's good. What have you done since I haven't been seeing you?

LAFONT. I've thought about you.

CLOTILDE. That's what you say, of course. What else?

LAFONT. What else? I've lived as usual.

CLOTILDE. You weren't away from home?

LAFONT. I needed a change of surroundings, but I haven't had the courage.

CLOTILDE. The ladies, they've been obliging? They've entertained you well?

LAFONT. I won't answer that.

CLOTILDE. Why? It's possible that previously an infidelity on your part would have been painful for me, very painful; but what was forbidden you then is surely permitted you now. As if I didn't know you, and you're just the man to deprive yourself of consolations. You weren't always very pleasant, my dear, or very cheerful, or very confident, but . . .

LAFONT. But . . .

CLOTILDE. Let's not discuss those things.

LAFONT. I'm suffering much too much, I assure you, to think of consolations. And besides, if fate wills that I've lost you forever, I won't seek someone to replace you in a society which I no longer frequent.

CLOTILDE. You're wrong. You ought to return to the company of those ladies. They're unrestrained; one's not embarrassed with them; they love prevarications, tears and battles; you'll never find it so with us. We can offer you only a quiet affection, sincere . . . and disinterested.

LAFONT. That's what I desire. That's what we all desire.

CLOTILDE. Then, my dear, you ought to have taken care and not risked what you had, for the pleasure of doing something impulsive.

LAFONT. Clotilde?

CLOTILDE. What, my dear?

LAFONT. Give me your hand.

CLOTILDE. No.

LAFONT. You surely can give me your hand.

CLOTILDE. Later, we'll see. Don't put on that face, or I'll send you away this very instant.

LAFONT. Give me your hand.

CLOTILDE. Well, there it is. You need the other one now.

LAFONT. You're very cool.

CLOTILDE. How's that, cool? I ask you to sit near me and I let you put your arm around me; you didn't think that I would throw myself about your neck as soon as you entered.

LAFONT. I'm here as a culprit. I accept all the criticisms you've given me; I think that you've earned some, too.

CLOTILDE. None.

LAFONT. Is it my fault or yours, if our relations have changed all of a sudden? There was no man happier than I till the day when your life was turned upside-down.

CLOTILDE. What's that you say? My life turned upside-down! It could have been only by you, if I hadn't stopped you in time.

LAFONT. You're right. I don't know why I've begun on that again. Let's leave what's happened.

CLOTILDE. What *has* happened? You're incorrigible. I receive you, I listen to you, I believe that you sincerely regret your inexplicable behavior, I tell myself that later, if you seriously reform, it would not be impossible that I'd forgive you, and you still anger me with that ill-humor in you which I detest and which I've never managed to overcome; nothing at all has happened, you understand, nothing, nothing, nothing, absolutely nothing! Move away.

LAFONT. Why?

CLOTILDE. Move away. I wish to get up.

LAFONT. No.

CLOTILDE. Yes.

LAFONT. Let's stay as we are.

CLOTILDE. Let me get up a moment. . . . You're not leaving yet. . . .

LAFONT. Let's go on.

CLOTILDE. How unreasonable!

LAFONT. You're not uncomfortable?

CLOTILDE. I'm nervous and agitated.

LAFONT. All the more reason.

CLOTILDE. What did you say?

LAFONT. I'm finding it difficult to control myself, too.

CLOTILDE. Come now, don't get excited; I'll remain seated.

LAFONT. Then you've thought of forgiving me just a bit?

CLOTILDE. I said so and I was wrong.

LAFONT. Let's take up our good old life again.

CLOTILDE. What's the good of that? You'd never be happy with me and I'd never have peace with you; you don't wish to understand my position.

LAFONT. What position?

CLOTILDE. *My* position. Don't I have a husband on whom I'm entirely dependent, and who ought to find me here every time he so desires? It's certainly the least I can do, you'll admit. There's still one very great offense on your part which you would avoid if you understood me better.

LAFONT. With what do you reproach me?

CLOTILDE. You don't like my husband.

LAFONT. But I do, I assure you.

CLOTILDE. Oh, no, you don't, I guarantee it to you. You don't like Adolph; I see it in many things. It's perhaps your temperaments which aren't in accord, or even the circumstances which have caused it.

LAFONT. What injustice! Your husband! He's never had but two friends in this world!

CLOTILDE. Two?

LAFONT. Yes, two.

CLOTILDE. Who?

LAFONT. You and me.

[*They laugh.*]

Let's leave the others behind and talk about ourselves. Come, Clotilde, be honest, isn't it true that you pleased me?

CLOTILDE. As for that, yes. I believe that I'm to your taste.

LAFONT. An affection like mine is not met with every day; have you taken account of that?

CLOTILDE. Certainly. It's precisely because it does affect me and because I do take account of it, that I've put up with all your tempests.

LAFONT. I'm very gentle usually, very tender. . . .

CLOTILDE. I don't deny it. You know perfectly well how to please, when you really wish to do so, and you sometimes think of extremely pretty things which are very pleasant to hear. . . . It's not you who'd talk to a woman about guns.

LAFONT. What does that mean?

CLOTILDE. Nothing. A piece of nonsense that someone told me. Pay no attention.

LAFONT [*moving in closer to her*]. Tell me that you forgive me.

CLOTILDE [*softly*]. Yes. . . . Be good, won't you?

LAFONT. You forgive me . . . completely?

CLOTILDE. Completely. . . . Don't pester me; I'll come to see you.

LAFONT. Soon?

CLOTILDE. Whenever you wish. . . . Take care, I'm not alone here.

LAFONT. Clotilde!

CLOTILDE. You love me?

LAFONT. I adore you.

CLOTILDE [*rising again*]. The needless words we shall have uttered in order to get back to the same point.

LAFONT [*going to her*]. Do you regret it?

CLOTILDE. Not yet.

LAFONT. I was quite dejected in coming here; I'll leave you with a better disposition.

CLOTILDE. Well, let that little lesson profit you! No more scenes, agreed, no more of those frightful suspicions which alienate a woman and which are so fruitless. When something goes badly, or you're troubled, tell me about it; I'm always disposed to listen to reason. Listen. I'll give you a piece of news which will not displease you.

LAFONT. Go on.

CLOTILDE. I believe that my fine days with Madame Simpson are ended.

LAFONT. Nonsense!

CLOTILDE. Yes.

LAFONT. You've had to complain of her?

CLOTILDE. No. On the contrary, I've had only praise for her. It's not exactly Madame Simpson whom I no longer wish to see; it's her house which it seems preferable not to visit.

LAFONT. What did I tell you at first?

CLOTILDE. You're more shrewd than I, that's all.

LAFONT. I know another person whose company is not very good for you, and whom you also ought to discard.

CLOTILDE. You're about to say something silly, I see it now. That person is . . .

LAFONT. Madame Beaulieu.

CLOTILDE. Me, be on bad terms with Pauline; I should indeed like to know why? Why?

LAFONT. It seems to me . . .

CLOTILDE. It seems to you what?

LAFONT. Monsieur Mercier!

CLOTILDE. Well? Monsieur Mercier?

LAFONT. I've been informed of who he is, and that you surely know, too.

CLOTILDE. Yes, I know him. So what?

LAFONT. You don't defend Madame Beaulieu, I presume.

CLOTILDE. Ah, that! Do you believe even a bit of what you're saying? Do you intend to reproach Pauline for doing for Monsieur Mercier what I'm doing for you?

LAFONT. It's not the same thing.

CLOTILDE. Are you sure of that? Explain the difference to me.

LAFONT. I see one.

CLOTILDE. What is it? Go on. Tell me a bit. What is it . . . ? You're all the same, you gentlemen. For you, we can permit ourselves everything, but you become indignant when there are others who profit from it. Rather than troubling yourself about Pauline, you ought to think about my husband, who has complained every day that we no longer see you and who intends to ask you for an explanation.

LAFONT [*gesturing toward the second door upstage*]. It's Adolph that we chanced to hear returning?

CLOTILDE. Yes, it's Adolph. Have you thought a bit about what you'll say to him?

LAFONT. No.

CLOTILDE. No. It makes you laugh. So much the worse for you, my dear; extricate yourself as best you can.

Scene 7

DU MESNIL [*entering*]. You, there you are!

LAFONT [*embarrassed*]. Good afternoon, my dear friend.

DU MESNIL. Good afternoon. Why haven't we seen you for such a long time?

LAFONT [*embarrassed*]. How are you?

DU MESNIL. I'm in splendid health. You're not answering my question. Tell me, whatever happened that you disappeared overnight?

CLOTILDE. Don't torment him. He's had a great vexation, isn't that so, Monsieur Lafont?

LAFONT. Yes, Madame.

DU MESNIL. What vexation?

CLOTILDE. Is it all right if I tell my husband?

LAFONT. If you wish.

DU MESNIL. Then tell me.

CLOTILDE. He was jealous.

DU MESNIL. Jealous! [*To* LAFONT.] What! You're still jealous at your age? [*To his wife.*] And who the devil was he jealous of? Some woman who doesn't belong to him, of course. These celibates! They deny themselves nothing. They're jealous, into the bargain. Should I tell you the opinion of a noted economist on jealousy? Jealousy is a deprivation, nothing else. If you were married, you wouldn't be deprived, and you wouldn't be jealous. It's true, isn't it, Clotilde?

CLOTILDE. Come now, let up a bit.

DU MESNIL. Jealous! [*To his wife.*] You've told him?

CLOTILDE. About what?

DU MESNIL. That I was appointed.

CLOTILDE. Monsieur Lafont was the first one who'd written to congratulate you.

DU MESNIL. Indeed. I'd forgotten that. He wrote me rather than coming to see me. [*To* LAFONT, *while intentionally looking at his wife.*] It's my uncle, my good old uncle, who's brought off the campaign.

CLOTILDE. Everyone's well aware that it's your uncle; you've no need to shout it from the housetops.

DU MESNIL [*to* LAFONT]. Well? Isn't it better to be a receiver than to be jealous, eh? [*To his wife.*] This poor Lafont! He's still not completely recovered. He doesn't have his usual nose. Now, then, has she deceived you, or *hasn't* she deceived you?

LAFONT. Leave me alone!

DU MESNIL. Come now, you can surely tell *me*. Has she deceived you, *or hasn't* she deceived you?

CLOTILDE. My husband's asking you a question; reply.

LAFONT. What should I reply? Is there any man, even one, who would swear that his mistress has *not* deceived him? Mine tells me that she hasn't; she couldn't tell me that she had. We're reconciled; that's no doubt what we both desired.

CLOTILDE. Really! It's quite unfortunate that the lady's not present to hear you; she would learn the opinion that you have of her, and of all women. Trust, Monsieur Lafont, trust; that's the only system which succeeds with us.

DU MESNIL. It's always been mine, my love. . . .

MICHEL DE GHELDERODE

1898–1962

MICHEL DE GHELDERODE was a Belgian playwright and novelist who wrote in French. He is now gradually coming to be known—and, alas, in some quarters even fashionable—throughout the world, but, in fact, he began to write his plays in the second decade of this century. Ghelderode, like García Lorca in Spain, is a unique figure in the modern theatre. It is unlikely that he will have any heirs, but it seems increasingly certain that history will show him to have been one of the most powerful and significant dramatists of our age.

Part of his uniqueness resides in the fact that he really does not seem to belong to our times—Lionel Abel refers to him as "our man in the sixteenth century"; but this is misleading, for his almost apocalyptic visions, so much like those of the Flemish painters Hieronymus Bosch and Pieter Breughel whom Ghelderode so greatly admired and by whom he was profoundly influenced, strike like lightning to the core of our twentieth-century nightmares.

With some notable exceptions—and *Christopher Columbus* is one—the world of Ghelderode's theatre is the darkly, yet coldly, sensual world of Flanders. It is a baroque world in which all the materials of God's creation, from the richest crimson velvets to the vilest stench of excrement, are heaped upon each other until they create their own explosive heat, resulting in plays which, in language and image, are paroxysms of the sensuous. In all that he writes, Ghelderode reminds us of the brutal fact that there are eternal things—things which cannot be classified, desiccated or demonstrated—and that humanity exists in the midst of this mystery, this fear. His theatre is the celebration of this mystery, and like his medieval blood brothers, he too uses shock and incantation as his central dramatic techniques. Where most contemporary playwrights attempt to discover rational explanations for these mysteries, Ghelderode discovers the demon, and in so doing *reveals* the mystery.

Finally, however, Ghelderode's plays are ruled by the powers of Death and Sin. But these forces have very special characteristics, for Ghelderode was always as much aware of the buffoonery and grotesqueness of evil as he was conscious of its monstrousness. Death may give his plays an atmosphere of darkness, but it is a gloom that is streaked with the colorful and antic shades of farce's absurdity. As a result, his is an almost primordial drama, a drama in which tragic horror and the frankest guffaws are indissolubly mixed. This combination produced plays so unlike most of those written in our time that it is hard for us to think of them as plays at all. They are, as I have suggested, apocalyptic visions. But this playwright of the Apocalypse may have seen much more deeply into the nature of the human condition than any of his colleagues. Ghelderode stopped writing for the theatre just before the outbreak of the Second World War; the theatre is still catching up to him.

THE OSTEND INTERVIEWS[1]

In 1951–1952 Le Club d'Essai de la Radiodiffusion Télé-vision Françaises broadcast some recorded interviews with Michel de Ghelderode. These interviews had taken place at Ostend in August 1951. Ghelderode was ill at the time, and it seems that the interviews would never have occurred had they not finally proved less of a strain on him than fighting off the would-be interviewers. He is not pleased with the record of questions and answers, which was published in 1956 as Les Entretiens d'Ostende, *since it reminds him of a period of great physical and mental discomfort. Also, he regards many of the questions put to him as irrelevant or stupid. Such questions were a source of great irritation to this writer who has always insisted that his private life ought to be private in fact as well as in name, and that his works ought to stand or fall alone, without being aided or hampered by apologies or explanations from their author. Ghelderode's reticence toward being drawn into what he considers fruitless discussion about himself is demonstrated by his frequent re-ply of "That's my business" (or some similar expression) to personal questions. His refusal to be lured into argument by references to his works is illustrated by part of his answer to a question about Mademoiselle Jaire: "You are free to reject a poetical work of this kind that proceeds from the irra-tional, from clairvoyance—but you haven't the right to ask me to justify it. I didn't ask that you call the public to go to see this undesirable play which I didn't ask anyone to put on —any more than I asked you into this room."*

The following selections from Les Entretiens d'Ostende *give some idea of Ghelderode's views on life and art, and*

[1] From *Les Entretiens d'Ostende* by Michel de Ghelderode, translated by George Hauger. Reprinted by permission of L'Arche SA, Paris, and *The Tulane Drama Review*. This translation of these extracts was first published in *The Tulane Drama Review*, Volume III, No. 3, March 1959, pp 3–23.

some idea of his emergence as a dramatist. It would have
been possible to group the extracts according to their topics;
but it has seemed better to leave them in the order in which
they appear in Les Entretiens. *Thus reprinted, they preserve*
something of the informality of the original comments. All
that follows this introductory note was spoken by Ghelderode.
The questions that he was asked have been omitted. In some
places a succession of dots will be noted: if the dots are en-
closed by square brackets, they have been introduced by the
translator to indicate an ommission from the text; otherwise,
they have been transposed from the original version. Finally,
it should be noted that the titles of Ghelderode's works have
not been translated. This is to facilitate reference to the
original texts. Already at least one translator has furnished a
play by Ghelderode with a title that the author did not
supply.

GEORGE HAUGER

If I have a legend, I have had no part in it. It has been
made for me. I have not contributed to it; but I shall not
stoop to contradict it. The matter leaves me indifferent. The
world has need of fables.

What am I?

I am going to tell you, and it is very simple.

I am a man who writes in a room—all alone—and who
does not trouble about the fate of his works, who does not
allow himself to be bothered by the row, the admiration or
the anger that his works may some day provoke. In short, a
man who asks nothing from men except friendliness, a little
tolerant understanding.

Even the theatrical representation of the world of my mind
goes on apart from me. It goes on in a place where there are
too many people, and on a physical plane, in the midst of an
often aggressive crowd; and that makes me uncomfortable,
even frightens me a little. That is why I am hardly ever seen
in theatres—not from diffidence, or because of a pose; but by
the fact of incompatibility, and because from the outset I
chose solitude, the hard road.

Of course, dealings with men, social contacts, are necessary and valuable to us. If one denied oneself these, one
would become arid, inhuman, incomprehensible: one would
be analphabetic. Nevertheless, like the act of love, the work

of art must be accomplished, not in darkness, but behind closed doors, in secret, away from witnesses and their curiosities, whether these be genuine or idle, away from confessions and confidences, gossip and interviews.

I must derive my taste for the supernatural from my mother. She was a timid soul who had remained close to nature, a primitive soul adept at the perception of the mysteries of nature, but also of certain extra-physical phenomena, and she was attracted by past ages and by the arts in their popular forms—images, for example. She was rich in proverbs, in forgotten songs, in haunted stories.

She had been at first brought up very freely in the country. Afterwards she grew up in a convent at Louvain, and there she was taught the lives of the saints, there she was the witness of little miracles. She knew liturgical chant, spoke ecclesiastical Latin, and believed in the devil whom, she said, she had seen many a time.

Be that as it may, it was during this conventual period that she matured, that she really took possession of traditions, hair-raising stories, and ancient legends, which she recounted to me, and recounted to me alone. My brothers and my sister hardly bothered themselves about them.

My father was principal clerk at the *Archives Générales*. He spent a lifetime there, and after his retirement he carried on his researches and his Benedictine tasks, to which he never put his signature. He worked as a subordinate for historians and genealogists, deciphering and copying for them dusty documents, charters, ancient obituary registers, letters patent, magistratic acts—work without glory, but of good account.

Such was our everyday background—parchments, yellowed papers, illegible or faded writings that my father succeeded in reading, as though hypnotized, through a huge magnifying glass. As for seals, they were his specialty. All of this in a sepulchral silence, and also there was a smell. . . .

The house was overrun by the souls of these ancient papers.

Was it the odor of History, the odor of the Past?

Once I put the question.

"Rat's piddle," the dear man replied.

But this odor saturated me forever. And I came across it again when in my turn I became an archivist, as I was during twenty or so years. But, more venturesome in spirit than my author, I used these peaceful years to create my Theatre, hiding behind files and bundles of papers to preserve appearances.

I fell in love with things of the past as every other child falls in love with his toys. I saw nothing else around me—the great wax or metal seals, and those fine counter-seals in their wooden box, these greasy sheets of parchment, these diplomas in weird writing, these letters patent ornamented with coats of arms, at the bottom of which tremendous signatures displayed themselves, the empress Maria Theresa, Philip II, Charles V, and others—from time to time, a Duke of Burgundy.

My father showed me these astounding relics in all artlessness. With his spectacles on his nose, he would laugh contemptuously, "Fuerunt." He also laughed that way because I sat with my behind on a great register in which the sentences of death of the Council of Troubles, or rather the Tribunal of Blood, created by the sinister Duke of Alba, were written. Yes, in this bloody book you could find the minutes of the condemnations to capital punishment of the Counts Egmont and Horn, among hundreds of others. And, in all innocence, I was sitting on it! Again, there were papers that had been pushed away to one corner of the table between the bread and the plates at the evening meal. I remember bundles of letters from Peter Paul Rubens, to some canon, to some Flemish or Italian Maecenas, about the purchase of a canvas, about the disposal of works of art, about grievances, about disputes, with grandiloquent formulas of politeness such as they loved at that time, "Your Lordship's most humble servant. . . ."

My father talked to me a little about these things because I was the only one who happened to be close by him and to listen to him. I was something of his reflection during these evening hours, his shadow, like the dog or the cat on the hearth. I loved him for these rare things, just as, at other times, I hated him for having killed a sparrow and a cricket.

Pedagogues fancy, quite wrongly, that a dreaming child dreams exclusively unclean things. What do they know of the world of childhood which they left prematurely and whose paths they would not be able to find again?

I dreamed wildly, but I watched the flight of a bee, a distant window on fire, or the progress of a white cloud shaped like a swan. "What are you dreaming about, sir?"—"About Lohengrin, sir,"—for I had treated myself to Wagner's opera at the *Monnaie* one fine Sunday. I read—something that was little appreciated by my teachers—but I didn't read forbidden books. I didn't understand them. They remained foreign to me. I think I have told you, I didn't awaken to the things of the flesh until late. I was not born to be of the Don Juan type, not in the least. Woman has been no more the eternal driving power in my life than she has been the inevitable subject of my plays. I have been reproached for this as a defect: yes, indeed!

I have always loved old churches, in the same way as theatres. I willfully say old, not the others; in the same way as old-fashioned theatres, gilded and purple, with a crystalline prism chandelier. Places of enchantment!

Yes, I have always admired rites, the stage management of offices, the glamor of processions and funerals. Somewhere in *Fastes d'Enfer*, I think, I made one of my characters say, "Only the church buries well," and that is true enough.

I cannot go past one of the churches of the past, one of our old chapels, without going inside, even at the risk of being promptly driven out by what I find there in the way of wretched prayer books and abominable pieces of art, and because I don't find the lively and radiant solitude without which the presence of the divine does not operate. What do I do in these holy places? What would I do other than tell the golden beads of dreams? And if you allow that meditation is a form of prayer, you will see me attentive to the call of the angels, to the secret signal from a mystic country whither I shall go when the flame has left the ashes. You should also know that at certain moments I hear an aerial music which, for me, is another sign, an everlasting language which accompanies the whole of my life: I hear bells living, breathing and wandering. I am a lover of bells. A strange passion, isn't it? Not only religious bells, but civil bells also, those carillons that Flanders invented, both the tragic bells with bloody mouths and the triumphant with golden tongues.

Many a time I have traveled to a very ancient and altogether hieratic city of the North, Bruges, where the bells and the carillons are innumerable and where, more than anywhere else, they speak well, are eloquent. And there, in this medieval city which hasn't changed much, I lived in the sound of these carillon recitals, storms of chimes, funeral forges of All Saints. The bells celebrated by Poe and Verhaeren were not yet electrified.

The Flanders I loved abided in this, nothing but this: bells and their towers. It could not be but so. The Flanders that bowled over Rainer Maria Rilke with its ghostly beauties.

Furthermore, you will frequently come across them in my writings, in my plays. They are like an obbligato accompaniment. They are a musical sign announcing the intrusion, the imminence of the supernatural, the approach of mystery.

My work is no more anticlerical than it is proclerical. If I deal with persons of the cloth in a way that rouses your indignation, I am not aiming at institutions or dogmas—neither those of the Roman religion nor those of any other religion.

[. . . . . .]

Why shouldn't people make a Catholic author of me, while they are about it, on the excuse that I have put saints on the stage?

Yes, why shouldn't the fact of having written works with biblical inspiration such as *Barabbas,* or having been the author of plays such as *Saint François d'Assise* prove me a purveyor of Catholic literature?

No, I don't practice that profession: I don't create that kind of theatre. It is a propagandist theatre, a theatre of patronage.

I no more think of edifying than of corrupting—or of convincing.

My second life began the day I realized that I was destined for one or other of the shabby occupations toward which my brothers were heading, banking, business, commerce and what-not. And my worthy father hoped for something similar for his youngest, something safe and respectable. He assumed me to be of mediocre intelligence. In his eyes, a civil servant was the best thing there was in this conformist world.

But, in fact, I was not bothering myself about the future.
More than anything else, I was dreaming.
I had plenty of time, and I believed life was long.
It is.

Moreover, I was already feeling the need for this second life, a secret life that I kept dark, like a hidden treasure. It was the realm of dreams to which, alone, I had found the magic keys. Paternal sermons were obliterated by those of Eulenspiegel, by the preaching of Reynard. And the extravagant discourses of the ingenious Hidalgo completed this topsy-turvy education. Somewhat intoxicated by the discovery of my coming autonomy, I thought about painting, I thought about music, not knowing exactly what, and I was the prey of confused and contradictory aspirations like the young German romantics whose drama was not being able to make up their minds between an artistic and an intellectual discipline.

I served the apprenticeship of a painter. Like other youngsters, I daubed about for some years—without result, if not without conviction.

Fervently, I went in for music; but the study of an instrument soon left me disappointed and did not offer an end in itself.

Then I turned toward writing—since that was what I was to do. But I was still unaware of that. One must take it that the time had not yet arrived.

I no longer go to concerts—I, who was so fond of virtuosi! I deny myself this delight. That is because I am very receptive and it has happened that I have been plunged into an inexpressible condition after certain hearings, certain revelations of important works. Prolonged euphoria became a means of atrophying the creative will.

So, I avoid music as one avoids pleasures that are too violent, too powerful. . . .

Still, it continues to help me in the form of phonograph records that I sometimes listen to in my solitude; but I no longer reckon to move out of a particular musical world which is my proper domain and which I do not seek to enlarge, although I am heedful of new forms.

It is the polyphonic world of the Flemings and the Italians, the medieval and pre-Renaissance polyphony of Guillaume de Machaut, of Dufay, Obrecht, Orlandus Lassus, Palestrina and others. It leads up to him who dominates all in the past and the future—Bach.

There is my great man of music, Johann Sebastian Bach.

I also retain a very great attachment to sacred music,

which is a way of religion to me. Art as religion, and perfectly so.

As for liturgical chant, that is my luxury on selected occasions—like reading *Ruysbroeck l'admirable*.

But equally there are kinds of popular music that very often enlighten me—Spanish, for example. And when I am *available*, as M. Gide put it, I very much enjoy fairground cacophonies, orchestrions, street organs, mechanical pianos, not forgetting nostalgic accordions. I followed a one-man band for days through the alleys of my old city. What a creature!

As for the music of my own time, syncopated music, I acknowledge its existence, but never when I am working. It wearies me very quickly: it distresses me. The silence that follows it is that of the morgue, its odor is that of human carrion. I feel a kind of incurable sadness in it, and I flee this misery of the soul because it is too contagious, too insinuating, and rarely in a pure state as in music taken from its popular sources. They say to me, *Rhythm;* I reply, *Spasm*.

These grindings make me think of outer darkness of the jerkings of *danses macabres*.

But music, yes! *The Mass of Pope Marcellus, The Pastoral Symphony,* and the sublime Berlioz, and my friend Moussorgsky. Yes, I would give a half-century of contemporary music for an air by the chevalier Gluck! But music is constantly present, believe me, it is always there, and it provides, if I may say so, a deep pedal to the whole of my toilsome existence.

A kind of education of the ear leads me to demand a certain music in human speech.

On the stage you can feel very strongly that a musical requirement is prevalent in my prose, in my theatrical language.

Then again, many works have come to me with music in their interstices, an underlying music. This is a fact that has often struck me—while I was writing certain plays, I had old refrains in my head and they followed me and pursued me the whole length of my work.

I can give examples.

The writing of my first theatrical work of any importance, *La Mort du Docteur Faust,* was accompanied in this way by a tune from the fair—a sort of Rhenish dance that a Limonaire organ played doggedly not far from my window.

If such a tune did not really furnish the climate of sound of my play, it helped me to write it, all the same. It was sufficient for me, at about three o'clock in the afternoon, to hear this orchestrion which painfully awoke, yawned, then suddenly burst out like a catastrophe, submerging the neighborhood, to be hurled roughly, headfirst, into the suspended play. The music literally bore me along, like the torrent from a lock that has been suddenly opened.

I have often introduced refrains and songs into my plays, not as tricks, but from necessity.

That was the case in *La Balade du Grand Macabre* and in *Mademoiselle Jaire*, where singing actors appeared. I heard them coming. I hummed their verses, their laments, with them. Sometimes the tunes were of my invention, to be sure, and they were probably incoherent; but what mattered to me was that they were in place and held me bound to my writing.

Yet another example: *Escurial* made me play over in my mind a record I possessed at that time, a harsh and dreary song, somewhat Gipsy, somewhat Arab—dreadfully Spanish. I found in it the mephitic, savage and gloomy atmosphere of a Spain that I wished to raise up, that of a Philip II and contemporary with the building of the Escorial and, indeed, the blazing days of the Holy Inquisition.

But this phenomenon is not very peculiar to me. Many writers as well as the poets have these solicitudes of a harmonic order, admit to similar manias. And if music has helped me a great deal in my work, I will add that it has at the same time remained a kind of recompense and a lasting aspect of my disquiet.

I have already told you, I do not misuse it, and most often I do without it because it torments me. When I am impressed by a work, by a concert that pleases me, I do not sleep. All night I reconstitute the music received as a gift from heaven, in the same way that I reconstitute poems I have heard and which have ricocheted in my heart as in the depths of a well.

It is, moreover, this same eternal music that we demand from poems that I want to find again in the best theatre, welling up, hidden in the dramatic prose, and running beneath it, murmuring and invisible.

There is indeed a certain *Poetic Theatre*—or allegedly so—which is rarely a vehicle for poetry. Let us beware of Poetry announced by placards.

Without the verbal incantation which renders it dependent on Magic, the Theatre disintegrates of itself, crumbles away in words, renounces its priority over other forms of literature and disclaims its obsessional or possessional power, its marvels.

A kind of serious accident was necessary in my young life for me to discover my true territory.

This happened towards my sixteenth year, at the beginning of the 1914-1918 war.

I was gravely ill from a contagious malady that almost carried me off, and after having been hanging between life and death during a whole winter, I had to leave my classical studies in the lurch, on the verge of finishing them. It was like a metamorphosis, for, on coming out of convalescence, childhood had gone for me, or, at least, was making off very quickly with long strides; and I awoke a man.

It was then that I took up a pen for the first time, immediately feeling the enchantment and the pathos of this new gesture.

Here, then, was a means of getting to know myself better, of living more generously, of resisting my native sadness better, or of denying the encompassing tragedy, or holding out against meanness and against the ugliness of the so common life—by the somewhat magical use of the Little Stump of Wood, as Jarry called the penholder!

Doubtlessly, like all young folk who pledge themselves to the writing-desk, I must have begun by writing poems; but I haven't the faintest recollection of them. I can no longer find any of these attempts—and so much the better.

Similarly, I must have kept a *Journal*. And why not *Memoirs,* after the fashion of all adolescents who haven't yet begun to live?

Meanwhile, I read a great deal, and in a happy enough way. I didn't devour books. I wasn't an avid reader; but I remained under the spell, and I don't know if it was a grace of Destiny's, but I came across decisive works which revealed the existence of myth, of the mythical character, to me. I breathed at a certain altitude to which one doesn't have access until older, and after certain trials.

Thus it was that I discovered *Don Quixote*—and not as an adolescent thirsting after action. I was struck forcibly by the size and the humanity of this intoxicating work which overwhelmed me to the extent of tears. All my life I have reread Cervantes, who never leaves my side, and I always read him in the same way—in the tragic vein. This is one of the works that resolutely pushed me toward pure literature, as the *Colloquies* of dear Erasmus pushed me toward a more theatrical art.

But it wasn't until after the discovery of that other epic tale, Charles de Coster's *Legend of Eulenspiegel,* that I set about writing in a determined way, in 1916-1917—and, to tell the whole truth, the discovery at the same time of the adorable *Gil Blas.*

At the same time, I was reading a lot of other things as well, notably the works of Belgians—of Camille Lemonnier, of Georges Eekhoud, who afterward became my master and my friend, of Max Elskamp, of Franz Hellens too, that incomparable tale-teller who was going to help me on so importantly. But it was principally *The Legend and the Heroic, Joyful and Glorious Adventures of Eulenspiegel and Lamme Goedzak in the Land of Flanders and Elsewhere* that gave me the desire to practice an autochthonic art, to try to write a work of some resonance—a work which might not be national (a term covering so many mediocrities that it is preferable to ignore it), but a work which might be *patriale,* if I dare use this adjective which is not at all French, but which expresses so well what I want to say: a *patriale* work, in short, a work that might be ancestral and traditionally of my home, whilst still being accessible to men of my time everywhere.

You can't separate my works whether prose, theatre, or even essay. It all comes from the same mind, from the same sensibility, and I have never attached importance to difference of forms, even though the theatre has taken precedence over the rest.

I went to the theatre from necessity, because this form turned out to suit me: unless the theatre came to me! I didn't take hold of this form: it took hold of me. That is the truth. One doesn't choose. Or so little!

Today it seems that my stories are a preparation for my plays, and that in these plays is the substance of stories.

But what is the point of seeking out these cross-references?

I sum up for you: I believe my work, looked at from the standpoint that my age permits, is one whole.

[. . . . .] I hold that to be authentic a play must be able to be recounted, to be communicated as a story—even if it is a cock-and-bull story. Failing this there would only be an incomplete structure, clouds in the flies, smoke on the stage —plays that never begin.

Take note, then, that a being endowed with any poetic sense is sensitive to the supernatural.

It is around us: it is in us.

Have you come across your image already present in an old mirror?

That some people never perceive the encompassing supernatural proves nothing. Let us say that they are impervious to everything, to poetry, to music, to light, to love, to the cries of the world, to the chorus of the dead, to the phosphorescence of the living, to metamorphosis, to anamorphosis.

Only the brute can deny that we are surrounded by the supernatural, that we lose our footing to the extent that reason advances into its sloping territories, its nocturnal borderlands.

You can perceive it, unexpectedly come across its messages in the humblest things, the most everyday things. I have an angel on my shoulder and a devil in my pocket! In order to reassure you, I don't say that everything breathes the supernatural; but could you dissociate it from art without great damage?

I love this solitude in all purity for its own sake. It is necessary to me. It is my security. I can do nothing without it. It is my collaborator, and I believe the artist can do nothing really great outside solitude.

Without solitude I am unable to write—not only at the moment of writing, but well before then, and even afterward, from the time that the dream kindles on my brow until it grows cold again, burnt out.

I have need of these long shores of silence and solitude, otherwise I wander endlessly.

It is a purification, a hygiene of the soul. And even now I still jealously guard this solitude that nothing will make me leave.

I tell you again, my destiny is to be alone, to work in my room.

Montaigne speaks truth. Solitude has its pitfalls. It is a way of life I wouldn't impose upon anyone; but this way of life suits me and confers upon me the state of bilocation indispensable to spiritual adventure and to the writing of art that records it.

[. . . . .] Death can be put off, one can receive a respite from Destiny, but Death will be back, rest assured of it! Even if you do not love him, he stays with you, and he is the only person of whose constancy you can be sure. Crown him with roses!

From the time I began to think, I have found myself in the face of enigmas. To the extent that I have had faith, a reply has been made for me, the Church has replied for me.

But when this faith became diverted, I had to rethink the essential problems of our life, of our human condition—what all things would become, and what would be their end.

And it is with infinite curiosity that I advance slowly toward this last ending—curtain-fall or curtain-rise! Is that clearly put?

I shall finish by knowing what is behind.

And this fear of the night gives value to our days.

But what name can we rightly give to this fear? Let us say anxiety. This anxiety shows through all my works. Without it, what would be their meaning? They would consist of literary games, little tales more or less neatly parceled up.

And I do not write little tales, for if I take up my pen, committing outrage on my idleness, it is more to fix this fear than to deliver myself from it—this fear so old that I believe it was born with the Earth, which is so old.

Fear of that fear which took hold of me at the very beginning and which doesn't leave me, of that fear which each man has on him and which has his odor.

Now you know why I write pages that sometimes appear to be unpleasant and that seem to be cruel; but I cannot do otherwise. This is my art. And not the art of an egoist, for my own private use. I give all to everyone, the sweat of my brow. This art is worth what it is worth; but it helps me to live, in the way I describe—always seeking the puppet-master and the meaning of the play we are acting.

[. . . . .] I discovered the world of shapes before discovering the world of ideas.

When I was quite a child, I was sensitive to public demonstrations—processions, parades, fairs, strikes, popular disturbances—to all open-air entertainments, funerals as well, triumphal entries, liturgical pomps, carnivals, masked balls. Equally, I allowed a great deal of importance to furniture, to clothes, to decoration, to the world of things that are believed to be dead. I was struck by everything that ordinarily doesn't surprise other children: dummies in shop windows, electric signs, statues in gardens, the enigmatic Hermes in the old park, the gesticulations of the trees, all that was color or movement—or seemed to contain mystery. And then, I was curious about entertainments that were still forbidden me because of my age. I might have been twelve years old when I made my way into fascinating halls—where I passed unnoticed. There I gazed on operas which I little understood but which enchanted me. I initiated myself into ballet. I witnessed bloody melodramas like *La Tour de Nesle.* So, little by little, this vocation for the theatre strengthened itself in me. And I must have been well-bitten when, at about seventeen or eighteen, I set about reading a great amount of dramatic literature, whose impression I still retain—notably the plays of Schiller and those of Victor Hugo. In spite of his redundancy and all that is laughable today, Victor Hugo greatly impressed me in his time: *Ruy Blas,* fairly enough, and even works which are less defensible but which contain good moments, highly contrived scenes which I accepted without discussion because, at the same time, I was discovering the underground theatre, the world of popular marionettes, where grandiloquence is obligatory, like the plume and the dagger, the poison and the sealed letter!

However, all of this hadn't yet been very decisive, and I insist that it was painting, giving colors to form, that led me toward the art of the theatre.

I had already very quickly made my choice in the galleries.

Naturally, I went to the works of my country, those of the master Hieronymus Bosch, of Pieter Breughel, of Teniers, of Jordaens. And this application accustomed me to the portrayed characters, settings and lightings that I later found once more when I put my feet on the stage. All was familiar to me, known, on the scale of the vast compositions that I had lately admired.

So, in spite of its small size—but what does that mean?—the Breughel canvas called *The Parable of the Blind Men* let me with so intense a memory of it that after many years, in 1933, I transposed this touching pictorial anecdote for the theatre—in a few hours, and with great enjoyment.

It was the same with *La Pie sur le Gibet*. A Breughel painting was the origin. Yes, Breughel again. You see that this master has played a very great part in my career. For me he is always present, for his work is not only wonderful painting; equally, it offers a vision of the world, a philosophy.

Yet another of my plays, *Masques Ostendais*, was also inspired in me by a painting; but this time it was a contemporary master, James Ensor, who was born and who died in this very city of Ostend where we are.

The Anglo-Flemish Ensor painted low women, down-and-outs, the fishermen of the port, all the maritime common people who work hard and who allow themselves no less rough compensations.

It is in one of the old interiors of the houses of these fine folk that I set the frenzied carnival of *Masques Ostendais*.

Once again, I have only transposed the vision of a painter.

For me, a theatrical work does not exist without the sensuousness proper to the plastic arts, or only exists as a dialogue which can be read and does not call for realization on the stage.

[. . . . .] Possessing a perfect knowledge of the English language, literature, and, above all, the theatre of the Elizabethan age, [Georges Eckhoud] published several translations and certain scholarly works which, even now, can still be read with profit—notably *Le Siècle de Shakespeare*.

It is thanks to Georges Eckhoud that I was able to recognize the greatness of this age, when passions were extreme, when life was perilous, the counter-Reformation not yet having carried out its ravages.

It was the Renaissance in all its purple glory—but for so little a time.

Also, in spite of the political censorship which must not be forgotten, the authors of the time—these extraordinary

contemporaries of Shakespeare—were able to bring on to
the stage the picture of the manners of their time, and these
manners were juicy in a way different from our own.

This was true for England and equally so for Italy. You
only need to read Stendhal's *Chroniques Italienne* to assure
yourself of it. Life had the same savor in Florence and in
London. And do you think that it was insipid in Paris under
the Valois?

That was what Georges Eckhoud revealed to me, the
hugeness of the men of yesterday. It's not so much a matter
of the works of an age as the spirit of that age. And that is
what has made me say that since the Renaissance man has
never stopped on his downward road, losing his autonomy,
losing face. . . .

What mattered to me was finding access to an authentic
world, to men of great size and powerful voice, with whom
nothing was small or mean.

Examine the historical events of that time, reread what the
Elizabethan theatre tells us of them, and we are soon forced
to admit that in our poor state as modern men we could not
any longer bear this way of complete living, in the best and
in the worst. And, after all, what are two or three centuries?

Georges Eckhoud, applying himself to *Le Siècle de Shakespeare,* showed me that these playwrights were not hindered
by rules, by academic instruction. He opened my eyes not on
the theatre, but on the size of the theatre. He taught me that
the theatre was in truth *the mirror of nature.* An integral
nature and in a state of expansion, rather than a conformist
nature read over and corrected for the use of a society that
thinks itself decent because it has disowned all passions.

A total nature—with all the horror and sublimity that
this entails, for the men of the Renaissance were the an-
nouncers of Romanticism and they swung between two ex-
tremes, the ecstasy of living and the horror of living. They
were perhaps full of sentimentality, especially in their elegies
and their elegant plays; but for the rest they were prepared
for anything, to protect their individuality. To sum up, this
age holds up to us an infinitely complex and contradictory
humanity, florid in colors and strong in odor. On Fortune's
wheel, a man is high or low—the average man is of our
time. This is the lesson held out to me by the Elizabethans,
Shakespeare essentially (or whoever hides under his name—

it matters little, and you can't get away from him) and then Kyd, Marlowe and Ben Jonson and Cyril Tourneur, and others as well, Massinger, John Ford. . . .

However, at the same time, I underwent another influence which was as elevating although of a different kind: that of Spain. The Spain of a Philip II and of a Theresa of Avila; but also the Spain of Cervantes and of a hundred other "fools" of the theatre, the dramatists of the Golden Age, Lope de Vega, Tirso de Molina, Alarcon, Calderon and all that illustrious assembly led not only by the Cervantes of *Don Quixote,* but also by the dramatist of *Numantia* and *The Two Chatterboxes.*

I was even more attracted by all of these writers because they freely spoke of Flanders. The theatre of the Golden Age is hypnotized by Flanders and includes many military plays in which it is merely a question of honor and of prodigious exploits, seen from the Spanish point of view, of course, and always to the glory of the King, the army, Don John of Austria, Farnese, Alvarez of Toledo.

This theatre, notably because of its action, remains thrilling today. It is little known in French, and the more's the pity. It contains odd plays that ought to be brought to light again, considering what some nations have "borrowed" from these lively fellows.

Naturally, I was unable to read all of these English and Spanish writers in their original tongue. I was only able to know them through more or less faithful translations. What did that matter since in these go-betweens there was the essential lesson—set the rules at naught!

Yes, all these dramatists, the Elizabethans in the van, taught the fledgling author to free himself from these rules, which are paralyzing, and it is thanks to them that I have always written plays as it suited me, in accordance with my perspective, and not in accordance with an eventual audience. And since one does not write plays for oneself, I have written for an imaginary public which, perhaps, had existed or could exist one day—not for the immediate public.

No doubt this is why I called this theatre, which was free from the worry of probable performance, *experimental.* It was a poetic form that suited me, a very versatile and a very rich instrument, much more thrilling than the story as I practiced it, or the novel which I didn't "feel."

As a result of the childhood that I have already told you about, that solitary childhood, I loved mystery, I loved drama, I even loved, as I have confessed, my own fear.

That is why, quite young, I came across a whole literature toward which my yearnings were pushing me, and if I haven't the least recollection of the novels of Horace Walpole or Ann Radcliffe, I still feel the dread I experienced during my reading of *The Monk*, by Lewis.

Equally, I remember *Notre-Dame de Paris* and *L'Homme qui rit,* which I very much want to read again.

And then, certain of Balzac's stories, his admirable metaphysical stories written under the influence of Jean-Paul. But, more prominently, there were the German romantics. I retain a very vivid recollection of Arnim, and above all of Hoffmann, the master Hoffmann, who was one of my bedside authors, and to whom, furthermore, I remain faithful.

Hoffmann, that staggering man who is so close to us, is badly translated, and it's a great pity. *Le Chat Mürr* and *La Princesse Brambilla* apart, we have only been given abridged versions, adapted to the French taste, as the translators of yesterday put it.

Finally, one must set down among these gloomy writers Barbey d'Aurevilley, Petrus Borel, Charles Baudelaire, Villiers de l'Isle-Adam, and the master of them all, Edgar Allan Poe.

We are relatives. We make up a huge family. It isn't possible not to be the friend of Edgar Allan Poe. Modern literature is indebted to him for his most acute perceptions.

He was the very first to be able to put down the inexpressible, the unutterable.

His influence has been considerable. Through Baudelaire, for example, Villiers de l'Isle-Adam, and many others, it shines as far as us, it affects our contemporaries. I dare to assert this!

I don't know the theories of Freud. I distrust these specious operations and I protect myself against all the works of science as against the Plague.

Likewise, I don't read philosophers. Nor sociologists. In my opinion, the dramatic author has no need to know so much. The theatre is an art of instinct. The intrusion of psychoanalysis, or of any analytical element, into the theatre seems to me harmful. The dramatic author must live by vision and divination only, the part played by the intellect remaining auxiliary. Reason serves to supervise the facts supplied by instinct.

Freud? This must be a fashion, a precarious idea of Man defrauded of divine direction. And a fashion is slavery. I saw the birth of this fashion. I have seen the ravages of this fashion. In my opinion, the author who submits his work to a system of this kind is infected, lost. Such a one reverts to political or denominational theatre, always the same mistake: he will create one-way and transitory theatre that may be profitable to the literary man but which objects to Man and denies all liberty of creation.

Directed, premeditated, this theatre makes its food of marginal references and hints, of countersigns and annotations. It is a theatre that opens the door to all literatures and to the worst of literatures. No.

My characters are what they are, just as they have come, incorrigible. I don't know if they are psychoanalyzable, as they say, or if they bear with them cholera or poetry. I don't know the current jargon and I don't bother myself about it. To the title of intellectual, which stinks, I prefer that of artisan—which has a good smell. . . .

But beyond this infatuation [with the expressionist novelties of the 1920's] there was the theatre. It was very necessary to return to it, and the principal motive of the theatre was not stage technique, the discovery of unknown accents and strange gestures, the discovery of an unexpected perspective or of lighting of a kind never seen before: the profound motive of the theatre remained man, or humanity. To express the man of one's time, and through him man eternal.

And it was to this unconditional and timeless theatre that I very quickly returned after wandering about for five or six years like all the dramatists of my time for whom the theatre wasn't an industry.

My first work for the Flemish Popular Theatre was *Saint François d'Assise*. Johan de Meester, the director and founder of the company, had ordered from me a commemorative play that put the life of the Poverello on the stage. I accepted on condition that there was no question whatsoever of an edifying play—the work would be such, naturally, since I was putting the life of a saint on the stage—but I remained free in the face of my inspiration. No style was imposed on me.

Then it became possible to see an astounding thing, a play (which was apparently religious) putting a saint on the stage in the most unexpected ways, the most modern ways, ways borrowed from music hall, pantomime, and ballet. Whence the joy and surprise of the artless country public, because the means set in action were very direct, very simple. Thus one saw at times angels swinging on trapezes, like acrobats. Thus were Francis' miracles expressed through pantomime. And there were clownish irruptions, the alternation of tragic and comic making up a play full of shocks that is still not forgotten to this moment. It was a kind of revolution.

There were incidents. The champions of the old romantic or realist theatre found my ideas of the representation of the life of a saint subversive, or even sacrilegious. The clergy protested, also a section of the press. Henri Ghéon, the well known author of edifying plays (some of which, moreover, are not without merit), Henri Ghéon, a Protestant converted to Catholicism, was not one of the least scandalized. He had seen Saint Francis dancing! Yes, in a transport of joy, Francis had danced among his brethren. He was happy, and this was his way of praising the Lord and creation: he danced.

That evening, Henri Ghéon asked me, "Would you dare, in the end, to make Christ dance?"

"And why not? I deny myself making him speak, but not making him dance. Do you know that he didn't dance, since he had a human nature like ours? He wept indeed, why shouldn't he have known joy? Is dancing immoral in itself? Isn't the mass, in a certain way, a sacred ballet? And is Catholicism a necessarily sanctimonious religion?"

Henri Ghéon made no reply to the infidel he suspected me of being. Since then I have come across many other critics in good faith—and in bad faith too.

To finish with *Saint François d'Assise*, this play was a complete success. From then onward, I was "set up," if I dare say so. I knew the public. Not only the collections of hybrid spectators in the capitals, and what is comically called the elite; but also the crowds in the little towns and in the country, in which there moves a collective spirit, or as much of it as remains in our day.

In the end, the essential thing about this experience [of having written plays for the Flemish Popular Theatre] was

that on going back into my ivory tower, in 1930, I was going
to be able to work comfortably. You must believe that I
was not disillusioned. For the future, I was very familiar with
the resources of actors, the possibilities of staging, up-to-date
equipment, the practical life and the economy of the theatre.
It was necessary that I should have gone through all this on
the other side of the footlights. But I also aspired to something else. This direct contact, these realizations, left me un-
satisfied. In fact, I was nostalgic for the theatrical dream that
I had lived in at the time of my studies and that success had
been unable to destroy. Now and again I even regretted not
having remained the poet, the storyteller, writing plays to be
read, plays that were theatrically inept, impractical. And it
was toward that, toward the work of art, that I turned back,
or at least thought I was turning back. Later, life offered me
a rude contradiction in bringing me, in spite of myself, to
those crowds from whom I saw myself forever separated. In
any case, I preserved the benefit of experience, and in the
future my plays were going to be marked by a certain virtue
that I shall style workmanlike. They would be organically
made for the stage: they would be playable. No doubt my
plays would be able to be read, as formerly; but also they
would have to be played: they would be above all for playing, even when I gave them an apparently difficult shape. Of
course, it has often been maintained that those plays that
outrage conventions and demand an effort of adaptation or
assimilation do not appear to be playable, even that they are
not playable. One has seen, since then: they were made for
the stage. But isn't it easier to declare unplayable that which
one hasn't the courage to put on because it demands work,
because it constitutes a risk of displeasing what is wrongly
held to be Public Opinion (never so stupid as directors, actors
. . . and authors take it to be)?

Yes, marionettes were the great concern of the whole of
my childhood, I'll even say of the whole of my career.

Even today I collect marionettes, dolls, puppets, little rag
creatures that the children of today scorn: also dummies
with lovely mortal faces of wax, models of hands, adorable
heads of young martyrs, severed by what executioner?

I welcome all these human shapes and reminders of human shapes to my home: I collect these image-beings as
treasures. They are silent presences—I say they are presences, presumptions.

All these effigies thrill me by the fact of their somewhat magical nature, and even though flesh and blood actors can weary me and often disappoint me, marionettes, because of their natural reserve and silence, manage to console me for the cacophony of the play and the crazy glibness of the impudent creatures that theatre people most often are.

Furthermore, I owe them the disclosure of the theatre, the theatre in its pure state, the theatre in its savage state, the original theatre.

Naturally, I wasn't able to understand all this from my first playtime. The marionette was then a toy, my favorite toy, even my passion—other toys gave me no pleasure. But even then I believed—and this strange belief is not yet dead in me—that objects were sensitive, living.

"Objects," says a poet, "objects are signs." Have you never noticed that there are objects that are hostile to us, and others that are benevolent? And there are some which are still neutral and waiting to reveal themselves.

One has seen objects seeking to do one ill, to hurt one physically, and Jerome Bosch has depicted very well for us the inscrutable, redoubtable world of things. He shows you a knife, for example, an innocent and terrible knife, from which legs have suddenly sprung and which comes toward you hypocritically—today it would be called radio-controlled.

Most certainly you yourself have such a knife. Suddenly it wounds you. You don't know why. You will never know why. You will say, "An accident!" but at the same time you can't help noticing how strange all accidents are, and their circumstances.

Aren't there sounds that the human ear cannot hear? Also certain colors remain imperceptible to our eyes. And do you think that we have smelt all the perfumes, all the odors?

You know what I think of the imperfection of our senses. Well, couldn't the most customary objects have a secret life that we haven't the power to make out, a capacity for joy and suffering, a memory and even nerves?

Listen, I remember having searched in the rain—I was still quite a child—for a wooden horse that I had left outside. I felt how much the horse must be suffering to be thus abandoned, and in the night I went to him and brought him back into the house, to where it was dry. I was at last relieved, and only then was I able to go to sleep. Forty years later, the horse came back, bright-eyed and laughing heartily! It was he, who had grown up—but I too had grown up!

It was the same with the "smaller than I" dolls. Moreover, by their shape and their structure, marionettes and dolls cannot be other than the objects that are the closest to us. I regard them as friends, as little familiar spirits. I gave them a name, a part to play in my life, a part that they still play, since I have never been able to dispense with them. Yes, one often has need of something smaller than oneself—the wisdom of the nations affirms as much.

Columbus became a synthesis of all the travelers, all the wanderers, all the "erratics" of his age and of all ages. To my mind, Columbus was the man who escapes. *Escape!* An expression that was fashionable twenty years ago and which has been much abused. However, it's the only one I find suitable at the moment—escape—but isn't this the worry of all men today, isn't it our daily worry? One must believe that the age in which we live, and that the present for the young people of all times, must be hard to spend one's life in and must give few joys in exchange for a great deal of pain, effort, and anxiety, since man has always tried to escape. In my sense, the expulsion—Biblical version—of Adam and his mate from the original Paradise is in fact an escape—otherwise the Creator's great anger wouldn't have its meaning. Adam escaped. Why? Go and ask his descendants . . . !

There isn't enough love-making in my plays doubtlessly because there was too much love-making and nothing but that—making love and going to bed—in all the French plays that poisoned us and whose fleshy odor still persists. There is a great deal of dying in my plays, but, after all, there is a great deal of dying in real life also. And if we take our age, not to talk of the past to which we so often turn back, don't you see that our age has the color and smell of the corpse, that it accumulates heaps, mountains of corpses? Look, death is everywhere, but they hide it from us, or try to. Happy ending to the innocents marked down for the great slaughter! But it's still the Death of the Middle Ages: it's still the same. It's no longer made into a carnival character or a character in a popular play. People can give it a scientific appearance, if they like. They can put a white apron and rubber gloves on it, make it a kind of super-scientist, Doctor Miracle in reverse. Parsifal has given way to a melodious gangster. In any case, if there is a great deal of dying in my plays, I believe there is a great deal of dying in all plays from the time plays were first made. Moreover, why must everything end happily? I don't write for the box office.

The aim of the theatre—and of mine in particular—is not comfort, no more is it to grieve. The theatre is a fact. And the definition given to it by Shakespeare remains true across the centuries. I will add that, if it is bad, the theatre gives rise to pleasure, if it is good, to joy. Low theatre can corrupt, high theatre raises up, gives the spectator the possibility of levitation. Morals have nothing to do with the matter.

Am I lovely? And you? Men are not lovely, not often, and it's very well that they are not even more ugly: but I believe in *Man*, and I think that this can be felt in my work. I don't despair of him, and I find him very interesting, capable of everything—and of its opposite.

Translated by George Hauger

CHRISTOPHER COLUMBUS

A Dramatic Fairy Tale in Three Scenes

by MICHEL DE GHELDERODE

1928

CHRISTOPHER COLUMBUS[1]

Translated by George Hauger

CHARACTERS

CHRISTOPHER COLUMBUS	THE WOMAN
THE CROWD-MAN	THE LOOK-OUT
THE REPORTER	MONTEZUMA
A FRIEND	THE ANGEL AZURET
THE SLEEPWALKER	VISQUOSINE
THE LEARNED MAN	THE POET
THE MINISTER	ADMIRAL DEATH
THE KING	THE AMERICAN
FOLIAL	BUFFALO BILL

And: SAILORS, INDIANS, A BOMBARDON PLAYER, A BIG-DRUM
    BEATER, A BALLERINA, THREE INDIAN DANCERS.

[1] From *Ghelderode: Seven Plays*, Vol. II translated and with an Introduction by George Hauger. © Editions Gallimard 1950, 1952, 1955, 1957. Copyright © 1964 Hill and Wang, Inc. Reprinted by permission of Hill and Wang.

Scene 1

[A plain wall on which there are some trite posters, and one which reads:

> Is the earth round?
> Fierce Controversy!

When the curtain goes up, COLUMBUS *is alone, sitting on his suitcase and occupied in blowing soap bubbles. He is lost in delight and wrapped in thought.]*

COLUMBUS. Bubbles! Little spheres! It's a strange sign that I should still be playing, at my age. My thoughts shape themselves into spheres and fly away. Where do they go? *[He blows bubbles.]* Geometry causes deep emotion in me. I can't explain. I blow bubbles. They justify themselves and vanish. *[More bubbles.]* Little spheres, logical, perfect! Sphere, ideal volume, shape of my dream, one must be like a child to understand you. *[He puts his clay pipe in his pocket and ponders.]* I am haunted by the horizon, tormented by distances. I am full of anguish, as at the onset of love, and my face is no doubt lit up with madness. Do traces of an ancient knowledge still linger in me? I have a recollection of a lost world. I do not know. I know nothing. Tomorrow I shall know, and I shall no longer be in anguish; but I shall be less happy. *[He takes out his pipe and begins to blow bubbles again.]* All of one's actions must be carried out with great seriousness. One must be born, brought up and disappear with simplicity. *[More bubbles.]* I am going to leave without a good-by, perhaps never to return, and I have no boat. Nevertheless, I pass my last night on this continent without giving a thought to the journey. I am not disillusioned; but people are insolent, and the air smells of the charnelhouse. *[Bubbles.]* I must go, for what fate will society appoint me if I go on blowing bubbles, bubbles that I cannot explain? I must go under

[117]

the cloak of my mysteriousness, letting people think I have designs. I am going to enter a great silence, a long darkness. I am going to sail upon supernatural waters. It is a good thing for a man to busy himself. . . . [*No more soapy water. He clutches his forehead. Someone arrives, walking on the wall.*]

REPORTER. Christopher Columbus?

COLUMBUS. I have an uncommon name that sounds like a famous one.

REPORTER. Bubbles, Columbus? You make such lovely ones!

COLUMBUS. Bubbles? . . . Yes . . . [*He stirs his pipe in the empty cup. Magnesium flash.*] Eh?

REPORTER. Thank you.

COLUMBUS [*standing*]. Who are you?

REPORTER. The press. The earth is round, isn't it?

COLUMBUS. I am a little mad.

REPORTER. You are extraordinary.

COLUMBUS. For having found out that the earth is round?

REPORTER. For daring to maintain it. Men like you are sensational, and that's what's wanted—sensational men.

COLUMBUS. Broadcast it throughout the universe, go on. I'm tired.

REPORTER. Nothing would go, you know. I am the organizer of public emotions. Nothing would go—neither the comet nor the coming of the Antichrist—so I announced a new heaven and a new earth. Speak, Columbus: the time has come.

COLUMBUS. The wind seems good.

REPORTER. Are you convinced?

COLUMBUS. I have faith in the stars.

REPORTER. The stars? Indeed, what a lovely night! [*Magnesium flash.*] Your face at those words. . . . You were sublime.

COLUMBUS. I wasn't thinking of anything.

REPORTER [*annoyed*]. Oh! [*Friendly.*] So, it's round? [*With some excitement.*] It's stupid. It's tragic. You realize that this will upset people's habits?

COLUMBUS [*who has had enough*]. It's only tragic for idiots. As for habits, people will acquire others. [*Bowing to the* REPORTER.] And the sphere, calmly indifferent, harmonious and satisfied with itself, makes great fun of our observations.

REPORTER. A joke? . . . [*Aside.*] Well, that was his chance to make his mark. [*He goes; but someone else has already come as* COLUMBUS *tightens the straps of his case.*]

FRIEND. Good evening! Fastening up your case, Columbus?

COLUMBUS. Where have I seen you?

FRIEND. We were at school together. You weren't very well up in geography, old chap. Do you persist in maintaining that it's round?

COLUMBUS. They'll finish up by making me doubt it.

FRIEND. After all, why shouldn't it be round? Here's five francs. [*He throws a coin which* COLUMBUS *catches in the air.*]

COLUMBUS. Charity?

FRIEND. An investment. I am a financier, God forgive me. I'm putting five francs into your venture. Who knows? . . . But if it is round, if you find the alleged new land, remember that henceforth you will have to play the part of civilizer, and that you can't civilize without the help and the backing of Finance. These five francs are symbolic, a token of the confidence Finance places in your genius. What do they prove?—Your lack of aptitude for geography! Goodby. [*He goes.* COLUMBUS *picks up his case and looks around, trying to decide in which direction to make off.*]

COLUMBUS. A little solitude, oh my spirit, a little solitude. . . . [*He is going off when a man in a nightshirt appears on the wall. The man carries a lighted candle and a suitcase.* COLUMBUS *seems rooted to the spot.*]

SLEEPWALKER. A little solitude that I may reflect on your roundness. . . . For it is round. I maintain that it must be round. Sphere on which I walk. . . .

COLUMBUS. What are you trying to make out? Impostor! I alone can declare that it is round.

SLEEPWALKER. It is round, just as I am pointed.

COLUMBUS. And who told you it was round?

SLEEPWALKER [*ambiguously*]. Revelation, revelation. . . . It's no longer a mystery. And that is why I am going. . . .

COLUMBUS [*alarmed*]. Have you a boat? Where are you going?

SLEEPWALKER. Elsewhere . . . where my spirit, full of sails, of compasses and of routes, leads me. My spirit dances on the waves. But I shall return to the very place from which I set out, because the earth is round.

COLUMBUS. They know; but they only know in their dreams, and they wake up ignorant.

SLEEPWALKER [*going out*]. Bubble . . . bubble . . . bubble. . . .

COLUMBUS. And when they wake up, I shall know the salt kiss of the high seas. It's time I went. [*Determined.*] A ship, ahoy! A ship?

[*Two men have come in, one to the right, one to the left. One is dressed like a* MINISTER *in an operetta, the other like a fairground astrologer.*]

MINISTER. A ship!

LEARNED MAN. Give him a ship!

COLUMBUS. Supporters?

MINISTER. It would be wise to give you a ship, that's all.

LEARNED MAN. Science agrees.

COLUMBUS. I beg your pardon?

MINISTER [*beginning a speech*]. Political sagacity. . . .

COLUMBUS. Excuse me, the ship. . . . [*An alarm clock rings loudly.* COLUMBUS *opens his case, takes out the clock, and goes pale. The other two take out their watches.*] My moment already? It gains: it always gains. It's a present from my mother. [*Thoughtful.*] What time will it be on the other side of the world? A homing pigeon or a bottle in the sea will no doubt one day tell you what sort of dawn I have seen breaking. [*He winds the alarm clock and puts it back in his case. The* MINISTER *has put on a compassionate air.*]

MINISTER. Are you accessible to reason, Columbus? Let us be frank. Among its many tasks the State has to look after those of its citizens who indulge in strange behavior. No one knows what these people may lead to, either for good or ill. The State does not like initiative, either. That is a monopoly which it claims for itself. The State does not willingly encourage innovators and discoverers. The State likes to bide its time. However, in your case, the State has made an unusual decision—neither to encourage nor to discourage you in anything: it will remain strictly neutral, while expressing the wish to see you succeed. If you do not succeed, your example will serve as a warning to youth; if you do succeed, we shall appoint a commission to consider a suitable way of rewarding you. In any case, we insist on your going, if only for the sake of public opinion. The State will always be able to turn your adventure to some account. You understand, don't you? You are intelligent. [COLUMBUS *bows. The* LEARNED MAN *presses forward.*]

LEARNED MAN. The learned societies have decided to bestow their kindly attention and their sympathy on you, as on one of their members. It was officially agreed that the earth was flat. You maintain that you will demonstrate that that is not so. Our assemblies will continue to uphold the idea of platitude. In the event of your theory turning out correct, remember that our assemblies venture to foresee that the earth could be spherical or cubic. [*Confidentially*.] Let me know first, so that I can write about it. You understand? You are. . . .

COLUMBUS [*courteously*]. I am of modest origin and of average intelligence. I did not suspect that the State and the learned assemblies would attach any importance to my voyage, which is a journey of convenience. The true motive for this journey is that I am weary. If I discover the new world, I shall not come back to say so. If I discover nothing, ask the laconic fishes for my address. Your confidence is delightful to me; but . . . the smallest boat would have been more to my purpose.

[*The* MINISTER *and the* LEARNED MAN *stand sadly. They are getting ready to justify themselves when a bugle sounds.* MINISTER *and* SAVANT, *bowing and scraping and loudly crying "The King!" go out backward.*]

COLUMBUS. The King?

[*The* KING *arrives. He has a golden crutch and a fantastic crown, and is followed by his fool,* FOLIAL, *who is in motley.*]

I've had enough of interviews. The ship?

FOLIAL. It's yours. Thank his Majesty.

COLUMBUS. It was my due.

KING. Pooh! It was to please the Queen. The Queen is an odd individual.

COLUMBUS. I am deeply moved.

KING. As far as I am concerned, I give you the boat willingly. It saves me the trouble of shutting you up. Set off quickly and sail toward oblivion. My subjects talk of nothing but the Eden you want to discover—as if my kingdom wasn't Eden! What do you think about it, Folial?

FOLIAL. Let the people have filth and mirages. Promise them Eden.

COLUMBUS. And if I discover Eden?

KING. That will be because God wishes to bless my reign by

your act. Haven't I given you the boat? [*He ponders.*] Columbus, it has always been men of your kind who have spoiled my life. Artists, in a way. I have my reasons for admiring them and for not thinking much of them. Is that not so, Folial?

FOLIAL. Sire, great minds don't understand little things.

KING. Still, I have need of them. You see there would be difficulty in writing the chronicle of my reign. And after all, it wouldn't be a bad thing if you discovered this Eden —which we would make into a well-managed colony.

COLUMBUS. Sire, by my holy scapular, I shall find this Eden, which you shall make a tribute to the Queen. Thank you . . . I see the ship. What memorable phrase can I pronounce?

FOLIAL. This is an historic evening; but it is for you, Sire to speak royally. Come!

KING [*warmly*]. Hail, Columbus! You who are sound in body and mind; what an ailing world it is. Find a new world. I reign over a neurasthenic kingdom. Happy are you to possess the sea, mighty misanthrope! As for me. . . .

COLUMBUS. Are you troubled?

KING. I am moved. You have a ship. I have only a throne. [*He grasps* COLUMBUS' *hand.*] I lied to you. It was I, not the Queen, who gave you this ship. And, no, my kingdom is not Eden. Ah, you far-sighted traveler. . . . [*The* FOOL *weeps.*] Shut up, Folial. It's your job to be gay.

FOLIAL. And yours to be courteous.

KING. You are right. [*He too weeps.*]

COLUMBUS. I would have liked to have gone without tears.

KING. Indeed. Dignity, Folial.

FOLIAL. This is an historic evening.

[*The overall dressing of the ship appears across the stage, enlivening it with multicolored flags.*]

COLUMBUS. Thank you for the ship. [*A murmuring begins.*] It's no good, it makes your heart swell. One may as well empty the vase. . . .

[*A* WOMAN *enters and begins to cross the stage.*]

Not so fast!

WOMAN. What?

COLUMBUS. You are my mother, and no mistake.

WOMAN. So what?

COLUMBUS. Good-by, mother. [*He kisses her, wipes away a tear, takes several steps, then comes back.*] I made a mistake. You are my fiancée. Good-by, darling. [*He kisses her, wipes away another tear, and makes off.*]

WOMAN. That suits me better.

COLUMBUS [*coming back*]. Pardon?

WOMAN. Go ahead.

COLUMBUS. You are my country!

WOMAN. Come to my arms, you confused young man. Give me children.

COLUMBUS. Out, strumpet! [*He pushes her out.*]

WOMAN. Tramp!

KING. I don't get it.

COLUMBUS. Tramp! that's a title. My eyes are dry. At last I am pure. At last I am alone.

[*A gangway is slid on the stage.* COLUMBUS *begins to climb it. The* KING *waves good-by with his handkerchief. The* CROWD *arrives—that is, a single actor, who gives the impression of many people in tumult.*]

CROWD-MAN. There he is! Good luck! Bravo!

COLUMBUS [*modestly acknowledging*]. Here I am.

CROWD-MAN. Stupendous! Stupid! Right! Wrong! Where is he? Him? Yes! No! Encore! Daredevil! Opportunist! Martyr!

COLUMBUS. Well, get it over with, go on.

CROWD-MAN. Speech!

COLUMBUS. I haven't prepared anything.

KING. Be a good fellow, Columbus.

COLUMBUS. People. . . .

REPORTER [*coming into view on the wall*]. Hasn't this chap gone yet?

CROWD-MAN. He is speaking. He has spoken. Marvelous! Bravo!

COLUMBUS. I have little to say, and much to do.

CROWD-MAN. He's beginning again. We've had enough.

REPORTER. Is he going? Much to do, did you say?

COLUMBUS. Make my testament, for example. Here it is. O King, O people. . . . Having destroyed a surface and created a volume, I make light of the critics who maintain that the object of my life is to make an egg stand on end. Excuse me for adding nothing more, and for appearing absentminded. I see things from above. Yes, I am from another world. I do not belong to yours. I am setting out for another world. But you must realize that it is not my ambition to discover one. It is a much more serious matter. I have a taste for unhappiness. I am fleeing the reasonable nations. [*He makes a gesture with his hand, and goes.*]

CROWD-MAN. The departure! Lovely! Thrilling!

VOICE OF COLUMBUS. Ocean, old friend. . . .

CROWD-MAN. Up the navy!

[*Some national fanfare or other sounds somewhere. A clamor breaks out and dies away.*]

KING. Let's get to hell. It's dismal. . . . [*He goes, with his* FOOL *at his heels.*]

CROWD-MAN [*wildly*]. The boat! He's off! Good luck! Fair winds! Out of sight! Done with! [*He rushes off as fast as his legs will carry him.*]

REPORTER [*still on the wall, finishing his notes*]. Carrying away hope. . . . launching out toward hope. . . . [*He goes, singing:—*] A little ship was on the sea. . . .

Scene 2

[*A sailing ship seen in cross section. The audience is looking from the poop forward. Red and green lights on the deck (practical), white lights in the rigging, where the* LOOK-OUT *is in position.* COLUMBUS *sits at a table in the hold. This narrow place is bathed in bluish light. At the back, toward the prow, are the quarters where the sleeping crew is. Ropes and ladders run up and down almost everywhere.*]

LOOK-OUT. Nothing to report, nothing, still nothing! Gulfs and darkness to port, gulfs and darkness to starboard, gulfs and darkness at the zenith, gulfs and darkness at the nadir. The stars are dead, except for one with a peculiar glitter. . . .

COLUMBUS. Mine!

LOOK-OUT. Night. . . . Is it night? Silence. . . . Is it silence? The sea and its gulfs. . . . Horrible! The sea. . . .

COLUMBUS. The orchestral sea whose melody escapes me. Our Lady of the mariners, protect my ship! They are asleep. The winds are bearing us along. Unexpectedly, I came across strange scents in the breeze. This is the sea of delusions. [*One of the sleeping sailors begins to struggle.*]

SLEEPER. Shipwreck!

COLMUBUS. Sleep, sailors. This ship is a cradle. Bye, bye, sailor, bye, bye. . . . [*He sings softly:*—] A little ship was on the sea. . . .

VOICES OF SLEEPERS. No, not that! It's too sad. We want to go home. We want a love song or something funny. . . .

COLUMBUS [*authoritatively*]. What? Sleep! I order it! You will awaken in the new world. There's no danger, except to your brains. Men without mystery! The little ship has its destiny. Get to bed, captain's orders! [*He fills his pipe and smokes.*]

LOOK-OUT. No moon. White moon in the sky at my birth! Laughing moon! Me, I weep.

COLUMBUS. Put on a diving suit, my spirit, and slip under the waters, turn about in the currents, swim among the flowers of the deep, loiter among the worm-eaten stage setting of old disasters, follow the trail of the drowned nonchalants, those who were drowned on voyage, like my voyage, without design, without timetable. Good Nautilus protect you, my little ship, my absurd boat! May God direct the winds and the sails! The sea is absolute. I am all the time moved. . . .

LOOK-OUT. It is warm. There are fanfares sounding beneath the waves.

COLUMBUS. This is my ship's record book, a collection of monologues. [*He begins to write.*]

LOOK-OUT. A lighthouse? No. Lights? One, two. . . . No. [*Pause.*] Lord have mercy on us! Christ have mercy on us! Holy Trinity have mercy. . . . [*His voice dies away.*]

VOICES OF SLEEPERS. Sleep. There are flies. Sailor's sorrow. The accordion has pegged out. More music, more hope. Where are we? Thirst, thirst! See my little girl again, ah!

COLUMBUS. Fever. . . . [*He stands.*]

VOICES OF SLEEPERS. She's called Julie. Hang him from the yardarm. Eden has seven springs. [*The voices become incoherent. Sound of an accordion.*] In Europe! Enough lies! Are you asleep, Jack? The captain's in the drink! [*Various kinds of grunts.*]

COLUMBUS [*shrugs his shoulders and says forcibly*]. If they knew that this world is at hand! [*The voices grow still.*]

LOOK-OUT. Perfumes . . . birds. . . .

COLUMBUS. In the old days, monks lost themselves on the ocean and discovered the supposedly unknown lands, whose maps they drew. Nature was so lovely there, and life so sweet that they thought they had found the Biblical paradise. [*Dead silence around.*] Strange flowers, oils, palms, gold nuggets! Gold, gold everywhere, rivers of gold, cities of gold, gold and feasting, wines, tall lascivious women! Feasting and sacrifice! Purple wine and blood! It is understood that no one ever works there. What rapture! It will be Eden indeed that those companions in fortune who maintain their courage and patience will share out between them. They have no idea of the orgies that threaten, of the sins, dreadful sins that they will commit. And they have doubts about me? They suspect my genius? Blind men who allow themselves to be led astray by the legends of a deluded middle ages! Nightmares of pitch and foam, waters of terror, the mouths of hell, the gruesome vessel that sails in the height of the storm, with its crew of the dead! They have read the tales of Edgar Allan Poe. All of that, the chaos, the gymnastic octopuses, the hordes of Leviathans, the submarine craters, is tremendously literary—and quite beside the point. Let them sleep and dream in their guileless perversity. I am guiding the boat across enchanted waters. Their awakening will be marvelous. Poor ragtime sailors! [*He goes to the crew's quarters, spits in it and comes back.*]

LOOK-OUT. Dawn's going to break.

COLUMBUS. Fools! I strongly doubt whether the dawn will bring you the promised land. And if, by that chance which no one calls to mind in the event of success, I should discover this world whose whereabouts I do not know, nor even whether it exists, all would be finished for me, the adventure and its adorable anguish.

[*The peaceful snoring of the sailors is heard, then silence. Someone sings.*]

Not very good, this artist.

[*A porthole, at the left, is pushed open from outside, allowing the face of a sixty-year-old, purple and bloated after long immersion, to appear in profile.*]

VISQUOSINE. Love?

COLUMBUS. Of course! [*He catches sight of the head and starts.*] What a horror! [*He goes to the porthole.*] What do you want?

VISQUOSINE. Permission, nice captain, to render the successes of my repertoire in honor of your gallant crew.

COLUMBUS. Who are you?

VISQUOSINE. Visquosine, the famous siren with the voice of the Atlantic.

COLUMBUS. What do you sing that is really bewitching?

VISQUOSINE. You shall hear. . . . [*She begins to sing raucously:—*]

> I am a pretty little fish,
>   Sticky, lithe and naughty,
> And unto those who live in hope
>   I sing of love at forty.
> [*Gurgling and ogling, she continues:—*]
> I charm the lonely bachelor. . . .

COLUMBUS. Really? [*He throws a handful of coins in her face.*] Swim off and don't let's have any more, you boiled-beef beauty.

VISQUOSINE. What an insult to my art. [*Sob.*] I shall drown myself at daybreak. [*She squirts a jet of water from her mouth at* COLUMBUS *and disappears from the porthole.*]

COLUMBUS. Here it is, daybreak, a difficult moment. [*He sits and writes.*] Another dawn. I hope that it lasts. We are somewhere. My crew is a little disturbed and its spirit is not of the best. As for myself, it is a matter of indifference whether I sail on or under the waters, or in the clouds, toward the paradise. I sail. And, in truth, I am afraid to see the end of the ocean. My delusion is dear to me. I would not like the earth to be round, because it is pleasant to go nowhere and to be conscious of being nothing, to be lost to the eyes of men. Sailing for a hundred years and a hundred years more, I shall find the Eden that is at the center of myself, perfect silence, perfect solitude. I shall know the happiness that is without words. I shall be a crab or a whiff of this perfume that has caught my senses. I write in . . . [LOOK-OUT *gives a tremendous yawn.* COLUMBUS *yawns similarly*] . . . in this book that I ask God to forgive this inexpressible desire of not-being. . . .

[*The deck is caressed by a pink light. Pause.* COLUMBUS *is going to doze off; but there is a cautious knocking in the timbers.*] Come in! [*He waits.*] Whoever knocks and doesn't come in can't be a thing of flesh. Are you there, spirit?

VOICE OF AZURET. One knock for yes. Lift the trap.

COLUMBUS. The classic scene of the stowaway revealing his presence!

[*He lifts a trap and a mournful and insipid creature comes into view. He is very true to type. He wears a clerical gown and his wings rigged up at his shoulder-blades.*]

Good evening, sir, or madame. I'll settle your hash for you. You're just another useless mouth to feed, so I'm going to pitch you overboard.

THE ANGEL AZURET. I don't eat, and water doesn't disagree with me. I am amphibious, from the Greek *ampho* and *bios*. What pleasure would you get from throwing me in the sea if I didn't die from it?

COLUMBUS. None. Name and profession?

THE ANGEL AZURET. Azuret, guardian angel.

COLUMBUS. And you guard . . . ?

THE ANGEL AZURET. You, Columbus.

COLUMBUS [*shakes hands*]. Pleased to meet . . . [*Puzzled.*] One is always being watched, spied on. . . . [*Pause.*] What have we to tell each other in particular? You know everything. That is annoying.

THE ANGEL AZURET. I am an excellent guardian, but you can set yourself at rest: I have a lamentable memory. If I have had the indelicacy to show myself, it is because of curiosity. Are you really going to discover America?

COLUMBUS. I imagine so.

THE ANGEL AZURET. Look out for the consequences. I have it on good authority that the Jesuits have their eyes on these future territories. And the Jesuits, you know. . . .

COLUMBUS. Are the enemy. Thank you.

[*Voices in the crew's quarters are heard.*]

Hide yourself, my dear angel. It can't be comfortable down there? Go back, for if my men saw your gown, they could make a mistake. As a matter of fact, are you a boy or a girl?

THE ANGEL AZURET. Nasty little devil! [*He disappears through the trap.*]

COLUMBUS. Wouldn't it be that angel who, in the end, gave me this ship? [*He goes back and sits at the table. His head nods. Sleep lays hold of him. He resists.*] Fatigue! I saw a Jesuit wearing a black robe and with wings on his back. I heard cries. . . .

LOOK-OUT. Land!

COLUMBUS. I dreamt that the look-out shouted. . . .

LOOK-OUT. Land! I see land!

COLUMBUS [*coming back to reality, leaps to his feet and climbs nimbly to the deck*]. What? Ahoy! Flying sailor, below!

LOOK-OUT [*clattering down to the deck*]. I saw it captain, and I'm still trembling from it. . . .

COLUMBUS. You saw?

LOOK-OUT. Captain. . . .

COLUMBUS. Sleep! [*He makes hypnotic passes. The* LOOK-OUT *immediately stiffens.*] Up the mast! Keep watch!

LOOK-OUT. I sleep . . . up the mast . . . keep watch. . . .

COLUMBUS. And when you sight America, for that is what it is, you will keep your trap shut. To your post! [*The* LOOK-OUT *climbs in the rigging and disappears.*] Helmsman!

HELMSMAN [*coming*]. Captain . . .

COLUMBUS. Sleep! [*Hypnotic passes. The* HELMSMAN *stiffens.*] When you sight America, you will turn about and set her head toward Europe. Fall out! [*The* HELMSMAN *goes.*] To hell with America! I say, to hell with it! [*He goes down into the hold. There is a murmur of voices from the crew's quarters.*] I have had a narrow escape. And one mustn't think of going back to Europe. We shall go to the devil. This is the real voyage! I have got plenty of liquor aboard. Farewell, America! You were too easy to discover. . . . [*He stations himself near the crew's quarters and listens to the voices which have become very clear.*]

1ST VOICE. Eat.

2ND VOICE. Eat what?

1ST VOICE. The captain.

3RD VOICE. How old is the captain?

2ND VOICE. Not eat, drink.

1ST VOICE. Drink what?

3RD VOICE. That is the question.

COLUMBUS [*in a loud voice*]. Whiskey. [*He takes a flat flask from his pocket.*] Very good whiskey! Oh, solace of clowns and navigators! [*He drinks.*]

[*The deck grows light. Muffled music with a persistent rhythm begins in the distance. In the hold, the shaven heads of the sailors, looking as though they have been cut off, appear in line above the partition of the crew's quarters. Their eyes are like those of attentive dogs, and their tongues are hanging out.*]

[COLUMBUS *walks about and takes nips of his whiskey.*] Everyone to his illusion. Mine is harsh, unalterable, more beautiful than art, than love. Magic figures, my dear illusion, what is your name? $V = \frac{4}{3} \pi R^3$! Sphere, I call you forth like a woman, and I wed your finished shape. I slip along your insensible sides. But you, Earth, are no longer the ideal sphere. I shall leave you for another where I shall be alone, a more advanced sphere. . .

[*The rhythm has become obsessive. The night is gone at last.*]

VOICE. Land!

COLUMBUS. Calamity! He wasn't asleep, the shammer! Sleepers, it's over. All on deck.

[*The sailors leap from their quarters and scatter about the ship, but gaudy, bawling Indians appear everywhere on deck —an invasion of magnificent feathers. They dance to the rhythm of the music and excitedly embrace the astounded sailors.* COLUMBUS *goes on deck.*]

What is this show, this carnival? And what about your orders, helmsman?

SAILORS. The new world! Victory!

COLUMBUS [*dominating the tumult and the situation*]. Let us get things clear! Are we really in America, savage gentlemen?

MONTEZUMA [*gorgeous, comes forward and bows*]. In South America, to be exact.

COLUMBUS. I have no luck. You speak English?

MONTEZUMA. It is an elegant language. Would you rather have French?

COLUMBUS. It doesn't matter. We were made to understand each other. How ornamental you are! But, tell me, what are your intentions? Have you come to cut our throats?

MONTEZUMA. I ask *you* that. We are peacefully celebrating your arrival, as we do everytime a navigator discovers America.

COLUMBUS. Then I am not the first?

MONTEZUMA. Alas, Christopher Columbus!

COLUMBUS. And you know my name?

MONTEZUMA. The oracles told it to me. We were awaiting your arrival. The oracles also revealed that there was a lot of whiskey in the hold.

COLUMBUS. I had a presentiment that you were superior to and contemptuous of our civilization?

MONTEZUMA. So what? We despise your civilization, but not whiskey. No fibs, friend. You come to civilize us. That is in order. It will soon be done—I mean that we shall be exterminated. What does it matter? It is written on our oldest stones. In you, we celebrate the agents of Destiny. We dance our death among our out-of-date pyramids and our tarnished suns. Perish our plumes and our millenary wisdom! You understand? We need whiskey in order to despair better.

COLUMBUS. Exterminate you, you lovely carnival characters? You seem to me to be excellent fellows, very fine, but a bit pessimistic. Great chief, I shall take you to Europe.

MONTEZUMA. No thank you, dear barbarian. You shall go back alone. I want to die beneath the debris of my empire. My race is finished—and my dynasty. Make way for the archaeologists!

COLUMBUS. I want to share your plumes and your dancing death.

MONTEZUMA. A hopeless desire! Death is a vocation. Whiskey!

THE INDIANS. Whiskey! Whiskey!

[*The sailors, laden with bottles, which they distribute, come up from the hold. Everyone drinks.*]

COLUMBUS. Since it is too late, I drink to America, to the last of the Aztecs, to your plumes. . . .

MONTEZUMA. Wipe us out—you may do that; but make speeches, oh no!

COLUMBUS. You are right, great chief. The Jesuits will come and preach to you. My feathered and fated friends, I drink to the sphere.

MONTEZUMA. Drink to this America, which opens its arms to

you—in a way. . . . [*He laughs heartily.* COLUMBUS *hugs him. The crew and the* INDIANS *dance to the accordion in an excess of irresistible fraternity.*]

Scene 3

[*A building occupies the back of the stage. It has three doors. That on the right is red, with the inscription SHAME. That on the left is black, with the inscription SILENCE. That in the center is gilt, with the inscription GLORY. Thus, one has, for the requirements of this scene, a triumphal arch in the center, a jail on the right, and a tomb on the left. At the top of the building is the base for a statue, on which one can read "In honor of. . . ." The* CROWD-MAN *brandishes newspapers and dances about.*]

CROWD-MAN. Hurrah! Day of triumph! Superman! What boldness! See him! Touch him! Crown him! Flowers! National Subscription! Banquet! Down with the cops! Long live Lord Roberts!

[*The gilt door lights up. It opens to allow* CHRISTOPHER COLUMBUS *to come through. He carries his case, and has a raincoat over his period costume.*]

COLUMBUS. It's me.

CROWD-MAN [*turning his back on the new arrival*]. Here he is! It's him! The conqueror! The conquistador! The toreador! Ah, magnificent fellow!

COLUMBUS. Thank you, ladies and gentlemen. Your acclamation. . . .

CROWD-MAN. Is he going to crash, or isn't he?

COLUMBUS. Who?

CROWD-MAN [*indicating the sky*]. The man who has discovered Europe! Long live Lindbergh! [*He takes stock of* COLUMBUS.] Are you a globe-trotter?

COLUMBUS. Exactly that. I am Christopher Columbus returning from America.

CROWD-MAN. Have you made a fortune?

COLUMBUS. No, but I am famous.

CROWD-MAN. In that case, long live Christopher Columbus. [*He dances.*] Long live the Grand Turk! Down with the Jews! Vive la France!

[*He has gone. Silence.* COLUMBUS *looks sadly at the triumphal arch, goes and puts out its light, then comes back and sits on his case.*]

COLUMBUS. The fickleness of people! If I hadn't come back, they might have sung an oratorio in my honor. My mistake was in being homesick on the strength of a fantasy, whereas my homeland is the ocean. If only I had stayed with the pipe-smoking Indians, among the carved gods and the angry little monkeys! I end up without beauty, without gold, and, for all one knows, without reputation. A little adventurer! I dreamed of the sphere, whereas it was a matter of something quite different. Showing that the earth was round wasn't a very sharp thing to do: the business of standing an egg on its end would have been more profitable to me. [*He sighs.*] I am old and I have not lived, because I have conceded too much to dreams. I have been far and I find myself nowhere. I have seen much and I have learned nothing. I only know that the world is small and illusion is great. I am neither conceited nor grasping nor lucky. I have neither the virtues of fools nor those of heroes. The scholarly books will say that I was an intrepid voyager, but the young will remember the business about the egg. After death, that won't matter. But now? Times are hard for anyone whose sole possession is merely the formula for the volume of a sphere. [*He gets up.*] My dear savages with your pretty plumes, forgive me for not having followed your advice at all. I shall think of you, but I shan't write about your last dance nor your nostalgic death, for it's not a good thing to reveal everything when you are begging for a pension and when the Jesuits wish you well. [*He walks up and down.*] Let these disappointments strengthen me. Let me find in myself that philosophy of the humble which suggests an acceptable explanation for calamitous happenings. What does this ingratitude, this indifference, matter to me if I think myself famous, if I alone understand the meaning of my destiny? Why shouldn't I celebrate myself? [*He leaps up and throws his hat in the air.*] Long live Christopher Columbus! Glory and honor! Long live the famous navigator! [*He puts his hat on again.*] There! Knowing glory, it only remains for me to enjoy it in some quiet place where, unknown to anyone, I shall finish my days. [*He is going, dragging his feet.*] Oh glory! so like

that America one has come back from. . . . [*But someone
is at his heels.*]

MINISTER. Hey! Columbus?

COLUMBUS. He has just gone.

MINISTER. It's you. I recognize you! [*He takes three steps
backward, then, ceremoniously:*—] Christopher Columbus,
in my voice, the State offers you its most spontaneous felic-
itations. It is aware of your worth, and hazards a guess at
the consequences of your discoveries. The America which
you give it is an excellent land for development, and con-
sequently you contribute to the elevation of national pres-
tige. Also, the State rewards you by decorating you with
this coveted order, which is only bestowed on men of
letters, on life-savers, and on agronomists. Let your bosom
swell with legitimate pride! On this occasion, the State has
set the man of letters, the life-saver, and the agronomist
on the same footing, for you are eminently all of these. As
a man of letters, you have sent a report to the Geographi-
cal Society, who find it properly drawn up. As a life-saver,
you have shown proof of civic courage in setting sail, when
it was known you can't swim, and in saving the kingdom's
finances by the contribution of these magnificent colonies,
which we have mortgaged without delay. As for agron-
omy, it owes you recognition for your samples of rare
seeds and your observation on the *doryphore,* the enemy of
agriculture. No more decoration has been more deserved,
and your modesty can exhibit it without blushing. Let me
embrace you, my dear Columbus. . . . [*Embrace and be-
stowing of decoration.*]

COLUMBUS. This will be a constant source of pleasure. Besides, you are very nice.

MINISTER. Excuse me. I have to be. But, tell me, this America, where is it? There are animals there, aren't there?
What do you think, now you are back?

COLUMBUS. That one is never better off than when in the
bosom of one's own family.

MINISTER [*shaking his hand*]. I am touched by those words.
[*A bugle sounds the "Attention." The* MINISTER *makes
off.*]

COLUMBUS. Wait! [*He picks up his case and is going, but
the* KING, *on crutches and furnished with a bunch of keys,
has arrived.*] He has seen me. Is he going to ask for his
ship?

KING. Not long ago, an individual called Columbus set out across the sea. I envied him. This man has come back. I pity him. To have found Eden, and to have come back to my kingdom. . . .

COLUMBUS. Sire, I am the man. How are you getting along?

KING. On crutches, my friend. And the kingdom is getting along badly, too. It is in trouble through your fault. Here I am in conflict with all the powers, as though the internal quarreling weren't enough. What need have we of colonial Edens. And I who dreamed of hanging gardens to promenade my infirmities! Anyway, everything considered, you have deserved well of the Nation. [*Familiarly.*] You must be tired, Columbus.

COLUMBUS. My bones, not my spirit.

KING. My council has decided that you should rest yourself. The Nation is going to house and feed you. Since this decision could be misinterpreted, I myself wanted to lead you to your retreat. Come, Columbus. [*He goes toward the red door, which lights up.*] The King asks you to come to prison.

COLUMBUS. Don't be distressed, Sire. I was just on the lookout for a hermitage. Providence wills that your Majesty should offer me it. [*He goes into the prison.*] And . . . the reason, Sire?

KING. Here is a profound one. It is human to belittle you and crush you in order to be able to glorify you all the better afterward. Then people will say there is justice after all.

COLUMBUS. But . . . the reason, Sire?

KING. Since you persist. . . . It's to please the Jesuits. Don't go and think that they don't wish you well and that your freedom has been taken from you. Nothing of the sort!

COLUMBUS [*thoughtfully*]. My dear savages. . . .

KING. This freedom. . . .

COLUMBUS. As a sailor, I have heard of it.

KING. [*pulling down a grille in front of* COLUMBUS]. What are you going to do from now on?

COLUMBUS. Travel.

KING. Good-by, Columbus. Your chains weigh the same as my crown. [*He goes off on his crutches.* COLUMBUS *sits in his jail.*]

COLUMBUS. The beginning of wisdom. And I am going to make the loveliest of voyages. It will be enough merely to close my eyes. [*He becomes still.*]

[*Pause. The* POET, *wearing high heels, enters.*]

POET. Columbus, whom the world forgets, the poet remembers you!

COLUMBUS. Forgive me.

POET. You are suffering. I can sense it.

COLUMBUS. Not at all.

POET. So! You are not suffering?

COLUMBUS. No—and you?

POET. I? . . . Ah, you have been decorated?

COLUMBUS. That is my least offense. You will be, one day, if you suffer suitably.

POET. Nonsense! But tell me, what remarkable things did you see yonder in the new world?

COLUMBUS. Poets.

POET. God! What school? What kind?

COLUMBUS. Poets who are neither civil servants nor pimps. They have infinite culture and tact. They know the most ancient fables on earth. The stars are their concern and are the burden of their songs. These poets live in solitude and have no names. They make the beasts obey them. They are chaste. They write nothing, and they never reveal the secret of their ecstasies to the common folk.

[*During this monologue, the* POET *has gone out on tiptoe.* COLUMBUS, *lost in his memories, goes on with his speech, and music, tender and sad, begins.* MONTEZUMA *and three Indian dancers, resplendent in jewels, come in and dance to its rhythm. Under the burden of their plumes, they mime what seem to be the agonies of hieratic birds.*]

From them I learned amazement—at the symphony of the seashores, the choir of the forests, the marriage of the constellations, the harps of the priests, the courage of the bee, the laments of women, the scent of spices, the lightning from God, the hills and plains of slumber, the dialogue of the serpent and the beetle, the tears and jewels of the betrothed, Life, Death, Metamorphosis, Numbers, Trance, the cure for all ills, the everlasting dance on the tombs. . . . [*He stands up in his prison.*] It is time to go. It is the auspicious time. It is the carnival of blood and plumes. The magnificent shadows act the farewell, the eternal departure. Like them, I have acquired the smiling indifference of ghosts. Only dead friends are kind. A new world isn't a

long way off any more. Oh, disquieting navigation! Let us
forget civilization and geography. I see signals.

[*The dancers have disappeared. A bell rings. The prison
grille rises. A ship's siren moans.* COLUMBUS *comes forward
on the stage.* DEATH, *an ageless naval officer, enters. Hands
in pockets, he dances springily to the music whose rhythm
has quickened.*]

Great Admiral, Captain Columbus salutes you.

ADMIRAL DEATH. Come aboard, captain. Leave your human
baggage at the harbor. Smash your compass. God is the
pole. Fleming, Breton or Spaniard, the infinite is a slack
water with neither joy nor pain. Come aboard, soul of a
captain. [*He dances off. The music has stopped. The prison light goes out. It is almost night.*]

COLUMBUS. I have loved adventure too much not to love
dying. It is with a light foot that I leave you, ancient
earth, and your obsolete sphere where everything is ashes,
puerile and perverse. This time I am going to travel without returning, among the luminous bubbles which God
blew on the first day that ever was. . . .

[*He enters, through the black door, into the tomb. He has
hardly gone from sight when a raging march in the manner
of Sousa rings out. Everything lights up brutally. A human
form covered by a sheet slowly climbs up the building. It
stations itself on the base and remains motionless. Then come
—the* AMERICAN, *wearing a dress coat made from his national
flag, and an opera hat of the 1840 style;* BUFFALO BILL—*the
most authentic cowboy of all, promoted colonel by the grace
of children—with his goatee and revolvers, shooting in evidence of joy; a pretty girl of a dancer in a tutu; a*
BOMBARDON PLAYER; A BIG-DRUM BEATER.

The procession halts facing the building. The musicians
stop playing. The* AMERICAN *takes out a paper, and* BUFFALO
BILL *tears down the sheet covering the statue. It is*
CHRISTOPHER COLUMBUS. *He looks petrified and abstract. He
holds one hand on his breast, the other he stretches out to
see if it is raining. The* AMERICAN *yaps. . . .*]

AMERICAN. Ladies and Gentlemen. In the name of America,
I come to salute you, Columbus—but not the great man,
only the statue. Stop. America does you great honor in

saluting you, because you are not an American, which is regrettable. In America there are not many great men. Americans are neither great nor small, but middling and of sound constitution. Stop. This tribute has its reservation. You discovered America four centuries too soon. You ought to be coming there now, yes sir! Still, it's all right as it is. It only remains for me to wish you good luck in this age in which it is possible that it will be shown that you did not exist, and in which statues go out of fashion remarkably quickly. Full stop.

[*At a signal from the speaker, the musicians attack Luther's chorale,* Ein feste Burg. *The* AMERICAN, *the* BALLERINA, *and* BUFFALO BILL—*the last of these punctuating the song with revolver shots—howl the following quatrain to the rudimentary music:*—]

> Columbus, we extol thy name,
> Nor ask we therefore pardon.
> We sing to thy immortal fame
> With voice and with bombardon.

[*The procession goes off cacophonically. Silence. The lights go out and the stage is drowned in shadow. On the base,* CHRISTOPHER COLUMBUS *moves. He takes out handkerchief and begins to weep.*]

COLUMBUS. It's no good seeing things from up above. It does something to you . . . when you are sensitive like me. There's nothing you can do about anything. You have to be a statue to understand. . . .

JEAN GIRAUDOUX

1882–1944

JEAN GIRAUDOUX described the theatre in his *Paris Impromptu* as "a world of light, poetry, and imagination," a magical place where reality resides in the unreal. And no dramatist in the modern theatre was more of a magician than this diplomat turned playwright who revitalized the French theatre. Today we think of the French as having one of the most exciting and alive theatres in the world, but we tend to forget that from the time of Victor Hugo and Dumas *fils* until the opening of Giraudoux's *Siegfried* in 1928, France produced only one playwright of international repute—Henri Becque. It can be said without fear of exaggeration that no one man was more responsible for the renaissance of the contemporary French theatre than Jean Giraudoux.

Giraudoux's theatre is a strange mixture combining the spirit of German romanticism with the traditions of French classicism. He used legends, history, and classical myths as the basic framework for most of his plays and then infused them with a delicate fantasy which is gay and pixie-ish at the same time that it is bitter, sad, and even ironic. The result is a gossamer theatrical world which is hospitable to every form of free-wheeling irrationality and at the same time is extremely close to the most somber aspects of everyday reality. However, Giraudoux was first of all a poet, and the most noticeable aspect of his drama is the verve and polish of the language. It is a language which has been transformed in such a way that it is capable of expressing in dramatic terms Giraudoux's belief in the essential goodness of life. "The theatre," he wrote, "is not an algebraic formula but a show; not arithmetic but magic. It should appeal to the imagination and the senses, not the intellect. For this reason the playwright must have literary ability, for it is his style that shines into the minds and hearts of the audience. Its poetry need not be understood any more than sunlight need be understood to be enjoyed." If the playwright–magician succeeds in communicating to his audiences through feelings, Giraudoux believed the theatre can do a great deal to make the world a better place in which to live. He insisted "that the real life of a people can only be great if their unreal life, the life of the imagination and the spirit, is great. A people's force lies in its dreams." Whether the theatre has made the world a better place in which to live is questionable, but there is no doubt that Giraudoux was in large measure responsible for unleashing those forces that have brought the French theatre to its position of dominance in our time.

TWO LAWS[1]

By Jean Giraudoux

Two laws govern—if I may thus express myself—the eternal status of the playwright.

The first law defines the sad and slightly ridiculous position of the playwright toward those of his characters he has created and given to the theatre. Just as a character, before being played by an actor, is docile toward the author, familiar, and a part of him—as you may judge from my own creations—so once he appears before the audience he becomes a stranger and indifferent. The first actor who plays him represents the first in a series of reincarnations by which the character draws further and further away from his creator and escapes him forever.

In fact, this is true of the play in its entirety. From the first performance on, it belongs to the actors. The author wandering in the wings is a kind of ghost whom the stagehands detest if he listens in or is indiscreet. After the hundredth performance, particularly if it is a good play, it belongs to the public. In reality the only thing the playwright can call his own is his bad plays. The independence of those of his characters who have succeeded is complete: the life they lead on road tours or in America is a constant denial of their filial obligations. So while the hero of your novels follows you everywhere, calling you "father" or "papa," those of your stage characters you chance to meet—as I have—in Carcassonne or Los Angeles, have become total strangers to you.

It was largely to punish them for this independence that Goethe, Claudel, and so many other writers wrote a new ver-

[1] *Two Laws* is from *Visitations* by Jean Giraudoux (Neuchâtel and Paris: *Ides et Calendes*). This translation, by Joseph Bernstein, appeared in *Playwrights on Playwriting* published by Hill & Wang, © 1961 by Toby Cole, and is reprinted here by permission of Toby Cole.

sion for their favorite heroines—but in vain. The new Marguerite, the new Hélène, or the new Violaine left their creators just as quickly. Once I was at a performance of Claudel's *Tidings Brought to Mary*. That day, at least, this law operated in my favor: I noted that the play belonged more to me than to Claudel.

How many playwrights are forced to seek in an actor or actress the memory or reflection of their sons and daughters who have escaped; just as, in daily life, other parents look for the same thing in a son-in-law or daughter-in-law. . . . On the terrace of the Café Weber, in the lobby during a dress rehearsal, on the lawn of the country house of a noted actress, how often we have met such couples: Feydeau and Mme. Cassive, Jules Renard and Suzanne Desprez, Maurice Donnay and Réjane. The woman slightly inattentive, the man alert, reminiscing, chatty, full of questions, was talking of his absent "child."

The second law, a corollary and inverse of the first, defines the wonderful position of the playwright toward his era and its events, and indicates his role therein. Here, if I wish to be sincere, I must strip myself and my colleagues of all false modesty. The figure who in the play is merely a voice, without personality, without responsibility, implacable, but a historian and an avenger, exists in a given era in flesh and blood: the playwright himself. Of all writers in the theatre worthy of the name, one should be able to say, when they appear: Add the archangel! It is futile to believe that a year or a century can find the resonance and elevation ultimately befitting the emotional debate and effort represented by each period of our passage on earth, if it does not have a spokesman of its tragedy or drama in order to reach its heights or plumb its depths. Tragedy and drama are the confession which humanity—this army of salvation and ruin—must also make in public, without reticence and in loudest tones, for the echo of its voice is clearer and more real than its voice itself. Make no mistake about it. The relationship between the theatre and religious ceremonial is obvious; it is no accident that in former times plays were given on all occasions in front of our cathedrals. The theatre is most at home on the open space in front of a church. That is what the audience goes to, on gala evenings in the theatre: toward the illuminated confession of its petty and giant destinies.

Calderón is humanity confessing its thirst for eternity,

Corneille its dignity, Racine its weakness, Shakespeare its appetite for life, Claudel its state of sin and salvation, Goethe its humanity, Kleist its vividness. Epochs have not come to terms with themselves unless crowds, dressed in their most striking costumes of confession, so as to increase the solemnity of the occasion, come to these radiant confessionals called theatres and arenas, to listen to their own avowals of cowardice and sacrifice, hatred and passion. And unless they also cry: Add the prophet!

For there is no theatre save that of divination. Not that false divination which gives names and dates, but the real thing: the one which reveals to men these amazing truths— that the living must live, that the living must die, that autumn follows summer, spring follows winter, that there are four elements, happiness, millions of catastrophes, that life is a reality, that it is a dream, that man lives by peace, that man lives by blood; in short, what they will never know.

That is theatre: the public recall of those incredible splendors whose visions disturb and overwhelm audiences by night. But—and this it is which heartens me—already by dawn the lesson and the memory are diluted, no doubt in order to make the writer's mission a daily one. Of such is the performance of a play: the sudden awareness in the spectator of the permanent state of this living and indifferent humanity— passion and death.

Translated by Joseph M. Bernstein

ELECTRA

A Play in Two Acts

by JEAN GIRAUDOUX

1937

ELECTRA[1]

Translated by Winifred Smith

CHARACTERS

ORESTES

THE EUMENIDES, *first as three little girls, later as fifteen-year-olds*

GARDENER

PRESIDENT OF THE COUNCIL

AGATHA, *his young wife*

AEGISTHUS

BEGGAR

CLYTEMNESTRA

ELECTRA

YOUNG MAN

CAPTAIN

NARSES' WIFE

GUESTS, SERVANTS, MAIDS, SOLDIERS

[1] Copyright, 1955, by Winifred Smith. Printed by permission of Ninon Tallon Karlweis. Published in French as *Elèctre*, Copyright, 1937, by B. Grasset, Paris. Caution: No part of this play may be written or performed without application in writing to Ninon Tallon Karlweis, 57 West 58th Street, New York, N.Y. 10019, exclusive agent for the works of Jean Giraudoux.

ACT ONE

Scene 1

[*A stranger,* ORESTES, *enters, escorted by three little girls,
just as, from the opposite side, the gardener comes in dressed
for a festival, and accompanied by guests from the village.*]

FIRST LITTLE GIRL. How fine the gardener looks!

SECOND LITTLE GIRL. Of course! It's his wedding day.

THIRD LITTLE GIRL. Here it is, sir, your Agamemnon's palace!

STRANGER. What a strange façade! Is it straight?

FIRST LITTLE GIRL. No. There's no right side to it. You think
you see it, but that's a mirage. Like the gardener you see
coming, who wants to speak to you. He's not coming. He
won't be able to say a word.

SECOND LITTLE GIRL. Or he'll bray—or meow——

GARDENER. The façade is perfectly straight, stranger. Don't
listen to these liars. You are confused because the right
side is built of stones from Gaul and sweat at certain seasons; that the people say the palace is weeping. The left
side is built of marble from Argos, which—no one knows
why—will suddenly be flooded with sunshine, even at
night. Then they say the palace laughs. Right now the
palace is laughing and crying at the same time.

FIRST LITTLE GIRL. So it's sure not to be mistaken.

SECOND LITTLE GIRL. It's really a widow's palace.

FIRST LITTLE GIRL. Or of childhood memories.

STRANGER. I can't remember seeing such a sensitive building
anywhere.

GARDENER. Have you already visited the palace?

FIRST LITTLE GIRL. As a baby.

SECOND LITTLE GIRL. Twenty years ago.

THIRD LITTLE GIRL. He couldn't walk yet.

GARDENER. But he must remember if he saw it.

STRANGER. All I can remember of Agamemnon's palace is a mosaic. They set me down on a square of tigers when I was naughty and on a hexagon of flowers when I was good —and I remember creeping from one to the other across some birds.

FIRST LITTLE GIRL. And over a beetle.

STRANGER. How do you know that, child?

GARDENER. And did your family live in Argos?

STRANGER. And I remember many, many bare feet. Not a face, faces were way up in the sky, but lots of bare feet. I tried to touch the gold rings under the edges of the skirts; some ankles were joined by chains, slaves' ankles. I remember two little feet, very white ones, the barest, the whitest. Their steps were always even, timid, measured by an invisible chain. I imagine they were Electra's. I must have kissed them, mustn't I? A baby kisses everything it touches.

SECOND LITTLE GIRL. Anyway that would have been the only kiss Electra ever had.

GARDENER. It surely would!

FIRST LITTLE GIRL. Jealous, gardener?

STRANGER. Electra still lives in the palace?

SECOND LITTLE GIRL. Still. But not much longer.

STRANGER. Is that her window, the one with jasmine?

GARDENER. No. That's the room where Atreus, the first king of Argos, killed his brother's sons.

FIRST LITTLE GIRL. The dinner when he served up their hearts took place in the room next to it. I'd love to know how they tasted.

THIRD LITTLE GIRL. Did he cut them up or cook them whole?

SECOND LITTLE GIRL. And Cassandra was strangled in the sentry box.

THIRD LITTLE GIRL. They caught her in a net and stabbed her. She yelled like a crazy woman, through her veil. I'd love to have seen it.

FIRST LITTLE GIRL. That all happened in the laughing wing, as you see.

STRANGER. The one with roses?

GARDENER. Stranger, don't try to connect the windows with flowers. I'm the palace gardener. I plant them at random. They're just flowers.

SECOND LITTLE GIRL. Not at all. There are flowers and flowers. Phlox doesn't suit Thyestes.

THIRD LITTLE GIRL. Nor mignonette Cassandra.

GARDENER. Oh, be quiet! The window with the roses, stranger, is the one of the rooms where our king, Agamemnon, coming back from the war, slipped into the pool, fell on his sword and killed himself.

FIRST LITTLE GIRL. He took his bath after his death. About two minutes after. That's the difference.

GARDENER. That's Electra's window.

STRANGER. Why is it so high up, almost on the roof?

GARDENER. So she can see her father's tomb.

STRANGER. Why is she there?

GARDENER. Because it's Orestes' old room, her brother's. Her mother sent him out of the country when he was two and he's not been heard of since.

SECOND LITTLE GIRL. Listen, sisters, listen! They're talking about Orestes!

GARDENER. Will you clear out! Leave us! You're just like flies.

FIRST LITTLE GIRL. We certainly won't leave. We're with this stranger.

GARDENER. Do you know these girls?

STRANGER. I met them at the door. They followed me in.

SECOND LITTLE GIRL. We followed him because we like him.

THIRD LITTLE GIRL. Because he's a lot better looking than you are, gardener.

FIRST LITTLE GIRL. No caterpillars in his beard.

SECOND LITTLE GIRL. Nor June bugs in his nose.

THIRD LITTLE GIRL. If flowers are to smell sweet, the gardener has to smell bad.

STRANGER. Be polite, children, and tell us what you do all the time.

FIRST LITTLE GIRL. What we do is, we're not polite.

SECOND LITTLE GIRL. We lie, we slander, we insult.

FIRST LITTLE GIRL. But specially, we recite.

STRANGER. And what do you recite?

FIRST LITTLE GIRL. We never know ahead of time—we invent as we go along. But we're very, very good.

SECOND LITTLE GIRL. The king of Mycenae, whose sister-in-law we insulted, said we were very, very good.

THIRD LITTLE GIRL. We say all the bad things we can think up.

GARDENER. Don't listen to them, stranger. No one knows who they are. They've been wandering about the town for two days without friends or family. If we ask who they are, they pretend they're the little Eumenides. And the horrible thing is that they grow and get fat as you look at them. Yesterday they were years younger than today. Come here, you!

SECOND LITTLE GIRL. Is he rude, for a bridegroom!

GARDENER. Look at her! See how her eyelashes grow. Look at her bosom. I understand such things, I've seen mushrooms grow. They grow fast, like an orange.

SECOND LITTLE GIRL. Poisonous things always win out.

THIRD LITTLE GIRL [to the FIRST LITTLE GIRL]. Really? You're growing a bosom?

FIRST LITTLE GIRL. Are we going to recite or not?

STRANGER. Let them recite, gardener.

FIRST LITTLE GIRL. Let's recite Clytemnestra, Electra's mother—You agree? Clytemnestra?

SECOND LITTLE GIRL. We agree.

FIRST LITTLE GIRL. Queen Clytemnestra has a bad color. She uses rouge.

SECOND LITTLE GIRL. Her color is bad because she sleeps badly.

THIRD LITTLE GIRL. She sleeps badly because she's afraid.

FIRST LITTLE GIRL. What is Queen Clytemnestra afraid of?

SECOND LITTLE GIRL. Of everything.

FIRST LITTLE GIRL. What's everything?

SECOND LITTLE GIRL. Silence. Silences.

THIRD LITTLE GIRL. Noise. Noises.

FIRST LITTLE GIRL. The idea that midnight is near. That the spider on its thread is about to pass from the time of day when it brings good luck to the time when it brings bad luck.

SECOND LITTLE GIRL. Of everything red, because blood is red.

FIRST LITTLE GIRL. Queen Clytemnestra has a bad color. She puts on blood.

GARDENER. What a silly story!

SECOND LITTLE GIRL. Good, isn't it?

FIRST LITTLE GIRL. See how the end goes back to the beginning—couldn't be more poetic!

STRANGER. Very interesting.

FIRST LITTLE GIRL. As you're interested in Electra we can recite about her. You agree, sisters? We can recite what she was like at our age.

SECOND LITTLE GIRL. We certainly do agree!

THIRD LITTLE GIRL. Even before we were born, before yesterday, we agreed.

FIRST LITTLE GIRL. Electra amuses herself by making Orestes fall out of his mother's arms.

SECOND LITTLE GIRL. Electra waxes the steps of the throne so her uncle, Aegisthus, will measure his length on the marble.

THIRD LITTLE GIRL. Electra is preparing to spit in the face of her little brother, Orestes, if he ever returns.

FIRST LITTLE GIRL. Of course, *that* isn't true, but it'd be a good story.

SECOND LITTLE GIRL. For nineteen years she's prepared poisonous spittle in her mouth.

THIRD LITTLE GIRL. She's thinking of your slugs, gardener, to make her mouth water more.

GARDENER. Now stop, you dirty little vipers!

SECOND LITTLE GIRL. Oh, ha, ha, the bridegroom gets mad!

STRANGER. He's right. Get out!

GARDENER. And don't come back!

FIRST LITTLE GIRL. We'll come back tomorrow.

GARDENER. Just try to! The palace is forbidden to girls of your age.

FIRST LITTLE GIRL. Tomorrow we'll be grown up.

SECOND LITTLE GIRL. Tomorrow will be the day after Electra's marriage to the gardener. We'll be grown up.

STRANGER. What are they saying?

FIRST LITTLE GIRL. You've not defended us, stranger. You'll be sorry for that.

GARDENER. Horrible little beasts! You'd think they were three little Fates. Dreadful to be a child Fate!

SECOND LITTLE GIRL. Fate shows you her tail, gardener. Watch out if it grows.

FIRST LITTLE GIRL. Come, sisters. Let's leave them both in front of their tainted wall.

[*The little* EUMENIDES *go out, the* GUESTS *shrinking away from them in terror.*]

Scene 2

[*The* STRANGER. *The* GARDENER. *The* PRESIDENT OF THE COUNCIL *and his young wife,* AGATHA THEOCATHOCLES. VILLAGERS.]

STRANGER. What did these girls say? That you are marrying Electra, gardener?

GARDENER. She'll be my wife an hour from now.

AGATHA. He'll *not* marry her. We've come to prevent that.

PRESIDENT. I'm your distant cousin, gardener, and the Vice President of the Council; so I've a double right to advise you. Run away to your radishes and squashes. Don't marry Electra.

GARDENER. Aegisthus orders me to.

STRANGER. Am I crazy? If Agamemnon were alive, Electra's wedding would be a festival for all Greece—and Aegisthus gives her to a gardener, whose family, even, objects! Don't tell me Electra is ugly or hunchbacked!

GARDENER. Electra is the most beautiful girl in Argos.

AGATHA. Oh, she's not too bad looking.

PRESIDENT. And she's perfectly straight. Like all flowers that grow in the shade.

STRANGER. Is she backward? Feeble-minded?

PRESIDENT. She's intelligence personified.

AGATHA. An especially good memory. Not always for the same thing, though. I don't have a good memory. Except for your birthday, darling, *that* I never forget.

STRANGER. What can she have done, or said, to be treated this way?

PRESIDENT. She does nothing, says nothing. But she's always *here*.

AGATHA. She's here now.

STRANGER. She has a right to be. It's her father's palace. It's not her fault he's dead.

GARDENER. I'd never have dreamed of marrying Electra, but as Aegisthus orders me to, I don't see why I'd be afraid.

PRESIDENT. You have every reason to be afraid. She's the kind of woman that makes trouble.

AGATHA. And you're not the only one! Our family has everything to fear.

GARDENER. I don't understand you.

PRESIDENT. You will understand. Life can be pleasant, can't it!

AGATHA. Very pleasant! Immensely so!

PRESIDENT. Don't interrupt me, darling, especially just to repeat what I say. It *can* be very pleasant. Everything has a way of settling itself in life—spiritual suffering can be cured more quickly than cancer, and mourning than a sty.

Take any group of human beings at random, each will have the same percentage of crime, lies, vice, and adultery.

AGATHA. That's a horrid word, adultery, darling.

PRESIDENT. Don't interrupt me, especially to contradict! How does it happen that in one group life slips by softly, conventionally, the dead are forgotten, the living get on well together, while in another there's hell to pay? It's simply that in the latter there's a woman who makes trouble.

STRANGER. That means there's a conscience in the second group.

AGATHA. I can't help thinking of your word, adultery—such a horrid word!

PRESIDENT. Be quiet, Agatha. A conscience, you say! If criminals don't forget their sins, if the conquered don't forget their defeats, if there are curses, quarrels, hatreds, the fault is not with humanity's conscience, which always tends toward compromise and forgetfulness, it lies with ten or fifteen women who make trouble.

STRANGER. I agree with you. Those ten or fifteen women save the world from egoism.

PRESIDENT. They save it from happiness! I know Electra. Let's agree that she is what you say—justice, generosity, duty. But it's by justice, generosity, duty, and not by egoism and easy going ways, that the state, individuals, and the best families are ruined.

AGATHA. Absolutely! But why, darling? You've told me, but I forget.

PRESIDENT. Because those three virtues have in common the one element fatal to humanity—implacability. Happiness is never the lot of implacable people. A happy family makes a surrender. A happy epoch demands unanimous capitulation.

STRANGER. You surrendered at the first call?

PRESIDENT. Alas, no! Some one else got in first. So I'm only the vice president.

GARDENER. Against what is Electra implacable? She goes every night to her father's tomb, is that all?

PRESIDENT. I know. I've followed her. Along the same road which my duty made me take one night, pursuing our most dangerous murderer, along the same river I followed and saw the greatest innocent in Greece. A horrible walk, behind the two of them. They stopped at the same places, at the yew, at the corner of the bridge, at the thousand-year-old milestone, all made the same signs to innocence and to crime. But because the murderer was there, the night was bright, peaceful, clear. He was the kernel taken out of the fruit, which, in a tart, might have broken your tooth. Electra's presence, on the contrary, confused light and darkness, even spoiled the full moon. Have you seen a fisherman who, before going out to fish, arranges his bait? All the way along the river, that was she. Every evening she spreads her net for everything that without her would have abandoned this pleasant, agreeable earth—remorse, confessions, old blood stains, rust, bones of murdered men, a mass of accusations. In a short time everything will be ready for the fisherman to pass by.

STRANGER. He always comes, sooner or later.

PRESIDENT. That's not so.

AGATHA [*much taken by the* STRANGER.] A mistake!

PRESIDENT. This child herself sees the leak in your argument. A triple layer of earth daily piles up over our sins, our failures, our crimes, and stifles their worst effects! Forgetfulness, death, human justice. It is madness to remember those things. A horrible country, one where because of an avenger of wrongs, ghosts walk, dead men, half asleep—where no allowance is ever made for human weakness, or perjury, where a ghost and an avenger constantly threaten. When guilty men's sleep continues to be more troubled after legal prosecution than the sleep of an innocent, society is terribly disturbed. When I look at Electra, I'm troubled by the sins I committed in my cradle.

AGATHA. And I by my future sins. I'll never commit them, darling. You know that. Especially that adultery, which you will talk about. But those other sins already bother me.

GARDENER. I'm rather of Electra's opinion. I don't much care for wicked people. I love truth.

PRESIDENT. Do you know what truth is for our family that you proclaim it so openly? A quiet, well-thought-of family, rising fast. You'll not deny my assertion that you are the least important member of it. But I know by experience that it's not safe to venture on thin ice. It won't be ten days, if you marry Electra, before the discovery—I'm just inventing this—that our old aunt, when a young girl, strangled her baby so her husband wouldn't find out about it, and in order to quiet suspicion, stopped hushing up the various aspersions on her grandfather's virtue. My little Agatha, in spite of being gaiety itself, can't sleep because of all this. You are the only one who doesn't see Aegisthus' trick. He wants to pass on to the Theocathocles family everything that might some day throw a sinister light on the Atrides.

STRANGER. And what have the Atrides to fear?

PRESIDENT. Nothing. Nothing that I know of; it's like every happy family or couple, every satisfied person. Yet it does have to fear the most dangerous enemy in the world, who would eat it through to the bone, Electra's ally, uncompromising justice.

GARDENER. Electra loves my garden. If she's a little nervous, the flowers will do her good.

AGATHA. But she'll not do the flowers good.

PRESIDENT. Certainly. You'll get to know your fuchsias and geraniums. You'll see that they're not just pretty symbols. They'll show their knavery and their ingratitude. Electra in the garden is justice and memory among the flowers—that means hatred.

GARDENER. Electra is devout. All the dead are for her.

PRESIDENT. The dead! The murdered, half melted into the murderers, the shades of the robbed mingled with those of the thieves, rival families scattered among each other, and saying, "Oh, Heavens! here's Electra! And we were so peaceful."

AGATHA. Here comes Electra!

GARDENER. No, not yet. It's Aegisthus. Leave us, stranger; Aegisthus doesn't like strange faces.

PRESIDENT. You, too, Agatha. He's rather too fond of well-known women's faces.

AGATHA [*with marked interest in the* STRANGER'S *good looks.*] Shall I show you the way, handsome stranger?

[AEGISTHUS *enters, to the hurrahs of the* GUESTS, *as* SERVANTS *set up his throne, and place a stool beside a pillar.*]

Scene 3

[AEGISTHUS. *The* PRESIDENT. *The* GARDENER. SERVANT.]

AEGISTHUS. Why the stool? What's the stool for?

SERVANT. For the beggar, my lord.

AEGISTHUS. What beggar?

SERVANT. The god, if you prefer. This beggar has been wandering through the city for several days. We've never seen a beggar who's so much a beggar, so it's thought he must be a god. We let him go wherever he likes. He's prowling around the palace now.

AEGISTHUS. Changing wheat to gold? Seducing the maids?

SERVANT. He does no harm.

AEGISTHUS. A queer god! The priests haven't found out yet whether he's a rascal or Jupiter?

SERVANT. The priests don't want to be asked.

AEGISTHUS. Friends, shall we leave the stool here?

PRESIDENT. I think it will be better to honor a beggar than to insult a god.

AEGISTHUS. Leave the stool there. But if he comes, warn us. We'd like to be just a group of human beings for a few minutes. And don't be rude to him. Perhaps he is delegated by the gods to attend Electra's marriage. The gods invite themselves to this marriage, which the President considers an insult to his family.

PRESIDENT. My lord . . .

AEGISTHUS. Don't protest. I heard everything. The acoustics in this palace are extraordinary. The architect apparently wanted to listen to the council's discussions of his salary and bonus; he built it full of echoing passages.

PRESIDENT. My lord . . .

AEGISTHUS. Be quiet. I know everything you're about to say on the subject of your fine honest family, your worthy sister-in-law, the baby-killer, your uncle, the satirist, and our nephew, the slanderer.

PRESIDENT. My lord . . .

AEGISTHUS. An officer, in a battle, to whom the King's standard is given to turn the enemy's fire on him, carries it with more enthusiasm. You're losing your time. The gardener will marry Electra.

SERVANT. Here is the beggar, my lord.

AEGISTHUS. Detain him a moment. Offer him a drink. Wine is appropriate for a beggar or a god.

SERVANT. God or beggar, he's drunk already.

AEGISTHUS. Then let him come in. He'll not understand us, though we must speak of the gods. It might even be amusing to talk about them before him. Your notion of Electra, President, is true enough, but it's peculiar, definitely middle-class. As I'm the Regent, allow me to give you more elevated philosophical ideas. You believe in the gods, President?

PRESIDENT. Do you, my lord?

AEGISTHUS. My dear President, I've often asked myself if I believe in the gods. Asked myself because it's the only problem a statesman must decide for himself. I do believe in the gods. Or rather, I believe I believe in the gods. But I believe in them, not as great caretakers and great watchmen, but as great abstractions. Between space and time, always oscillating between gravitation and emptiness, there are the great indifferences. Those are the gods. I imagine them, not constantly concerned with that moving mould on the earth which is humanity, but as having reached the stage of serenity and universality. That is blessedness, the same thing as unconsciousness. They are unconscious as at the top of the ladder of being, as the atom is at the bottom. The difference is that theirs is the unconsciousness of lightning, omniscient, thousand-faceted, so that in their normal state, like diamonds, powerless and deaf, they only *react* to light, to omens, without understanding them.

BEGGAR [*at last seated, feels he must applaud*]. Well said! Bravo!

AEGISTHUS. Thanks. On the other hand, President, it's undeniable that sometimes there seem to be interruptions in human life so opportune and extensive that it's possible to believe in an extraordinary superhuman interest or justice. Such events have something superhuman or divine about them, in that they are like coarse work, not at all well designed. The plague breaks out in a town which has sinned by impiety or folly, but it also ravages the neighboring city, a particularly holy one. War breaks out when a nation becomes degenerate and vile, but it destroys all the just, the brave, and preserves the cowards. Or, whose ever the fault, or by whom committed, it's the same family that pays, innocent or guilty. I know a mother of seven children, who always spanked the same child—she was a divine mother. This fits our idea of the gods, that they are blind boxers, always satisfied by finding the same cheeks to slap, the same bottoms to spank. We might even be surprised if we understood the confusion that comes from a sudden waking to beatitude, that their blows weren't given more at random; that the wife of a good man, and not a per-

jurer's, is brained by a shutter in a wind storm; that accidents strike down pilgrims and not troops. Always humanity
suffers. . . . I'm speaking generally. We see crows or deer
struck down by an inexplicable epidemic—perhaps the
blow intended for mankind went astray, either up or
down. However it be, it's certain that the chief duty of a
statesman is to watch fiercely that the gods are not shaken
out of their lethargy, and to limit the harm they do to such
reactions as sleepers snoring, or to thunder.

BEGGAR. Bravo! That's very clear! I understand it very well!

AEGISTHUS. Charmed, I'm sure.

BEGGAR. It's truth itself. For example, look at the people
walking along the roads. Sometimes every hundred feet
you'll see a dead hedgehog. They go over the roads at
night by tens, male and female, and get crushed. You'll
say they're fools, that they could find their mates on their
side of the road. I can't explain it, but love, for hedgehogs,
begins by crossing a road. What the devil was I trying to
say? I've lost the thread. . . . Go on, it'll come back to me.

AEGISTHUS. Indeed! What is he trying to say!

PRESIDENT. Shall we talk about Electra, my lord?

AEGISTHUS. What do you think we've been talking about?
Our charming little Agatha? We were talking only about
Electra, President, and about the need I feel to get her out
of the royal family. Why, since I've been Regent, while
other cities are devoured by dissension, other citizens by
moral crises, are we alone satisfied with other people and
with ourselves? Why are we so rich? Why in Argos alone
are raw materials so dear and retail prices so low? Why,
when we're exporting more cows, does butter go down in
price? Why do storms pass by our vineyards, heresies our
temples, animal diseases our barns? Because, in this city,
I wage merciless war against all who signal to the gods.

PRESIDENT. What do you mean, signal to the gods?

BEGGAR. There! I've found it!

AEGISTHUS. Found what?

BEGGAR. My story, the thread of my story. I was speaking of
the death of hedgehogs.

AEGISTHUS. One moment, please. We're speaking of the gods.

BEGGAR. To be sure! Gods come first, hedgehogs second. But
I wonder if I'll remember.

AEGISTHUS. There are no two ways of signaling, President:
it's done by separating one's self from the crowd, climbing

a hill and waving a lantern or a flag. The earth is betrayed, as is a besieged city, by signals. The philosopher signals from his roof, the poet or desperate man signals from his balcony or his swimming pool. If for ten years the gods have not meddled with our lives, it's because I've kept the heights empty and the fairgrounds full. I've ordered dreamers, painters, and chemists to marry; and because, in order to avoid racial trouble between our citizens—something that can't help marking human beings as different in the eyes of the gods—I've always given great importance to misdemeanors and paid slight attention to crimes. Nothing keeps the gods so quiet as an equal value set on murder and on stealing bread. I must say the courts have supported me splendidly. Whenever I've been forced to be severe, they've overlooked it. None of my decisions has been so obvious as to allow the gods to avenge it. No exile. I kill. An exile tends to climb up a steep road, just like a ladybird. I never execute in public. Our poor neighboring cities betray themselves by erecting their gallows on the top of a hill; crucify at the bottom of a valley. Now I've said everything about Electra.

GARDENER. What have you said?

AEGISTHUS. That there's just one person in Argos now to give a signal to the gods, and that's Electra. What's the matter?

[BEGGAR *moves about among the* GUESTS.]

BEGGAR. Nothing's the matter. But I'd better tell you my story now. In five minutes, at the rate you're talking, it won't make sense. It's just to support what you say. Among those crushed hedgehogs you'll see dozens who seem to have died a hedgehog's death. Their muzzles flattened by horse's hoofs, their spines broken under wheels, they're just smashed hedgehogs, nothing more. Smashed because of the original sin of hedgehogs—which is crossing the main or side road on the pretext that the snail or partridge egg on the far side tastes better but actually to make hedgehog love. That's their affair. No one stops them. Suddenly you see a little young one, not flattened like the others, not so dirty, his little paw stretched out, his lips closed, very dignified, and you feel that he's not died a hedgehog's death, but was struck down for someone else, for you. His cold little eye is your eye. His spikes, your beard. His blood, your blood. I always pick up those little

ones, they're the youngest, the tenderest to eat. A year
goes by, a hedgehog no longer sacrifices himself for mankind. You see I understand. The gods were mistaken, they
wanted to strike a perjurer, a thief, and they kill a hedgehog. A young one.

AEGISTHUS. Very well understood.

BEGGAR. And what's true of hedgehogs holds for other
species.

PRESIDENT. Of course! Of course!

BEGGAR. Why, of course? That's all wrong. Take the martin.
Even though you're a President of the Council, you'll
never pretend to have seen birds dying for you?

AEGISTHUS. Will you let us go on talking about Electra?

BEGGAR. Talk! Talk! But I must add, when you see dead men,
many seem to have died for bulls or pigs or turtles, not
many for mankind. A man who seems to have died for
man, he's hard to find, or even for himself. Are we going
to see her?

AEGISTHUS. See whom?

BEGGAR. Electra. I'd like to see her before she's killed.

AEGISTHUS. Electra killed? Who says Electra's to be killed?

BEGGAR. You.

PRESIDENT. There's been no thought of killing Electra.

BEGGAR. I have one gift. I don't understand words—I've had
no education—but I do understand people. You want to
kill Electra.

PRESIDENT. You don't understand at all, beggar. This man is
Aegisthus, Agamemnon's cousin, and Electra's his darling
niece.

BEGGAR. Are there two Electras? The one he was talking
about who ruins everything, and the other one, his darling
niece?

PRESIDENT. No! There's only one.

BEGGAR. Then he wants to kill her. No doubt of it. He wants
to kill his darling niece.

PRESIDENT. I repeat, you don't understand in the least.

BEGGAR. Oh, I move about a lot. I knew a couple, he was
called Narses. She was better than he. She was sick, her
breathing bad. But a great deal better than he. No comparison.

GARDENER. He's drunk, a beggar, you know.

PRESIDENT. He's raving. He's a god.

BEGGAR. No. I started to tell you they had a wolf cub. It was their darling little pet. But one day around noon, wolf cubs, you know, grow up. They couldn't foretell the day. Two minutes before noon they were petting her, one minute after twelve she jumped at their throats. I didn't mind about him!

AEGISTHUS. Well?

BEGGAR. Well, I was just passing by. And I killed the wolf. She was beginning to eat Narses' cheeks, she liked them. Narses' wife got away, not too badly hurt. Thanks! You'll see her. She's coming for me pretty soon.

AEGISTHUS. What's the connection . . . ?

BEGGAR. Oh, don't expect to see an Amazon queen. Varicose veins age a person.

PRESIDENT. He asked, what's the connection?

BEGGAR. The connection? It's because I think this man, as he's head of the state, must be more intelligent than Narses. No one could imagine such stupidity as Narses'. I never could teach him to smoke a cigar except by the lighted end. And what about knots? It's terribly important to know how to make knots. If you make a curlycue where you ought to have a knot, and vice versa, you're lost. You lose your money, you catch cold, you choke, your boat veers away or collides, you can't pull off your shoes. I mean if you want to pull them off. And the laces? You know Narses was a poacher.

PRESIDENT. We've asked you, what is the connection?

BEGGAR. Here's the connection. If this man distrusts his niece, if he knows that one of these days she'll give a signal, as he said, she'll begin to bite, to turn the city upside down, push up the price of butter, start a war, et cetera, he can't hesitate. He ought to kill her dead before she reveals herself. When will she reveal herself?

PRESIDENT. What do you mean?

BEGGAR. What day, at what time will she reveal herself? When will she turn into a wolf? When will she become Electra?

PRESIDENT. But nothing tells us she'll turn into a wolf.

BEGGAR [*pointing to* AEGISTHUS.] Yes. He thinks so. He says so.

GARDENER. Electra is the gentlest of women.

BEGGAR. Narses' wolf cub was the gentlest of wolves.

PRESIDENT. Your expression "reveals herself" doesn't make sense.

BEGGAR. My expression doesn't make sense? You know nothing about life. The 29th of May, when you see the hills astir with thousands of little red, yellow, and green balls flying, squawling, quarreling over every little bit of thistle fluff, never making a mistake nor going after dandelion down, aren't the butterflies revealing themselves? And June 14th when you see on the river bank two reeds move without wind or wave till June 15th, and, too, without bubbles made by carp, isn't the pike revealing himself? And judges like you, the first time they condemn to death, when the condemned man appears, distraught, don't they reveal themselves by the taste of blood on their lips? Everything in nature reveals itself. Even the king. And the question today, if you'll believe me, is whether the king will reveal himself as Aegisthus before Electra reveals herself as Electra. So he has to know the day when it will happen to the girl, so he can kill her on the eve, down in a valley, as he said, down in a little valley, the handiest and least visible, in her bath.

PRESIDENT. Isn't he awful?

AEGISTHUS. You're forgetting the wedding, beggar.

BEGGAR. True. I am forgetting the wedding. But a wedding, if you want to kill someone, isn't as sure as death. Especially as a girl like her, sensitive, rather retarded, et cetera, will reveal herself the moment a man takes her in his arms for the first time. You're marrying her?

AEGISTHUS. At once. Right here.

BEGGAR. Not to the king of a neighboring city, I hope?

AEGISTHUS. Not on your life! To this gardener.

PRESIDENT. To this gardener.

BEGGAR. She'll take him? I'd not reveal myself in the arms of a gardener. But everyone to his taste. I revealed myself in Corfu, at the fountain near the bakery, under the plane trees. You should have seen me that day! In each tray of the scales I weighed a hand of the baker's wife. They never weighed the same. I evened them up in the right tray with flour, in the left with oatmeal. . . . Where does the gardener live?

GARDENER. Outside the walls.

BEGGAR. In a village?

GARDENER. No. My house stands alone.

BEGGAR [to AEGISTHUS]. Bravo! I catch your idea. Not bad!

It's quite easy to kill a gardener's wife. Much easier than a princess in a palace.

GARDENER. Whoever you are, I beg you . . .

BEGGAR. You'll not deny that it's easier to bury someone in compost than in marble?

GARDENER. What are you imagining? For one thing she'll not be a minute out of my sight.

BEGGAR. You'll bend down to plant a pear tree. Transplant it again because you hit a hard clod. Death has passed by.

PRESIDENT. Stranger, I fear you don't know where you are. You're in Agamemnon's palace, in his family.

BEGGAR. I see what I see; I see this man is afraid; he lives with fear, fear of Electra.

AEGISTHUS. My dear guest, let's not misunderstand each other. I'll not deny I'm anxious about Electra. I know misfortunes and troubles will come to the family of the Atrides the day she reveals herself, as you say. And to us all, for every citizen is affected by what happens to the royal family. That's why I'm handing her over to a lowly family, unseen by the gods, where her eyes and gestures will not inflame, where the harm will be only local and in the middle class, the Theocathocles family.

BEGGAR. A good idea, a good idea! But the family ought to be especially lowly.

AEGISTHUS. It is, and I'll see that it stays so. I'll see that no Theocathocles distinguishes himself by talent or courage. As for boldness and genius, I'm not afraid they'll make their mark.

BEGGAR. Take care! This little Agatha is not exactly ugly. Beauty too can give a signal.

PRESIDENT. I beg you to leave Agatha out of our argument.

BEGGAR. Of course it's possible to rub her face with vitriol.

PRESIDENT. My lord!

AEGISTHUS. The case has been argued.

PRESIDENT. But I'm thinking of fate, Aegisthus! It's not a disease. You think it's infectious?

BEGGAR. Yes. Like hunger among the poor.

PRESIDENT. I can hardly believe that fate will be content with one obscure little clan instead of the royal family, or that it will become the fate of the Theocathocles instead of the Atrides.

BEGGAR. Don't worry. A royal cancer spreads to the middle classes.

AEGISTHUS. President, if you don't want Electra's entrance
into your family to mark the disgrace of its members, don't
add a word. In a third-class zone the most implacable fate
will do only third-class harm. I personally am distressed,
because of my great esteem for the Theocathocles family,
but the dynasty, the state, and the city can no longer take
risks.

BEGGAR. And perhaps she can be killed a little anyway, if an
occasion arises.

AEGISTHUS. I have spoken. You may fetch Clytemnestra and
Electra. They're waiting.

BEGGAR. It's not too soon. Without blaming you, I must say
our talk lacks women.

AEGISTHUS. You'll have two, and talkers!

BEGGAR. And they'll argue with you a little, I hope?

AEGISTHUS. You like arguing women?

BEGGAR. Adore them. This afternoon I was in a house where
a dispute was going on. Not a very high-toned discussion.
Not compared to here. Not a plot of royal assassins as
here. They were arguing whether they ought to serve
guests chickens with or without livers. And the neck, of
course. The women were furious. Had to be separated.
Now I think of it, it was a fierce dispute. Blood flowed.

Scene 4

[*The Same.* CLYTEMNESTRA, ELECTRA, MAIDS.]

PRESIDENT. Here they both are.

CLYTEMNESTRA. Both! That's a manner of speaking. Electra
is never more absent than when she's present.

ELECTRA. No. Today I'm here.

AEGISTHUS. Then let's make the most of it. You know why
your mother has brought you here?

ELECTRA. It's her habit. She's already led a daughter to
sacrifice.

CLYTEMNESTRA. There's Electra to the life! Never a word
that's not treason or insinuation.

ELECTRA. Excuse me, mother. The allusion is quite apropos
in the family of the Atrides.

BEGGAR. What does she mean? Is she angry with her mother?

GARDENER. It would be the first time anyone has seen Electra angry.

BEGGAR. All the more interesting!

AEGISTHUS. Electra, your mother has told you of our decision. We've been anxious about you for a long time. I hardly think you realize that you're like a sleepwalker in broad daylight. In the palace and the city people speak of you only in whispers, they're so afraid you'd wake and fall if they raised their voices.

BEGGAR [*shouting*]. Electra!

AEGISTHUS. What's the matter with him?

BEGGAR. Oh, I'm sorry, it's just a joke. Excuse it. But you were scared, not she. Electra's no sleepwalker.

AEGISTHUS. Please——

BEGGAR. At least the experiment has been made. You were the one who flinched. What would you have done if I'd shouted, "Aegisthus"?

PRESIDENT. Let our Regent speak.

BEGGAR. I'll shout "Aegisthus" pretty soon, when nobody expects it.

AEGISTHUS. You must get well, Electra, no matter what it costs.

ELECTRA. To cure me, that's easy. Give life to a dead man.

AEGISTHUS. You're not the only one who grieves for your father. But he'd not ask you to make your mourning an offense to the living. We wrong the dead to attach them to our lives, for that deprives them of the freedom of death, if they know it.

ELECTRA. He's free. That's why he comes.

AEGISTHUS. Do you really think he's pleased to see you weep for him, not like a daughter but like a wife?

ELECTRA. I am my father's widow, for lack of another.

CLYTEMNESTRA. Electra!

AEGISTHUS. Widow or not, today we'll celebrate your marriage.

ELECTRA. Yes, I know your plot.

CLYTEMNESTRA. What plot? Is it a plot to marry a twenty-one-year-old daughter? At your age I had the two of you in my arms, you and Orestes.

ELECTRA. You carried us badly. You let Orestes fall on the marble floor.

CLYTEMNESTRA. What could I do? You pushed him.

ELECTRA. That's a lie. I never pushed him.

CLYTEMNESTRA. What do you know about it? You were only fifteen months old.

ELECTRA. I did not push Orestes! I remember it, far back in my memory. Oh, Orestes, wherever you are, hear me! I did not push you.

AEGISTHUS. That's enough, Electra.

BEGGAR. This time they're really at it! It'd be funny if the little girl revealed herself right in front of us.

ELECTRA. She lies. Orestes, she lies!

AEGISTHUS. Please, Electra!

CLYTEMNESTRA. She did push him. Obviously at her age she didn't know what she was doing. But she did push him.

ELECTRA. With all my strength I tried to hold him: by his little blue tunic, by his arm, by the end of his fingers, by his shadow. I sobbed when I saw him on the floor, with the red mark on his forehead.

CLYTEMNESTRA. You shouted with laughter. The tunic, by the way, was mauve.

ELECTRA. It was blue. I know Orestes' tunic. When it was drying you couldn't see it against the sky.

AEGISTHUS. Can *I* get a word in? Haven't you had time these twenty years to settle this debate?

ELECTRA. For twenty years I've waited for this chance. Now I have it.

CLYTEMNESTRA. Why can't she understand that she might be wrong, even honestly?

BEGGAR. They're both honest. That's the truth.

PRESIDENT. Princess, I beg of you! Of what interest is this question today?

CLYTEMNESTRA. Of none, I grant you.

ELECTRA. What interest? If I had pushed Orestes I'd rather die, I'd kill myself. My life would have no meaning.

AEGISTHUS. Must I force you to keep quiet? Are you as mad as she, queen?

CLYTEMNESTRA. Electra, listen. Let's not quarrel. This is exactly what happened: he was on my right arm.

ELECTRA. On your left!

AEGISTHUS. Have you finished, Clytemnestra, or haven't you?

CLYTEMNESTRA. We've finished. But a right arm is a right arm, a mauve tunic is mauve, not blue.

ELECTRA. It was blue. As blue as Orestes' forehead was red.

CLYTEMNESTRA. That is true. Very red. You touched the
wound with your finger and danced around the little prone
body. You laughed as you tasted the blood.

ELECTRA. I? I wanted to bruise my head on the step that
hurt him. I trembled for a week.

AEGISTHUS. Silence!

ELECTRA. I'm still trembling.

BEGGAR. Narses' wife tied hers with an elastic rope that had
some play. Often it was askew, but he didn't fall.

AEGISTHUS. Enough. We'll soon see how Electra will carry
hers. For you agree, don't you? You accept this marriage?

ELECTRA. I agree.

AEGISTHUS. I must admit not many suitors throng around
you.

BEGGAR. They say . . .

AEGISTHUS. What do they say?

BEGGAR. They say you've threatened to kill the princes who
might marry Electra. That's what they say in the city.

ELECTRA. Good! I don't want any prince.

CLYTEMNESTRA. You'd rather have a gardener?

ELECTRA. I know you two have decided to marry me to my
father's gardener. I accept.

CLYTEMNESTRA. You shall not marry a gardener.

AEGISTHUS. Queen, we settled that. Our word is given.

CLYTEMNESTRA. I take mine back. It was a wicked word. If
Electra is ill we'll care for her. I'll not give my daughter to
a gardener.

ELECTRA. Too late, mother. You have given me.

CLYTEMNESTRA. Gardener, you dare to aspire to Electra?

GARDENER. I'm unworthy, queen, but Aegisthus commands
me.

AEGISTHUS. I do command you. Here are the rings. Take
your wife.

CLYTEMNESTRA. If you persist, gardener, it's at the risk of
your life.

BEGGAR. Then don't persist. I'd rather see soldiers die than
gardeners.

CLYTEMNESTRA. What's that man saying? Marry Electra, gardener, and you die.

BEGGAR. It's your business. But go into the garden a year
after the death of the gardener. You'll see something. You'll

see what's happened to the endive, widowed by its gardener. It's not like kings' widows.

CLYTEMNESTRA. The garden won't suffer. Come, Electra.

GARDENER. Queen, you can deny me Electra, but it's not nice to say bad things about a garden you don't know.

CLYTEMNESTRA. I know it—empty land, with scattered plantings.

GARDENER. Empty? The best tended garden in Argos.

PRESIDENT. If he begins to talk about his garden we'll never finish.

AEGISTHUS. Spare us your descriptions!

GARDENER. The queen provoked me, and I answer. My garden is my dowry and my honor.

AEGISTHUS. Never mind! Enough of quarrels.

GARDENER. Empty, indeed! It covers ten acres of hilly land, and six of valley. No, no, you'll not silence me! Not a sterile inch, is there, Electra? On the terraces I have garlic and tomatoes, on the slopes grape vines and peach trees. On the level land vegetables, strawberries, and raspberries. A fig tree at the bottom of each slope against the wall, which warms the figs.

AEGISTHUS. Fine! Let your figs get warm and take your wife.

CLYTEMNESTRA. You dare talk of your garden! I've seen it from the road. It's all dry, a bald skull. You shall not have Electra.

GARDENER. All dry! A brook flows between the box and the plane trees, never dry in hottest weather; I've dug two little trenches from it—one turned on the meadow, the other cut in the rock. Try to find skulls like that! And scattered plantings! In spring it's full of narcissus and jonquils. I've never seen Electra really smile, but in my garden, I saw something on her face almost like a smile.

CLYTEMNESTRA. See if she's smiling now!

GARDENER. I call that Electra's smile.

CLYTEMNESTRA. Smiling at your dirty hands, your black nails. . . .

ELECTRA. Dear gardener. . . .

GARDENER. My black nails? Look, see if my nails are black! Don't believe it, Electra. You're unlucky today, queen, I spent this morning whitewashing my house, so there's not a sign of mice there, and my nails came out, not black, as you say, but mooned with white.

AEGISTHUS. That's enough, gardener.

GARDENER. I know, I know it's enough. And my dirty hands! Look! Look at these dirty hands! Hands that I washed after taking down the dried mushrooms and onions, so nothing would trouble Electra's nights. I'll sleep in the outhouse, Electra; there I'll keep guard so that nothing disturbs your sleep, whether an owl, or the open floodgate, or a fox, hunting in the hedge, with a chicken in his mouth. I've said my say.

ELECTRA. Thanks, gardener.

CLYTEMNESTRA. And that's how Electra will live; Clytemnestra's daughter, watching her husband going around his border, two pails in his hands. . . .

AEGISTHUS. There she can weep for her dead to her heart's content. Get ready your wreaths of everlasting tomorrow.

GARDENER. And there she'll escape from anxiety, torture, and perhaps tragedy. I don't understand people, queen, but I do know the seasons. It's time, full time, to transplant misfortune from our city. The Atrides won't be grafted on our poor family, but on the seasons, the fields, the winds. I think they'll lose nothing by that.

BEGGAR. Be persuaded, queen. Don't you see that Aegisthus hates Electra so much he'll be driven to kill her, giving her to the earth by a kind of play on words: he gives her to a garden. She gains by that, she gains life.

[AEGISTHUS *rises*.]

What? Was I wrong to say that?

AEGISTHUS [*to* ELECTRA *and the* GARDENER]. Come here, both of you.

CLYTEMNESTRA. Electra, I beg you!

ELECTRA. You're the one who wanted it, mother.

CLYTEMNESTRA. I no longer want it. You see I don't want it now.

ELECTRA. Why don't you want it? Are you afraid? Too late!

CLYTEMNESTRA. How can I make you remember who I am and who you are?

ELECTRA. You'll have to tell me I didn't push Orestes.

CLYTEMNESTRA. Stupid girl!

AEGISTHUS. Are they beginning again?

BEGGAR. Yes, yes, let them begin again.

CLYTEMNESTRA. And unjust! And stubborn! I let Orestes

fall! I who never break anything! Never let fall a glass or
a ring! I'm so steady that birds light on my arms. It's possible to fly away from me but not to fall. That's just what
I said when he lost his balance, "Why, why did an ill fate
bring his sister so near him?"

AEGISTHUS. They're crazy!

ELECTRA. And I said to myself, as soon as I saw him slipping,
"If she's a true mother she'll stoop to soften his fall, or
she'll bend to make a slope and catch him on his thigh or
her knees. We'll see if they'll catch him, the noble knees
and thighs of my mother. I'm not sure. I'll see."

CLYTEMNESTRA. Be quiet!

ELECTRA. "Or she'll bend backward, so little Orestes will
slip off her like a child from a tree where he's picked off
a nest, or she'll fall so *he* won't, or so he'll fall on her. She
knows all the ways a mother uses to catch her son, she
still knows them. She can still be a curve, a shell, a motherly slope, a cradle." But she stood fixed, straight, and he
fell right down from the full height of his mother.

AEGISTHUS. The case is heard. Clytemnestra, we'll leave.

CLYTEMNESTRA. Just let her remember what she saw when she
was fifteen months old and what she didn't see. That's the
point.

AEGISTHUS. Who but you believes her or listens to her?

ELECTRA. There are a thousand ways of preventing a fall,
and she did nothing.

CLYTEMNESTRA. The slightest movement, and *you* would
have fallen.

ELECTRA. Just as I said. You calculated. You figured it all
out. You were a nurse, not a mother.

CLYTEMNESTRA. My little Electra . . .

ELECTRA. I'm not your little Electra. Your motherly feeling is
tickled awake by your rubbing your two children against
you. But it's too late.

CLYTEMNESTRA. Please———!

ELECTRA. There you are! Open your arms, see what you've
done. Look, everybody. That's just what you did.

CLYTEMNESTRA. Let's go, Aegisthus. [*She leaves.*]

BEGGAR. I believe the mother is frightened.

AEGISTHUS [*to the* BEGGAR]. What's that you say?

BEGGAR. I? I say nothing. I never say anything. When I'm
hungry I talk, everyone hears me. Today I've drunk a little
something.

Scene 5

[ELECTRA, BEGGAR, GARDENER, STRANGER, AGATHA.]

AGATHA. This is the right time, Aegisthus isn't here. Get out, gardener.

GARDENER. What do you mean?

AGATHA. Get out, fast. This man will take your place.

GARDENER. My place with Electra?

STRANGER. Yes, I'll marry her.

ELECTRA. Let go my hand.

STRANGER. Never.

AGATHA. Just look at him, Electra. Before you turn your back on a man, at least look at him. I'm sure you'll lose nothing by that.

ELECTRA. Gardener, help!

STRANGER. I owe you nothing, gardener. But look me in the eye. You understand species and kinds. Look at me and see the kind I am. So! Look, with your poor peasant eyes, with the gaze of humble folk, a blear-eyed mixture of devotion and fear, the sterile look of the poor, unchanged by sunshine or misfortune, see if I can give way to you. Fine! Now give me your ring. Thanks!

ELECTRA. Agatha, cousin! Help me! I swear I'll not tell about your rendezvous, your quarrels, I'll tell nothing.

AGATHA [leading off the GARDENER]. Come, the Theocathocles are saved. Let the Atrides work it out.

BEGGAR. She runs away—like a wood louse, hiding under a stone to escape from the sun.

Scene 6

[ELECTRA, STRANGER, BEGGAR.]

STRANGER. Struggle no more.

ELECTRA. I'll struggle till I die.

STRANGER. You think so? In a minute you'll take me in your arms.

ELECTRA. No insults!

STRANGER. In a minute you'll embrace me.

ELECTRA. Shame on you for profiting from two infamies!

STRANGER. See how I trust you. I let you go.

ELECTRA. Farewell forever!

STRANGER. No! I'll say one word to you and you'll come back to me, tenderly.

ELECTRA. What lie is this?

STRANGER. One word, and you'll be sobbing in my arms. One word, my name.

ELECTRA. There's only one name in the world that could draw me to anyone.

STRANGER. That's the one.

ELECTRA. Are you Orestes?

ORESTES. Ungrateful sister, only recognizing me by my name!

[CLYTEMNESTRA *appears.*]

Scene 7

[CLYTEMNESTRA, ELECTRA, ORESTES, BEGGAR.]

CLYTEMNESTRA. Electra!

ELECTRA. Mother?

CLYTEMNESTRA. Come back to your place in the palace. Leave the gardener. Come!

ELECTRA. The gardener has left, mother.

CLYTEMNESTRA. Where is he?

ELECTRA. He's given me to this man.

CLYTEMNESTRA. What man?

ELECTRA. This man. He's my husband now.

CLYTEMNESTRA. This is no time for jokes. Come!

ELECTRA. How can I come? He's holding my hand.

CLYTEMNESTRA. Hurry!

ELECTRA. You know, mother, those clogs they put on the legs of foals to prevent their running away? This man has put them on my ankles.

CLYTEMNESTRA. This time I command you. You must be in your room by tonight. Come!

ELECTRA. What? Leave my husband the night of my wedding?

CLYTEMNESTRA. What are you doing? Who are you?

ELECTRA. He'll not answer you. This evening my husband's mouth belongs to me, and all the words he speaks.

CLYTEMNESTRA. Where do you come from? Who is your father?

ELECTRA. A misalliance maybe. But not such a bad one.

CLYTEMNESTRA. Why do you look at me like that? Why the challenge in your eyes? Who was your mother?

ELECTRA. He never saw her.

CLYTEMNESTRA. She's dead?

ELECTRA. Perhaps what you see in his eyes is that he never saw his mother. Handsome, isn't he?

CLYTEMNESTRA. Yes. He looks like you.

ELECTRA. If our first married hours make us look alike, that's a good omen, isn't it, mother?

CLYTEMNESTRA. Who are you?

ELECTRA. What does it matter to you? Never was a man less yours.

CLYTEMNESTRA. Whatever or whoever you are, stranger, don't give in to her caprice. We'll see tomorrow if you're worthy of Electra. I'll win over Aegisthus. But I've never known a less propitious night. Leave this man, Electra.

ELECTRA. Too late! His arms hold me.

CLYTEMNESTRA. You can break iron if you want to.

ELECTRA. Iron, yes, *this* iron, no!

CLYTEMNESTRA. What has he said against your mother that you accept him this way?

ELECTRA. We've had no time yet to speak of my mother or his. Go, we'll begin!

ORESTES. Electra!

ELECTRA. That's all he can say. If I take my hand from his mouth, he just says my name without stopping. You can't get anything else out of him. Oh, husband, now that your mouth is free, kiss me!

CLYTEMNESTRA. Shame! So this madness is Electra's secret!

ELECTRA. Kiss me, before my mother.

CLYTEMNESTRA. Farewell! But I didn't think you were a girl to give yourself to the first passer-by.

ELECTRA. Nor I. But I didn't know what the first kiss was like.

Scene 8

[ELECTRA, ORESTES, BEGGAR.]

ORESTES. Why do you hate our mother so, Electra?

ELECTRA. Don't speak of her, above all not of her! Let's imagine for a minute that we were born without a mother. Don't talk.

ORESTES. I have everything to tell you.

ELECTRA. You tell me everything just by being here. Be
quiet. Close your eyes. Your words and your look touch
me too poignantly, they wound me. I often wished that I'd
find you in your sleep, if I ever found you. Now I can't
bear to have all at once the look, the voice, the life of
Orestes. I ought to have stumbled on your image, dead at
first, then coming alive little by little. But my brother was
born like the sun, a golden animal at his rising. Either I'm
blind or I find my brother by groping—oh, the joy of
being blind for a sister who finds her brother! For twenty
years my hands have fumbled over mean or indifferent
things, and now they touch—a brother—a brother in whom
everything is true. Some dubious or some false bits might
have been in this head, this body, but by a wonderful
chance, everything in Orestes is brotherly, everything is
Orestes.

ORESTES. You smother me.

ELECTRA. I don't smother you. I don't kill you. I caress you.
I'm calling you to life. From this brotherly shape which my
dazzled eyes have scarcely seen I'm making my brother in
all his features. See, how I've made my brother's hand,
with its straight thumb. See how I've made my brother's
chest, which I'm animating so it swells and breathes, giving
life to my brother. See how I make this ear, little, curled,
transparent like a bat's wing. One last touch and the ear is
finished. I make the two alike. Quite a success, these ears!
And now I'll make my brother's mouth, gentle and dry,
and fasten it on his face. Take your life from me, Orestes,
not from our mother.

ORESTES. Why do you hate her? Listen . . .

ELECTRA. What's the matter with you? Are you pushing me
away? That's the ingratitude of sons. They're hardly finished before they get away and escape.

ORESTES. Someone is watching us from the staircase.

ELECTRA. It's she, certainly she. From jealousy or fear. It's
our mother.

BEGGAR. Yes, yes, it's she.

ELECTRA. She suspects we're here, creating ourselves, freeing
ourselves from her. She thinks that my caresses will cover
you, wash you clear of her, make you an orphan. Oh,
brother, who else could do me such a service!

ORESTES. How can you speak so of her who bore you?
Though she was harsh to me, I'm less hard on her.

ELECTRA. That's just what I can't stand about her, that she
bore me. That's my shame. I feel that I came into life in
a dubious way, that her motherhood is only a plot to bind
us together. I love everything that comes from my father.
I love the way he put off his fine wedding garment and
lay down to beget me, from his thought and from his body.
I love his eyes, and his surprise the day I was born; I came
from him far more than from my mother's pains. I was
born from his nights of deep sleep, his nine months' eman-
cipation, the comfort he found with other women while
my mother was carrying me, his fatherly smile when I
was born. I hate everything about my birth that comes
from my mother.

ORESTES. Why do you detest women so?

ELECTRA. I don't detest women, I detest my mother. And I
don't detest men, I detest Aegisthus.

ORESTES. Why do you hate him?

ELECTRA. I don't know yet. I only know it's the same hatred.
That's why it's so hard to bear, that's why I'm suffocating.
Many times I've tried to find out why I hate both of them
with a special hatred. Two little hatreds could be borne—
like sorrows—one balances the other. I tried to think I
hated my mother because she let you fall when you were a
baby, and Aegisthus because he stole your throne. But it's
not true. I really pitied this great queen, who ruled the
world, yet suddenly, frightened and humble, let her child
fall, like a feeble grandmother. I pitied Aegisthus, that
cruel tyrant, whose fate is to die miserably from your
blows. All the reasons I had for hating them made me
think them human, pitiable, but no sooner had my hatred
washed them clean and re-clothed them and I found myself gentle, obedient before them, than a yet heavier wave,
charged with a yet more virulent hatred, flowed over them.
I hate them with a hatred that is not really me.

ORESTES. I'm here. It will vanish.

ELECTRA. You believe that? I used to think your return
would free me of this hatred. I thought my illness was because you were far away. I prepared for your return by
becoming all tenderness, tenderness for everyone, for
them too. I was wrong. My pain tonight is caused by your

being here and all the hatred in me laughs and welcomes
you, it is my love for you. It caresses you as a dog does the
hand that frees him. I know that you have given me the
sight, the smell of hatred. The first scent, and now I follow
the trail. Who's there? Is it she?

BEGGAR. No, me. You're forgetting the time. She's gone up.
She's undressing.

ELECTRA. She's undressing. Before her mirror, looking long
at herself, our mother, Clytemnestra, undresses. Our
mother, whom I love for her beauty and pity because she's
aging, whose voice and looks I admire, our mother, whom
I hate.

ORESTES. Electra, sister darling, please calm yourself.

ELECTRA. Then I'm to follow the trail?

ORESTES. Calm yourself.

ELECTRA. I? I'm perfectly calm. I'm all sweetness. Sweet to
my mother, very sweet. It's this hatred for her that swells
up and kills me.

ORESTES. Now it's your turn not to talk. We'll think about
that hatred tomorrow. This evening let me taste, for an
hour at least, the sweetness of the life I've never known
and now return to.

ELECTRA. An hour. All right, one hour.

ORESTES. The palace is so beautiful beneath the moon. My
palace. All the power of our family is emanating from it.
My power. In your arms let me imagine all the happiness
these walls might have held for calmer, more reasonable
people. Oh, Electra, how many of our family's names
were originally sweet and tender, and should have been
happy names!

ELECTRA. Yes, I know. Medea, Phaedra.

ORESTES. Even those, why not?

ELECTRA. Electra. Orestes.

ORESTES. Isn't there still time? I've come to save them.

ELECTRA. Silence! She's there.

ORESTES. Who?

ELECTRA. She with the happy name: Clytemnestra.

Scene 9

[ELECTRA, ORESTES, BEGGAR, CLYTEMNESTRA, *then* AEGIS-
THUS.]

CLYTEMNESTRA. Electra?

ELECTRA. Mother?

CLYTEMNESTRA. Who is this man?

ELECTRA. Guess.

CLYTEMNESTRA. Let me see his face.

ELECTRA. If you can't see it at a distance you'd see him less well near to.

CLYTEMNESTRA. Electra, let's stop fighting. If you really want to marry this man, I'll agree. Why do you smile? Wasn't it I who wanted you to marry?

ELECTRA. Not at all. You wanted me to be a woman.

CLYTEMNESTRA. What's the difference?

ELECTRA. You wanted me in your camp. You didn't want the face of your worst enemy constantly before you.

CLYTEMNESTRA. You mean my daughter's?

ELECTRA. Chastity, rather!

ORESTES. Electra . . . !

ELECTRA. Let me alone, let me alone. I've found the trail.

CLYTEMNESTRA. Chastity! This girl who's devoured by desire talks about chastity! This girl at two years old couldn't see a boy without blushing. It was because you wanted to embrace Orestes, if you want to know, that you pulled him out of my arms.

ELECTRA. Then I was right. I'm proud of it. It was worth while.

[*Trumpets. Shouts. Faces in the windows.* AEGISTHUS *leans down from a balcony.*]

AEGISTHUS. Are you there, queen?

BEGGAR. Yes, she's here.

AEGISTHUS. Great news, queen. Orestes is not dead. He's escaped. He's coming toward Argos.

CLYTEMNESTRA. Orestes!

AEGISTHUS. I'm sending my bodyguard to meet him. I've posted my most faithful men around the walls. You say nothing?

CLYTEMNESTRA. Orestes is coming back?

AEGISTHUS. Coming back to seize his father's throne, to prevent my being regent, and you being queen. His emissaries are preparing a revolt. But don't worry. I'll keep order. Who's down there with you?

CLYTEMNESTRA. Electra.

AEGISTHUS. And her gardener?

BEGGAR. And her gardener.

AEGISTHUS. I hope you're not still trying to separate them? You see how well founded my fears were! You agree now?

CLYTEMNESTRA. No. I'm not trying any more.

AEGISTHUS. Don't let them leave the palace. Them especially. I've ordered the gates closed till the soldiers return. You hear me, gardener?

ELECTRA. We'll not leave.

AEGISTHUS. Queen, come upstairs. Go back to your room. It's late and the Council is to meet at dawn. I wish you a good night.

ELECTRA. Thanks, Aegisthus.

AEGISTHUS. I was speaking to the queen, Electra. This is no time for irony. Come, queen.

CLYTEMNESTRA. Good-by, Electra.

ELECTRA. Good-by, mother.

[CLYTEMNESTRA *goes, then turns back.*]

CLYTEMNESTRA. Good-by, my daughter's husband.

BEGGAR. What you see in families! You see everything!

ELECTRA. Who spoke?

BEGGAR. No one! No one spoke. You think someone would speak at a time like this?

Scene 10

[ELECTRA, ORESTES, BEGGAR.]

ORESTES. Tell me, Electra! Tell me!

ELECTRA. Tell you what?

ORESTES. Your hatred. The reason for your hatred. You know it now, when you were talking to Clytemnestra a moment ago you almost fainted in my arms. It might have been from joy—or horror.

ELECTRA. It was both joy *and* horror. Are you strong or weak, Orestes?

ORESTES. Tell me your secret and I'll find out.

ELECTRA. I don't know my secret yet. I hold only one end of the thread. Don't worry. Everything will follow. Take care! Here she is.

[CLYTEMNESTRA *appears at the back of the stage.*]

Scene 11

[ELECTRA, CLYTEMNESTRA, ORESTES, BEGGAR.]

CLYTEMNESTRA. So it's you, Orestes?

ORESTES. Yes, mother, it's I.

CLYTEMNESTRA. Is it sweet to see a mother when you're twenty?

ORESTES. A mother who sent you away? Sad and sweet.

CLYTEMNESTRA. You look at her from far away.

ORESTES. She's just as I imagined her.

CLYTEMNESTRA. My son. Handsome. Regal. And yet I draw near.

ORESTES. Not I. At a distance she's a magnificent mother.

CLYTEMNESTRA. Who tells you that near to her magnificence remains?

ORESTES. Or her motherliness? That's why I don't move.

CLYTEMNESTRA. The mirage of a mother is enough for you?

ORESTES. I've had so much less until today. At least I can tell the mirage what I'd never tell my real mother.

CLYTEMNESTRA. If the mirage deserves it, that's all right. What will you tell her?

ORESTES. Everything I never tell you. Everything that would be a lie if said to you.

CLYTEMNESTRA. That you love her?

ORESTES. Yes.

CLYTEMNESTRA. That you respect her?

ORESTES. Yes.

CLYTEMNESTRA. That you admire her?

ORESTES. That the mother and the mirage can share.

CLYTEMNESTRA. It's the opposite for me. I don't love the mirage of my son. But when my son is actually before me, speaking, breathing, I lose my strength.

ORESTES. Think of hurting him, you'll recover it.

CLYTEMNESTRA. Why are you so hard? You don't look cruel. Your voice is gentle.

ORESTES. Yes, I'm exactly like the son I might have been. You too, of course. You look so like a wonderful mother. If I weren't your son, I'd be deceived.

ELECTRA. Why are you both talking? Where does this horrible maternal coquetry get you, mother? At midnight the little window which allows a mother and son to see each other as they are not opens for a minute. Shut it, the minute has passed.

CLYTEMNESTRA. Why so quickly? How do you know one minute of maternal love is enough for Orestes?

ELECTRA. Everything tells me you have no right to more than a minute of your son's love in your whole life. You've had it. And that's the end. What a comedy you're playing! Go!

CLYTEMNESTRA. Very well. Good-by.

FIRST LITTLE GIRL [*appearing from behind the columns*]. Good-by, truth of my son!

ORESTES. Good-by.

SECOND LITTLE GIRL. Good-by, mirage of my mother!

ELECTRA . You might say au revoir. You'll meet again.

Scene 12

[ELECTRA *and* ORESTES *asleep. The little* EUMENIDES. BEGGAR. *The* EUMENIDES *now seem to be about twelve or thirteen years old.*]

FIRST GIRL. They're asleep. It's our turn to play Clytemnestra and Orestes. But not the way they played. Let's play it truly.

BEGGAR [*to himself, though out loud*]. The story of push or not push—I'd like to know. . . .

SECOND GIRL. You there, let us play. We're playing.

[*The three little* EUMENIDES *take the positions of the actors in the preceding scene and play it as a parody. Masks could be used.*]

FIRST GIRL. So it's you, Orestes?

SECOND GIRL. Yes, it's me, mother.

FIRST GIRL. You've come to kill me and Aegisthus?

SECOND GIRL. News to me!

FIRST GIRL. Not to your sister. You've done some killing, little Orestes.

SECOND GIRL. The things one kills when one is good! A doe. And to be a little kind, I killed her fawn too, so it wouldn't be an orphan. But to kill my mother, never! That would be—parricide.

FIRST GIRL. Was that the sword you did your killing with?

SECOND GIRL. Yes. It will cut iron. See, it went through the fawn so fast he felt nothing.

FIRST GIRL. I'm not suggesting anything. I don't want to influence you. But if a sword like that were to kill your sister, we'd all be at peace!

SECOND GIRL. You want me to kill my sister?

FIRST GIRL. Never! That would be—fratricide. If the sword were to kill her by itself, that would be ideal. Let it come out of its scabbard, like this, and kill her by itself. I'd just quietly marry Aegisthus. We'd call you home; Aegisthus is getting old. You'd succeed him very soon. You'd be King Orestes.

SECOND GIRL. A sword doesn't kill by itself. It needs an assassin.

FIRST GIRL. Certainly! I should know! But I'm talking about the times when swords will kill by themselves. People who avenge wrongs are the curse of the world. And they get no better as they get older, I beg you to believe that. As criminals improve with age, good people always become criminals. Surely this is a fine moment for a sword to think for itself, move of itself, and kill by itself. They'd marry you to Alcmena's second daughter, the laughing one, with the fine teeth—you'd be Orestes, the married man.

SECOND GIRL. I don't want to kill my sister, I love her, nor my mother, I detest her.

FIRST GIRL. I know, I know. In a word you're weak and you have principles.

THIRD GIRL. Why are you two talking? Because the moon is rising, the nightingale singing here in the middle of this night of hatred and threats; take your hand off the hilt of your sword, Orestes, and see if it will have the intelligence to act by itself.

FIRST GIRL. That's right. Take it off . . . it's moving, friend, it's moving!

SECOND GIRL. It really is! It's a thinking sword. It thinks so hard it's half out!

ORESTES [asleep]. Electra!

BEGGAR. Off with you, screech owls! You're waking them.

ELECTRA [asleep]. Orestes!

Scene 13

[ELECTRA, ORESTES, BEGGAR.]

BEGGAR. I'd love to get straight that story of pushed or not pushed. For whether it's true or false, it would show whether Electra is truthful or lying and whether she lies knowingly or whether her memory plays her false. I don't believe she pushed him. Look at her: two inches above ground she's holding her sleeping brother as tight as if they were over an abyss. He's dreaming that he's falling, evidently, but that's not her fault. Now the queen looks like those bakers' wives who never stoop, even to pick up their money, or like those bitches who smother their prettiest pup while they sleep. Afterward they lick it as the queen licked Orestes, but no one ever made a child with saliva. I can see the story as if I'd been there. It's understandable, if you imagine the queen had put on a diamond pin and a white cat had passed by. She's holding Electra on her right arm, for the girl was getting heavy, and the baby on the left, a bit away from her so he'll not scratch himself on the brooch or drive it into him. It's a queen's pin, not a nurse's. And the child sees the white cat, a magnificent creature—a white life, white hair—his eyes follow it, he rocks himself, and she's an egotistical woman. Anyway, seeing the child capsizing, in order to hold him she need only free her arm of little Electra, throw little Electra off on the marble floor, get rid of little Electra. Let little Electra break her neck, so the son of the king of kings be unhurt! But she's an egotist. For her a woman is as good as a man, she's a woman; the womb as good as the phallus, and she's a womb; she wouldn't dream for a second of destroying her daughter to save her son, so she keeps Electra. Now look at Electra. She's revealed herself in her brother's arms, and she's right. She couldn't wish for a better moment. Fraternity is the mark of human beings. Beasts know only love . . . cats, parrots, et cetera, they only recognize fraternity by the hair. To find brothers they have to love men, to turn to men. . . .What does the duckling do when he gets away from the other ducks and, with his tender little eye shining on his slanting duck's cheek, he looks at us humans, eating and playing games, because he knows men and women are his brothers? I've taken little ducks in my hands, and could have wrung their necks, because they came to me so fraternally, trying to understand what I was doing, I, their brother, cutting my bread and cheese and adding an onion. Brother of ducks, that's our real title, for when they raise the little heads they've plunged into the water and look at a man, they're all neatness, intelligence and tenderness—not eatable except for their brains. I could teach those little duck heads to weep! . . . So Electra didn't push Orestes! That makes everything she says legitimate, everything she undertakes irrefutable. She's unadulterated truth, a lamp without a wick. So if she kills, as looks likely, all happiness and peace around her, it's because she's right. It's as if the soul of a girl, in bright sunlight, felt a moment of anguish, as if she sniffed escaping gas in the midst of splendid festivals, and had to go after it, for the young girl is the guardian of truth; she has to go after it whether or not the world bursts and cracks down to its foundations, whether innocents die the death of innocents to let the guilty live their guilty lives. Look at those two innocents! What will be the fruit of their marriage? To bring to life, for the world and for ages to come, a crime already forgotten, the punishment of which will be a worse crime? How right they are to sleep away this hour that is still theirs! Leave them. I'm going for a walk. If I stayed, I'd wake them. I always sneeze three times when the moon is full, and, right now, to sneeze would be taking a frightful risk. But all you who remain here, be quiet, now. This is Electra's first rest, and the last rest of Orestes.

INTERLUDE: THE GARDENER'S LAMENT

I'm not in the play any more. That's why I'm free to come and tell you what the play can't tell you. In stories like this the people won't stop killing and biting each other in order to tell you that the one aim of life is to love. It would be awkward to see the parricide stop, with upraised dagger, and make a speech praising love. That would seem artificial. A

lot of people wouldn't believe him. But I really don't see what
else I can do here in this loneliness and desolation. And I
speak impartially. I'll never marry anyone but Electra, and
I'll never have her. I was made to live with a woman day
and night, but I'll always live alone. I was meant to give myself fully, and yet I have to keep myself to myself. This is
my wedding night that I'm living through, all alone—but
thank you for being here—and the orangeade I'd prepared
for Electra I had to drink up myself; there's not a drop left,
and this was a long wedding night. Now who will doubt my
word? The trouble is that I always say the opposite of what
I mean, and that would be miserable today when my heart is
so heavy and my mouth so bitter—oranges are really bitter
—and if I forgot for an instant that I must speak to you of
joy. Yes, love and joy. I come to tell you they're preferable
to bitterness and hate. That's a motto to carve on a porch,
or to put on a handkerchief, or better, in dwarf begonias
in a clump. Of course, life is a failure, yet it's very, very
good. Of course nothing ever goes right, never is well
planned, yet you must confess, sometimes everything comes
out splendidly, is splendidly planned. . . . Not for me . . . or
perhaps just for me. . . . If I can judge from my wish to love
everything and everyone, which is the result of the greatest
misfortune in my life! What will happen to people who've
had less bad luck? How much love must men feel who marry
wives they don't love, what joy must those feel who leave a
wife they adore, after having had her in their home one
hour? And people whose children are ugly? Of course, tonight in my garden, I wasn't very happy. As a little festival
it didn't come off. I pretended sometimes that Electra was
near me, I talked to her and said: "Come in, Electra! Are
you cold, Electra?" But no one was deceived, not even the
dog, not to say myself. The dog thought: "He promised us a
bride, and he only gives us a word. My master has married
a word; he put on his white garment, the one my paws soil,
which keeps me from caressing him, just to marry a word! He
gives his orangeade to a word. He scolds me for barking at
shadows, real shadows which aren't alive, yet he tries to embrace a word."

And I didn't lie down: to sleep with a word was impossible.
I can speak with a word, that's all! But if you were sitting
like me in this garden, where everything is confused at night,
where the moon is shining on the sundial, and the blind owl

tries to drink the cement walk instead of the brook, you'd
understand what I've understood: the truth! You'd understand that the day your parents died, that day your parents
were born; the day you were ruined, that day you were rich;
when your child was ungrateful, he was gratitude itself; when
you were abandoned, the whole world was coming to you in
rapture and tenderness. That was what happened to me in
this empty, silent suburb. All these stony trees, these im-
movable hills, rushed toward me. This all applies to our play.
To be sure, we can't say Electra is all love for Clytemnestra.
But note the difference: she tries to find a mother and would
see one in the first comer. She was marrying me because I
was the only man who could be a kind of mother to her,
though I'm not *really* the only one. There are men who'd be
glad to carry a child nine months, if they had to, just to have
daughters. All men, actually. Nine months are rather long,
but . . . a week, or a day . . . any man would be proud. Perhaps to find a mother in *her* mother she'd have to cut her
breast open, though with royalty that's rather theoretical.
Among kings there are experiences never found among humble folk, pure hatred, for instance, and pure wrath. Always
purity. That's tragedy, with its incests and parricides: purity,
meaning—innocence. I don't know if you're like me, but to
me, in tragedy, Pharaoh's daughter killing herself means
hope, the treasonous Marshall means faith, the Duke-Assassin
speaks of tenderness. Cruelty is a deed of love—excuse me, I
mean: tragedy is a deed of love. That's why I'm sure this
morning, that if I asked, Heaven would approve me, would
give a sign that a miracle is near, which would show you
that joy and love are written in heaven, and that they echo
my motto, though I'm abandoned and alone. If you wish,
I'll ask. I'm as sure as I'm here that a voice from on high
would answer me, that loud-speakers and amplifiers and
God's thunder are all prepared by God himself to shout, if I
ask: "Love and joy." But I'd rather you didn't ask. First it
would be indecent. It's not the gardener's role to demand of
God a storm, even a storm of tenderness. Moreover it would
be useless. We know so well that at this moment, and yesterday and tomorrow and always, they're all up there, as many
as there are, or perhaps only one, or even if that one is
absent, they're all ready to shout: "Love and joy." It's
much better for a man to take the gods at their word—this
is euphemism—without forcing them to underline it, or to be

held by it, or to create among themselves obligations of
creditor and debtor. I'm always convinced by silences. Yes,
I've begged them, haven't I? not to shout love and joy. But
let them shout it if they really want to. Yet I'd rather conjure them, I conjure you, God, as a proof of your affections,
of your voice and all your shouting, to keep silent, silent for
one second. . . . That's much more convincing. . . . Listen!
. . . Thanks!

ACT TWO

Scene 1

[*The same setting, shortly before dawn.* ELECTRA, *seated, holding* ORESTES, *asleep.* BEGGAR. *A cock. Sound of a trumpet in the distance.*]

BEGGAR. It won't be long now, eh, Electra?

ELECTRA. No. It's not far away.

BEGGAR. I said "it," I meant the day.

ELECTRA. I meant the light.

BEGGAR. It's not enough for you that liars' faces are shining in the sun? That adulterers and murderers move about freely? That's what the day brings—not too bad.

ELECTRA. No. But I want their faces to look blank at noon, and their hands red. That's what light brings out. I want their eyes to be rotten, their mouths diseased.

BEGGAR. As you say, one can't ask too much!

ELECTRA. There's the cock . . . shall I wake him?

BEGGAR. Wake him if you wish, but if I were you, I'd give him another five minutes.

ELECTRA. Five minutes of nothingness! A poor gift!

BEGGAR. You never know. I believe there's an insect that lives only five minutes. In five minutes he's young, adult, senile; he runs through childhood and adolescence, to the time of lame knees and cataract, and legitimate and morganatic unions. While I'm speaking he must be having measles and growing to puberty.

ELECTRA. Let's wait till he dies. That's all I'll agree to.

BEGGAR. Our brother sleeps well.

ELECTRA. He went to sleep right away. He escaped from me. He slipped into sleep as though that were his real life.

BEGGAR. He's smiling. It *is* his real life.

[189]

ELECTRA. Tell me anything you like, beggar, except that Orestes' real life is a smile.

BEGGAR. Loud laughter, love, fine clothes, happiness. I guessed that as soon as I saw him. Orestes would be gay as a lark, if life were good to him.

ELECTRA. He has bad luck.

BEGGAR. Yes, he's not very lucky. All the more reason for not hurrying him.

ELECTRA. Good! As he was made to laugh, to dress well, as he's a lark, I'll give Orestes five minutes, for he'll wake to a lifetime of horror.

BEGGAR. In your place, since you can choose, I'd see to it that this morning light and truth depart at the same time. That doesn't mean much, but it would be a young girl's role and would please me. Man's truth is part of his habits, it leaves him somehow, whether at nine o'clock in the morning when workers strike, or at six in the evening, when women confess, et cetera; these are always bad things, always unclear. Now I'm used to animals. They know when to leave. A rabbit's first jump in the heather, the very second the sun rises, the plover's first flight, the young bear's first run from his rock, these, I can tell you, go toward the truth. If they don't get there, that's because they don't have to. A mere nothing distracts them, a gudgeon, a bee. Do as they do, Electra, go toward the dawn.

ELECTRA. A fine kingdom where gudgeons and bees are liars! But your animals are moving already!

BEGGAR. No. Those are the night creatures turning in. Owls. Rats. The night's truth turning in. Hush! Listen to the last two, the nightingales, of course the nightingales' truth.

Scene 2

[*The same.* AGATHA. *A* YOUNG MAN.]

AGATHA. Darling, you do understand, don't you?

YOUNG MAN. Yes, I have an answer for everything.

AGATHA. If he sees you on the stairs?

YOUNG MAN. I have come to see the doctor on the top floor.

AGATHA. You forget already! He's a veterinary. Buy a dog. ... If he finds me in your arms?

YOUNG MAN. I've picked you up in the street, you've sprained your ankle.

AGATHA. If it's in our kitchen?

YOUNG MAN. I'll pretend to be drunk—I don't know where I am. I'll break the glasses.

AGATHA. One will be enough, darling, a small one, the large ones are crystal. If it's in our room and we're dressed?

YOUNG MAN. I'm looking for him, to talk politics. I had to go there to find him.

AGATHA. If it's in our room and we're undressed?

YOUNG MAN. I entered unexpectedly, you're resisting me, you are perfidy itself, you treat as a thief a man who's pursued you six months. . . . You're a tart!

AGATHA. Darling!

YOUNG MAN. A real tart!

AGATHA. I understand. It's almost day, my love, and I've hardly had you for an hour, and how many more times do you think he'll believe I walk in my sleep, and that it's less dangerous to let me stroll in the grove than on the roof? Oh, my love, can you think of any pretext for letting me have you in *our* bed at night, me between you two, so it would seem quite natural to him?

YOUNG MAN. Think! You'll invent something.

AGATHA. A pretext for letting you two talk about your elections and the races over the body of your Agatha, so he'd not suspect anything. That's what we need—that's all.

YOUNG MAN. All!

AGATHA. Oh dear! Why is he so vain? Why is his sleep so light? Why does he adore me?

YOUNG MAN. The eternal litany! Why did you marry him? Why did you love him?

AGATHA. I? Liar! I never loved anyone but you!

YOUNG MAN. I? Remember in whose arms I found you day before yesterday!

AGATHA. That was only because I'd sprained my ankle. The man you mention was picking me up.

YOUNG MAN. First I've heard of any sprain.

AGATHA. You! You understand nothing. You don't realize that accident gave me an idea for us to use.

YOUNG MAN. When I meet him on the stairs he has no dogs, I can tell you, and no cats.

AGATHA. He rides horseback. You can't take a horse to the doctor upstairs.

YOUNG MAN. And he's always leaving your room.

AGATHA. Why do you force me to betray a state secret? He comes to consult my husband. They're afraid of a plot in the city. Please don't tell anyone, that would mean his dismissal. You'd bring me to the stake.

YOUNG MAN. One evening he was hurrying, his scarf not fastened, his tunic half unbuttoned. . . .

AGATHA. Of course, that was the day he tried to kiss me. I fixed him!

YOUNG MAN. You didn't let him kiss you, and he so powerful? I was waiting downstairs. He stayed two hours. . . .

AGATHA. He did stay two hours, but I didn't let him kiss me.

YOUNG MAN. Then he kissed you without your leave. Confess, Agatha, or I'll go away.

AGATHA. Force me to confess! That's a fine reward for my frankness. Yes, he did kiss me . . . once . . . on my forehead.

YOUNG MAN. And that seems dreadful to you?

AGATHA. Dreadful? Frightful!

YOUNG MAN. And you don't suffer for it?

AGATHA. Not at all! . . . Ah, do I suffer? It's killing me, killing me! Kiss me, darling. Now you know everything, and I'm glad of it. Aren't you happy everything is cleared up between us?

YOUNG MAN. Yes. Anything is better than a lie.

AGATHA. What a nice way you have of saying you prefer me to everything else, darling!

Scene 3

[ELECTRA, ORESTES, BEGGAR. *Then the* EUMENIDES. *They are taller than before, and seem fifteen years old.*]

BEGGAR. A dawn song, at the dawn of such a day! It's always like this.

ELECTRA. The insect is dead, beggar?

BEGGAR. Dispersed in the universe. His great-grandchildren are now fighting gout.

ELECTRA. Orestes!

BEGGAR. You see he's no longer asleep. His eyes are open.

ELECTRA. Where are you, Orestes? What are you thinking about?

FIRST FURY. Orestes, there's just time. Don't listen to your sister.

SECOND FURY. Don't listen to her. We have learned what life holds for you, it's wonderful!

THIRD FURY. Just by chance. As we grew up during the night.

SECOND FURY. We're not saying anything about love to you, does that seem strange?

FIRST FURY. She's going to spoil everything with her poison.

THIRD FURY. Her poison of *truth,* the only one that has no antidote.

FIRST FURY. You're right. We know what you're thinking. Royalty is magnificent, Orestes: young girls in the royal parks, feeding bread to the swans, King Orestes' miniature hanging on their blouses—they kiss it secretly; soldiers going to war, the women on the roofs, the sky like a veil over them, a white horse prancing to music; the return from war, the king's face looking like the face of a god, just because he's chilly or hungry or a little frightened, or pitying his people. If the truth is going to spoil all that, let it perish!

SECOND FURY. You're right. And love is magnificent. Orestes! Lovers, it seems, will never part. They're never separated but they rush back to each other, to clasp hands. Or if they go away, they find each other face to face again immediately. The earth is round for the sake of lovers. Everywhere I run into him I love, though he's not yet alive. All this Electra wants to take from you, and from us too, with her Truth. We want to love. Flee Electra!

ELECTRA. Orestes!

ORESTES. I'm awake, sister.

ELECTRA. Wake from your awakening. Don't listen to these girls.

ORESTES. Are you sure they aren't right? Are you sure that it's not the worst kind of arrogance for a human being to try to retrace his steps? Why not take the first road and go forward, at random? Trust yourself to me. At this moment I can see so clearly the track of the game called happiness.

ELECTRA. Alas! That's not what we're hunting today.

ORESTES. The only thing that's important is not to leave

each other. Let's go to Thessaly. You'll see my house, covered with roses and jasmine.

ELECTRA. Darling Orestes, you've saved me from the gardener not just to give me to flowers!

ORESTES. Be persuaded! Let's slip out of the trap which will soon catch us! Let's rejoice that we woke up before it did! Come!

FIRST FURY. It's awake! Look at its eyes!

THIRD FURY. You're right. The spring is wonderful, Orestes. When you can see over the hedges only the moving backs of the beasts grazing in the new grass, and the donkey's head looking at you over them. That donkey's head would look funny if you murdered your uncle. Pretty funny, a donkey looking at you when your hands are red with your uncle's blood——

ORESTES. What's she saying?

THIRD FURY. Talk on about the spring! The buttery mould that floats on the watercress in the brooks—you'll see what a comfort that will be for a man who kills his mother. Spread your butter that day with a knife, even if it's not the knife that killed your mother, and you'll see!

ORESTES. Help! Electra!

ELECTRA. So! You're like all men, Orestes! The least little flattery relaxes them, the slightest breath captivates them. Help you? I know what you'd like me to say.

ORESTES. Then tell me.

ELECTRA. That on the whole human beings are good, that life, too, after all, is good.

ORESTES. Isn't that true?

ELECTRA. That it's not a bad fate to be young, handsome, and a prince, to have a young sister who's a princess. That it's enough to leave men alone in their mean, vain business —not lancing human ulcers, but living for the beauty of the earth.

ORESTES. Isn't that what you're telling me?

ELECTRA. No! I'm telling you our mother has a lover.

ORESTES. You lie! That's impossible.

FIRST FURY. She's a widow. She has the right.

ELECTRA. I'm telling you our father was murdered.

ORESTES. Agamemnon! Murdered!

ELECTRA. Stabbed, by assassins.

SECOND FURY. Seven years ago. It's ancient history.

ORESTES. You knew that and let me sleep all night!

ELECTRA. I didn't know it. It's the night's gift to me. These truths were tosssed to me by the night. Now I know how prophetesses work. They hold their brother close to their heart through one night.

ORESTES. Our father killed! Who told you?

ELECTRA. He himself.

ORESTES. He spoke to you before he died?

ELECTRA. Dead, he spoke to me. The very day of his death, but it's taken seven years for his word to reach me.

ORESTES. He appeared to you?

ELECTRA. No. His corpse appeared to me last night, looking like him the day he was murdered, but illuminated; I just had to read. There was a fold of his garment which said, I'm not a fold of death but of murder. And on his shoe there was a buckle which repeated, I'm not an accidental buckle but a criminal buckle. And on his eyelid there was a wrinkle which said, I didn't see death, I saw regicides.

ORESTES. And about our mother, who told you that?

ELECTRA. She herself, herself again.

ORESTES. She confessed?

ELECTRA. No I saw her dead. Her body betrayed her. There's no possible doubt. Her eyebrow was the eyebrow of a dead woman who'd had a lover.

ORESTES. Who is this lover? Who is this murderer?

ELECTRA. I've waked you so you can find out. Let's hope they're both the same, then you'll have to strike just one blow.

ORESTES. Girls, I think you'll have to clear out. My sister presents me as I wake with a harlot queen and a murdered king . . . my parents.

FIRST FURY. That's not too bad. Add nothing more.

ELECTRA. Forgive me, Orestes.

SECOND FURY. Now she's excusing herself.

THIRD FURY. I'm killing you, but excuse it, please.

BEGGAR. She's wrong to excuse herself. This is the kind of awakening we generally reserve for our wives and sisters. They seem to be made for that.

ELECTRA. They are made just for that. Wives, sister-in-law, mothers-in-law, they're the ones to shake up the men who, barely awake, see nothing but purple and gold, till the women give them, with their coffee and hot water, a hatred of injustice and a scorn for small joys.

ORESTES. Forgive me, Electra!

SECOND FURY. It's his turn to beg pardon. Aren't they polite in this family!

FIRST FURY. They take off their heads and bow to each other.

ELECTRA. And they watch for their waking. For men put on the armor of happiness if they sleep no more than five minutes: and with it satisfaction, indifference, generosity, appetite. And a spot of sunlight reconciles them to all blood spots. And a bird song to all lies. But the women are there, all of them, worn by insomnia, with jealousy, envy, love, memory and truth. Are you awake, Orestes?

FIRST FURY. And we'll be as old as he in an hour! Let's hope heaven makes us different!

ORESTES. I believe I'm waking up.

BEGGAR. Here comes our mother, children.

ORESTES. Where's my sword?

ELECTRA. Bravo! That's what I call a good awakening. Take up your sword. Take up your hatred. Take up your strength.

Scene 4

[The same. Enter CLYTEMNESTRA.*]*

CLYTEMNESTRA. Their mother appears. And they turn into statues.

ELECTRA. Orphans, rather.

CLYTEMNESTRA. I'm not going to listen to an insolent daughter any longer.

ELECTRA. Listen to your son.

ORESTES. Who is it, mother? Confess.

CLYTEMNESTRA. What kind of children are you, turning our meeting into a melodrama? Leave me, or I'll call.

ELECTRA. Whom will you call? Him?

ORESTES. You struggle too much, mother.

BEGGAR. Be careful, Orestes. An innocent creature struggles as much as a guilty.

CLYTEMNESTRA. Creature? What kind of creature am I for my children? Speak, Orestes, speak!

ORESTES. I don't dare.

CLYTEMNESTRA. Electra, then. She'll dare.

ELECTRA. Who is it, mother?

CLYTEMNESTRA. Of whom, of what are you speaking?

ORESTES. Mother, it is true you have . . . ?

ELECTRA. Don't specify, Orestes. Just ask who it is. There's a name somewhere in her. However you ask your question, the name will come out.

ORESTES. Mother, it is true you have a lover?

CLYTEMNESTRA. That's your question too, Electra?

ELECTRA. It might be put that way.

CLYTEMNESTRA. My son and daughter ask if I have a lover?

ELECTRA. Your husband can't ask it now.

CLYTEMNESTRA. The gods would blush to hear you.

ELECTRA. That would surprise me. They've not been doing much blushing lately.

CLYTEMNESTRA. I have no lover. But watch your step. All the evil in the world is caused by the so-called pure people trying to dig up secrets and bring them to light.

ELECTRA. Rottenness is born of sunshine. I grant that.

CLYTEMNESTRA. I have no lover, I couldn't have a lover if I wanted one. But take care. Curious people have had no luck in our family: they tracked down a theft and found a sacrilege; they carried on a love affair and ran into an incest. You'll not find out I have a lover, because I haven't, but you'll stumble on a stone which will be fatal to your sisters and yourselves.

ELECTRA. Who is your lover?

ORESTES. Electra, at least listen to her.

CLYTEMNESTRA. I have no lover. But who would call it a crime if I had?

ORESTES. Oh, mother, you're a queen.

CLYTEMNESTRA. The world is not old and day is just dawning. But it would take us at least till twilight to recite the list of queens who've had lovers.

ORESTES. Mother, please! Fight on this way. Convince us. If this struggle restores a queen to us, it's blessed, everything is restored.

ELECTRA. Don't you see you're giving her weapons, Orestes?

CLYTEMNESTRA. That's enough. Orestes, leave me alone with Electra, will you?

ORESTES. Must I, sister?

ELECTRA. Yes, yes. Wait there, under the arch. And run back to me as soon as I call, Orestes. Run as fast as you can. It will mean I know all.

Scene 5

[CLYTEMNESTRA, ELECTRA. *The* BEGGAR.]

CLYTEMNESTRA. Help me, Electra!

ELECTRA. Help you to what? To tell the truth or to lie?

CLYTEMNESTRA. Protect me.

ELECTRA. It's the first time you stoop to your daughter, mother. You must be afraid.

CLYTEMNESTRA. I'm afraid of Orestes.

ELECTRA. You lie. You're not the least afraid of Orestes. You see what he is: passionate, changeable, weak—still dreaming of an idyl in the Atrides family. It's I you're afraid of, it's for me you're playing this game, the meaning of which still escapes me. You have a lover, haven't you? Who is he?

CLYTEMNESTRA. He knows nothing. And he's not in question.

ELECTRA. He doesn't know he's your lover?

CLYTEMNESTRA. Stop acting like a judge, Electra. Stop this pursuit. After all, you're my daughter.

ELECTRA. After all! Exactly after all! That's why I'm questioning you.

CLYTEMNESTRA. Then stop being my daughter. Stop hating me. Just be what I look for in you—a woman. Take up my cause, it's yours. Defend yourself by defending me.

ELECTRA. I'm not a member of the Women's Association, and someone other than you would have to recruit me.

CLYTEMNESTRA. You're wrong. If you betray your equal in body, in misfortune, you're the first one Orestes will loathe. Scandal always strikes back at the people who start it. What good does it do you to bespatter all women by bespattering me? In Orestes' eyes you'll sully all the qualities you get from me.

ELECTRA. I'm not like you in anything. I never look in my mirror except to be certain of that piece of luck. All the shiny marble, all the fountains of the palace have cried out to me, your own face cries it: Electra's nose is not the least like Clytemnestra's nose. My forehead is my own. My mouth's my own. And I have no lover.

CLYTEMNESTRA. Listen! I have no lover. I'm in love.

ELECTRA. Don't try that trick. You throw love at me the way drivers pursued by wolves throw them a dog. Dog meat is not my food.

CLYTEMNESTRA. We're women, Electra. We have a right to love.

ELECTRA. There are many rights in the sisterhood of women. I know. If you pay the entrance fee, which is steep, which means admission only for weak, lying, base women, you have a right to be weak, lying, and base. Unfortunately women are strong, loyal, and noble, so you're wrong. You had the right to love my father only. Did you? On your wedding night, did you love him?

CLYTEMNESTRA. What are you driving at? Do you want me to say that your birth owes nothing to love, that you were conceived in indifference? Be satisfied. Not everyone can be like your Aunt Leda, and lay eggs. You never spoke in me. We were indifferent to each other from the first. You didn't even cause me pain at your birth. You were small and withdrawn, your lips tight. When you were a year old, your lips were sealed, so "mother" wouldn't be your first word. Neither of us cried that day. We've never wept together.

ELECTRA. Weeping parties don't interest me.

CLYTEMNESTRA. You'll weep soon, perhaps over me.

ELECTRA. Eyes can weep by themselves. That's what they're there for.

CLYTEMNESTRA. Yes, even yours, which look like two stones. Some day tears will drown them.

ELECTRA. I hope that day comes! But why are you trying to hold me by cold words instead of by love?

CLYTEMNESTRA. So you'll understand I have a right to love. So you'll know that my whole life has been as hard as my daughter from her very first day. Since my marriage I've never been alone, never at peace. I never went to the forest except for festivals. No rest, even for my body which was covered every day by golden robes and at night by a king. Always mistrust, even of things, animals, plants. I often said to myself, as I looked at cross, silent lindens, smelling like a wet nurse: "They're like Electra's head, the day she was born." No queen has ever suffered so deeply the fate of queens, a husband's absence, a son's suspicions, a daughter's hatred. What had I left?

ELECTRA. What the others had left: waiting.

CLYTEMNESTRA. Waiting, for what? Waiting is horrible.

ELECTRA. For her who has caught you today, perhaps.

CLYTEMNESTRA. Can you tell me what you're waiting for?

ELECTRA. I no longer wait. For ten years I've waited—for my father. Waiting is the only happiness in the world.

CLYTEMNESTRA. A virgin's happiness, a solitary happiness.

ELECTRA. You think so? Except for you and the men, everything in the palace awaited my father with me, everything was party to my waiting. It began in the morning with my early walk under the lindens which hate you, which waited for my father with an eagerness they tried in vain to repress; they were sorry to live by the year and not by the decade, ashamed every spring that they couldn't hold back their flowers and perfume, that they grew weak with me over his absence. It went on till noon when I went to the brook that was the luckiest of us all, for it awaited my father as it ran to the river that ran to the sea. And in the evening, when I wasn't strong enough to wait near his dogs and his horses, poor short-lived beasts, that couldn't wait for centuries, I took refuge with the columns and the statues. I modeled myself on them. I waited in the moonlight for hours, motionless like them, without thought, lifeless. I awaited him with a stony heart—marble, alabaster, onyx—though it was beating, shattering my breast. Where would I be if there weren't still hours to wait, to wait for the past, wait for him still?

CLYTEMNESTRA. I'm not waiting. I love.

ELECTRA. Everything goes well with you now?

CLYTEMNESTRA. Very well.

ELECTRA. Flowers obey you? Birds talk to you?

CLYTEMNESTRA. Yes, your lindens signal to me.

ELECTRA. Quite likely. You've robbed me of everything in life.

CLYTEMNESTRA. Fall in love. We'll share.

ELECTRA. Share love with you? Are you offering to share your lover with me? Who is he?

CLYTEMNESTRA. Electra, have pity! I'll tell you his name, though it will make you blush. But wait a few days. What good will a scandal do you? Think of your brother. Can you imagine the Argives letting Orestes succeed an unworthy mother?

ELECTRA. An unworthy mother? What are you getting at with this confession? What time do you want to gain? What trap are you setting for me? What brood are you hoping to save, limping off like a partridge, toward love and unworthiness?

CLYTEMNESTRA. Spare me public disgrace! Why do you force me to confess I love someone below me in rank?

ELECTRA. Some little nameless lieutenant?

CLYTEMNESTRA. Yes.

ELECTRA. You're lying. If your lover were some little nameless, inglorious officer, or a bathhouse attendant, or a groom, you'd love him. But you're not in love, you've never loved. Who is it? Why do you refuse to name him, as you'd refuse a key? What piece of furniture are you afraid of opening with that name?

CLYTEMNESTRA. Something of my own, my love.

ELECTRA. Tell me the name of your lover, and I'll tell you if you love. And we'll keep it to ourselves forever.

CLYTEMNESTRA. Never!

ELECTRA. You see! It's not your lover but your secret that you're hiding from me. You're afraid his name would give me the one proof I'm lacking in my pursuit.

CLYTEMNESTRA. What proof? You're mad.

ELECTRA. The proof of the crime. Everything tells me, mother, that you committed it. But what I don't yet see, what you must tell me, is why you committed it. I've tried all the keys, as you say. Not one opens it—yet. Not love. You love nothing. Not ambition. You scoff at queenship. Not anger. You're deliberate, calculating. But your lover's name would clear up everything, tell us everything, wouldn't it? Who do you love? Who is he?

Scene 6

[*The same.* AGATHA, *pursued by the* PRESIDENT.]

PRESIDENT. Who is he? Who do you love?

AGATHA. I hate you.

PRESIDENT. Who is it?

AGATHA. I tell you that's enough. Enough lies. Electra's right. I'm on her side. Thanks, Electra, you give me life.

PRESIDENT. What is this song?

AGATHA. Wives' song. You'll soon know it.

PRESIDENT. So, she's going to sing!

AGATHA. Yes, we're all here, with our unsatisfactory husbands or our widowhood. And we all kill ourselves, trying to make life and death pleasant. And if they eat cooked lettuce they have to have salt and a smile with it. And if they smoke we have to light their horrid cigars with the flame of our hearts.

PRESIDENT. Who are you talking about? I never ate cooked lettuce.

AGATHA. Sorrel, if you prefer.

PRESIDENT. Your lover doesn't eat sorrel or smoke cigars?

AGATHA. The sorrel my lover eats turns into ambrosia, and I lick up what's left. And everything soiled by my husband's touch is purified by his hands or lips. I myself! God knows!

ELECTRA. I've found out, mother, I've found out!

PRESIDENT. Collect yourself, Agatha.

AGATHA. Precisely. I've done just that. Twenty-four hours a day we kill ourselves to please someone whose displeasure is our only joy, for a husband whose absence is our only delight, for the vanity of the only man who humiliates us daily by showing us his toes and his shirt tails. And he has the gall to reproach us for stealing from him one hour a week of this hell! But, sure enough, he's right. When this wonderful hour comes, we don't greet it with a dead hand!

PRESIDENT. Electra, this is your work. This very morning she kissed me!

AGATHA. I'm pretty and he's ugly. I'm young and he's old. I'm bright and he's stupid. I have a soul and he hasn't. Yet he has everything. At least he has me. And I have nothing, though I have him! Until this morning, I gave everything and had to seem grateful. Why? I black his shoes. Why? I brush off his dandruff. Why? I make his coffee. Why? The truth might be that I'm poisoning him, rubbing his collar with pitch and ashes. Of course you can understand about the shoes. I spit on them. I spit on you. But it's all over, finished. Welcome, truth! Electra has given me her courage. I'm through. I'd as soon die.

BEGGAR. Don't these wives sing well!

PRESIDENT. Who is it?

ELECTRA. Listen, mother! Listen to yourself. It's you talking.

AGATHA. Who is it? All husbands think it's just one person.

PRESIDENT. Lovers? You have lovers?

AGATHA. They think we deceive them only with lovers. Of course we have lovers, too. But we deceive you with everything. When I wake and my hand slips along the wooden bedstead, that's my first adultery. Let's use your word for

once, adultery. How often, when I'm wakeful, I've caressed
that wood—olive wood, so soft! What a pretty name! I start
when I hear an olive tree mentioned in the street—I hear
my lover's name! And my second adultery is when I open
my eyes and see daylight through the blinds. And my third,
when my foot touches the bathwater and when I jump in. I
betray you with my fingers, with my eyes, with the soles of
my feet. When I look at you, I deceive you. When I listen
to you and pretend to admire you in court, I'm deceiving
you. Kill the olive trees, the pigeons, the five-year-old children, boys and girls, and water and earth and fire! Kill this
beggar. You're betrayed by all of them.

BEGGAR. Thanks!

PRESIDENT. And yesterday this woman was still pouring my
tea! And finding it too cool, having the water boiled again!
You're all pleased, aren't you? This little scandal within a
great one can't displease you!

BEGGAR. No. It's like the squirrel in a big wheel. It gives the
right rhythm.

PRESIDENT. And this scene before the queen herself. You'll
pardon it?

ELECTRA. The queen envies Agatha. The queen would give
her life to have the chance Agatha has today. Who is it,
mother?

BEGGAR. Sure! Don't let anything distract you, President. It's
almost a minute since you asked her who it is.

PRESIDENT. Who is it?

AGATHA. I've told you. Everybody. Everything.

PRESIDENT. It's enough to drive me to suicide, to make me
bash my head against the wall.

AGATHA. Don't stop on my account. The Mycenean wall is
solid.

PRESIDENT. Is he young? Or old?

AGATHA. A lover's age—between 16 and 80.

PRESIDENT. And she thinks she's disgracing me by insulting
me! Your insults only hurt yourself, abandoned woman!

AGATHA. I know, I know. Outrage is called majesty. In the
streets the most respectable people slip on dung.

PRESIDENT. At last you'll find out who I am! Whoever your
lovers are, I'll kill the first one I find here.

AGATHA. The first one you find here? You choose the place
badly.

PRESIDENT. I'll make him kneel down and kiss the marble.

AGATHA. You'll see how he'll kiss the marble when he comes into this court in a minute and sits on the throne.

PRESIDENT. Wretch, what are you saying?

AGATHA. I'm saying that at present I have two lovers, and one is Aegisthus.

CLYTEMNESTRA. Liar!

AGATHA. What! She too!

ELECTRA. You too, mother?

BEGGAR. That's funny. I'd have thought, if Aegisthus had a liking, it was for Electra.

PAGE [*announcing*]. Aegisthus!

ELECTRA. At last!

THE FURIES. Aegisthus!

[AEGISTHUS *comes in. Much more majestic and calm than in the first act. Far above him, a bird hovers in the air.*]

Scene 7

[*The same. Enter* AEGISTHUS. *A* CAPTAIN. SOLDIERS.]

AEGISTHUS. Electra is here. . . . Thanks, Electra! I'll stop here, Captain. Headquarters are here.

CLYTEMNESTRA. I, too, am here.

AEGISTHUS. I'm glad. Welcome, queen!

PRESIDENT. I too, Aegisthus!

AEGISTHUS. Good, President. I need your help.

PRESIDENT. And now he insults us!

AEGISTHUS. What's the matter with you all, that you stare at me so?

BEGGAR. What's the matter is that the queen is waiting for a perjurer, Electra for an infidel, Agatha for a faithless lover. He's more humble, he's waiting for the man who seduced his wife. They're all waiting for you, but it's not you that's come!

AEGISTHUS. They have no luck, have they, beggar?

BEGGAR. No, they have no luck. Waiting for a rascal, they see a king enter! I don't care about the others, but for our little Electra, the situation is complicated.

AEGISTHUS. You think so? I think not.

BEGGAR. I knew it would happen. I told you so yesterday. I

knew the king would reveal himself in you. He has your strength and your years. He finds the right moment. Electra is near. That might have involved a bloody act. But you've revealed yourself. Fine for Greece! But not so gay for the family.

CLYTEMNESTRA. What do these riddles mean? What are you talking about?

BEGGAR. Lucky for us, too! Since there has to be *some* kind of meeting, better let Electra meet nobility than wickedness. How did you get this way, Aegisthus?

AEGISTHUS [*looking at* ELECTRA]. Electra is here! I knew I'd find her looking toward me, her statuesque head, her eyes which see only when the lids are closed, deaf to human speech.

CLYTEMNESTRA. Listen to me, Aegisthus!

PRESIDENT. How well you choose your lovers, Agatha! What impudence!

CAPTAIN. Aegisthus, there's no time!

AEGISTHUS. Your ears are ornaments, aren't they, Electra? Mere ornaments. . . . The gods said, we gave her hands so she'd not touch, eyes so she'd be seen, we can't let her head be without ears! People would soon discover that she hears only us. . . . Tell me, what would we hear if we placed our ears near hers? What roaring! And where from?

CLYTEMNESTRA. Are you mad? Take care! Electra's ears do hear you.

PRESIDENT. They blush for it.

AEGISTHUS. They hear me. I'm sure of that. Since what happened to me just now in the outskirts of Argos, my words come from beyond myself. And I know she sees me too, she's the only one who does see me. The only one to guess what I've become since that moment.

CLYTEMNESTRA. You're talking to your worst enemy, Aegisthus!

AEGISTHUS. She knows why I galloped toward the city from the mountains. Electra, you'd have thought my horse understood. He was beautiful, that light chestnut, charging toward Electra, followed by the thunder of the squadron, in which the knowledge of rushing toward Electra grew less, from the white stallions of the trumpeters to the piebald mares of the rear guard. Don't be surprised if my horse sticks his head between the pillars, neighing to you.

He knew that I was strangling, with your name in my
mouth like a golden stopper. I had to shout your name,
and to you—shall I shout it, Electra?

CLYTEMNESTRA. Stop this outrageous behavior, Aegisthus.

CAPTAIN. Aegisthus! The city is in danger!

AEGISTHUS. True! Pardon me! Where are they now, Captain?

CAPTAIN. You can see their lances coming over the hills. I've
never seen a harvest grow so fast. Nor so thick. There are
thousands of them.

AEGISTHUS. The cavalry's no use against them?

CAPTAIN. Repulsed, prisoners taken.

CLYTEMNESTRA. What's happening, Aegisthus?

CAPTAIN. The Corinthians are surrounding us, no declaration
of war, no reason for it. Their regiments entered our territory last night. The suburbs are on fire already.

AEGISTHUS. What do the prisoners say?

CAPTAIN. Their orders are to leave no stone standing in
Argos.

CLYTEMNESTRA. Show yourself, Aegisthus, and they'll flee!

AEGISTHUS. I fear, queen, that wouldn't be enough.

CAPTAIN. They have friends in the city. The reserves of pitch
have been stolen, so the middle-class quarters can be
burned. Gangs of beggars are gathering around the markets ready to start pillaging.

CLYTEMNESTRA. If the guard is loyal, what is there to fear?

CAPTAIN. The guard is ready to fight. But they're muttering.
You know, they've never willingly obeyed a woman. The
city's the same way. They both demand a king, a man.

AEGISTHUS. They're right. They shall have one.

PRESIDENT. Who ever wants to be king of Argos, Aegisthus,
must first kill Clytemnestra.

BEGGAR. Or simply marry her.

PRESIDENT. Never!

AEGISTHUS. Why, never? The queen can't deny that's the only
way to save Argos. I don't doubt she'll consent. Captain,
tell the guard the wedding has this moment taken place.
Keep me informed of events. I'll wait here for your bul-
letins. And do you, President, go meet the rioters and tell
them this news most enthusiastically.

PRESIDENT. Never! I must first speak to you, man to man,
no matter what happens.

AEGISTHUS. No matter if Argos falls, if war comes? You're
outrageous.

PRESIDENT. My honor, the honor of all Greek judges, is at stake.

BEGGAR. If Greek justice lies in Agatha's lap, that's just what it deserves. Don't hinder us at such a time. Look at Agatha, see if she cares for the honor of Greek judges, with her nose in the air.

PRESIDENT. Her nose in the air! Agatha is your nose in the air?

AGATHA. My nose *is* in the air. I'm looking at that bird hovering over Aegisthus.

PRESIDENT. Lower it!

AEGISTHUS. Queen, I'm waiting for your reply.

CLYTEMNESTRA. A bird? What is that bird? Get from under that bird, Aegisthus.

AEGISTHUS. Why? He's not left me since sunrise. He must have his reasons. My horse noticed him first. He kicked without any provocation. I looked all around and then up there. He was kicking at that bird, and plunging and rearing. It's exactly above me, isn't it, beggar?

BEGGAR. Exactly above. If you were a thousand feet tall, your head would be there.

AEGISTHUS. Like a mark on a page, isn't it? A black mark.

BEGGAR. Yes, at the moment you're the most marked man in Greece. We'll have to find out whether the mark is over the word "human" or the word "mortal."

CLYTEMNESTRA. I don't like this hovering bird. What is it? A kite or an eagle?

BEGGAR. He's too high up. I might recognize him by his shadow, but so high up we can't see it, it's lost.

CAPTAIN [*returning*]. The guards are delighted, Aegisthus. They're joyfully getting ready to fight. They're waiting for you to appear on the balcony with the queen, so they can cheer you.

AEGISTHUS. My oath, and I'll go.

PRESIDENT. Electra, help me! Why should this rake teach us courage?

BEGGAR. Why? Listen! . . .

AEGISTHUS. Oh, Heavenly Powers, since I must pray to you on the eve of battle, I thank you for the gift of this hill which overlooks Argos the moment the fog evaporates. I dismounted, weary from the night patrol, I leaned against the battlement, and suddenly I saw Argos as I had never before seen it—new, rebuilt by me; you have given it to

me. You've given it all to me, its towers, its bridges, the
smoke from its farm machines, the flying pigeons, its first
movements, the grinding of its locks, its first cry. Everything in your gift has equal value, Electra, the sunrise over
Argos, the last lantern in the city, the temple, the ruins,
the lake, the tanneries. And the gift is forever! This morning I was given my city for eternity, as a mother her child,
and in agony I asked myself if the gift were not even
greater, if you hadn't given me far more than Argos. In
the morning God never counts his gifts: he might even
have given me the whole world. That would have been
dreadful. I should have felt a despair like that of a man
who expects a diamond on his birthday and is given the sun.
Electra, you see my anxiety! I anxiously stretched my foot
and my thoughts beyond Argos. What joy! I had not been
given the Orient, its plagues, earthquakes, famines: I
realized that with a smile. My thirst was not like that of
men who quench it in the great, warm rivers flowing
through the desert, but, I discovered, I could quench it at
an icy spring. And nothing in Africa is mine! Negresses
can pound millet at the doors of their huts, the jaguar
drive his claws into the crocodile's flank, not a drop of
their soup or their blood is mine. I'm as happy over the
gifts not given me as over the gift of Argos. In a fit of
generosity the Gods have not given me Athens or Olympia
or Mycenae. What joy! They have given me the Argive
cattle markets, not the treasures of Corinth; the short noses
of the Argive girls, not the nose of Athena; the wrinkled
prune of Argos, not the golden fig of Thebes! That's what
they gave me this morning; me, the wastrel, the parasite,
the knave, a country where I feel myself pure, strong, perfect; a fatherland; a country where, instead of being a
slave, I am king, where I swear to live and die—you hear me,
judge—a country I swear to save.

PRESIDENT. I rely on you only, Electra!

ELECTRA. Rely on me. No one should save his fatherland with
impure hands.

BEGGAR. A coronation purifies everything.

ELECTRA. Who crowned you? Who witnessed your coronation?

BEGGAR. Can't you guess? Just what he begged of you. For
the first time he sees you in your truth and power. The

thought has suddenly dawned on him that Electra is included in this gift of Argos.

AEGISTHUS. Everything on my way consecrated me, Electra. As I galloped I heard the trees, the children, the streams shout to me: I was king. But the holy oil was lacking. I was a coward yesterday. A rabbit, whose trembling ears showed over a furrow, gave me courage. I was a hypocrite. A fox crossed the road, his eyes crafty, and I became frank. And a couple of magpies gave me independence, an ant hill, generosity. And if I hurried back to you, Electra, it was because you are the only creature who can give me her very being.

ELECTRA. And that is——?

AEGISTHUS. I think it is rather like duty.

ELECTRA. My duty is certainly the mortal enemy of yours. You shall not marry Clytemnestra.

PRESIDENT. You shall not marry her.

CLYTEMNESTRA. And why shan't we marry? Why should we sacrifice our lives to ungrateful children? Yes, I love Aegisthus. For ten years I've loved Aegisthus. For ten years I've postponed this marriage for your sake, Electra, and in memory of your father. Now you force us to it. Thanks! But not under that bird. That bird annoys me. As soon as the bird flies away, I consent.

AEGISTHUS. Don't worry, queen. I'm not marrying you in order to create new lies. I don't know if I still love you, and the whole city doubts that you ever loved me. For ten years our liaison has dragged along between indifference and neglect. But marriage is the only way to cast a little truth over our past lies, and it will safeguard Argos. It must take place, this very hour.

ELECTRA. I don't believe it will take place.

PRESIDENT. Bravo!

AEGISTHUS. Will you be quiet? Who are you in Argos? A deceived husband or the chief justice?

PRESIDENT. Both, of course.

AEGISTHUS. Then choose. I have no choice. Choose between duty and prison. Time is short.

PRESIDENT. You took Agatha from me.

AEGISTHUS. I'm not the one who took Agatha.

PRESIDENT. Weren't you given all the deceived husbands in Argos this morning?

BEGGAR. Yes. But he's not the man who deceived them.

PRESIDENT. I understand. The new king forgets the outrages he committed as regent.

BEGGAR. Agatha looks like a rose. Outrages make her rosy?

AEGISTHUS. A king begs you to pardon today the insult a rake inflicted on you yesterday. That must satisfy you. Listen to my orders. Go quickly to your courtroom, try the rebels, and be severe with them.

AGATHA. Be severe. I have a little lover among them.

PRESIDENT. Will you stoop looking at that bird? You irritate me.

AGATHA. I'm sorry. It's the only thing in the world that interests me.

PRESIDENT. Idiot! What will you do when it goes away?

AGATHA. That's what I'm wondering.

AEGISTHUS. Are you disobeying me, President? Don't you hear those shouts?

PRESIDENT. I'll not go. I'll help Electra prevent your marriage.

ELECTRA. I don't need your help, President. Your role ended when Agatha gave me the key to everything. Thanks, Agatha!

CLYTEMNESTRA. What key?

AEGISTHUS. Come, queen.

CLYTEMNESTRA. What key did she give you? What new quarrel are you trying to start?

ELECTRA. You hated my father! Oh, everything is clear in the light of Agatha's lamp.

CLYTEMNESTRA. There she goes again! Protect me, Aegisthus!

ELECTRA. How you envied Agatha just now! What joy to shout out your hatred to the husband you hate! That joy was not allowed you, mother. Never in your life will you have it. Till the day of his death he believed you admired and adored him. At banquets and festivals I've often seen your face harden, your lips move soundlessly, because you wanted to cry out you hated him. You wanted passers-by, guests, the servant pouring wine, the detective guarding the silver, to hear you, didn't you? Poor mother, you could never go to the country alone to cry out to the bushes! All the bushes say you adored him!

CLYTEMNESTRA. Listen, Electra!

ELECTRA. That's right, mother, cry it out to me! Though he's

not here, I'm his substitute. Cry to me! That will do you
as much good as to say it to him. You're not going to die
without letting him know you hated him.

CLYTEMNESTRA. Come, Aegisthus! Never mind the bird!

ELECTRA. If you take one step, mother, I'll call.

AEGISTHUS. Whom will you call, Electra? Is there anyone in
the world who can take from us the right to save our city?

ELECTRA. Save our city from hypocrisy, from corruption?
There are thousands. The purest, the handsomest, the
youngest is here, in this courtyard. If Clytemnestra takes
a step, I'll call.

CLYTEMNESTRA. Come, Aegisthus!

ELECTRA. Orestes! Orestes!

[*The* EUMENIDES *appear and bar the way*.]

FIRST FURY. Poor girl! You're too naive! Do you think we'll
let Orestes run around sword in hand? Accidents happen
too quickly in this palace. We've gagged him and chained
him up.

ELECTRA. That's not true! Orestes! Orestes!

SECOND FURY. You, too, it will happen to you.

AEGISTHUS. Electra, dear Electra, listen to me. I want to
persuade you.

CLYTEMNESTRA. You're losing precious time, Aegisthus.

AEGISTHUS. I'm coming! Electra, I know you're the only one
who understands what I am today. Help me! Let me tell
you why you must help me!

CLYTEMNESTRA. What is this craze to explain, to argue? Are
we roosters in this courtyard or human beings? Do we have
to go on explaining till our eyes are gouged out? Must the
three of us be carried off by force, to separate us?

PRESIDENT. I think that's the only way, queen.

CAPTAIN. I beseech you, Aegisthus! Hurry!

BEGGAR. Don't you understand? Aegisthus must settle once
and for all the business about Agamemnon—Clytemnestra
—Electra. Then he'll come.

CAPTAIN. In five minutes it will be too late.

BEGGAR. We'll all do our bit. It will be settled in five minutes.

AEGISTHUS. Take this man away.

[*Guards take out the* PRESIDENT. *All the spectators leave.
Silence*.]

AEGISTHUS. Now, Electra, what do you want?

Scene 8

[ELECTRA, CLYTEMNESTRA, AEGISTHUS, BEGGAR.]

ELECTRA. She's not late, Aegisthus. She just won't come.

AEGISTHUS. Of whom are you speaking?

ELECTRA. Of her you're waiting for. The messenger of the
gods. If divine justice absolves Aegisthus because he loves
his city, and is marrying Clytemnestra because he despises
lies and wants to save the middle class and the rich, this is
the moment for her to appear before the two of you, bearing her diplomas and her laurels. But she'll not come.

AEGISTHUS. You know she has come. This morning's sunbeam on my head was she.

ELECTRA. That was a morning beam. Every scurvy child
thinks he's a king when a morning sunbeam touches him.

AEGISTHUS. Do you doubt my sincerity?

ELECTRA. I don't doubt it. I recognize in it the hypocrisy and
malice of the gods. They change a parasite into a just
man, an adulterer into a husband, a usurper into a king.
They thought my task not painful enough, so they made a
figure of honor out of you, whom I despise! But there's one
change they can't carry through! They can't transform a
criminal into an innocent man. They bow to me there.

AEGISTHUS. I don't know what you mean.

ELECTRA. You have an inkling. Listen to the small voice beneath your heroic soul. You'll understand.

AEGISTHUS. Who can explain what you're talking about?

CLYTEMNESTRA. Of whom *can* she talk? What has she always talked about her whole life long? Of a father she
never knew.

ELECTRA. I? I never knew my father?

CLYTEMNESTRA. You touched a corpse, ice that had been
your father. But not your father.

AEGISTHUS. Please, Clytemnestra! How can you quarrel at
such a moment!

CLYTEMNESTRA. Everyone must have a turn in this debate.
It's my turn now.

ELECTRA. For once you're right. We've come to the heart of
the matter. If I'd not touched my living father, from
whom would I have drawn my strength, my truth?

CLYTEMNESTRA. Precisely. But now you're talking wildly. I wonder if you ever kissed him. I took care he didn't lick my children.

ELECTRA. I never kissed my father?

CLYTEMNESTRA. Your father's dead body, perhaps, not your father.

AEGISTHUS. I beg you . . . !

ELECTRA. Ah, now I see why you're so firm as you face me. You thought me unarmed, you thought I'd never touched my father. What a mistake!

CLYTEMNESTRA. You're lying.

ELECTRA. The day my father came home you two waited for him a minute too long on the palace stairs, didn't you?

CLYTEMNESTRA. How do you know? You weren't there!

ELECTRA. I was holding him back. I was in his arms.

AEGISTHUS. Now listen, Electra . . .

ELECTRA. I'd waited in the crowd, mother. I rushed toward him. His escorts were frightened, they feared an attempt on his life. But he recognized me, smiled at me. He understood Electra's attempt, and, brave father, went to meet it. And I touched him.

CLYTEMNESTRA. You may have touched his leg armor, his horse, leather and hair!

ELECTRA. He got down, mother. I touched his hands with these fingers, his lips with these lips. I touched a skin you'd never touched, purified from you by ten years of absence.

AEGISTHUS. That's enough. She believes you!

ELECTRA. My cheek on his, I felt my father's warmth. Sometimes in summer the whole world is just as warm as my father. I faint from it. And I did hug him in these arms. I thought I was taking the measure of my love—it was also that of my vengeance. He freed himself, mounted his horse, more agile, more resplendent than before. Electra's attempt on his life was over. He was more alive, more golden, because of it. And I ran to the palace to see him again, but I was really running not toward him, but toward you, his murderers.

AEGISTHUS. Pull yourself together, Electra!

ELECTRA. Perhaps I am out of breath. I've reached my goal.

CLYTEMNESTRA. Rid us of this girl, Aegisthus. Give her back to the gardener. Or turn her over to her brother.

AEGISTHUS. Stop, Electra! Why, at the very moment that I

see you, that I love you, when I'm at the point of understanding you—your scorn for abuses, your courage, your
disinterestedness—why do you persist in fighting?

ELECTRA. I have only this moment.

AEGISTHUS. Don't you know Argos is in danger?

ELECTRA. We don't see the same dangers.

AEGISTHUS. Don't you know that if I marry Clytemnestra,
the city will quiet down, the Atrides will be saved? If not,
riots, conflagrations?

ELECTRA. Perhaps.

AEGISTHUS. Don't you know that I alone can defend the city
against the Corinthians who are already at the gates? If
not, pillage, massacre?

ELECTRA. Yes. You'd be victor.

AEGISTHUS. Yet you are obstinate! You ruin my work. And
you sacrifice your family and your country to a dream!

ELECTRA. You're mocking me, Aegisthus! You pretend to
know me yet you think I'm the kind to whom you can say,
"If you lie and let other people lie, you'll have a prosperous
country. If you hide your crimes, your country will be
victorious." What is this poor country that you're all of a
sudden placing between us and truth?

AEGISTHUS. Your country—Argos.

ELECTRA. You're wrong, Aegisthus. This morning, at the very
hour you were given Argos, I also received a gift. I expected it, it had been promised me, but I still didn't know
just what it would be. I had already been given a thousand
gifts, which seemed incomplete, I couldn't see their ap-
propriateness, but last night, near Orestes as he slept, I
saw they were all one and the same gift. I'd been given
the back of a truck driver, the smile of a laundress suddenly stopped in her work, watching the river. I'd been
given a fat, naked little child, running across the street as
his mother and the neighbors shouted to him. I'd been given
the cry of a caged bird set free, and that of a mason I one
day saw fall from a scaffold, his legs sprawling. I was given
the water plant, resisting the current, fighting and dying;
the sick young man, coughing, smiling and coughing; and
my maid's red cheeks, puffed up each winter morning as
she blows on the ashes of the fire. I too thought I was given
Argos, everything in Argos that is modest, tender, beautiful and wretched, but just now I found out that it's not so.
I knew I'd been given all the servants' cheeks as they blow

on wood or coal, all the laundresses' eyes, whether round or almond-shaped, all the falling masons, all the water plants which seem lost and grow again in streams or the sea. But Argos is only a speck in this universe, my country only a village in that country. All the light and the cries in sad faces, all the wrinkles and shadows on joyful faces, all the desires and despair on indifferent faces—these are my new country. And this morning, at dawn, when you were given Argos and its narrow borders, I also saw it as tremendous, and I heard its name, which is not to be spoken, but which is both tenderness and justice.

CLYTEMNESTRA. So that's Electra's motto! Tenderness! That's enough. Let's go.

AEGISTHUS. And you dare call this justice, that makes you burn your city, damn your family, you dare call this the justice of the gods?

ELECTRA. Far from it! In this country of mine, concern for justice is not the gods' business. The gods are only artists. A beautiful light from a conflagration, beautiful grass on a battle field, such is their justice. A magnificent repentance for a crime is the gods' verdict on your case. I don't accept it.

AEGISTHUS. Electra's justice consists in re-examining every sin, making every act irreparable?

ELECTRA. Oh, no! Some years, frost is justice for the trees, other times it's injustice. There are criminals we love, murderers we embrace. but when the crime is an assault on human dignity, infects a nation, corrupts its loyalty, then—no pardon is possible.

AEGISTHUS. Have you any idea what a nation is, Electra?

ELECTRA. When you see a huge face fill the horizon and you look straight at it with pure, brave eyes, that's a nation.

AEGISTHUS. You talk like a young girl, not like a king. There's also a huge body to rule and to nourish.

ELECTRA. I speak like a woman. There's a bright look to sift, to gild. And the only gold is truth. Those great eyes of truth, they're so beautiful, when you think of the real nations of the world.

AEGISTHUS. There are truths that can kill nations, Electra.

ELECTRA. Sometimes, the eyes of a dead nation shine forever. Pray Heaven that will be the fate of Argos! But since my father's death, since our people's happiness came to be founded on injustice and crime, since everyone has

become a cowardly accomplice in murder and lies, the city
can prosper, sing, dance, conquer, heaven may shine on it,
but it will be only a cellar where eyes are useless. Infants
suck the breast without seeing it.

AEGISTHUS. A scandal can only destroy it.

ELECTRA. Possibly. But I can no longer endure the dim,
lusterless look in its eyes.

AEGISTHUS. That will cost thousands of glazed, dead eyes.

ELECTRA. That's the price. It's not too high.

AEGISTHUS. I must have this day. Give it to me. Your truth,
if there is such a thing, will find a way to be revealed at a
time more suitable for it.

ELECTRA. The revolt shows this day is made for it.

AEGISTHUS. I beseech you! Wait till tomorrow.

ELECTRA. No. This is the day for it. I've seen too many
truths fade away because they were a day too late. I know
young girls who waited one second before saying no to an
ugly, vile thing, and could then say nothing but yes, yes.
The beautiful and cruel thing about truth is that she is
eternal, but is also like a flash of lightning.

AEGISTHUS. I must save the city and Greece.

ELECTRA. That's a small duty. I'm saving their soul.—You
did kill him, didn't you?

CLYTEMNESTRA. How dare you say that, daughter? Everyone
knows your father slipped on the tiles.

ELECTRA. Everyone knows it because you said so.

CLYTEMNESTRA. Crazy girl, he slipped and fell.

ELECTRA. He did not slip. For one obvious reason. Because
my father never slipped.

CLYTEMNESTRA. How do you know?

ELECTRA. For eight years I've been asking the grooms, the
maids, his escort in rain and hail. He *never* slipped.

CLYTEMNESTRA. The war came after.

ELECTRA. I've asked his fellow soldiers. He crossed Scaman-
der without slipping. He took the battlements by assault
without slipping. He never slipped, in water or in blood.

CLYTEMNESTRA. He was in haste that day. You had made
him late.

ELECTRA. I'm the guilty one, am I? That's Clytemnestra's
kind of truth. Your opinion, too, Aegisthus? Electra murdered Agamemnon?

CLYTEMNESTRA. The maids had soaped the tiles too well. I
know. I almost slipped myself.

ELECTRA. Ah, you were in the bathroom, too, mother? Who held you up?

CLYTEMNESTRA. What's wrong in my being there?

ELECTRA. With Aegisthus, of course?

CLYTEMNESTRA. With Aegisthus. And we weren't alone. Leo, my counsellor, was there, wasn't he, Aegisthus?

ELECTRA. Leo, who died the next day?

CLYTEMNESTRA. Did he die the next day?

ELECTRA. Yes. Leo slipped, too. He lay down on his bed and in the morning was found dead. He found a way to slip into death—sleeping, not slipping! You had him killed, didn't you?

CLYEMNESTRA. Aegisthus, defend me. I call on you for help.

ELECTRA. He can do nothing for you. You've come to the place where you must defend yourself.

CLYTEMNESTRA. Oh, God! Have I come to this? A mother! A queen!

ELECTRA. Where is "this"? Tell us where you've come.

CLYTEMNESTRA. Brought there by this heartless, joyless daughter! Happily, my little Chrysothemis loves flowers.

ELECTRA. Don't I love flowers?

CLYTEMNESTRA. To come to this! Through this idiotic journey called life, to come to this! I, who as a girl loved quiet, tending my pets, laughing at mealtime, sewing! . . . I was so gentle, Aegisthus, I swear I was the gentlest. . . . There are still old men in my birthplace who call gentleness Clytemnestra.

ELECTRA. If they die today, they needn't change their symbol. If they die this morning!

CLYTEMNESTRA. To come to this! What injustice! Aegisthus, I spent my days in the meadows behind the palace. There were so many flowers I didn't have to stoop to pick them. I sat down. My dogs lay at my feet, the one who barked when Agamemnon came to take me away. I teased him with flowers and he ate them to please me. If I only had him! Anywhere else, if my husband had been a Persian, or an Egyptian, by now I'd be good, careless, gay! When I was young I had a voice, I trained birds! I might have been an Egyptian queen, singing gaily; I'd have had an Egyptian aviary! And we've come to this! What has this family, what have these walls done to us?

ELECTRA. Murderers! . . . These are wicked walls.

MESSENGER. My lord, they've forced an entrance. The postern gate gave way.

ELECTRA. All right. Let the walls crumble.

AEGISTHUS. Electra, heed my final word. I forgive everything—your foolish fancies, your insults. But can't you see your country is dying?

ELECTRA. And I don't love flowers! Do you imagine flowers for a father's grave are picked sitting down?

CLYTEMNESTRA. Well, let this father return! Let him stop being dead! What nonsense, this absence, this silence! Let him come back, in his pomp, his vanity, his beard! That beard must have grown in the grave—a good thing, too!

ELECTRA. What are you saying?

AEGISTHUS. Electra, I promise that tomorrow, as soon as Argos is saved, the guilty, if there are any, shall disappear, for good and all. But don't be stubborn. You're gentle, Electra, in your heart you're gentle. Listen! The city will perish.

ELECTRA. Let it! I can already feel my love for a burnt and conquered Argos! No! My mother has begun to insult my father, let her finish!

CLYTEMNESTRA. Why are you talking about the guilty? What do you mean, Aegisthus?

ELECTRA. He's just told me in a word all that you deny!

CLYTEMNESTRA. And what do I deny?

ELECTRA. He's told me that you let Orestes fall, that I love flowers, and that my father didn't slip.

CLYTEMNESTRA. He did slip. I swear he slipped. If there's a truth in the world, let lightning from heaven show it to us. You'll see it revealed in all its brilliance.

AEGISTHUS. Electra, you're in my power. Your brother too. I can kill you. Yesterday I should have killed you. Instead of that I promise, as soon as the enemy is repulsed, to step down from the throne and place Orestes on it.

ELECTRA. That's no longer the question, Aegisthus. If the gods for once change their methods, if they make you wise and just in order to ruin you, that's their affair. The question now is, will she dare tell us why she hated my father!

CLYTEMNESTRA. Oh, you want to know that?

ELECTRA. But you'll not dare tell.

AEGISTHUS. Electra, tomorrow, before the altar where we celebrate our victory the guilty man shall stand, for there is only one guilty man, in a parricide's coat. He'll confess his crime publicly and determine his punishment himself. First let me save the city.

ELECTRA. You've "saved" yourselves today, Aegisthus, and in my presence. That's enough. Now I want her to finish!

CLYTEMNESTRA. So, you want me to finish!

ELECTRA. I dare you to!

MESSENGER. They're entering the court yards, Aegisthus!

AEGISTHUS. Come, queen!

CLYTEMNESTRA. Yes, I hated him. Yes, you shall know what this fine father was like. Yes, after twenty years I'll have the joy that Agatha had today. A woman might belong to anyone, but there was just one man in the world to whom I couldn't belong. That man was the king of kings, father of fathers! I hated him from the first day he came to wrench me from my home, with his curly beard and the hand with the little finger always sticking up. He raised it when he drank, when he drove, when he held his scepter . . . and when he held me close I felt on my back only four fingers. It drove me wild, and the morning he sacrificed your sister, Iphigenia—horrible—I saw the little fingers of both his hands sticking out, dark against the sun—king of kings! What nonsense! He was pompous, indecisive, stupid. He was the fop of fops, the most credulous creature. The king of kings was never anything more than that little finger and the beard that nothing could soften. The bathwater I soaked his head in didn't soften it, nor did the nights of false love when I pulled and tangled it, nor the storm at Delphi which turned the dancers' hair into manes; it came out in gold ringlets from water, bed, and rain. He would beckon me with his little finger and I would go smiling. . . . Why? He would tell me to kiss his mouth in that fleece and I would run to kiss it. . . . Why? And when I woke and was unfaithful to him, like Agatha, with the wooden bedstead—a royal bed—and he bade me talk to him, though I knew he was vain, empty, tiresome, I told him he was modest, strange, even splendid. . . . Why? And if he persisted, stammering, pathetic, I swore to him he was a god. King of kings! The only excuse for that title is that it justifies a hatred of hatreds. Do you know what I did, Electra, the day of his departure, when his ship was still in sight? I sacrificed the curliest ram I could find and toward midnight I stole into the throne room quite alone, and took the scepter in my hands! Now you know everything. You wanted a hymn to truth, and here's a beautiful one.

ELECTRA. Oh, father, forgive!

AEGISTHUS. Come, queen.

CLYTEMNESTRA. Take this girl first and chain her up.

ELECTRA. Father, will you ever forgive me for listening to her? Aegisthus, should she not die?

AEGISTHUS. Farewell, Electra.

ELECTRA. Kill her, Aegisthus. And I'll forgive you.

CLYTEMNESTRA. Don't let her go free, Aegisthus. They'll stab you in the back.

AEGISTHUS. We'll see about that. Leave Electra alone. . . . Unbind Orestes.

[AEGISTHUS *and* CLYTEMNESTRA *go out.*]

ELECTRA. The bird is coming down, beggar, the bird is coming down.

BEGGAR. Look, it's a vulture!

Scene 9

[ELECTRA, NARSES' WIFE, BEGGAR. *Then* ORESTES.]

BEGGAR. You here, Narses' wife?

NARSES' WIFE. All of us beggars, the lame, the halt, and the blind, have come to save Electra and her brother.

BEGGAR. Justice, eh?

NARSES' WIFE. There they are, untying Orestes.

[*A crowd of* BEGGARS *enters, a few at a time.*]

BEGGAR. This is how they did the killing, listen, woman. This is the way it all happened, I never invent anything. It was the queen who had the steps soaped that go down to the bath; the two of them did it. While all the housewives in Argos scrubbed their thresholds, the queen and her lover soaped the doorsill to his death. Think how clean their hands were when they greeted Agamemnon at his entrance! And your father slipped, Electra, as he reached out his arms to her. You were right except on this one point. He slipped on the steps, and the noise of his fall, because of his golden cuirass and helmet, was that of a king falling. And she threw herself on him, he thought, to raise

him up, but she held him down. He didn't understand why
his darling wife was holding him down, he wondered if it
was a love transport, but then why did Aegisthus stay?
Young Aegisthus was awkward and indiscreet. (We'll consider his promotion.) The ruler of the world, the conqueror
of Troy, who had just reviewed the army and navy parade,
must have been humiliated, to fall like that, on his back
and in his noisy armor, even if his beard was untouched, in
the presence of his loving wife and the young ensign. All
the more annoyed because this might be a bad omen. The
fall might mean he'd die in a year, or in five years. And he
was surprised that his beloved wife caught his wrists and
threw herself on him to hold him down, as fisherwomen
do with big stranded turtles on the shore. She was strong,
and not so beautiful, her face flushed, her neck wrinkled.
Not like young Aegisthus, who was trying to extricate his
sword for fear he'd hurt himself, apparently, he looked
handsomer every minute. What was strange, though, was
that the two of them were silent. He said "Dear wife, how
strong you are!" "Young man," he said, "pull out the sword
—by its handle!" But they said nothing, the queen and the
squire had become mutes in the last ten years, and no one
had told him. They were as mute as travelers hurrying to
pack a trunk when time is short. They had to do something
quickly, before anyone else came in. What was it? Suddenly
Aegisthus kicked his helmet as a dying man kicks his dog,
and the truth was plain. And he cried, "Wife, let me go.
Wife, what are you doing?" She took care not to answer,
she couldn't say aloud, "I'm killing you, murdering you!"
But she said to herself, "I'm killing you because there's not
one gray hair on your beard, because it's the only way to
murder that little finger."

She undid the laces of his cuirass with her teeth, and the
gold turned scarlet, and Aegisthus—beautiful with the
beauty of Achilles killing Hector, of Ulysses killing Dolon
—approached, with drawn sword. Then the king of kings
kicked Clytemnestra's back, and she shook all over, her
silent hand shook, and he shouted so loud Aegisthus had to
roar with laughter to cover the noise. Then he drove in the
sword. And the king of kings was no longer the mass of
bronze and iron he'd thought himself, he was just soft
flesh, as easy to pierce as a lamb, and the sword cut so
deep it split the marble. The murderers were wrong to

hurt the marble, for it revenged itself. I found out about
the crime from that split tile.

So he stopped struggling, let himself go between the woman, who became uglier every moment, and the man, who
was handsomer and handsomer. One good thing about
death is that you can trust yourself to her, death is your
only friend in an ambush, she has a familiar look, he saw
that and called on his children, first the boy, Orestes, then
the girl, Electra, to thank them for avenging him in future, lending their hands of death. Clytemnestra, foam on
her lips, did not let go of him, and Agamemnon as willing
to die but not to have this woman spit in his face, on his
beard. She didn't spit because she was walking around the
corpse, trying not to get blood on her sandals; her red
dress looked to the dying man like the sun. Then the
shadow fell, because each of them took an arm and turned
him over on the floor. On his right hand four fingers were
already stiff. Then, as Aegisthus had pulled out the sword
without thinking, they turned him over again and put it
gently, deliberately, back in the wound. Aegisthus was
grateful to the dead man for having let himself be killed
so very easily. Dozens of kings of kings could be killed
like that, if murder was so easy.

But Clytemnestra's hatred of the man who'd struggled so
fiercely, so stupidly, grew as she foresaw how every night
she would dream of this murder. That's just what happened. It's seven years since she killed, she's killed him
three thousand times.

[ORESTES *has come in during this speech.*]

NARSES' WIFE. Here's the young man! Isn't he handsome?
BEGGAR. As beautiful as Aegisthus when young.
ORESTES. Where are they, Electra?
ELECTRA. Dear Orestes!
NARSES' WIFE. In the southern courtyard.
ORESTES. I'll see you soon, Electra, and we'll never part.
ELECTRA. Go, my lover.
ORESTES. Don't stop, beggar. Go on, tell them about the
death of Clytemnestra and Aegisthus. [*He goes out, sword
in hand.*]
NARSES' WIFE. Tell us, beggar.
BEGGAR. In two minutes. Give him time to get there.
ELECTRA. He has his sword?

NARSES' WIFE. Yes, daughter.

BEGGAR. Are you crazy? Calling the princess your daughter!

NARSES' WIFE. I call her daughter, I don't say she's my daughter. I've often seen her father, though. Heavens, what a fine man!

ELECTRA. He had a beard, hadn't he?

NARSES' WIFE. Not a beard, a sun. A wavy, curly sun, a sun just rising from the sea. He stroked it with his hand. The most beautiful hand in the world.

ELECTRA. Call me your daughter Narses' wife! I am your daughter. . . . I heard a cry!

NARSES' WIFE. No, my daughter.

ELECTRA. You're sure he had his sword? He didn't go to them without a sword?

NARSES' WIFE. You saw him going. He had a thousand swords. Be calm, be calm!

ELECTRA. What a long minute, mother, you waited at the edge of the bath!

NARSES' WIFE. Why don't you tell us? Everything will be over before we know it.

BEGGAR. One minute! He's looking for them. Now! He's found them.

NARSES' WIFE. Oh, I can wait. Little Electra is soft to touch. I had only boys, gangsters. Mothers who only have girls are happy.

ELECTRA. Yes . . . happy. . . . This time I do hear a cry!

NARSES' WIFE. Yes, my daughter.

BEGGAR. So, here's the end. Narses' wife and the beggars untied Orestes. He rushed across the courtyard. He didn't touch or embrace Electra. He was wrong, for he'll never touch her again. He found the murderers on the marble balcony, calming the rioters. As Aegisthus leaned down to tell the leaders that everything was going well, he heard behind him the cry of a wounded beast. But it wasn't a beast crying, it was Clytemnestra. She was bleeding. Her son had stabbed her. He struck at the couple blindly, his eyes closed. A mother, though, even when unworthy, is sensitive and human. She didn't call on Electra or Orestes but on her youngest daughter, Chrysothemis, so Orestes thought he had killed another, and an innocent, mother. She clung to Aegisthus' arm; she was right, that gave her a last chance to stand up. But she prevented Aegisthus from drawing his sword. He shook her, to free his arm. She was too heavy to serve as a shield. And that bird was beating his head with its wings and attacking him with its beak, so he struggled. Just with his unarmed left arm, the dead queen, loaded with necklace and pendants, on his right arm. He was in despair over dying like a criminal, when he had become pure and holy; to be fighting because of a crime which was no longer his; to find himself, though loyal and innocent, infamous before this parricide. He struggled with one hand, which the sword was cutting little by little, but the lacing of his cuirass caught on a brooch of Clytemnestra's, and it opened. Then he resisted no longer; he only shook his right arm to rid himself of the queen, not only to fight but to die alone, to lie far from Clytemnestra in death. He didn't succeed. Forever Clytemnestra and Aegisthus will be coupled. He died, calling a name I'll not repeat.

[AEGISTHUS' *voice off stage*. Electra!]

BEGGAR. I talked too fast. He caught up with me.

Scene 10

[ELECTRA, BEGGAR, NARSES' WIFE, *the* EUMENIDES, *who are of exactly the same height and figure as* ELECTRA.]

SERVANT. Flee, everybody, the palace is on fire!

FIRST FURY. That's what Electra wanted. Three things: daylight, truth—and this fire!

SECOND FURY. Satisfied, Electra? The city's dying.

ELECTRA. I'm satisfied. I know now that it will be born again.

THIRD FURY. And the people killing each other in the streets, will they be born again? The Corinthians have started the attack, and it's a massacre.

FIRST FURY. Your pride has brought you to this, Electra. You have nothing left, nothing.

ELECTRA. I have my conscience, I have Orestes, I have justice, I have everything.

SECOND FURY. Your conscience! Will you listen to your conscience in the early mornings to come? For seven years you've not slept because of a crime that others committed. Now you're the guilty one.

ELECTRA. I have Orestes, I have justice, I have everything.

THIRD FURY. Orestes! You'll never see Orestes again. We're leaving *you*—to pursue *him*. We've taken on your age and your shape—to pursue him. Good-by! We'll not leave him until he's been driven to madness or suicide, cursing his sister.

ELECTRA. I have justice. I have everything.

NARSES' WIFE. What are they saying? They're back. What have we come to, my poor Electra, what have we come to?

ELECTRA. What have we come to?

NARSES' WIFE. Yes, tell me. I'm not very quick to understand. I know something's happened but I don't know just what. How can you explain it, when a day begins like today, and everything's ruined and pillaged—though we're still breathing, we've lost everything, the city's burning, innocent people are killing each other, the guilty are dying, too —and the sun still rises?

ELECTRA. Ask the beggar. He knows.

BEGGAR. It all has a beautiful name, Narses' wife, it is called the dawn.

JEAN ANOUILH

1910–

JEAN ANOUILH is one of the most productive playwrights in modern times. Since his first work appeared in 1931, he has published more than thirty plays, and now each new theatrical season in Paris can count on an Anouilh play as one of its highlights. Anouilh himself has divided his work into four general categories: Black, Rose, Brilliant, and Grating; but such distinctions are not very helpful in dealing with his plays. In all of them we find the same mixture of sombre bitterness and broad, lighthearted farce played within the traditional structures of nineteenth-century melodrama. Maurice Valency succinctly described the typical Anouilh play when he wrote that they "look a bit like *The Importance of Being Earnest* played for tragedy." Like Wilde, Shaw, Pirandello, and Giraudoux, the playwrights he seems to admire the most, Anouilh has a magnificent sense of the theatre and a crisp and lucid style of writing. He sees life itself as theatrical, and when watching or reading his plays one can never be certain whether the life presented on the stage is an image of life outside of the theatre or whether the reverse is true.

But for all of Anouilh's theatrical and verbal dexterity, each of his plays is in some way concerned with the same single theme: the fact that the realities of man's day-by-day existence tend to distort, deform, and finally destroy the ideals by which he would live. This theme is usually presented in the form of an individual's struggle with some force or institution of society, but in every case the individual fails, and all that remains for him as he stands amidst the ruins of his shattered ideals is a gnawing residue of yearning for his past innocence. At the end of *Antigone*, Anouilh's Creon has the following dialogue with a young page:

CREON. In a hurry to grow up, are you?
THE PAGE. Oh yes, sir.
CREON. I shouldn't be, if I were you. Never grow up if you can help it.

Like Creon, Anouilh despairs of the contemporary world which he finds so inhospitable to the verities of his lost childhood; but he, like his character, knows that we do grow up and must get on with the business of daily life. So, with sadness and a wry hope, each year Anouilh writes a new play that deals with another aspect of this theme which has haunted so many writers of the twentieth century.

TO JEAN GIRAUDOUX[1]

Fortunate are those young men who have had masters!

Fortunate are the nervous youngsters who went and rang doorbells and received with flushed faces the encouraging word from the man whom they admired!

I grew up without any masters; in the years around 1928, I had a warm place in my heart for Claudel and I carried dog-eared copies of Shaw and Pirandello in my pockets, and yet, I was all alone. Alone with the anguish of one soon to be twenty years old, with a love for the theatre, and all the awkwardness of youth. Who would divulge to me the secret in those days in which only well made plays were performed? Musset, Marivaux reread a thousand times? They were too far off. They were from an era already fabulous in which spoken French still had periods and commas, from an era in which the very sentences danced. And yet, there was a secret, a secret doubtless lost for a long time and which I was much too small ever to find again by myself. Eighteen years old! And my studies which were already becoming hazy, and a livelihood to earn somehow, and this anguish, these stiff fingers. Of course, Claudel before me was to have found the secret again or rather he had found another one, one suited only to him; but he was like a great inaccessible statue, a saint of wood upon a mountain whom one could ask for nothing.

It was then that an incomparable springtime came, warming and bringing into flower the Avenue Montaigne.

In all of my life, I believe that I shall never again see such chestnut trees, such balminess in the air. There were evenings when, in those lights which tinted the leaves above

[1] *To Jean Giraudoux*, by Jean Anouilh, translated by Arthur Evans, from Volume 3, Number 4, May, 1959 of *The Tulane Drama Review*, is reprinted here by permission of *The Tulane Drama Review*. Copyright © 1959.

with blue, I pressed close to the gods, when I joined in the bustling throng of long automobiles, of women in evening clothes, in that sudden perfection which everything took on for me in that corner of Paris.

Oh the exits from *Siegfried*. . . . Dear Giraudoux, who will tell you now, since I never dared or wished to tell you, what strange encounters of despair and the harshest joy, of pride and the tenderest humility, took place in this young man who stumbled down from the upper gallery of the *Comédie des Champs-Elysées*?

Because of you that avenue and that thoroughfare, isolated by invisible signs in the midst of a detestable quarter, will always remain for me the streets of my village. Nowadays, I never pass through this landscape, zigzagging between the white barriers of the war and my memories, without being inundated with happiness.

The theatre, my life of beauty (oh the terrace of the "Francis" where Jouvet and Renoir would sit and drink and behind which I imagined God knows what sort of lavish display!), poetry, indeed, the inaccessible, caused me to choose my domicile between the Métro Alma and the Plaza Hotel, in that almost spa-like elegance, with its women in diamonds in the warm shadows, its men in white dress shirts. In the heat of a precocious summer, what château suddenly loomed forth from amidst the middle-class barracks, and what entertainment was presented there which compelled this young fellow to remain there, without the strength to leave, after everyone else had left?

Even though others have found their poetry in the quiet streets of a sleepy town, along the banks of a still lake, under the vaults of a church or forest, in a poetic setting, my poetry was to have its *rendezvous* with me, because of you, in that Parisian landscape for rich foreigners with its accessory figures scarcely suited to please me.

I still know *Siegfried* by heart, dear Giraudoux. Did I tell you that at the only dinner which I had with you, the only time when I was with you for more than five minutes? Did I tell you that I can still imitate all the voices? Boverio as Zelten, "It is you, dark-skinned brachycephalic one, with too many spectacles and too many woolen waistcoats"? and Bouquet, the poor Bouquet, "Son of Arminius, Glutton of carnage, it is I . . ." and Jouvet-Fontgeloy, whose accent of a

"Hussard general of death" you'd swear was authentic, and
their patron—just a minute now—"is never far away." And
Renoir and Bogaert and Valentine and the inimitable Simon
himself as the customs inspector.

Dear Giraudoux, I didn't tell you something else, it was
the evening of *Siegfried* that I understood. As a consequence,
I was to enter into a long night from which I have not yet
completely emerged, from which, perhaps, I shall never
emerge, but it is because of those spring evenings in 1928
when I, the only spectator, wept, even at the amusing dialogue, that I have been able to move somewhat out of myself.

Then came *Amphitryon, Intermezzo,* both farther from
me; then, irritated with the man who produced them and
intransigent as innocence is wont to be, I no longer saw your
plays performed. I would read them, overwhelmed, without
opera *décor*, without glitter, without excess of magic tricks,
without that imposing air of gala which your *premières* always managed to take on somewhat too lavishly. I would talk
about them with Pitoëff—my other master, but with whom
I was on familiar terms—who regretted so much your admirable *Elèctre* and then, finally, I experienced that tender
despair a last time with *Ondine.*

When Jouvet—detested (I was his secretary) and then
suddenly pardoned for so much just nobleness of spirit—lay
down in his black armor upon that long gray stone, a despair
rent me which I shall never forget.

It was not only too beautiful, it not only made ridiculous
everything I had wanted to do, it was tender, solemn, and
definitive like a farewell. I had a very certain feeling about
it: the farewell of Hans to Ondine took on the meaning of
another farewell which wrenched my heart. It was the time
of the phony war and we dreamed about lives in danger. I
believed, naively, that this mysterious farewell concerned me.

Dear Giraudoux, it was you whom I was leaving, owing
you so much without ever having told you, having known
you so little and so well.

I am happy, at least, that at the end of that dinner, last
winter, where for the first time I was with you for more than
five minutes, and where I still said nothing to you, I took
hold of your overcoat and I helped you on with it. This is
something I never do, and I surprised myself in doing it and in
fixing your coat collar so that you would be warmer. Then,

this familiarity coming from I know not where suddenly bothered me and I left you. . . .

But now I am happy that I served you, at least once, as the schoolboys used to serve their masters, in exchange for that evening of *Siegfried*.

Translated by Arthur Evans

EURYDICE

(Legend of Lovers)

by JEAN ANOUILH

1941

EURYDICE[1]

(Legend of Lovers)

Translated by Kitty Black

CHARACTERS

FATHER
ORPHEUS
EURYDICE
MOTHER
STATION WAITER
VINCENT
MATHIAS
THE GIRL
DULAC
ANOTHER GIRL
THE YOUNG MAN, *Monsieur Henri*
THE MANAGER
THE CASHIER
HOTEL WAITER
THE CLERK
LOUDSPEAKER
VOICE

Scenes: The action of the play takes place in the refreshment room of a French provincial railway station and in a hotel bedroom in Marseilles.

[1] *Legend of Lovers* by Jean Anouilh, translated by Kitty Black. Copyright 1952 by Jean Anouilh and Kitty Black. Reprinted by permission of Coward McCann, Inc.

Legend of Lovers is fully protected by copyright and is the sole property of the authors. It may not be acted by either professionals or by amateurs without written consent. Public readings, radio and television broadcasts are likewise forbidden. All inquiries should be directed to Dr. Jan van Loewen, International Copyright Agency, 81–83 Shaftesbury St., London W.1, England.

ACT ONE

[*The refreshment room of a provincial station. Overdeco-rated, worn, and dirty. Marble-topped tables, mirrors, benches covered with threadbare red velvet.*

Seated at a too-high desk, like a Buddha on an altar, is the CASHIER, *with a large bun and enormous breasts. Aged* WAITERS, *bald and dignified, spittoons, and sawdust.*

Before the rise of the curtain we hear an accordion. It is ORPHEUS *playing quietly in the corner, beside his* FATHER, *absorbed in his miserable accounts in front of two empty glasses. In the background a single customer, a* YOUNG MAN *with his hat pulled down over his eyes, wearing a mackintosh, apparently lost in thought. Music for a moment, then the* FATHER *stops his additions and looks at* ORPHEUS.]

FATHER. My boy?

ORPHEUS [*still playing*]. Father?

FATHER. You don't expect your poor old father to go round with the hat in a station restaurant?

ORPHEUS. I'm playing for my own pleasure.

FATHER [*continuing*]. A station restaurant with only one customer, who's pretending not to notice anyway. I know their little ways. They pretend not to be listening, and not to see the plate when you hold it out. But I pretend not to see they're pretending. [*Pause, while* ORPHEUS *continues to play.*] D'you enjoy playing as much as that? I can't imagine how you, a musician, can still manage to like music. When I've been twanging away for a bunch of idiots playing cards in a café, there's only one thing I want to do. . . .

ORPHEUS [*without stopping*]. Go and play cards in another café.

FATHER [*surprised*]. Exactly. How did you know?

[237]

ORPHEUS. I guessed—nearly fifteen years ago.

FATHER. Fifteen years? Oh, come now! Fifteen years ago, I still had talent. . . . Fifteen years ago, when I played in the orchestra, who would have believed your old father would come down to playing his harp in the street? Who'd have thought he'd be reduced to going round afterward with a little saucer?

ORPHEUS. Mother would—every time you got yourself sacked from your current job. . . .

FATHER. Your mother never loved me. Neither do you. You spend all your time trying to humiliate me. But don't think I'll put up with it always. You know I was offered a job as a harpist at the casino at Palavas-les-Flots?

ORPHEUS. Yes, father.

FATHER. And I refused because they had no vacancy for you?

ORPHEUS. Yes, father. Or rather, no, father.

FATHER. No, father? Why, no, father?

ORPHEUS. You refused because you know you play abominably and you'd be sacked the next morning.

FATHER [turning away, hurt]. I shan't even answer you. [ORPHEUS goes back to his playing.] Must you?

ORPHEUS. Yes. Does it bother you?

FATHER. I can't concentrate. Eight times seven?

ORPHEUS. Fifty-six.

FATHER. Are you sure?

ORPHEUS. Quite sure.

FATHER. Isn't it odd? I hoped it might be sixty-three. Still, eight times nine are obviously seventy-two. . . . You know we've very little money left, my boy.

ORPHEUS. Yes, father.

FATHER. Is that all you can say?

ORPHEUS. Yes, father.

FATHER. You're thinking of my white hairs?

ORPHEUS. No, father.

FATHER. I thought not. Oh, I'm used to it. [He goes back to his additions.] Eight times seven?

ORPHEUS. Fifty-six.

FATHER [bitterly]. Fifty-six. . . . You didn't have to remind me. [He closes his notebook and gives up his accounts.] That wasn't such a bad meal for twelve francs seventy-five. . . .

ORPHEUS. No, father.

FATHER. You shouldn't have ordered a vegetable. If you

know how to do things, you get your vegetable with the main course and they let you have a second sweet instead. When you're having the set meal, it's always better to choose the two sweets. The Neapolitan ice was a dream. . . . In one sense, we did better tonight for twelve francs seventy-five than yesterday for thirteen francs fifty à la carte at Montpellier. . . . You could say they had linen serviettes instead of paper ones. It was a place that gave itself airs, but fundamentally it was no better. And did you see they charged us three francs for the cheese? If they had at least brought the tray along like they do in proper restaurants! Once, my boy, I was taken to dine at Poccardi's, you know, in Paris. They brought the tray along. . . .

ORPHEUS. You've told me about it before, father.

FATHER [*hurt*]. All right—I don't want to bore you. [ORPHEUS *goes back to his playing. After a moment the* FATHER *is bored and decides to stop sulking.*] I say, my boy—that's horribly sad.

ORPHEUS. So is what I'm thinking.

FATHER. What are you thinking about?

ORPHEUS. About you, father.

FATHER. About me? Well, what is it now?

ORPHEUS. Or rather, you and me.

FATHER. The outlook isn't very promising, of course, but we're doing our best, my boy.

ORPHEUS. I'm thinking that ever since mother died, I've followed you round the cafés with my accordion. I've watched you struggling with your accounts at night. I've listened to you discussing the menus of the set meals and then I've gone to bed. In the morning I get up again.

FATHER. When you get to my age, you'll see that that is life.

ORPHEUS. I'm thinking that if you were all alone, with your harp, you'd never be able to live.

FATHER [*worried suddenly*]. You don't want to leave me?

ORPHEUS. No. Probably I'll never be able to leave you. I'm a better musician than you are, I am young and I'm sure life has better things to offer; but I couldn't live if I knew you were starving somewhere else.

FATHER. That's good of you, my boy. Think of your old father.

ORPHEUS. Good, yes, but it's a big responsibility. Sometimes I dream something might come between us. . . .

FATHER. Now, now, we understand each other so well. . . .

ORPHEUS. There's the wonderful job where I earn enough to make you an allowance. But it's a dream. A musician never earns enough to pay for two rooms and four meals a day.

FATHER. Oh, my needs are very small, you know. A meal costing twelve francs seventy-five like today. A table at the café. A small glass of something, a ten-centime cigar, and I'm as happy as a sandboy. [*Pause, he adds.*] If I had to, I could quite well do without the small something.

ORPHEUS [*going on with his dream*]. Then there's the level crossing where one of us is knocked down by a train. . . .

FATHER. Good heavens . . . which one?

ORPHEUS [*gently*]. Oh, it doesn't really matter. . . .

FATHER [*starting*]. How strange you are. I don't want to die! You're full of gloom tonight, my boy. [*He burps genteelly.*] That rabbit was really excellent. Good heavens, you make me laugh! At your age, I thought life was wonderful. [*He suddenly studies the cashier.*] And what about love? Had you thought you might fall in love?

ORPHEUS. What is love? Girls I might get to meet with you?

FATHER. My dear boy, can any of us guess where and how love will find us? [*He comes a little closer.*] Tell me, you don't think I look rather too bald? She's quite charming, that girl. A little provincial, perhaps. More my type than yours. What would you put her at? Forty? Forty-five?

ORPHEUS [*Gives a pale little smile. He claps his father on the shoulder*]. I'm going outside for a bit. . . . We've still got an hour before the train.

[*When he has gone, the* FATHER *rises, walks all round the* CASHIER, *who blasts him with a look—the miserable customer. Suddenly, the* FATHER *feels he is old and ugly, poor and bald. He rubs his hand over his head and goes sadly back to pick up his instrument before going out. Exit.*

Outside on the platform a train arrives. The members of Dulac's company are seen for a moment. Then EURYDICE *enters and makes her way to a chair.*

Eurydice's MOTHER *enters in triumph. Boa and feather hat. Ever since 1920 she has grown younger every day.*]

MOTHER. There you are, Eurydice. . . . This heat . . . how I hate waiting at stations. The whole tour has been a disgrace—as usual. The manager ought to arrange that the leading actors don't spend all their time waiting for connections. When you've spent the whole day on a platform, how can you give your best in the evening?

EURYDICE. There's only one train for the whole company and it's an hour late because of the storm yesterday. The manager can't help it.

MOTHER. You always find excuses for these incompetents!

THE WAITER [*who has come up*]. May I take your orders, ladies?

MOTHER. Do you feel like something?

EURYDICE. After that star entrance of yours, it's the least we can do.

MOTHER. Have you any really good peppermint? I'll have a peppermint. In Argentine, or in Brazil where the heat was really exhausting, I always used to take a peppermint just before making my first entrance. The divine Sarah gave me the tip. A peppermint.

THE WAITER. And for mademoiselle?

EURYDICE. Coffee, please.

MOTHER. Why aren't you with Mathias? He's wandering about like a soul in torment.

EURYDICE. Don't worry about him.

MOTHER. It was very wrong of you to upset that boy. He adores you. It was your fault in the first place. You shouldn't have let him be your lover. I told you so at the time, but it's too late to worry about that now. Besides, we all begin and end with actors. When I was your age, I was much prettier than you. I could have been taken up by anyone I pleased. All I could do was waste my time with your father. . . . You see the charming results yourself.

WAITER [*who has brought the drinks*]. A little ice, madame?

MOTHER. Never—think of my voice! This peppermint is disgusting. I hate the provinces, I hate these second-rate tours. But in Paris nowadays, they only go mad over little idiots with no breasts, who can't say three words without fluffing. . . . What has the boy done to upset you? You didn't even get into the same compartment at Montélimar? My dear child, a mother is a girl's natural confidante, particularly when they're the same age—I mean, particularly when she's a very young mother. Come along, tell me. What has he done?

EURYDICE. Nothing, mother.

MOTHER. Nothing, mother. That doesn't make sense. Only one thing is sure—he adores you madly. Maybe that's why you don't love him. We women are all the same. Nothing can make us change. How's your coffee?

EURYDICE. You have it—I don't want it.

MOTHER. Thank you, darling. I like plenty of sugar. Waiter! Bring some more sugar for Mademoiselle. Don't you love him any more?

EURYDICE. Who?

MOTHER. Mathias.

EURYDICE. You're wasting your time, mother.

[*The* WAITER, *sulking, has brought the sugar.*]

MOTHER. Thank you. It's covered with flyblows! Charming. I, who have been round the world and stayed at all the best hotels—this is what I've come to. Oh, well, I suppose it will melt. . . . [*She drinks the coffee.*] I think you're absolutely right. You should always follow your instincts. I've always followed mine, like a thoroughgoing old pro. But then you're not really an actress by vocation. Do sit up! Ah, here's Vincent. Darling boy! He looks quite put out. Now do be nice to him. You know how fond of the boy I am.

[VINCENT *enters, silver-haired, handsome, and soft beneath a very energetic exterior. His gestures are ample, his smile full of bitterness. His eye a roving one. He kisses the* MOTHER'S *hand.*]

VINCENT. Ah, there you are! I've been looking for you everywhere.

MOTHER. I've been here, with Eurydice.

VINCENT. This little manager is absolutely useless! Apparently we've got to wait here for more than an hour. We shan't have time for dinner again before the performance. I call it really annoying. We may all have the patience of angels, but you must admit it's really annoying!

EURYDICE. It's not the manager's fault we had such a storm yesterday.

MOTHER. I wish I knew why you always stand up for the little idiot.

VINCENT. He's an incompetent—a real incompetent! I can't

think why Dulac keeps such a man in the job. The last thing I heard was that he's lost the basket with all the wigs. And tomorrow we've got a matinee of *The Burgomaster*. Can you imagine what it will be like?

EURYDICE. I'm sure he'll find it again. It probably got left behind at Montélimar. . . .

VINCENT. If it was, it'll probably arrive in time for tomorrow, but tonight—for *Guinevere's Disgrace*—what are we to do? He says it couldn't matter less because it's a modern play, but I've given Dulac my last word. I cannot play the doctor without my goatee.

WAITER [*who has come up*]. Can I take your order, sir?

VINCENT [*superb*]. Nothing, thank you. A glass of water. [*The* WAITER *retreats, beaten.*] The first and second acts, perhaps, but I'm sure you'll agree with me, dear friend. With the best will in the world, how can I play the big scene in the last act without my goatee? What on earth should I look like?

[EURYDICE *goes away bad temperedly.*]

MOTHER. Where are you going, darling?

EURYDICE. Just for a walk, mother. [*She goes out abruptly.*]

VINCENT [*watches her departure, haughtily. When she has gone*]. Dear friend, you know I'm not in the habit of getting on my high horse, but your daughter's attitude toward me is nothing short of scandalous.

MOTHER [*simpering and trying to take his hand*]. My big bear.

VINCENT. Our relationship toward each other is perhaps a little delicate, I agree—although you're perfectly free to do as you please, you're separated from her father—but really, anyone would say she delights in aggravating it.

MOTHER. She's a silly girl. You know how she protects that fool, as she protects all the lame things in the world, God knows why—old cats, lost dogs, helpless drunkards. The thought that you might persuade Dulac to send him away was too much for her, that's all.

VINCENT. It may have been too much for her, but there are ways of doing these things.

MOTHER. You know quite well that's what's wrong with her. . . . She's a good child, but she has no manners.

[MATHIAS *enters abruptly. He is badly shaven, somber, on edge.*]

Oh, hullo, Mathias.

MATHIAS. Excuse me, madame. Have you seen your daughter?

MOTHER. She's just gone down the platform.

[MATHIAS *exits. The* MOTHER *watches him go.*]

Poor boy. He's mad about her. She's always been good to him until just lately and now I don't know what's come over her. These last two or three days it's as though she were looking for something, or someone. . . . What? I don't know. . . . [*Faraway the music of* ORPHEUS.] Why must that man keep playing that thing? It's maddening.

VINCENT. He's waiting for his train.

MOTHER. That's no reason. That music and the flies . . . it's so appallingly hot!

[*The music has come nearer. They listen. During the next scene,* EURYDICE *walks across the back as though looking for the music.*]

MOTHER [*abruptly, in a different voice*]. Remember the casino at Ostend?

VINCENT. The year they launched the Mexican tango. . . .

MOTHER. How handsome you were!

VINCENT. I still had my figure in those days. . . .

MOTHER. And such an air about you. . . . Remember the first day? "Madame, will you give me the pleasure of this dance?"

VINCENT. "But, sir, I don't know how to dance the tango."

MOTHER. "Nothing simpler, madame. I hold you in my arms. You've only to let yourself go." The way you said that! Then you put your arms around me and everything swam together . . . the face of the old fool who was keeping me and was watching furiously . . . the barman—he was making love to me, too, at the time. He was a Corsican, and he said he'd like to kill me . . . the waxed mustaches of the gypsies, the big mauve irises and pale green ranunculuses decorating the walls . . . ah! it was delicious. It was the year everyone wore *broderie anglaise*. . . . I had an exquisite white dress. . . .

VINCENT. I wore a yellow carnation in my buttonhole, and a
bird's-eye check in green and brown. . . .

MOTHER. When we danced you held me so tightly the pattern of my dress was driven right into my flesh. . . . The
old fool noticed it and made a scene. I slapped his face
and found myself in the street without a farthing. You
hired a carriage with pink pompons and we drove all
round the bay alone till it was dark. . . .

VINCENT. Ah, the uncertainty, the delicious disturbance of
that first day of days. The searching, the awareness, the
groping toward the unknown. One does not yet know one's
love and yet one knows it will last for the rest of one's life.

MOTHER [*suddenly with a change of voice*]. Why on earth
did we quarrel a fortnight later?

VINCENT. I don't know. I can't remember.

[ORPHEUS *has stopped playing.* EURYDICE *is standing in front
of him and they look at each other.*]

EURYDICE. Was it you playing just now?

ORPHEUS. Yes.

EURYDICE. How beautifully you play!

ORPHEUS. Thank you.

EURYDICE. What was it called—what you were playing?

ORPHEUS . I don't know. I was improvising. . . .

EURYDICE [*in spite of herself*]. I'm sorry. . . .

ORPHEUS. Why?

EURYDICE. I don't know. I would have liked it to have had a
name.

[*A* GIRL *passes along the platform, sees* EURYDICE *and calls.*]

THE GIRL. Eurydice! Is that you?

EURYDICE [*without taking her eyes off* ORPHEUS]. Yes.

THE GIRL. I've just seen Mathias. He's looking for you,
darling. . . . [*She disappears.*]

EURYDICE. Yes. [*She looks at* ORPHEUS.] Your eyes are light
blue.

ORPHEUS. Yes. I don't know how to describe yours.

EURYDICE. They say it depends on what I'm thinking.

ORPHEUS. Just now they're dark green, like deep water beside
the stone steps of a harbor.

EURYDICE. They say that's when I'm happy.

ORPHEUS. Who's "they"?

EURYDICE. The others.

THE GIRL [*coming back, calling from the platform*]. Eurydice!

EURYDICE [*without turning round*]. Yes?

THE GIRL. Don't forget Mathias.

EURYDICE. Yes. [*Suddenly she asks.*] D'you think you'll make me very unhappy?

ORPHEUS [*smiling gently*]. I don't think so.

EURYDICE. I don't mean unhappy as I am at this moment. It's a sort of pain, but a sort of joy as well. What frightens me is being unhappy and lonely when you leave me.

ORPHEUS. I'll never leave you.

EURYDICE. Will you swear that?

ORPHEUS. Yes.

EURYDICE. On my head?

ORPHEUS [*smiling*]. Yes.

[*They look at each other.*]

EURYDICE [*suddenly she says gently*]. I like it when you smile.

ORPHEUS. Don't you ever smile?

EURYDICE. Never when I'm happy.

ORPHEUS. I thought you said you were unhappy.

EURYDICE. Don't you understand? Are you a real man after all? How strange it is! Here we are, the two of us, standing face to face, with everything that's going to happen drawn up ready and waiting behind us. . . .

ORPHEUS. D'you think much is going to happen?

EURYDICE [*gravely*]. Everything. All the things that happen to a man and woman on earth, one by one. . . .

ORPHEUS. Gay things, sweet things, terrible things?

EURYDICE [*gently*]. Shameful things and filthy things. . . . We're going to be so unhappy.

ORPHEUS [*taking her in his arms*]. How wonderful!

[VINCENT *and the* MOTHER, *dreaming cheek to cheek, continue softly.*]

VINCENT. Ah, *l'amour, l'amour!* You see my darling one, on this earth where all our hopes are shattered, where all is deception and pain and disappointment, it's a marvelous consolation to remember we still have our love. . . .

MOTHER. My big bear. . . .

VINCENT. All men are liars, Lucienne, faithless, false, hypocritical, vainglorious, or cowards; all women are perfidious, artificial, vain, capricious, or depraved; the world is nothing but a bottomless sink where the most monstrous beasts disport and distort themselves through oceans of slime. But there is one holy and sublime hope left in the world—the union of these two imperfect and horrible beings!

MOTHER. Yes, my darling. Perdican's big speech.

VINCENT [*stops, surprised*]. Is it? I've played it so often!

MOTHER. Remember? You played it that first evening at Ostend. I was in *The Foolish Virgin* at the Kursaal, but I was only in the first act. I waited for you in your dressing room. You came offstage still thrilling with the wonderful love scene you'd been playing and you took me there and then, in doublet and hose. . . .

VINCENT. Ah, those nights, those nights! The fusion of body and heart! The moment, the unique moment when you no longer know if it's the flesh or the spirit fluttering. . . .

MOTHER. You're a wonderful lover, dear boy!

VINCENT. And you, the most adorable of mistresses!

[EURYDICE *and* ORPHEUS *have listened to them, pressed together as if afraid.*]

EURYDICE. Make them stop. Please, please, make them stop.

ORPHEUS [*going to the couple while* EURYDICE *hides*]. Monsieur, madame, you certainly won't understand my attitude. It will seem strange to you. Even very strange. But I'm afraid you must both get out of here.

VINCENT. Out of here?

ORPHEUS. Yes, monsieur.

VINCENT. Is it closing time?

ORPHEUS. Yes, monsieur. Closing time for you.

VINCENT [*rising*]. Really, I. . . .

MOTHER [*also rising*]. But you don't belong here. I know you —you're the one who was playing. . . .

ORPHEUS. You must both go away at once. I promise if I could explain, I would, but I can't explain anything. You wouldn't understand. Something very important is happening here.

MOTHER. The boy's mad. . . .

VINCENT. But good gracious, I mean to say, it doesn't make sense! This place is open to everyone!

ORPHEUS. Not any more.

MOTHER. Well! really! This is too much! [*She calls.*] Madame, please! Waiter!

ORPHEUS [*pushing them toward the door*]. No, don't call them, it's no use. Go away. I'll settle your bill myself.

MOTHER. But you can't be allowed to treat us like this!

ORPHEUS. I'm a peaceful soul, madame, very kind, very shy even. I promise you I'm very shy, madame, and until this minute I'd never had dared to do what I'm doing. . . .

MOTHER. I've never seen such a thing!

ORPHEUS. No, madame, you've never seen such a thing. Anyway, I've never seen such a thing.

MOTHER [*to* VINCENT]. Can't you say something?

VINCENT. Come away. You can see he's not in a normal condition.

MOTHER [*disappears, calling*]. I shall report you to the stationmaster.

EURYDICE [*coming out of hiding*]. Ah! How horrible they were, weren't they? Horrible and stupid!

ORPHEUS [*turning to her smiling*]. Sh! Don't talk about them. How everything falls into place now that we are alone. How clear and simple everything has become. It's as though I were seeing the chandeliers and the palm . . . and the spittoons and the chairs for the first time. . . . Isn't a chair charming? You'd think it was an insect listening for the sound of our steps, ready to spring away on its four thin little legs. Careful! We mustn't move, or if we do, we must be very quick. . . . [*He makes a spring, dragging* EURYDICE.] Got it! Isn't a chair a clever invention. You can even sit on it. . . . [*He hands her to the chair with comical ceremony, then looks at her sadly.*] What I don't understand, is why they invented the second chair. . . .

EURYDICE [*pulling him down and making room for him on her chair*]. It was for people who didn't know each other. . . .

ORPHEUS [*taking her in his arms and crying out*]. But I know you! Just now as I was playing and you came along the platform and I didn't know you. . . . Now everything's changed, and it's wonderful! Everything round us has suddenly become extraordinary. Look . . . how beautiful the cashier is with her big bosom resting delicately on her counter. And the waiter! Look at the waiter! His long flat feet in his button boots, his distinguished mustache, and his noble, noble air. . . . This is an extraordinary evening; we were fated to meet each other, and to meet the noblest waiter in France. A waiter who might have been a governor, a colonel, a member of the *Comédie Française*. Waiter. . . .

WAITER [*approaching*]. Monsieur?

ORPHEUS. You are quite charming.

WAITER. But, monsieur. . . .

ORPHEUS. Yes, yes, don't protest. I'm very sincere, you know, and I'm not used to paying compliments. You're quite charming. And we shall always remember you and the cashier, Mademoiselle and I. You'll tell her so, won't you?

WAITER. Yes, monsieur.

ORPHEUS. Isn't it wonderful to be alive! I didn't know it was so exciting to breathe, to have blood rushing through your veins, muscles that can move. . . .

EURYDICE. Am I heavy?

ORPHEUS. Oh, no! Just the right weight to keep me down to earth. Until now I was too light. I floated. I bumped into furniture and people. My arms were stretched too wide, my fingers were losing their grip. . . . How funny it is, and how lightly the experts make their calculations of weight! I've just realized I was short of exactly your weight to make me part of the atmosphere. . . .

EURYDICE. Oh, my darling, you're frightening me! You really are part of it now? You'll never fly away again?

ORPHEUS. Never again.

EURYDICE. What should I do, all alone on the earth, if you were to leave me? Swear you'll never leave me?

ORPHEUS. I swear.

EURYDICE. That's so easy to say. I hope you don't really mean to leave me. If you really want to make me happy, swear you'll never even want to leave me, even for a minute, even if the prettiest girl in the world looked at you.

ORPHEUS. I swear that too.

EURYDICE [*rising abruptly*]. You see how false you are! You swear that even if the prettiest girl in the world looked at you, you wouldn't want to leave me. But to know that she looked at you, you'd have to look at her. Oh, dear God, how unhappy I am! You've only just begun to love me, and already you're thinking of other women. Swear you wouldn't even see the idiot, my darling. . . .

ORPHEUS. I should be blind.

EURYDICE. Even if you don't see her, people are so wicked, they'd tell you about her as quickly as they could, just so as they could hurt me. Swear you won't listen to them!

ORPHEUS. I should be deaf.

EURYDICE. I know—there's something much simpler. Swear to me straightaway, sincerely, of your own free will and not just to please me, that you won't ever think another woman pretty. . . . Even the ones supposed to be beautiful. . . . It doesn't mean a thing, you know.

ORPHEUS. I swear it.

EURYDICE [*suspiciously*]. Not even one who looked like me?

ORPHEUS. Even that one. I'll watch out for her.

EURYDICE. You swear it of your own free will?

ORPHEUS. Of my own free will.

EURYDICE. Good. And you know you've sworn it by my head?

ORPHEUS. By your head.

EURYDICE. You know, don't you, that when you swear by someone's head, it means that person dies if you don't keep your word?

ORPHEUS. Yes, I know.

EURYDICE [*going to him*]. Good. Now I'll tell you. I only wanted to test you. We haven't really sworn anything. To swear properly, it's not enough to lift your hand, a vague little gesture you can interpret how you like. You must stretch out your arm like this, spit on the ground—don't laugh. This is very serious. We must do it properly. Some people say that not only does the person die suddenly if you break your word, but that she suffers horribly as well.

ORPHEUS [*gravely*]. I've made a note of it.

EURYDICE. Good. Now, you know what you'll make me risk if you lie, even a very little; you'll swear to me now, please, darling, stretching out your hand and spitting on the ground, that everything you've sworn was true.

ORPHEUS. I spit, I stretch out my hand, and I swear.

EURYDICE [*with a great sigh*]. Good. I believe. Besides, it's so easy to deceive me, I'm very trusting. You're smiling. Are you laughing at me?

ORPHEUS. I'm looking at you. I've just realized I haven't had time to look at you before.

EURYDICE. Am I ugly? Sometimes, when I've been crying, or laughing too much, I get a tiny red spot on the side of my nose. I'd rather tell you straightaway, so you don't get a shock later on.

ORPHEUS. I'll remember.

EURYDICE. And I'm very thin. Not so thin as I look; when I'm in the bath, I don't think I'm too bad, but what I mean is, I'm not one of those women you can rest against comfortably.

ORPHEUS. I didn't expect to be very comfortable.

EURYDICE. I can only give you what I've got, can't I? So you mustn't imagine things. . . . I'm very stupid too—I never know what to say and you mustn't rely on me too much to make conversation.

ORPHEUS [smiling]. You never stop talking!

EURYDICE. I never stop talking, but I wouldn't know how to answer you. That's why I talk all the time, to prevent people asking me questions. It's my way of keeping quiet. You'll see you won't like anything about me.

ORPHEUS. You're quite wrong. I like it when you talk too much. It makes a little noise and it's very restful.

EURYDICE. Really! I'm sure you like mysterious women. The Garbo type. Six feet high, huge eyes, big mouths, big feet, who spend the whole day smoking in the woods. I'm not like that at all. You must say good-by to that idea straightaway.

ORPHEUS. I have.

EURYDICE. Yes, you say that, but I can see in your eyes. . . . [She throws herself into his arms.] Oh, darling, darling, it's too awful not to be the one you love! What can I do? Do you want me to grow? I'll try. I'll go in for exercises. Do you want me to look haggard? I'll put mascara on my eyelids, use much more make-up. I'll try and be somber, to smoke. . . .

ORPHEUS. Of course not!

EURYDICE. Yes, yes, I'll even try to be mysterious. It's not so very complicated. All you have to do is think of nothing. Any woman can do it.

ORPHEUS. What a little lunatic you are!

EURYDICE. I'll manage, you'll see! I'll be wise and extravagant and thrifty—sometimes—and obedient as a little odalisque, or terribly unjust the days you'd like to feel unhappy because of me. Oh, only those days, don't worry. . . . And then I'll make it up to you the days I'll be maternal—

so maternal I'll be a little annoying—the days you'll have boils or toothache. Then on rainy days, I can still be bourgeois, badly brought up, prudish, ambitious, highly strung, or just plain boring.

ORPHEUS. D'you think you can play all those parts?

EURYDICE. Of course, my darling, if I'm to keep you, I must be all the other women in one. . . .

ORPHEUS. And when will you be yourself?

EURYDICE. In between. Whenever I've got the time—I'll manage.

ORPHEUS. It'll be a dog's life!

EURYDICE. That's what love is! Anyway, it's easy for the lady dogs. All they have to do is let the other dogs sniff them a little, then trot along with a dreamy air, pretending they haven't noticed anything. Men are much more complicated!

ORPHEUS [pulling her to him, laughing]. I'm going to make you very unhappy!

EURYDICE [pressing herself to him]. Oh, yes! I shall make myself so small, I shan't make any demands on you. All you'll need to do is let me sleep at night against your shoulder, hold my hand all day. . . .

ORPHEUS. I like sleeping on my back, diagonally across the bed. I like taking long walks by myself. . . .

EURYDICE. We could both try and sleep across the bed, and when we go for walks, I'll walk a little behind you, if you like. Only a very little. Almost beside you all the same. But I shall love you so much, and I shall always be so true, so true. . . . Only you must always talk to me so I won't have time to think of stupid things. . . .

ORPHEUS [dreams for a moment in silence with her in his arms; murmurs]. Who are you? I feel I've known you always.

EURYDICE. Why ask me who I am? It means so little. . . .

ORPHEUS. Who are you? It's too late, I know quite well, I could never leave you now. You appeared quite suddenly in this station. I stopped playing my accordion, and now you're in my arms. Who are you?

EURYDICE. I don't know who you are, either. And yet I don't want you to explain. I'm happy. That's enough.

ORPHEUS. I don't know why I'm suddenly afraid of being hurt.

THE GIRL [*passing on the platform*]. What? Still there? Mathias is expecting you in the third-class waiting room. If you don't want a whole new series of rows, darling, you'd better go to him straightaway. . . . [*She has gone.*]

ORPHEUS [*who has let* EURYDICE *go*]. Who is this Mathias?

EURYDICE [*quickly*]. No one, darling.

ORPHEUS. This is the third time someone's said he's looking for you.

EURYDICE. He's one of the boys in the company. No one at all. He's looking for me. All right. He's probably got something to say.

ORPHEUS. Who is this Mathias?

EURYDICE [*crying out*]. I don't love him, darling, I've never loved him!

ORPHEUS. Is he your lover?

EURYDICE. These things are so quickly said, it's so easy to call everything by the same name. I'd rather tell you the truth at once, and tell you myself. Everything must be clear between us. Yes. He is my lover. [ORPHEUS *falls back a step.*] No, don't leave me. I so much wanted to be able to say, I'm only a girl. I've been waiting for you. Yours will be the first hand to touch me. I so much wanted to be able to tell you that—isn't it stupid?—it seemed to me it was true.

ORPHEUS. Has he been your lover long?

EURYDICE. I don't know. Six months perhaps. I've never loved him.

ORPHEUS. Then why?

EURYDICE. Why? Oh, don't keep asking me questions. When we don't know each other very well, when we don't know everything about each other, questions can become the most terrible weapons. . . .

ORPHEUS. Why? I want to know.

EURYDICE. Why? Because he was unhappy, I suppose, and I was tired. And lonely. He was in love with me.

ORPHEUS. And before?

EURYDICE. Before, my darling?

ORPHEUS. Before him?

EURYDICE. Before him?

ORPHEUS. You've never had another lover?

EURYDICE [*after imperceptible hesitation*]. No. Never.

ORPHEUS. Then he taught you how to make love? Answer

me. Why don't you say something? You said you only wanted the truth to be between us.

EURYDICE [*crying out in despair*]. Yes, but, my darling, I'm trying to decide what will hurt you least! If it was him, whom you'll probably see, or someone else, a long time ago, whom you'll never see. . . .

ORPHEUS. It's not a question of what hurts me least, but the truth!

EURYDICE. Well, when I was very young, a man, a stranger, took me, almost by force. . . . It lasted for a few weeks, and then he went away.

ORPHEUS. Did you love him?

EURYDICE. He hurt me, I was afraid. I was ashamed.

ORPHEUS [*after pause*]. Is that all?

EURYDICE. Yes, my darling. You see, it was very stupid, very sad, but very simple.

ORPHEUS [*in a low voice*]. I'll try never to think of them.

EURYDICE. Yes, darling.

ORPHEUS. I'll try never to think of their faces close to yours, their eyes upon you, their hands touching you.

EURYDICE. Yes, darling.

ORPHEUS. I'll try not to think they've already held you close. [*Takes her in his arms again.*] There, now it's all begun again. I'm the one who's holding you.

EURYDICE [*very gently*]. It's wonderful in your arms. Like a tiny house, snug and secure, in the middle of the world. A tiny house where no one can ever come. [*They kiss for the first time.*] Here? In this café?

ORPHEUS. In this café. I, who always feel embarrassed when people look at me, I wish it could be full of people . . . it will be a beautiful wedding! For witnesses we shall have had the cashier, the noblest waiter in France, and a shy little man in a mackintosh who pretends not to see us, though I'm sure he can. . . .

[*He kisses her. The* YOUNG MAN *in the mackintosh who has been sitting silently in the background from the beginning of the act, looks at them, then gets up noiselessly and comes to lean against a column nearer to them. They haven't seen him.*]

EURYDICE [*freeing herself suddenly*]. Now, you must leave me. There's something I must do. No, don't ask me. Go out for a moment, I'll call you back. [*She goes with him to the door, then goes back to the door that opens on to the platform; she stops and stands motionless for a moment on the threshold. One realizes she is looking at someone invisible who is also staring at her. Suddenly she says in a hard voice.]* Come in. *[MATHIAS enters slowly without taking his eyes off her. He stops on the threshold.]* You saw? I kissed him. I love him. What do you Want?

MATHIAS. Who is he?

EURYDICE. I don't know.

MATHIAS. You're mad.

EURYDICE. Yes.

MATHIAS. For a week now, you've been avoiding me.

EURYDICE. For a week, yes, but it wasn't because of him. I've only known him for an hour.

MATHIAS *[looks at her in sudden fear]*. What did you say? *[He draws back.]*

EURYDICE. You know, Mathias.

MATHIAS. Eurydice, you know I cannot live without you.

EURYDICE. Yes, Mathias. I love him.

MATHIAS. You know I'd rather die at once than go on living alone, now that I've had you with me. I don't ask anything of you, Eurydice, nothing except not to be left alone. . . .

EURYDICE. I love him, Mathias.

MATHIAS. Is that the only thing you can say?

EURYDICE *[softly, pitilessly]*. I love him.

MATHIAS *[going out suddenly]*. Very well. If that's the way you want it.

EURYDICE *[running after him]*. Listen, Mathias, try to understand. I like you very much, only—I love him. . . .

[They have gone. The YOUNG MAN in the mackintosh watches them go. He goes out slowly after them. The stage is empty for a moment. We hear a bell ringing, then the whistle of a train in the distance. ORPHEUS comes in slowly, watching EURYDICE and MATHIAS disappear. Behind him his FATHER bursts in with his harp, while the train whistles and the bell becomes more insistent.]

FATHER. The train's coming, my boy. Platform two. Are you ready? *[Takes a step, suddenly becomes absent-minded.]* Er . . . have you paid? I think you said it was your turn?

ORPHEUS *[gently, without looking at him]*. I'm not going, father.

FATHER. Why always wait until the last minute? The train
will be in in two minutes and we've got to take the subway.
With the harp, we've only just got time.

ORPHEUS. I'm not taking this train.

FATHER. What? You aren't taking this train? Why aren't you
taking this train? We want to get to Palavas tonight, it's
the only one.

ORPHEUS. Then take it. I'm not going.

FATHER. This is something new! What's the matter with you?

ORPHEUS. Listen, father. I'm very fond of you. I know you
need me, that it'll be terrible, but it had to happen one
day. I'm going to leave you. . . .

FATHER [a man fallen from the clouds]. What are you saying?

ORPHEUS [crying out suddenly]. You heard me quite well!
Don't make me say it again to give you a lead into a
pathetic scene. Don't hold your breath so that you can turn
pale; don't pretend to tremble and tear your hair! I know
all your tricks. It was all right when I was little. They don't
impress me now. [He repeats, in a low voice.] I'm going to
leave you, father.

FATHER [changing his tactics suddenly and wrapping himself
in an exaggerated dignity]. I refuse to listen to you. You're
not in your right mind. Come along.

ORPHEUS. Dignity doesn't work either. I told you I knew all
your tricks.

FATHER [hurt]. Forget my white hairs—forget my white
hairs! I'm used to it. . . . But I repeat, I refuse to listen to
you. That's clear enough, isn't it?

ORPHEUS. You must listen to me because you've only two
minutes to understand. Your train's whistling already.

FATHER [sneering nobly]. Ah! Ah!

ORPHEUS. Don't sneer nobly, I beg you! Listen to me. You've
got to catch that train, and catch it alone. It's your only
hope of arriving at Palavas-les-Flots in time to get the job
as harpist.

FATHER [babbling]. But I refused the job! I refused it on
your account!

ORPHEUS. You can say you've thought it over, that you're
deserting me, that you accept. Tortoni has probably not
had time to find another harpist. He's your friend. He'll
do his best for you.

FATHER. But I refused his offer. He's drunk his shame to the very dregs. You mustn't forget he's an Italian. Those people never forgive an insult.

ORPHEUS. Take the train, father. As soon as you've gone, I'll telephone to Palavas. I swear I'll make him forget you refused.

FATHER [*shouts in a voice the power of which is unsuspected in his frail body.*] Never!

ORPHEUS. Don't shout! He's not such a bad chap. I'm sure he will listen to me.

FATHER. Never, do you hear? Your father will never abase himself.

ORPHEUS. But I'm the one who's going to be abased! I'll say it was all my fault. I'll telephone Tortoni straightaway. [*Goes to desk.*] Madame, can I telephone from here?

FATHER [*catching him back*]. Listen, my boy. Don't telephone that animal. I'd rather tell you straightaway. The harpist's job. . . .

ORPHEUS. Well?

FATHER. Well—he never offered it to me.

ORPHEUS. What?

FATHER. I said it to make you think better of me. I got wind of the job and begged him to have me. He refused.

ORPHEUS [*after short pause*]. I see. . . . [*Says gently.*] I thought you could have had that job. It's a pity. It would have settled so many things.

[*Pause.*]

FATHER [*gently*]. I am old, Orpheus. . . .

[*The train whistles.*]

ORPHEUS [*suddenly, in a sort of fever*]. Take the train all the same, please, please, father; go to Palavas-les-Flots; there are plenty of cafés there. It's the height of the season, I promise you you'll be able to earn your living!

FATHER. With nothing but the harp . . . you're joking!

ORPHEUS. But that's what people like—they always noticed the harp. You see so few about. Every beggar plays the accordion in the street. But the harp—you've said it often enough yourself—that was what made us both look like artists.

FATHER. Yes, but you play extremely well, and the women thought you were young and charming. They dug their elbows into their escorts and made them put two francs into the plate. When I'm alone, they'll keep their elbows to themselves.

ORPHEUS [*trying to laugh*]. Of course they won't, father—the more mature ones. You're an old Don Juan still!

FATHER [*throwing a glance at the cashier who humiliated him earlier, and stroking his beard*]. Between ourselves, an old Don Juan for chambermaids in cheap hotels—and only ugly chambermaids. . . .

ORPHEUS. You're exaggerating, father—you're still successful when you choose!

FATHER. So I tell you, but it doesn't always happen as I say. Besides, I've never told you this, my boy. I brought you up, I had my paternal pride—I don't know if you've noticed . . . I . . . I play the harp very badly.

[*There is a terrible silence;* ORPHEUS *hangs his head; he cannot help smiling a little.*]

ORPHEUS. I couldn't help noticing, father.

FATHER. You see, you say so yourself. . . .

[*Another pause. The train whistles very close.*]

ORPHEUS [*shaking him suddenly*]. Father, I can't do anything more for you. If I were rich, I'd give you some money. But I haven't any. Go and take your train. Keep everything we've got, and good luck.

FATHER. Just now you said you couldn't leave me!

ORPHEUS. Just now, yes. Now I can.

[*The train is heard coming into the station.*]

ORPHEUS. Here's your train. Hurry, pick up the harp.

FATHER [*still struggling*]. You've met someone, haven't you?

ORPHEUS. Yes, father.

FATHER. The girl who came in just now?

ORPHEUS [*kneeling in front of the suitcases*]. Yes, father. [*Takes some things from one case, puts them into the other.*]

FATHER. I talked a little with those people. She's an actress, you know, a tenth-rate company that plays in flea pits. She's no better than she ought to be.

ORPHEUS. Yes, father. We really must hurry. . . .

FATHER. I shall curse you! This will cost you dear!

ORPHEUS. Yes, father.

FATHER [*rising*]. Laugh away. I've still got a few hundred francs. I can earn my living from day to day, you'll have nothing.

ORPHEUS [*laughing, in spite of himself, and catching him by the shoulders*]. My father, my dear old father, my terrible father. I'm very fond of you, but I can do nothing more for you.

LOUDSPEAKER [*outside*]. Passengers for Béziers, Montpellier, Sète, Palavas-les-Flots.

ORPHEUS. Quick, you're going to miss it. You've got the harp, the big suitcase? I've got two hundred francs, keep the rest.

FATHER. Don't be so generous!

LOUDSPEAKER. Passengers for Béziers, Montpellier, Sète, Palavas-les-Flots!

FATHER [*suddenly*]. Do you think I could get a rebate on your ticket?

ORPHEUS [*embracing him*]. I don't know. I'm so happy, father. I love her. I'll write to you. You ought to be a little pleased to see me happy. I so much want to live!

FATHER [*loading himself up*]. I'll never be able to manage alone.

ORPHEUS. I'll help you. You must get a porter at the other end.

FATHER [*crying from the doorway like a ridiculous curse, and dropping some of his parcels in the process*]. You're deserting your father for a woman! A woman who probably doesn't love you in return!

ORPHEUS [*crying out, following him*]. I'm so happy, father. . . .

VOICE [*outside*]. Mind the doors!

FATHER [*before going out*]. You're sending me away to die!

ORPHEUS [*pushing him*]. Hurry, father, hurry!

[*Whistles, noise of the porters, steam. Suddenly, the train is heard starting up.* EURYDICE *enters with a small suitcase and sits in a corner, making herself very inconspicuous.* ORPHEUS *comes back; he goes to her. She looks at him.*]

ORPHEUS. It's all over.

EURYDICE [*comically*]. It's all over with me, too.

ORPHEUS [*kissing her head*]. Forgive me. He's rather ridiculous. He's my father.

EURYDICE. You mustn't ask me to forgive you. The woman talking about love just now, with all those noises, was my mother. I didn't dare tell you.

[*They are facing each other, smiling gently. A bell rings, then the whistle of an approaching train.*]

LOUDSPEAKER. Passengers for Toulouse, Béziers, Carcassonne, platform seven. The train arriving now.

ANOTHER LOUDSPEAKER [*farther away*]. Passengers for Toulouse, Béziers, Carcassonne, platform seven. The train arriving now.

[*Through the door opening on to the platform, the members of the company pass with their baggage.*]

THE GIRL. Quickly, darling, or we'll have to stand all the way again. Naturally, the stars are traveling second. Who's paying the extra, I ask you? Who's paying the extra?

ANOTHER GIRL [*continuing a story*]. Then, d'you know what she said to me? She said, I don't give a damn. I've my position to consider. . . .

[*They have gone. The* MOTHER *and* VINCENT *pass, overloaded with hatboxes, enormous suitcases.*]

MOTHER. Vincent, darling boy, the big case and the green box?

VINCENT. I've got them both. Off we go!

MOTHER. Be very careful. The handle's not very secure. It reminds me of one day at Buenos Aires. Sarah's hatbox burst open in the middle of the station. There were ostrich feathers all over the track. . . .

[*They have gone. A fat man passes, puffing, behind them.*]

DULAC. Quickly, for God's sake, quickly! And check that the trunks have been loaded. Then get in the back. The rest of us will be up front.

EURYDICE [*gently*]. All the people in my life. . . .

[*Running, and unable to run, comic, lamentable, absurd, the little* MANAGER *comes last, tripping over too many suit-*

*cases, too many parcels slipping from his grasp. All in the
midst of distant cries and the approaching whistles of the
train.*]

EURYDICE [*gently, to* ORPHEUS]. Close the door. [ORPHEUS
  closes the door. A sudden silence covers them.] There.
  Now we're alone in the world.
LOUDSPEAKER [*farther away*]. Passengers for Toulouse,
  Béziers, Carcassonne, platform seven. The train arriving
  now.

[ORPHEUS *has gently come back to her. Noise of train reaching the station and a cry, a cry that becomes a noise that
swells and stops suddenly, giving place to a terrible silence.
The* CASHIER *has stood up and tried to see. The* WAITER *runs
across the stage, calling to them as he passes.*]

WAITER. Someone's thrown himself in front of the express
  —a young man!

[*People pass, running along the platform.* ORPHEUS *and*
EURYDICE *are facing each other, unable to look at one another. They say nothing. The* YOUNG MAN *in the mackintosh
appears on the platform. He comes in, then shuts the door
and looks at them.*]

EURYDICE [*gently*]. I couldn't help it. I love you and I didn't
  love him.

[*There is a pause. Each stares straight ahead without looking at the other.* THE YOUNG MAN *in the mackintosh comes
up to them.*]

THE YOUNG MAN [*in an expressionless voice, without taking
  his eyes off them*]. He threw himself in front of the en-
  gine. The shock itself must have killed him.
ORPHEUS. How horrible!
THE YOUNG MAN. No. He chose a fairly good method. Poison
  is very slow, and causes so much suffering. One vomits,
  and twists about, and it is all disgusting. It's the same with
  sleeping draughts. People think they'll go to sleep, but it's
  a death in the midst of hiccups and bad smells. [*He has
  come nearer, calm and smiling.*] Believe me . . . the easiest
  way when you're very tired, when you've nursed that

same idea for a long time is to slip into the water as if it were a bed. . . . You stifle for a moment, with a magnificent succession of visions . . . then you go to sleep. That's all!

EURYDICE. You don't think it hurt him to die?

THE YOUNG MAN [*gently*]. It never hurts to die. Death never hurts anybody. Death is gentle. . . . What makes you suffer when you take certain poisons, or give yourself a clumsy wound, is life itself.

[ORPHEUS *and* EURYDICE *are pressed against each other.*]

EURYDICE [*gently, like an explanation*]. We couldn't help ourselves. We love each other.

THE YOUNG MAN. Yes, I know. I've been listening to you. A fine young man, and a pretty girl. Two courageous little animals, with supple limbs and sharp white teeth, ready to fight till dawn, as they should, and fall together, mortally wounded.

EURYDICE [*murmuring*]. We don't even know you. . . .

THE YOUNG MAN. But I know you. I'm very glad to have met you both. You're leaving here together? There's only one more train tonight. The train for Marseilles. Perhaps you'll be taking it?

ORPHEUS. Perhaps.

THE YOUNG MAN. I'm going there myself. I hope I'll have the pleasure of meeting you again?

[*He bows and exits.* ORPHEUS *and* EURYDICE *turn to each other. They are standing, looking very small, in the middle of the empty hall.*]

ORPHEUS [*gently*]. My love.

EURYDICE. My dear love.

ORPHEUS. Our story is beginning. . . .

EURYDICE. I'm a little afraid. . . . Are you good, or wicked? What's your name?

ORPHEUS. It's Orpheus. What's yours?

EURYDICE. Eurydice.

ACT TWO

[*A room in a provincial hotel—huge, somber, and dirty. The ceilings are too high, lost in shadow, dusty double curtains, a big iron bed, a screen, a miserable light.*]

[ORPHEUS *and* EURYDICE *are lying on the bed, fully dressed.*]

ORPHEUS. To think everything might have gone wrong. . . . Supposing you'd turned to the right, I to the left, not even that. Nothing more important than the flight of a bird, a child's cry, to make you turn your head for a second. I'd be playing my accordion on the terraces at Perpignan with father.

EURYDICE. And I'd be playing *The Orphans of the Storm* at the municipal theater of Avignon. Mother and I play the two orphans.

ORPHEUS. Last night I thought of all the luck that brought us together. To think we might never have met; that we might have mistaken the day or the station.

EURYDICE. Or met while we were still too young.

ORPHEUS. But we didn't mistake the day, or the minute. We never missed a step during the whole eventful journey. We're very clever.

EURYDICE. Yes, my darling.

ORPHEUS [*powerful and gay*]. We're much stronger than the whole world, both of us.

EURYDICE [*looking at him with a little smile*]. My hero! All the same you were very frightened yesterday when we came into this room.

ORPHEUS. Yesterday we weren't stronger than all the people in the world. Now, at least, we know each other. We know how heavy a sleeping head feels, the sound of our laughter. Now we have our memories to protect us.

EURYDICE. A whole evening, a whole night, a whole day— how rich we are!

ORPHEUS. Yesterday, we had nothing. We knew nothing, and we came into this room by chance, under the eye of that terrible waiter with the mustache who was sure we were going to make love. We began to undress, quickly, standing, face to face. . . .

EURYDICE. You threw your clothes like a madman into the four corners of the room. . . .

ORPHEUS. You were shaking all over. You couldn't undo the little buttons of your dress and I watched you pull them off without making a movement to help you. And then, when you were naked, suddenly you were ashamed.

EURYDICE [*hanging her head*]. I thought I ought to be beautiful as well, and I wasn't sure. . . .

ORPHEUS. We stood like that for a long time, face to face, without speaking, without daring to speak. . . . Oh, we were too poor, too naked, and it was too unjust to have to risk everything like that on a single throw. Then suddenly a wave of tenderness took me by the throat because I saw you had a tiny red spot on your shoulder.

EURYDICE. Then afterward, it all became so simple. . . .

ORPHEUS. You laid your head against me and fell asleep. You said things in your dreams I couldn't answer. . . .

EURYDICE. Did I? I often talk in my sleep. I hope you didn't listen.

ORPHEUS. Of course I did.

EURYDICE. I call that very mean of you! Instead of sleeping honestly, you spy on me. How do you think I can know what I say when I'm asleep?

ORPHEUS. I only understood three words. You sighed a terrible deep sigh. Your lips trembled a little, and then you said, "it's so difficult."

EURYDICE [*repeating*]. It's so difficult.

ORPHEUS. What was so difficult?

EURYDICE [*stays for a moment without answering, then shakes her head and says in a little voice*]. I don't know, my darling. I was dreaming.

[*Knock at the door. It is the* WAITER, *who enters immediately. He has big gray mustaches, and a strange air.*]

WAITER. Did you ring, sir?

ORPHEUS. No.

WAITER. Oh! I thought you did. [*Hesitates for moment, then goes out, saying.*] Excuse me, sir.

EURYDICE [*as soon as he has gone*]. D'you think they're real?

ORPHEUS. What?

EURYDICE. His mustaches.

ORPHEUS. Of course. They don't look real. It's only false ones that look real—everyone knows that.

EURYDICE. He doesn't look as noble as the waiter at the station.

ORPHEUS. The one from the *Comédie Française*? He may have been noble, but he was very conventional. Under his imposing façade, I think he was a weakling. This one has more mystery about him.

EURYDICE. Yes. Too much. I don't like people with too much mystery. They frighten me a little. Don't they you?

ORPHEUS. A little, but I didn't like to tell you.

EURYDICE [*pressing herself to him*]. Oh, my darling, hold me very tight. How lucky it is that there are two of us.

ORPHEUS. There so many characters in our story already— two waiters, a noble weakling, a strange mustache, the lovely cashier and her enormous breasts. . . .

EURYDICE. Such a pity she never said anything to us!

ORPHEUS. In all stories there are silent characters like her. She didn't say anything, but she watched us all the time. If she hadn't been silent all the time, what a lot of stories she could tell about us. . . .

EURYDICE. And the porter?

ORPHEUS. The one who stammered?

EURYDICE. Yes, my darling. Wasn't he sweet? I'd have liked to put him in a box and keep him, with his fat watch chain and brand new cap.

ORPHEUS. Remember how he told us the names of all the stations where we didn't have to change, to make us remember, without any possible doubt, the name of the station where we really had to change!

EURYDICE. He was quite enchanting. I'm sure he brought us luck. But the other one, the brute, the conductor. . . .

ORPHEUS. That fool! The one who couldn't understand we had a third-class ticket for Perpignan and another for Avignon, so what we wanted was to pay the difference on two second-class tickets to Marseilles?

EURYDICE. Yes, that one. Wasn't he ugly and stupid with his greasy uniform, his self-importance, and his oily fat cheeks?

ORPHEUS. He is our first ignoble character. There'll be others, you'll see. . . . All happy stories are full of despicable characters.

EURYDICE. Oh, but I refuse to keep him. I'll send him away. You must tell him I don't want him any more. I won't have such an idiot in my memories of you.

ORPHEUS. It's too late, my darling, we have no right to reject anyone.

EURYDICE. Then, all our lives, this dirty, self-satisfied man will be a part of our first day together?

ORPHEUS. All our lives.

EURYDICE. Are you sure we couldn't just forget the bad ones and only keep the good?

ORPHEUS. Out of the question. They have happened now, the good with the evil. They've danced their little pirouettes, said their three words in your life . . . and there they are, inside you, as they are, forever.

EURYDICE [*suddenly*]. Then, you mean, if you've seen a lot of ugly things in your life, they stay inside you too?

ORPHEUS. Yes.

EURYDICE. And everything you've ever done, does one's body remember that too, d'you think?

ORPHEUS. Yes.

EURYDICE. You're sure that even the words we said without meaning them, the ones we can't recall, are still inside us when we talk?

ORPHEUS [*trying to kiss her*]. Of course, darling fool.

EURYDICE [*freeing herself*]. Wait, don't kiss me. Explain. Are you sure what you've just told me is true, or it is only what you think? Do other people say it too?

ORPHEUS. Of course.

EURYDICE. Clever people? I mean, people who ought to know, people one ought to believe?

ORPHEUS. Of course.

EURYDICE. Then we can never really be alone, with all that around us. We can never be sincere, even when we mean what we say with all our strength. . . . If all the words are there, all the filthy bursts of laughter, if all the hands that have ever touched you are still sticking to your flesh, none of us can really change?

ORPHEUS. What are you talking about?

EURYDICE [*after a pause*]. Do you think we'd do the same,

if when we were little, we knew that one day it would be vitally important to be clean and pure? And when we say these things—when we say, "I made that movement, I said those words, I listened to that sentence, I deserted that man. . . ." [*She stops.*] When one says those same things to someone else—to the man you love, for instance—do they think that kills all your memories around you?

ORPHEUS. Yes. They call that confessing yourself. Afterward, they say that we are washed clean again, shining and pure. . . .

EURYDICE. Oh! Are they very sure of that?

ORPHEUS. So they say.

EURYDICE [*after thinking for a little*]. Yes, yes, but if ever they were wrong, or if they just said that for the effect; supposing they go on living twice as strong, twice as powerful, for having been repeated; if ever the other person began to remember, for always. . . . You can tell your clever people I don't trust them, and I think it's better not to say a word. . . . [ORPHEUS *looks at her, she sees this and adds quickly, pressing herself against him.*] Or else, my darling, when it's simple, as it was for us two yesterday, to tell everything, like me.

[*The* WAITER *knocks and enters.*]

WAITER. Did you ring, sir?

ORPHEUS. No.

WAITER. Oh! Sorry I disturbed you. [*Turns to go, then adds.*] I ought to tell you, sir, the bell is out of order. If you want me at any time, it's better if you call.

ORPHEUS. Thank you.

[*They think the* WAITER *is going, but he changes his mind, crosses room and goes to double curtains; he opens and closes them again.*]

WAITER. The curtains work.

ORPHEUS. So we see.

WAITER. In some rooms it's the opposite. The bell works and the curtains don't. [*Starts to go, then says again.*] Still, if monsieur tries to make them work later, and they don't, you've only to ring. . . . [*Stops.*] I mean, call, because, as I said before, the bell. . . . [*Makes a gesture and exits.*]

ORPHEUS. He's our first eccentric. We'll have lots of others. I should think he's really a very good man, entirely without malice.

EURYDICE. Oh, no. He looked at me all the time. Didn't you see how he kept looking at me?

ORPHEUS. You're dreaming.

EURYDICE. Oh, I like the other much better—the nice one from the *Comédie Française.* . . . You could feel that even in a tragedy he wouldn't be very dangerous. . . .

[*The* WAITER *knocks and enters again. He gives very clearly the impression of having been behind the door.*]

WAITER. Excuse me, sir. I forgot to tell you, madame asks if you'll be good enough to go downstairs. There's something missing on your form. Madame must send it in tonight and it isn't complete.

ORPHEUS. Does she want me right away?

WAITER. Yes, sir, if you'll be so kind.

ORPHEUS. All right, I'll come with you. [*To* EURYDICE.] Get dressed while I'm gone, then we'll go out for dinner.

[*The* WAITER *opens the door for* ORPHEUS *and goes out after him. He comes back almost at once and goes to* EURYDICE, *who has raised herself on the bed.*]

WAITER [*holding out an envelope*]. Here's a letter for you. I was told to give it to you when you were alone. Madame isn't in her office. I was lying. There's only one floor to go. You have thirty seconds to read it.

[*He remains standing in front of her.* EURYDICE *has taken the letter, trembling a little. She opens it, reads it, tears it into tiny pieces without moving a muscle of her face. Then she throws away the bits.*]

Never use the basket. [*He goes to the basket, kneels down, and begins to pick up the pieces, which he stuffs into the pocket of his apron.*] Have you known each other long?

EURYDICE. One whole day.

WAITER. Then everything should still be fine.

EURYDICE [*gently*]. Yes, it should be.

WAITER. The numbers I've seen passing through this room lying on the bed, just like you. And not only good-looking ones. Some were too fat, or too thin, or real monsters. All using their saliva to say "our love." Sometimes, when it's getting dark, as it is now, I seem to see them all again—all together. The room is humming with them. Ah, love isn't very pretty.

EURYDICE [*hardly audible*]. No.

ORPHEUS [*entering*]. You still here?

WAITER. Just going, sir.

ORPHEUS. The manageress wasn't there.

WAITER. I must have taken too long coming up. I suppose she couldn't wait. It doesn't matter, sir, it will do this evening. [*Looks at them both again and goes out.*]

ORPHEUS. What was he doing here?

EURYDICE. Nothing. He was describing all the other lovers he's seen passing through this room.

ORPHEUS. Very amusing!

EURYDICE. He says sometimes he seems to see them all together. The whole room is humming with them.

ORPHEUS. And you listened to such stupidity?

EURYDICE. Perhaps it wasn't so stupid. You, who know everything, said that all the people one had ever met go on living in our memories. Perhaps a room remembers too. . . . All the people who have been here are around us, coupled together, the fat ones, the thin ones, real monsters.

ORPHEUS. Little lunatic!

EURYDICE. The bed is full of them. How ugly love can be.

ORPHEUS [*dragging her away*]. Let's go out to dinner. The streets are flushing with the first lamps of evening. We'll go and dine in a little restaurant smelling of garlic. You'll drink from a glass a thousand lips have touched, and the thousands of fat behinds that have hollowed out the leather bench will make a tiny place for you where you'll be very comfortable. Come, let's go.

EURYDICE [*resisting*]. You're laughing—you're always laughing. You're so strong.

ORPHEUS. Ever since yesterday! A hero! You said so yourself.

EURYDICE. Yes, yes, a hero who understands nothing, who feels nothing, who is so sure of himself he goes straight forward. Ah, you can take things lightly, you others—yes—now that you have made me so heavy. . . . You say things the moment you least expect them, you bring to life all the dirty lovers who have done things between these four walls, and then you don't give it another thought. You go out to dinner, saying, it's a fine day, the lamps are shining, and the restaurant smells of garlic.

ORPHEUS. So will you, in a minute. Come, let's get out of here.

EURYDICE. It isn't nice here any more. It doesn't feel nice. How brief it was. . . .

ORPHEUS. What's the matter? You're trembling.

EURYDICE. Yes.

ORPHEUS. You're quite pale.

EURYDICE. Yes.

ORPHEUS. How strange you look. I've never seen you look like this.

[*He tries to make her follow him; she turns away.*]

EURYDICE. Don't look at me. When you look at me, I can feel it. It's as if you had put your two hands on my back, and entered, burning, into me. Don't look at me.

ORPHEUS. I've been looking at you since yesterday.

[*He draws her away; she lets herself go.*]

EURYDICE [*murmuring, beaten*]. You are strong, you know. . . . You look such a thin little boy and you are stronger than anyone. When you play your accordion, like yesterday in the station, or when you talk, I turn into a little snake. . . . There's nothing I can do except crawl along slowly toward you.

ORPHEUS. Then you say, "It's so difficult."

EURYDICE [*crying out suddenly and freeing herself*]. Darling!

ORPHEUS. Yes.

EURYDICE. I'm so afraid it may be too difficult.

ORPHEUS. What?

EURYDICE. The first day, everything seems so easy. The first day all you have to do is invent. You're sure we haven't invented everything?

ORPHEUS [*taking her head in his hands*]. I'm sure I love you, and you love me. Sure as the stones, sure as the things made of wood and iron.

EURYDICE. Yes, but perhaps you thought I was someone else. And when you see me as I am. . . .

ORPHEUS. Since yesterday I've been looking at you. I've heard you talking in your sleep.

EURYDICE. Yes, but I didn't say much. Supposing I go to sleep tonight and tell you everything?

ORPHEUS. Everything? What's everything?

EURYDICE. Or if someone, one of our characters, came and told you. . . .

ORPHEUS. What could they come and tell me about you, I know you better than they do, now.

EURYDICE. Are you sure? [*She lifts her head and looks at* ORPHEUS, *who continues with joyous strength.*]

ORPHEUS. Sure. I haven't thanked you either for your courage. . . . For the days that will soon be here when we'll go without our dinner, smoking our last cigarette, one puff in turn. For the dresses you'll pretend not to see in the windows; for the beds made up, the rooms swept out, your reddened hands and the kitchen smell still caught up in your hair. Everything you gave when you agreed to follow me. [EURYDICE'S *head is lowered. He looks at her in silence.*] I didn't think it would be possible to meet a comrade who would go with you, a little silent companion who takes on all the chores and at night is warm and beautiful beside you. Tender and secret, a woman for you alone. I woke last night to ask myself if I really did deserve to have you.

[EURYDICE *has raised her head and stares at him in the growing darkness.*]

EURYDICE. You really think all that of me?

ORPHEUS. Yes, my love.

EURYDICE [*thinks a little, then says*]. It's true. She'd be a very charming Eurydice: the very wife for you. Mademoiselle Eurydice—your wife!

ORPHEUS [*putting his arms round her*]. Are you happy, little serpent? [*They remain embraced for a moment, then he springs up, strong and joyful.*] And now, will you come and eat? The snake charmer can't blow his flute any longer —he's dying of hunger.

EURYDICE [*in a different voice*]. Put on the lights.

ORPHEUS. There's a sensible thing to say! Lights up everywhere. Floods of light. Drive away the phantoms.

[ORPHEUS *turns on the switch. A hard light fills the room, making it ugly.* EURYDICE *has risen.*]

EURYDICE. Darling, I don't want to go to a restaurant, with all those people. If you like, I'll go downstairs, I'll buy something, and we can eat it here.

ORPHEUS. In the room humming with noises?

EURYDICE. Yes. It doesn't matter any more.

ORPHEUS [*moving*]. It'll be great fun. I'll come down with you.

EURYDICE [*quickly*]. No, let me go alone. [*He stops.*] I'd like to do your shopping for you, just this once, like a respectable married woman.

ORPHEUS. All right. Buy all sorts of things.

EURYDICE. Yes.

ORPHEUS. We must have a real party.

EURYLICE. Yes, darling.

ORPHEUS. Exactly as if we had plenty of money. It's a miracle the rich can never understand. . . . Buy a pineapple—a real one, just as the good Lord made it, not a sad American pineapple in a can. We haven't got a knife. We'll never be able to eat it. But that's the way pineapples protect themselves.

EURYDICE [*with a little laugh, her eyes filled with tears*]. Yes, my darling.

ORPHEUS. Buy some flowers too—lots and lots of flowers. . . .

EURYDICE [*falteringly, with her poor little smile*]. You can't eat flowers.

ORPHEUS. Nor can you. We'll put them on the table. [*Looks round.*] We haven't got a table. Never mind, buy lots of flowers all the same. And buy some fruit. Peaches, fat hothouse peaches, apricots, golden pears. A little bread to demonstrate the serious side of our nature, and a bottle of white wine we can drink out of the tooth glass. Hurry, hurry! I'm dying of hunger. [EURYDICE *fetches her little hat and puts it on in front of the mirror.*] You're putting on your hat?

EURYDICE. Yes. [*Turns round suddenly and says in a strange hoarse voice.*] Adieu, my darling.

ORPHEUS [*cries to her, laughing*]. But you're saying good-by!

EURYDICE [*from the doorway*]. Yes.

[*She looks at him for a second longer, smilingly and pityingly, and goes out abruptly.* ORPHEUS *stays for a moment without moving, smiling at the absent* EURYDICE. *Suddenly his smile disappears, his face looks drawn, a vague fear seizes him, he runs to the door, calling.*]

ORPHEUS. Eurydice!

[*He opens the door, and recoils, stupefied.* THE YOUNG MAN *who spoke to them at the station is on the threshold, smiling.*]

THE YOUNG MAN. She's just gone downstairs. [ORPHEUS *retreats, surprised, hesitating to recognize him.*] Don't you remember me? We met yesterday in the station restaurant, just after the accident. . . . You know, the young man who threw himself under the train. I've taken the liberty of coming to say good evening. I liked you both so much. We're neighbors. I'm in room eleven. [*Takes a step into the room, holding out a packet of cigarettes.*] Smoke? [ORPHEUS *takes a cigarette mechanically.*] I don't myself. [*Takes out a box of matches and lights one.*] Light?

ORPHEUS. Thanks. [*He closes the door again and asks mechanically.*] May I ask your name?

THE YOUNG MAN. When you meet people on journeys, half the charm is to know as little as possible about them. My name won't mean anything to you. Call me Monsieur Henri. [*He has come right into the room. He looks at* ORPHEUS *and smiles.* ORPHEUS *looks at him as if hypnotized.*] A fine town, Marseilles. This human ant heap, this collection of riffraff, this filth. There aren't as many suicides in the old port as they say, but all the same, it's a fine town. Do you expect to stay here long?

ORPHEUS. I don't know.

M. HENRI. I didn't wait to be introduced before speaking to you yesterday. But you were so touching, the two of you, holding each other so closely in the middle of that huge hall. . . . A beautiful setting, wasn't it? Somber and red, with the night falling and the station noises in the background. . . . [Looks at ORPHEUS for a long time, smiling.] Little Orpheus and Mademoiselle Eurydice. . . . One doesn't get such a stroke of luck every day. . . . I shouldn't have spoken to you. . . . Normally, I never speak to people. What's the good? But I couldn't resist the urge to know you better—I don't know why. You're a musician?

ORPHEUS. Yes.

M. HENRI. I like music. I like everything that is sweet and

happy. To tell the truth, I like happiness. But let's talk
about you. It's of no interest to talk about me. But first
let's have something to drink. It helps the conversation.
[*Rises and rings the bell. He looks at* ORPHEUS *and smiles
during the short wait.*] It gives me a great deal of pleasure to talk to you like this. [*The* WAITER *has entered.*]
What'll you have? Whisky? Brandy?

ORPHEUS. If you like.

M. HENRI. Some brandy, please.

WAITER. Just one?

M. HENRI. Yes. [*To* ORPHEUS.] Forgive me, won't you. I
never drink. [*The* WAITER *has gone out. He still watches*
ORPHEUS, *smiling.*] I'm really delighted to have met you.

ORPHEUS [*embarrassed*]. It's kind of you to say so.

M. HENRI. You must be wondering why I take such an interest in you. [ORPHEUS *makes a movement.*] I was at the
back of the restaurant yesterday when she came to you, as
if called by your music. These moments when we catch a
glimpse of Fate laying her snares are very exciting, aren't
they? [*The* WAITER *has returned.*] Ah, your brandy.

WAITER. Here you are, sir. One brandy.

ORPHEUS. Thank you.

[*The* WAITER *goes out.*]

M. HENRI [*who has watched him*]. Did you notice how
slowly and insolently the waiter went out of the room?

ORPHEUS. No.

M. HENRI [*going to listen at the door.*] He's certainly gone
back to his post behind the door. [*Comes back to*
ORPHEUS.] I'm sure he's been in here on several different
occasions with different excuses; I'm sure he's tried to speak
to you?

ORPHEUS. Yes.

M. HENRI. You see, I'm not the only one to take an interest
in you. . . . Haven't shopkeepers, porters, little girls in the
streets smiled at you oddly since yesterday? . . .

ORPHEUS. Everyone is kind to lovers.

M. HENRI. It isn't only kindness. Don't you think they look at
you a little too closely?

ORPHEUS. No. Why?

M. HENRI [*smiling*]. No reason. [*Dreams for a moment,
then suddenly takes his arm.*] Listen, my friend, there are

two races of beings. The masses, teeming and happy—common clay, if you like—eating, breeding, working, counting their pennies; people who just live; ordinary people; people you can't imagine dead. And then, there are the others—the noble ones, the heroes. The ones you can quite well imagine lying shot, pale and tragic: one minute triumphant with a guard of honor, and the next being marched away between two gendarmes. Hasn't that sort of thing ever attracted you?

ORPHEUS. Never; and this evening less than usual.

M. HENRI [*going to him and laying his hand on his shoulder; looking at him, almost tenderly*]. It's a pity. You shouldn't believe too blindly in happiness. Particularly not when you belong to the good race. You're only laying up disappointments for yourself.

[*The* WAITER *knocks and enters.*]

WAITER. There's a young lady here asking for Mademoiselle Eurydice. I told her she had gone out, but she doesn't seem to believe me. She insists on seeing you. May I ask her to come up?

THE GIRL [*entering and pushing the* WAITER *aside*]. I've already come. Where's Eurydice?

ORPHEUS. She's gone out, mademoiselle. Who are you?

THE GIRL. One of her friends from the company. I must talk to her at once.

ORPHEUS. I tell you she's gone out. Besides, I don't think she has anything to say to you.

THE GIRL. You're wrong. She's got plenty to say. How long ago did she go out? Did she take her suitcase with her?

ORPHEUS. Her suitcase? Why should she take her suitcase? She's gone out to buy our dinner.

THE GIRL. She may have gone out to buy your dinner, but she had very good reasons for taking her suitcase. She was supposed to meet us at the station to catch the eight-twelve train.

ORPHEUS [*crying out*]. Meet who?

WAITER [*who has pulled out a fat copper watch*]. It's ten minutes and forty seconds past eight now. . . .

THE GIRL [*as if to herself*]. She must be on the platform with him already. Thank you. [*She turns to go.*]

ORPHEUS [*catches her up in front of the door*]. On the platform with who?

THE GIRL. Let me go. You're hurting me. You'll make me miss the train.

WAITER [*still looking at his watch*]. Exactly eleven minutes past eight.

DULAC [*appearing in the doorway, to the* WAITER]. It's eight-thirteen. Your watch is slow. The train has gone. [*To* ORPHEUS.] Let the girl go. I can answer you. On the platform with me.

ORPHEUS [*retreating*]. Who are you?

DULAC. Alfredo Dulac. Eurydice's impresario. Where is she?

ORPHEUS. What do you want her for?

DULAC [*walking calmly into room, chewing his cigar*]. What do you want her for?

ORPHEUS. Eurydice is my mistress.

DULAC. Since when?

ORPHEUS. Since yesterday.

DULAC. She also happens to be mine. And has been, for a year.

ORPHEUS. You're lying!

DULAC [*smiling*]. Because she forgot to tell you? Because the child was in this bed last night instead of mine? You're a child, too, my boy. A girl like Eurydice has to be humored in her little caprices. She slept with the fool who killed himself yesterday too. I can understand her liking you. You're good looking, young. . . .

ORPHEUS [*crying out*]. I love Eurydice and she loves me!

DULAC. Did she tell you so?

ORPHEUS. Yes.

DULAC [*sitting calmly in armchair*]. She's an extraordinary girl. Luckily, I know her so well.

ORPHEUS. Supposing I know her better than you?

DULAC. Since yesterday?

ORPHEUS. Yes, since yesterday.

DULAC. I don't pretend to be an expert. If it were a question of anything else—you look much more intelligent than I am—I'd probably say "Good," but there are two things I really understand. First my job. . . .

ORPHEUS. And then, Eurydice?

DULAC. No, I don't make any such claims. I was going to use a much more modest expression: women. I've been an impresario for twenty years. I sell women, my boy, by the gross, to kick up their heels in provincial revues, or massacre the big arias from *La Tosca* in a casino. I don't give a damn—besides, I love them. That makes at least one good reason out of two for pretending to understand them. Eurydice is perhaps an odd little girl—I'm the first to admit it—but considering the opportunities we've both had to see, you'll agree with me that she is a woman. . . .

ORPHEUS. No.

DULAC. How do you mean, no? She seemed to be an angel, did she? Look at me squarely, my boy. Eurydice belonged to me for over a year. Do I look as though I could seduce an angel?

ORPHEUS. You're lying. Eurydice could never have belonged to you.

DULAC. You're her lover, so am I. Would you like me to describe her to you?

ORPHEUS [*recoiling*]. No.

DULAC [*advancing, ignoble*]. What's she like, your Eurydice? How do you get her out of bed in the morning? Can you drag her away from her thrillers and her cigarettes? Have you ever seen her for a moment without a scowl on her face like a little criminal? And her stockings? Could she find them when she once got up? Be frank with me. Admit her petticoat was hanging from the top of the cupboard, her shoes in the bathroom, her hat under the chair, and her bag completely lost. I've already bought her seven.

ORPHEUS. It isn't true.

DULAC. How do you mean, it isn't true? Is yours a tidy Eurydice? I'm beginning to think we're not talking of the same person, or else she thought it wouldn't last for long. . . . She told you it would be for life? I'm sure she must have been sincere. She thought: "It'll be for all my life, if he's strong enough to keep me, if Papa Dulac doesn't find my tracks again, if he doesn't want to take me back." And at the bottom of her heart, she must have known quite well that Papa Dulac would find her out. It's only what I would have expected of her.

ORPHEUS. No.

DULAC. Of course, my boy, of course . . . Eurydice is a girl in a million, but her mentality is exactly the same as any other girl of that sort.

ORPHEUS. It isn't true!

DULAC. You won't admit anything's true! You're very odd.
How long ago did she go downstairs?

ORPHEUS. Twenty minutes.

DULAC. Good. Is that true?

ORPHEUS. Yes.

DULAC. She insisted on going alone, didn't she?

ORPHEUS. Yes. She said it would be fun to buy our dinner
alone.

DULAC. Is that true, too?

ORPHEUS. Yes.

DULAC. Very well, listen to me. Five minutes before, I had
a letter given to her, asking her to meet me on the platform.

ORPHEUS. No one brought her a letter. I haven't left her
for an instant since yesterday.

DULAC. Are you sure?

[*He looks at the* WAITER; ORPHEUS *also looks at the* WAITER
without knowing why.]

WAITER [*suddenly worried*]. Excuse me, I think I'm being
called. [*He disappears.*]

ORPHEUS. I did leave her for a moment, yes. That man came
and told me I was wanted in the office.

DULAC. I told him to give my note to Eurydice when she was
alone. He gave it to her while you were downstairs.

ORPHEUS [*going to him*]. What did you say in your letter?

DULAC. I said I was expecting her on the eight-twelve train.
I didn't have to say anything else . . . because Fate had
knocked on her door and said, "Eurydice, it's over." I was
sure she would obey me. It's only men who jump out of
windows.

ORPHEUS. All the same, she didn't join you!

DULAC. That's true. She didn't come. But my Eurydice is
always late. I'm not very worried. Did you ask yours to
buy a lot of things?

ORPHEUS. Some bread and fruit.

DULAC. And you say she went out twenty minutes ago? It
seems a long time to me to buy bread and fruit. The street
is full of shops. Maybe your Eurydice is unpunctual too?
[*To the* GIRL.] She must be at the station looking for us.
Go and see.

ORPHEUS. I'm going with you!

DULAC. You're beginning to think she may have gone to meet us after all? I'm staying here.

ORPHEUS [*stops and cries to the* GIRL]. If you see her, tell her. . . .

DULAC. Quite useless. If she finds her at the station, then I'm right. Your faithful and tidy Eurydice was only a dream. And in that case, you have nothing more to say to her.

ORPHEUS [*calling to the* GIRL]. Tell her I love her!

DULAC. She may perhaps shed a tear; she's very sentimental. That's all.

ORPHEUS [*still calling*]. Tell her she isn't what the others think her. She is as I know her to be!

DULAC. Too complicated to explain at a railway station. Hurry along, and listen—I'm a sportsman—bring her here. In one minute she may be able to tell us herself what she is.

[*The* GIRL *goes out, bumping into the* WAITER.]

WAITER [*appearing in doorway*]. Excuse me, sir. . . .

ORPHEUS. What is it?

WAITER. There's an officer with a police van. . . .

ORPHEUS. What does he want?

WAITER. He's asking if there's anyone here related to the young lady. She's had an accident, sir—in the bus for Toulon. . . .

ORPHEUS [*crying like a madman*]. Is she hurt? Eurydice!

[*He hurls himself out into the corridor.* DULAC *follows him, throwing away his cigar with a stifled oath. The* GIRL *disappears as well.*]

DULAC [*as he goes out*]. What the devil was she doing in the but for Toulon?

[*The* WAITER *is left facing* MONSIEUR HENRI, *who hasn't moved.*]

WAITER. They'll never know what she was doing . . . she isn't hurt, she's dead. As they drove out of Marseilles the bus crashed into a gasoline truck. The other passengers were only cut by the glass. She's the only one . . . I saw her.

They've laid her out in the police van. There's a tiny mark on her temple. You'd say she was asleep.

M. HENRI [*does not seem to have heard; his hands driven into the pockets of his coat, he walks past the* WAITER; *in the doorway he turns round*].   Make out my bill. I'm leaving. [*He goes out.*]

ACT THREE

[*The station restaurant in shadow. It is night. A vague light only comes from the platform where only the signal lamps are lit. There is a strange humming noise coming from far-away. The restaurant is empty. The chairs are piled on the tables. The stage is empty for a moment.*]

[*Then one of the doors from the platform opens slightly.* M. HENRI *enters, bringing* ORPHEUS *behind him, hatless, wearing a mackintosh. He is haggard, exhausted.*]

ORPHEUS [*looking round without understanding*]. Where are we?

M. HENRI. Don't you know?

ORPHEUS. I can't walk any farther.

M. HENRI. You can rest now. [*Picks a chair off a table.*] Have a chair.

ORPHEUS [*sitting down*]. Where are we? What did I have to drink? Everything's been turning round and round. What's been happening since yesterday?

M. HENRI. It's still yesterday.

ORPHEUS [*realizing suddenly and crying out, trying to rise.*] You promised.

M. HENRI [*laying his hand on his shoulder*]. Yes, I promised. Keep still. Relax. Have a cigarette? [*He holds out a cigarette, which* ORPHEUS *takes mechanically.*]

ORPHEUS [*still looking round while the match burns*]. Where are we?

M. HENRI. Guess.

ORPHEUS. I want to know where we are.

M. HENRI. You told me you wouldn't be frightened.

ORPHEUS. I'm not frightened. All I want to know is if we've arrived at last.

M. HENRI. Yes, we've arrived.

ORPHEUS. Where?

[281]

M. HENRI. Just a little patience. [*He strikes another match, follows the wall round until he finds the electric light. A tiny noise in the shadows, and a bracket lights up on the back wall, throwing out a meager light.*] D'you know now?

ORPHEUS. It's the station restaurant. . . .

M. HENRI. Yes.

ORPHEUS. [*rising*]. You were lying, weren't you?

M. HENRI [*pushing him back in the chair*]. No. I never lie. Keep still. Don't make a noise.

ORPHEUS. Why did you come into my room just now? I was lying on that tumbled bed. Utterly wretched. I was almost happy, shut up in my misery.

M. HENRI [*in a low voice*]. I couldn't bear to see you suffer.

ORPHEUS. What difference could it make to you if I were suffering?

M. HENRI. I don't know. It's the first time it's happened. Something strange began to fail inside me. If you had gone on weeping, suffering, it would have begun to bleed like a wound. . . . I was almost leaving the hotel. I put down my suitcase and came back again to comfort you. Then, as you wouldn't be comforted, I made you that promise to keep you quiet.

ORPHEUS [*taking his head in his hands*]. I want to believe you with all my strength, but I don't believe you, no.

M. HENRI [*laughs a little silently, then he pulls* ORPHEUS' *hair*]. Stubborn as a mule, aren't you? You're crying, and groaning and suffering, but you don't want to believe me. I like you very much. If I hadn't liked you so much, I'd have gone away yesterday as I always do. I wouldn't have gone into that room where you were sobbing. I can't bear grief. [*He pulls his hair again with a strange sort of tenderness.*] Soon you won't be weeping any more—you won't have to ask yourself if you should or should not believe me.

ORPHEUS. Is she coming?

M. HENRI. She is already here.

ORPHEUS. Here? [*Crying out suddenly.*] But she's dead. I saw them carry her away.

M. HENRI. You want to understand, don't you? It's not enough that fate is making an enormous exception for you. You took my hand without a tremor, you followed me

without even asking who I was, without slackening speed
the whole night through, but on top of everything, you
want to understand.

ORPHEUS. No. I want to see her again. That's all.

M. HENRI. You aren't more curious than that? I bring you to
the doors of death, and you think of nothing but your little
friend. . . . You're perfectly right—death deserves nothing
but your scorn. She throws out her huge nets, grotesque,
enormous. An idiot, a clumsy reaper, capable of chopping
off her own limbs with the rest. [*He has sat down near*
ORPHEUS, *a little tired.*] I'm going to tell you a secret, just
for yourself, because I'm fond of you. There's just one
thing about death no one knows. She's very kindhearted,
horribly kindhearted. She's afraid of tears and grief. Every
time she can, whenever life allows her, she does it quickly
. . . she unties, relaxes, while life persists, clutching blindly,
even if the game is lost, even if the man cannot move, if
he is disfigured, even if he might suffer always. Death alone
is a friend. With the tip of her finger she can give the
monster back his face, soothe the soul in torment she delivers.

ORPHEUS. She has stolen Eurydice! This friend of yours!
With her finger she has destroyed the young Eurydice, the
gay Eurydice, the smiling Eurydice.

M. HENRI [*rising suddenly as if he has had too much, then
brusquely*]. She's giving her back to you.

ORPHEUS. When?

M. HENRI. At once. But listen carefully. Your happiness was
over anyway. Those twenty-four hours, that pitiful little
day, was all life had in store for you—your life—your
cherished life. Today you wouldn't have been weeping
because she was dead, but because she'd left you.

ORPHEUS. That's not true! She never went to meet that horrible man!

M. HENRI. No. But she didn't come back to you either. She
took the bus for Toulon alone, without money, without
baggage. Where was she flying to? What was she exactly,
this little Eurydice you thought you could love?

ORPHEUS. Whatever she is, I love her still. I want to see her
again. Ah, I beg you, give her back to me, however imperfect. I want to suffer and be ashamed because of her.
I want to lose her, and find her again. I want to hate her,

and rock her gently afterward, like a little child. I want to struggle, to suffer, to accept . . . I want to live.

M. HENRI [*annoyed*]. Of course you'll live. . . .

ORPHEUS. With the mistakes, the failures, the despair, the fresh starts . . . the shame.

M. HENRI [*looks at him, scornful and tender; murmurs*]. Poor boy. . . . [*He goes to him, and says in a different voice.*] Good-by. The moment has come. She's out there, on the platform, standing on the same spot where you saw her yesterday for the first time—waiting for you, eternally. Do you remember the condition?

ORPHEUS [*already looking at the door*]. Yes.

M. HENRI. Say it out loud. If you forget, I can do nothing more for you.

ORPHEUS. I mustn't look at her.

M. HENRI. It won't be easy.

ORPHEUS. If I look at her just once before the dawn, I lose her again forever.

M. HENRI [*stops, smiling*]. You don't ask me why or how any more?

ORPHEUS [*still looking at the door*]. No.

M. HENRI [*still smiling*]. Fine. Good-by. You can start again from the beginning. Don't try and thank me. I'll see you later.

[*He goes out.* ORPHEUS *stands for a moment without moving, then goes to the door and opens it on the deserted platform. First he says nothing, then in a low voice, he asks without looking.*]

ORPHEUS. Are you there?

EURYDICE. Yes, my darling. What a long time you've been.

ORPHEUS. I've been allowed to come back and fetch you. . . . Only I mustn't look at you before the morning.

EURYDICE [*appearing*]. Yes, I know. They told me.

ORPHEUS [*taking her hand and pulling her along without looking at her; they cross the stage in silence until they reach a bench*]. Come. We can wait for morning here. When the waiters arrive for the first train, at dawn, we shall be free. We'll ask them for some nice hot coffee and something to eat. You'll be alive. You haven't been too cold?

EURYDICE. Yes. That's the worst part. The terrible cold. But

I've been forbidden to talk about anything. I can only tell you what happened up to the moment when the driver smiled into his little mirror and the gasoline truck fell on us like a mad beast. [*Pause. She adds in a little voice.*] After that I can't tell you anything.

ORPHEUS. Are you comfortable?

EURYDICE. Oh yes—here against you.

ORPHEUS. Put my coat around your shoulders.

[*Puts his coat round her; pause; they are happy.*]

EURYDICE. Remember the waiter from the *Comédie Française*?

ORPHEUS. We'll see him again tomorrow.

EURYDICE. And the beautiful silent cashier? Maybe we'll know what she thought of us at last? It's so convenient to be alive again. . . . As if we'd just met for the first time. [*She asks him as she did that first time.*] Are you good, or wicked? What's your name?

ORPHEUS [*entering into the game and smiling*].   It's Orpheus. What's yours?

EURYDICE. Eurydice. . . . [*Then gently she adds.*] Only this time we've been warned. [*She hangs her head, then says after a tiny pause.*] Please forgive me. You must have been so afraid. . . .

ORPHEUS. Yes. When I saw you downstairs, lying in the van, it all stopped. I wasn't afraid any more.

EURYDICE. Did they put me in a van?

ORPHEUS. A police van. They laid you out on a bench at the back, with a policeman sitting beside you, like a little thief who had been arrested.

EURYDICE. Was I ugly?

ORPHEUS. There was a little blood on your temple. That's all. You seemed to be asleep.

EURYDICE. Asleep? If you knew how I was running. I was running as fast as I could go, like a mad thing. [*She stops; there is a tiny pause; she asks.*] You must have suffered horribly?

ORPHEUS. Yes.

EURYDICE. Please forgive me.

ORPHEUS [*in a low voice*]. There's no need.

EURYDICE [*after another pause*]. If they brought me back to the hotel it must have been because I was still holding my letter. I had written to you in the bus before we started. Did they give it to you?

ORPHEUS. No. They must have kept it at the police station.

EURYDICE. Ah! [*She asks, worried suddenly.*] Do you think they'll read it?

ORPHEUS. They may.

EURYDICE. D'you think we could stop them reading it? Couldn't we do something straightaway? Send someone there, telephone them, tell them they have no right?

ORPHEUS. It's too late.

EURYDICE. But I wrote that letter to you! What I said was only for you. How could anyone else possibly read it? How could anyone else say those words? A fat man, with a dirty mind, perhaps, an ugly, self-satisfied, fat old man? He'll laugh, he'll surely laugh when he reads my agony. Oh, stop him, stop him, please—please stop him reading it! It makes me feel as if I were naked in front of a stranger.

ORPHEUS. They may not even have opened the envelope.

EURYDICE. I hadn't time to close it! I was just going to when the truck crashed into us. Probably that's why the driver looked at me in the glass. I put my tongue out, it made him smile, and I smiled too.

ORPHEUS. You smiled. You could still smile?

EURYDICE. Of course not. I couldn't smile. You don't understand! I had just written you this letter where I told you I loved you, that I was suffering, but I had to go away. . . . I put out my tongue to lick the envelope, he made a crack as all those boys do, and everyone smiled. [*She stops, discouraged.*] Ah, it's not the same when you describe it. It's difficult. You see, it's too difficult.

ORPHEUS [*in a low voice*]. What were you doing in the bus for Toulon?

EURYDICE. I was running away.

ORPHEUS. You had the letter from Dulac?

EURYDICE. Yes, that's why.

ORPHEUS. Why didn't you show me the letter when I came back?

EURYDICE. I couldn't.

ORPHEUS. What did he say in the letter?

EURYDICE. To meet him on the eight-twelve train, or else he'd come and fetch me.

ORPHEUS. Is that why you ran away?

EURYDICE. Yes. I didn't want you to see him.

ORPHEUS. You didn't think he might come and I'd see him just the same?

EURYDICE. Yes, but I was a coward. I didn't want to be there.

ORPHEUS. You've been his mistress?

EURYDICE [crying out]. No! Is that what he told you? I knew he would, and you'd believe him! He's been chasing me for a long time, he hates me. I knew he'd tell you about me. I was afraid.

ORPHEUS. Why didn't you tell me yesterday, when I asked you to tell me everything? Why didn't you tell me you'd been his mistress?

EURYDICE. I wasn't.

ORPHEUS. Eurydice, now it would be better to tell me everything. No matter what happens, we are two poor wounded beings sitting on this bench, two poor souls talking without daring to look at each other——

EURYDICE. What must I say to make you believe me?

ORPHEUS. I don't know. That's what's so terrible. . . . I don't know how I'm ever going to believe you. . . . [Pause; he asks, gently, humbly.] Eurydice, so I won't have to worry afterward, when you tell me the simplest things—tell me the truth now, even if it is terrible. Even if it will hurt me horribly. It can't hurt any more than the air I haven't been able to breathe since I've known you lied to me. . . . If it's too difficult to say, don't answer me, but please don't lie. Did that man tell the truth?

EURYDICE [after an imperceptible pause]. No. He was lying.

ORPHEUS. You've never belonged to him?

EURYDICE. Never.

[There is a pause.]

ORPHEUS [in a low voice, staring straight in front of him.] If you're telling me the truth, it should be easy to see. Your eyes are as clear as a pool of water. If you're lying, or if you aren't sure of yourself, a dark green circle forms and shrinks around the pupil. . . .

EURYDICE. The dawn will soon be here, my darling, and you can look at me. . . . [Gently.] Don't talk any more. Don't think. Let your hand wander over me. Let it be happy all alone. Everything will become so simple if you just let your hand love me alone. Without saying anything more.

ORPHEUS. D'you think that's what they call happiness?

EURYDICE. Yes. Your hand is happy at this moment. It doesn't ask anything more of me than to be there, obedient and warm beneath it. Don't ask anything more of me, either. We love each other, we are young; we're going to live. Agree to be happy, please. . . .

ORPHEUS [*rising*]. I can't.

EURYDICE. If you love me. . . .

ORPHEUS. I can't.

EURYDICE. Be quiet, then, at least.

ORPHEUS. I can't do that either! All the words haven't yet been said. And we must say them all, one after the other. We must go now to the very end, word by word. And there are plenty of them!

EURYDICE. My darling, be quiet, I beg you!

ORPHEUS. Can't you hear? A swarm of them has been around us ever since yesterday. Dulac's words, my words, your words, all the words that brought us here. And the words of all the people who looked at us as if we were two animals being led along. The ones that haven't been spoken yet, but which are there, attracted by the aroma of the rest, the most conventional, the most vulgar, the ones we hate the most. We're going to say them; we're surely going to say them. They must always be said.

EURYDICE [*rises, crying out*]. My darling!

ORPHEUS. Ah, no! I want no more words—enough! We've choked ourselves with words since yesterday. Now I've got to look at you.

EURYDICE [*throwing herself against him, holding him close to her with her arms round his waist*]. Wait, wait, please wait. What we must do is get through the night. It will soon be morning. Wait. Everything will be simple again. They'll bring us coffee, rolls and butter. . . .

ORPHEUS. I can't wait till morning. It's too long to wait until we're old. . . .

EURYDICE [*still holding him, her head pressed to his back, imploringly*]. Oh, please, please, don't look at me, my darling, don't look at me just yet. . . . Maybe I'm not the person you wanted me to be. The one you invented in the happiness of the very first day. . . . But you can feel me, can't you, here against you? I'm here, I'm warm, I'm sweet, and I love you. I'll give you all the happiness that is in me.

But don't ask more of me than I can give. . . . Don't look at me. Let me live. . . . I so much want to live. . . .

ORPHEUS. Live! Live! Like your mother and her lover, perhaps, with baby talk, smiles, and indulgences, and then a good meal, a little love-making, and everything's all right. Ah, no! I love you too much to live! [*He has turned round and looked at her. They are standing face to face, separated by an appalling silence; suddenly he asks, in a low voice.*] Did he hold you to him, that horrible man? Did he touch you with those hands all covered with rings?

EURYDICE. Yes.

ORPHEUS. How long have you been his mistress?

EURYDICE [*replying to him now with the same eagerness to lacerate herself*]. For a year.

ORPHEUS. Is it true you were with him two days ago?

EURYDICE. Yes, the night before I met you; he called for me after the performance. He made a scene. He made a scene every time.

ORPHEUS. What scene?

[*The little* MANAGER *appears, in agony, awkward, clumsy. He raises his little hat before speaking.*]

MANAGER. He threatened to send me away, monsieur. I'm his company manager, and each time he threatened to dismiss me.

DULAC [*entering, and exploding when he sees the* MANAGER]. He's a fool! He loses everything! I won't keep such an idiot in my company.

MANAGER. Oh, Monsieur Dulac, I have to look after all the trunks, all the scenery, and I'm alone. I'll never manage! I'll never manage!

DULAC. He's a half-wit, I tell you. He's a half-wit!

EURYDICE. It's your fault—you're always shouting at him. I'm sure if you talked to him gently, he'd understand. Listen, Louis darling. . . .

MANAGER. I'm listening, Eurydice. . . .

EURYDICE. Listen, darling Louis, it's really very simple. You get to the station where we have to change. You get out of the train very quickly. You run to the baggage car. You count the trunks to make sure they haven't forgotten one. . . .

MANAGER. Yes, but the others put their suitcases down beside me and tell me to look after them and go away. And the platform is full of people hurrying along. . . .

EURYDICE. You mustn't let them go away! You must run after them!

MANAGER. I can't watch the trunks if I'm running after them! I'll never be able to manage, I tell you, I'll never be able to manage. I'd much better go away. . . .

DULAC [*roaring*]. He's a fool! A fool, I tell you! This time it's settled. He leaves at Châtellerault!

EURYDICE. Don't shout at him all the time. If you do, how can you expect him to understand?

DULAC. He'll never understand. I tell you he's an incompetent. He leaves the company at Châtellerault, and that's my final word!

MANAGER. Monsieur Dulac, if you fire me, I don't know what I shall do. I promise you I'll be very careful, Monsieur Dulac!

DULAC. You're fired! You're fired, I tell you!

EURYDICE. I'll help you! I promise I'll manage so that he doesn't lose anything. . . .

DULAC. I know what your promises are worth! No, no, he's quite useless. Sacked, fired! Get out! [*And he pushes the little* MANAGER *out into the darkness.*]

EURYDICE [*she fastens on to him, imploringly*]. I promise you he'll be careful. Dulac, I promise. . . .

DULAC [*looking at her*]. Oh, you're always promising, but you don't always keep your word.

EURYDICE [*in a lower voice*]. Yes.

DULAC [*going to her, softly*]. If I keep him just once more, you'll be good to me?

EURYDICE [*hanging her head*]. Yes.

[DULAC *embraces her roughly.*]

DULAC. Admit that that time you came with me because you wanted to, you little liar.

EURYDICE [*pulling herself away from him*]. Because I wanted to? I spat every time you kissed me.

DULAC [*calmly*]. Yes, my dove.

EURYDICE. As soon as you left me, I ran away. I undressed completely. I washed all over—changed my clothes. You never knew that, did you? [DULAC *laughs.*] Oh, I know you, my darling—you can laugh, but it's out of the wrong side of your face.

DULAC. You aren't going to tell me you believed in that scene for a whole year?

EURYDICE. Don't pretend to be so damn clever!

DULAC. Don't pretend to be stupid, Eurydice. You aren't stupid at all. Did you, yourself, believe in that scene for a whole year?

EURYDICE. What!

DULAC. It had become a mere formality, that threat. I made it so that you could save your dirty pride, and pretend you had a reason which forced you to follow me without admitting you enjoyed it.

EURYDICE. You mean, it wasn't true, you wouldn't really have fired him?

DULAC. Of course not. [*And he laughs again, as he disappears into the shadows.*]

EURYDICE. That's what happened every time. Forgive me, my darling.

ORPHEUS [*who has recoiled, in a low voice*]. I shall always see you with that man's hands on you. I shall always see you as he described you in that room.

EURYDICE [*humbly*]. Yes, my darling.

ORPHEUS. He wasn't even jealous when he came to fetch you. He even knew you were a coward. That if he came to fetch you, you wouldn't stay with me. Because you are a coward, aren't you? He knows you better than I do.

EURYDICE. Yes, my darling.

ORPHEUS. Explain, can't you? Why don't you try and explain?

EURYDICE. How can I explain? Do you want me to lie to you? I am untidy, I am a coward. Ah, it's too difficult.

[*There is a pause.* ORPHEUS *raises his head. He looks at* EURYDICE *who is standing humbly before him.*]

ORPHEUS. If you loved me, why were you going away?

EURYDICE. I thought I'd never be able to make you understand.

MOTHER [*exclaiming suddenly*]. What I don't understand is why everything seems so terribly sad to these children!

VINCENT. I've always said: a little love, a little money, a little success, and life is wonderful!

MOTHER. A little love? A great deal of love! That child thinks she's invented the whole thing with her little musician. We've adored each other too, haven't we? We've often wanted to kill ourselves for each other's sake. Remember the time I tried to swallow vinegar? I took the wrong bottle. It was wine.

VINCENT. Anyway, the details don't matter. What matters is that we've also loved each other passionately enough to die for it.

MOTHER. Well, are we dead?

EURYDICE [*As the* MOTHER *and* VINCENT *fade out of sight*]. No, mother. [*To* ORPHEUS.] You see, darling, we mustn't complain too much. . . . You were right. In trying to be happy, we might perhaps have become like them. . . .

ORPHEUS. Why didn't you tell me everything the first day? The first day I might have been able to understand. . . .

EURYDICE. There's no more time. . . . [*She runs up the steps at the back, turns to take him in her arms, then tears herself away. A figure appears in the light, and she turns toward him.*] The waiter from the *Comédie Française!* Our very first character. How are you?

WAITER [*with an overelaborate gesture*]. Farewell, mademoiselle!

EURYDICE [*smiling in spite of herself*]. You're very noble, very charming, you know. Good-by, good-by. [*The* WAITER *disappears. The* CASHIER *takes his place.*] Oh, you're the lovely silent cashier. I've always felt you had something to say to us.

CASHIER. How beautiful you were when you came together through the music. Beautiful, innocent and terrible—like love itself.

EURYDICE [*smiles at her and turns to go*]. Thank you, madame.

[*A* YOUNG MAN *appears and calls after her urgently.*]

THE YOUNG MAN. Mademoiselle! Mademoiselle!

EURYDICE. I think you're mistaken. I don't remember you at all.

THE YOUNG MAN. I'm a clerk at the police station, mademoiselle. You have never seen me.

EURYDICE. Ah! Then you must be the one who has my letter. Give it back to me, please, monsieur. Give it back.

THE YOUNG MAN. I'm afraid that's impossible, mademoiselle.

EURYDICE. I don't want that big, fat, dirty man to read it!

THE YOUNG MAN. I can promise you the Inspector won't read it, mademoiselle. I realized at once it would be impossible

for a man such as the Inspector to read that letter. I took
it out of the file. The case is closed, no one will ever notice.
I have it with me. I read it every day when I am alone.
. . . But it's different for me. [*He bows, noble and sad,
takes the letter from his pocket, and after putting on his
spectacles, begins to read in his somewhat flat voice.*] "My
darling, I'm in this bus, and you're waiting for me. I know
I'm never coming back to you, and I'm miserable, miserable on your account. The people in the bus are looking at
me. They think it's sad because I'm crying. I hate tears.
They're such stupid things. For the sorrow I feel now, I
would have liked not to cry. I'm much too miserable to
cry [*He resettles his voice, turns the page and continues.*]
"I'm going away, my darling. Ever since yesterday I've
been afraid, and when I was asleep you heard me say, 'It's
so difficult.' A man is coming. He has had a letter given
to me. I've never talked to you about this man, but he has
been my lover too. Don't believe I loved him—you'll see
him, no one could love him. But I thought so little of myself, and I didn't love you then, my darling. That's the whole
secret. I didn't love you then. That's the only reason I'm
going away. Not only because I'm afraid he'll tell you I
belonged to him, not only because I'm afraid you may
stop loving me. . . . I don't know if you'll ever understand,
but I'm going away because I'm red with shame. . . ."

ORPHEUS. Forgive me, Eurydice.

EURYDICE [*tenderly*]. There's no need, my darling. It's I who
ask you to forgive me. I must go. [*And she disappears into
the shadows.*]

ORPHEUS. Eurydice!

[*He runs to the back like a madman. She has disappeared.
ORPHEUS is alone. He does not move. The morning breaks. A
train whistles faraway. When the light of day is almost real,
the WAITER enters, looking very much alive.*]

WAITER. Good morning, sir. Bitterly cold day. Can I get you
some coffee, sir?

[*ORPHEUS does not reply. The WAITER takes this for a sign
of assent, and begins to lift the chairs down from the tables.
A TRAVELER passes on the platform, hesitates, then enters
timidly. He is overloaded with suitcases and musical instru-
ments. It is Orpheus' FATHER.*]

FATHER. Oh is that you, my boy? I didn't take the train to
Palavas, after all. Full. Full to bursting, my boy. And
those swine wanted me to pay the difference to travel
second. I got out. I'll complain to the management. A
traveler is entitled to a seat in all classes. They should have
let me travel second for nothing. Are you having some
coffee? [ORPHEUS *seems not to see him.*] I could do with
some myself. I spent the night in the waiting room. I was
anything but warm. [*He whispers in* ORPHEUS' *ear.*] To
tell you the truth, I slipped into the first class. An excellent leather sofa, my dear. I slept like a prince. [*The*
CASHIER *enters and goes across the restaurant, humming a
traditional sentimental song. She sees the* FATHER, *and stops
in her tracks, then tosses her head and hurries away.*] She
loses a lot by daylight, that woman. She's got a fine figure,
but she looks extremely common. . . . Well, my boy, what
are you going to do? Night brings good counsel. Are you
coming with me after all?

ORPHEUS [*with an effort*]. Yes, father.

FATHER. I knew you'd never desert your old father! We'll
celebrate by having a good dinner at Perpignan. I know of
a wonderful restaurant, the Bouillon Jeanne-Hachette,
where for fifteen francs seventy-five, you can have hors-
d'oeuvres (including wine) or lobster, if you pay an extra
four francs; main dish—very generous, vegetables, cheese,
sweet, fruit or pastries—wait, wait—coffee and brandy,
or sweet liqueurs for the ladies. The little menu at the
Jeanne-Hachette used to include a good cigar. . . .

[*During this speech,* M. HENRI *has come in quietly, and at
this point, he advances on the* FATHER, *holding out a cigar.*]

M. HENRI. Allow me?

FATHER [*looking at the cigar, and at* MONSIEUR HENRI].
What, what? Oh, thanks very much. [*He accepts the cigar,
and the light offered by* M. HENRI.] Ah, delicious. A
Merveillitas, isn't it?

M. HENRI. Yes.

FATHER. Must have cost a packet, a cigar like that.

M. HENRI. Yes.

FATHER. Don't you smoke?

M. HENRI. No.

FATHER. I don't understand why you carry such expensive

cigars if you don't smoke yourself. Maybe you're a traveling salesman?

M. HENRI. That's it.

FATHER. Big business, probably?

M. HENRI. Yes.

FATHER. Then I understand. You've got so soften up the customers. At the right moment, you pull out a Merveillitas. You ask him if he'll smoke? He accepts, of course. And bingo! it's in the bag. You're all so clever. I'd have adored to have been in business. Wouldn't you, my boy? [ORPHEUS *doesn't answer. He looks at him.*] You must snap out of it, my boy. Look, give him a Merveillitas too. If he doesn't finish it, I will. When I'm down in the mouth, a good cigar. . . . [*Neither* ORPHEUS *nor* MONSIEUR HENRI *gives any sign of having registered this remark. The* FATHER *sighs and adds more timidly.*] Well, we all have our tastes.

[*He goes back to smoking, with a glance now and then at the two silent men. The* WAITER *brings the coffee and sets it down on one of the tables.*]

M. HENRI [*gently, after a pause*]. You must go back with your father, Orpheus.

FATHER [*helping himself to coffee*]. Of course he must. I've just been telling him so. . . .

M. HENRI. You ought to listen to your father.

FATHER. I know how sad it is. I've suffered too. I lost a girl once I adored. A girl from Toulouse, a creature made of fire. Carried off in a week. Bronchitis. I sobbed like a child during the funeral. They had to take me into a café to recover. It hurts at first. Naturally. But one fine day—it took me like that—you have a bath, do up your tie, the sun is shining, you go into the street, and suddenly, bingo! you see the girls are pretty again. We're terrible, my boy, all the same, terrible scoundrels.

M. HENRI. Listen carefully, Orpheus. . . .

FATHER. I don't say you take the first one who comes along. No. We aren't animals after all, and you're bound to feel a little awkward when you open the conversation. You say how lonely you are, how lost. And it's true, it's sincere. Ah, you can imagine how much that sort of talk can influence a woman! You'll say, of course, that I'm an old rogue, but I was still using the same technique ten years afterward.

ORPHEUS. Be quiet, father.

M. HENRI. Why should you want him to be quiet? He's talking to you as life will talk to you through every mouth; he's saying what you'll see tomorrow in every eye, if you get up and try to start life again. . . . But Eurydice can be given back to you forever. The Eurydice of your first meeting, eternally pure and young, eternally herself.

ORPHEUS [*looks at him, after a pause, shaking his head*]. No.

M. HENRI [*smiling*]. Why not?

ORPHEUS. I hate death.

M. HENRI [*gently*]. You're unfair. Why should you hate death? She alone can create the proper setting for love. You heard your father talking about life just now. It was grotesque, wasn't it, but that's what it is like. Go and wander round life's side shows with your little Eurydice, and you'd meet her at the exit with her dress covered with finger marks. Life would never have allowed you to keep Eurydice.

ORPHEUS. I don't want to die.

M. HENRI. Then listen to your father, Orpheus. He can tell you about life.

FATHER [*who has been replenishing his coffee cup, turns at this*]. Life? But life is wonderful, my boy. When you have your health and strength, it's all so simple. The whole secret—daily exercise. Ten minutes every morning. You don't need more, but it's those ten minutes that count. [*He gets up, and with the butt of his cigar between his teeth, begins to go through a ridiculous form of Swedish drill.*] One, two, three, four. One, two, three, four. One, two, three, four. One, two. One, two. One, two. One, two. If you do that you'll never have a sagging stomach, or varicose veins. Health through joy, joy through health, and vice versa.

M. HENRI. You see, Orpheus. It's very simple!

FATHER [*sitting down again, puffing like a grampus*]. It's a question of will power. Everything in life is a question of will power. Now, you're unhappy, but you're young. I like a young man to be ambitious. Don't you want to be a millionaire? Oh, money, money! But that is life, my boy! Think that you might become very rich. Think of the women, my boy, think of love! Blondes, brunettes, red-heads, peroxides! Such variety, such choice! And all for you. You're the sultan, you lift your finger. That one! She comes to you. And then it's a succession of enchanted nights. . . . Passion, cries, bites, mad kisses. . . . Or else on the divans of secret boudoirs, from five to seven, wrapped in rich furs. . . . I've no need to tell you more, my boy! Sensations! Every possible sensation. A lifetime of sensa-tions. And where's your grief? Gone up in smoke. [*He makes a gesture, and becomes serious.*] That is not the whole of life. There's respectability, a social life. You're strong and powerful, a captain of industry. Board meet-ings with brilliant minds. You juggle with the economic safety of Europe. Then the strike. The armed workmen. Violence. You appear alone before the factory. A shot is fired and misses you. You don't move. In a voice of thunder, you speak to them. You castigate them. They hang their heads, go back to work. Beaten! It's magnifi-cent. Then, on the advice of your best friends, you go in for politics. Honored, powerful, decorated, a senator. Al-ways in the forefront. National funeral, flowers, a million flowers, muffled drums, long speeches. And I, modestly in a corner—a distinguished old man, but mastering my grief, erect and at attention. [*He declaims.*] "Let us pay the homage due to a father's grief!" [*It is too beautiful. He breaks down.*] Ah, my boy, my boy, life is wonderful.

M. HENRI. You see, Orpheus?

FATHER. The man talking to you has suffered. He has drunk his cup to the very dregs. You wonder sometimes at my bent back, my premature white hairs, my child. If you knew how heavy is the weight of a lifetime on the shoulders of a man. . . . [*He pulls in vain on the butt of his cigar. He looks at it, annoyed, then reaches for a match.*]

[M. HENRI *goes to him, holding out his case.*]

M. HENRI. Another cigar?

FATHER. Thank you. I'm embarrassed. Yes, yes, embar-rassed. What an aroma! Tell me, have you heard it said that the girls who make these roll them on their thighs? [*He sighs.*] Their thighs. . . . [*He lights the cigar.*] What was I saying?

M. HENRI. The weight of a lifetime. . . .

FATHER [*who has lost his lyric fervor*]. How do you mean, the weight of a lifetime?

M. HENRI. If you knew how heavy the weight of a lifetime can be on a man's shoulders.

FATHER. Ah! That's right. If you knew how heavy the weight of a lifetime can be. . . . [*He stops, takes a pull at his cigar, and concludes simply.*] Well, it's heavy, my boy. Extremely heavy. [*He inhales a deep breath with delight.*] Marvelous. [*He winks at* M. HENRI.] I feel as if I'm smoking the thigh itself! [*He starts to laugh and chokes on the smoke.* M. HENRI *returns to* ORPHEUS.]

M. HENRI. You've listened to your father, Orpheus? Fathers are always right. Even the foolish ones. Life is made in such a way that foolish fathers know as much, sometimes more than clever fathers. [*He moves away for a moment, then suddenly comes back to* ORPHEUS.] Supposing life had held in store for you a day when you would have found yourself alone beside your living Eurydice.

ORPHEUS. No.

M. HENRI. Yes. One day or the next, in a year, in five years, in ten, if you like, without stopping loving her, perhaps, you might have realized you didn't want Eurydice any more, that Eurydice didn't want you either.

ORPHEUS. No.

M. HENRI. Yes. It might have been as stupid as that. You'd have become the man who'd been unfaithful to Eurydice.

ORPHEUS [*crying out*]. Never!

M. HENRI. Why do you protest so loudly? For my benefit, or for yours? [*He makes a gesture.*] In any case, Eurydice might already have abandoned you.

ORPHEUS [*plaintively this time*]. No.

M. HENRI. Why not? Because she loved you yesterday?

ORPHEUS. We could never have stopped loving each other.

M. HENRI. Maybe she wouldn't have stopped loving you. It's not so easy to stop loving someone. Tenderness is a stubborn emotion, you know. She might perhaps have had a way of giving herself to you, before going to meet her lover, so humbly, so gently, that you might almost have known a little of the old happiness.

ORPHEUS. No! Her love for me would have lasted forever, until she was old beside me, and I was old beside her.

M. HENRI. No, little man. You're all the same. You thirst for eternity, and after the first kiss you're green with fear be-

cause you have a vague feeling it can never last. Vows
are soon exhausted. Then you build houses, because stones
at least will endure. You have a child. You lightly stake
the happiness of that tiny, innocent recruit to this uncertain
battle on the most fragile thing in the world—your love of
man and woman. And it dissolves and crumbles. It falls to
pieces exactly as if you'd made no vows at all. [*The*
FATHER *has fallen asleep. He begins to snore gently.*] Your
father's snoring, Orpheus. Look at him. He's ugly. And
pitiful. He has lived. Who knows? Maybe he hasn't been as
stupid as he seemed just now. Maybe there has been a moment when he touched the heights of love and beauty.
Look at him now, clinging to existence, with his poor snoring carcass sprawled over there. Look at him well. People
believe that the wear and tear on a face is the fear of death.
What a mistake! It's the fear of life. Take a good look at
your father, Orpheus, and remember Eurydice is waiting.

ORPHEUS [*suddenly, after a pause*]. Where? What must I do?

M. HENRI. Put on your coat, it's cold this morning. Walk out
of the station. Follow the main road. You'll see a little
wood of olives. That's the place.

ORPHEUS. What place?

M. HENRI. Your rendezvous with death. At seven o'clock. It's
nearly that now. Don't keep her waiting.

ORPHEUS. I'll see Eurydice again?

M. HENRI. Immediately.

ORPHEUS. Very well. [*He crosses to the door, then turns and
hesitates, looking at his* FATHER. *He bends down and kisses
the sleeping old man, then turns back to the door, with a
last look at* M. HENRI.] Good-by.

M. HENRI. Au revoir, my friend.

[ORPHEUS *has gone. Suddenly the lights change, leaving the
station in darkness, and* M. HENRI *standing quite still, his
hands in his pockets. He calls softly and urgently.*]

Eurydice!

[*She enters, and stands in a shaft of light.*]

EURYDICE. He's agreed?

M. HENRI. Yes, he's agreed.

EURYDICE. Will he be able to look at me?

M. HENRI. Yes. Without ever being afraid of losing you.

EURYDICE. Oh, my darling, come quickly, quickly.

[*In the distance a clock begins to strike. With the last strokes, the music begins to build to a crescendo, and* ORPHEUS *appears, hesitating, as if dazzled by the light. She turns, to take him in her arms.*]

My darling, what a long time you've been!

[M. HENRI *turns and walks away into the darkness, leaving the two lovers clasped in a long embrace.*]

HENRI DE MONTHERLANT

1896–

HENRI DE MONTHERLANT defies definition of any usual, co-herent sort, whether it be of life or of art. He has engaged in activities as varied as bullfighting and politics. He has ada-mantly supported one extreme of an issue only to write audaciously in favor of its opposite. (Montherlant is notori-ous for his denunciation of women in the novel *Les Jeunes Filles*; against which can be placed many moving, sympa-thetic, and poetic portraits of women characters—like Ines in *Queen After Death*.) To try to portray Montherlant in a consistent manner is, as he writes in *Queen After Death*, like trying to carve a statue out of sea water.

Montherlant, even more than other modern playwrights, has found it necessary to flaunt openly and flagrantly the so-called "rule" of consistency. Montherlant's lifelong interest has been in the wealth of possible activity and situations with which a man can be involved. He sees with a somewhat vain but frightening candor that opposing emotions, thoughts, and actions form the only consistency in the framework of man. And why not? For "Nature, within herself makes night alternate with day, heat with cold, rain with drought, calm with tempests; and, within bodies, fasting and food activity and sleep; but no one argues from this that Nature is inco-herent or that her variety leads to confusion. Like her, I re-fuse to make a choice." Out of this basic refusal to choose arises the incompatibilities that at once outrage our sensi-bilities, and yet give Montherlant's drama the curious quality of human diversity with which we so readily identify.

But for all of the apparent eclecticism of his attitudes, Montherlant is in actuality a classical writer and he has been termed, quite justifiably, the most conservative dramatist presently writing in France. He has a passion for trying to put new wine in old bottles. The themes of his plays suggest Genet, Pirandello, Lorca, and Ugo Betti, but unlike them he has been content to use the seventeenth-century forms of Corneille and Racine rather than invent new forms which might be more expressive to contemporary audiences. This has led to charges that he is merely academic and that his plays are impossible to produce in the theatre. Such charges are unjust. While it is true that Montherlant is a member of the Academy and that his plays have seldom been successfully produced outside of France, the fault may well be more ours than his. Few writers in the modern theatre can match Montherlant's ability to write powerful dramatic verse, and in Ferrante, the King in *Queen After Death*, he has created one of the greatest characters in the modern repertoire.

NOTES ON THE THEATRE[1]

There are no set rules for writing a good play. But a plentiful supply of sly wit is a prerequisite.

One must reach the universal through the most violent or the starkest particular.

"Isn't the tragic always based on the apprehension of intolerable objects?" (Goethe). Examples of intolerable objects: Alvaro, Georges Carrion, even Ferrante.

Greek and Roman tragedies deal not only with the family group, but also with the different selves within one being.

Critics are still improvising brilliant variations on *Comment on tue les femmes* (*How to Kill Women*), the subtitle of *La Reine Morte* (*Queen After Death*); for four years now, I have eliminated this subtitle from all new editions. And I also note that elaborate studies on my essay "Tibre et Oronte" ("Tiber and Oronte") are being published today; I eliminated that essay from the "Olympiques" (Olympics) twelve years ago.

The playwright moves through two stages of creativity: through emotion he creates substance; then, through art, he judges, chooses, combines, constructs.

If we could visualize the *mise en scène,* the costumes and the interpretation of Corneille's and Racine's plays in the seventeenth century we would be aghast; and Corneille and Racine, no doubt, would be just as astounded if they could see how they are played today.

I am convinced that lasting works of art endure only because of misunderstandings and because of the accumulated writings with which posterity surrounds them. Eventually, these writings drown out and hide the real intentions of the authors. This can happen during their own lifetime. At first, they fight back; they write prefaces and footnotes, they give

[1] From *Théâtre Complet* by Henri de Montherlant, Copyright © Editions Gallimard 1955. Translated by Danielle Hasse-Dubosc. Used by permission of Editions Gallimard.

interviews and information. And, because they love to create and writing commentaries takes time away from new creation, there comes a time when they tire of fighting and let the theories fall as they may. They see the distortion of their works taking place under their very eyes; at the same time, they see budding legends distort their personalities and their lives.

This situation is perhaps all to the good, and, in any case, nothing can be done about it . . . when something is distressing the wisest course of action is to begin to love it. If the *Ninth* Symphony were played today for the first time in a competition for the Prix de Rome, hardly anyone would be interested or pleased. But it has been gushed over for two hundred years; one goes to listen in a state of delighted anticipation, bringing—as one does to Spanish inns—all one seeks to find there. If Beethoven came back to life, he would surely do what we all do—he would leave current opinion alone. He would give a free rein to the players, who would perhaps interpret his work in a way that he had not considered and that would exasperate him.

When Racine's *Bérénice* was played years ago with Baty's absurd *mise en scène*, I, for one, was in favor of the undertaking. It was indeed absurd, but it created a great deal of interest in the play; it provoked indignation, discussions, and articles. For two months, everyone in France thought about *Bérénice*. Then, the said *mise en scène* was forgotten, and the play regained its original virginity. There was nothing for it but to wait until, once more, it could be for a few weeks the experimental object of a director's new whim which would put it again in the public eye. It is through errors that works survive.

There was a scene that I could have included in *La Reine Morte*; it would have fitted in perfectly with the spirit of the play. The old king deliberately keeps abreast of nothing and retreats into his quarters because of his insurmountable horror of any contact with the baseness of his grandees; he then finds himself in a state of isolation that is gradually compounded by his grandees who turn the tables on him and no longer keep him informed of anything. And finally he asks the treacherous young page Dino del Moro: "What are they talking about at court? How is the business with the pope coming along?" The scene should be played right up to the level of burlesque: "Do you think we're going to declare war

on Alphonse d'Aragon?" And I am not against pushing the
incongruity to the point when he would say: "I wonder if we
should declare war on him. What do you think?" The page
answers whatever comes to his mind, depending on his mood,
or his petty ambitions of the day. In that scene, tragedy and
ridicule would mingle as they do in real life, for I am convinced that such scenes really did happen, that the situation—
an old monarch who no longer has any link with his State
but the idle gossip of servants, of a mistress, or a page—
must have taken place time and time again in history.

To believe that anyone can be convinced of the excellence
of a play by being forced to attend in evening dress is as
obvious a trick as for a woman to make up in public: As one
cheats, one gives away the trick. All that is retrograde in a
society is revealed insofar as it lets itself be taken in by this
kind of game.

But to force an audience to come to an execrable play on
a winter day in full dress regalia is as grotesque as indecency
can be.

People think a play is "cold" when it is well written; they
want a great deal to be left to the imagination.

When I was asked to write the scenario for a film on
Ignatius of Loyola, I came to understand one of the hidden
reasons that had allowed me to portray Jansenism in *Port-
Royal*: No one was alive to represent and defend that faith.
No one, therefore, wanted to influence or control me, nor
win me over to their ranks and force me to say more than I
wanted to say.

They talk about "romantic love." But it is only love.

In a play that I am presently writing (*Celles qu'on prend
dans ses bras*) (*Those We Take in Our Arms*), a man comes
in a room and finds the woman he loves in tears; he has never
seen her cry before. I first write: "What's the matter? My
God! I see *you* crying!" I cross out and write: "What's the
matter? My God! You are *crying!*" I cross out again and
write: "What's the matter? My God! *I* see you crying!"

There is a kind of playwright who can be personally offended if he is told one of his actors is playing badly; he is
like the lady who is annoyed when someone tells her out of
kindness that she has just spotted her blouse.

Mrs. X . . . writing me about a radio broadcast of *La
Reine Morte*, said: "One word sounded ugly to me: Sweat."
Actually, Inès' line on her sweat is skipped by most of the

actresses who play the role at the *Comédie Française*. Sweat!
How vulgar! An actress with full tenure at the *Comédie
Française* does not sweat.

On *La Reine Morte*: They call "eloquence" and "rhetoric"
that part of my work that bursts forth from me like fire. Am
I to blame if, in my case, expression is commingled with the
jet of passion?

Modern theatre forbids monologues, asides, and set
speeches. But our classical theatre is full of such monologues,
asides, and set speeches. It even abounds with entire scenes
where the actors only declaim. Modern literature forbids us
to repeat the same word in the same context but Racine
doesn't worry at all about repeating words. (In *Alexandre*
the hero recites a long speech where the word "beautiful" or
"beauties" is repeated three times within fifteen verses; I
could find *fifty* such examples.) The same is true about as-
sonance which is forbidden today:

> Grâces au *ciel*, mes mains ne sont point crimin*elles*.
> Je *sens* bien que *sans* vous je ne saurais plus vivre.

I spent thirty years of my writing life changing "like" to
"just as." Then I realized that the "Masters" had never worried about such things, and that we were fools. . . .

Mony Dalmès was rehearsing the kissing scene of *La
Reine Morte* with Renée Faure. They got to the part where
they have to kiss: "This is the best part," whispers Mony
Dalmès, half joking, half in earnest, in an aside between two
lines, with a charming expression on her face.

A play is considered flawed if its plot is known in advance,
but to give away the denouement and even the plot at the
beginning of the play is to make the art of playwriting even
more gloriously difficult. That way, the playwright is forced
to win back the advantage that is relinquished when he fore-
goes surprise effects by his deeper analysis of evolving characters and passions.

In any case, is the audience ever truly surprised? After the
first ten performances of any play the town and the country
have learned its plot, either through hearsay or the reviews.

One of my friends, a gifted author and reporter, read the
manuscript of *La Reine Morte* and returned it to me, saying:
"It's magnificent . . . " It was hard to decide whether the few
words he added were more banal than brief, or more brief
than banal. Clearly, the play did not interest him, and he did

not have a thought on the subject, not a single one. The play was then published and performed. Soon thereafter my friend wrote three or four lengthy reviews of it; they were full of admiring and penetrating analyses. He began thinking about the play only after reading what others had written and hearing what others had said; then, in all good faith, he could either repeat or disagree with what was said, or say whatever came into his head. Such casual remarks, added to many other similar remarks, make a play famous and launch it toward posterity.

Some playwrights believe that in a love scene the lovers must repeat each other's name whenever they address one another: they think this "establishes love."

Some playwrights believe that a character must repeat the same line, and even the same answer, several times: They think this "establishes depth."

Some playwrights believe that ellipsis can be substituted for emotion; because the words begin with the same letter, no doubt.

In my plays I have proclaimed loudly the lofty secrets that only can be whispered.

I was always telling Henri-Rollant when we worked on *Le Maître de Santiago* (*The Master of Santiago*): "You don't need to stage that." "You're right," he would answer, "I felt it all along. We're always tempted to do too much."

A bad actor, a bad writer, a bad painter, a bad torero: They always want to add one more touch. The good ones simplify more and more.

Modern French authors cannot rest until they have convinced their audience that they are not carried away by the characters they have invented. "For God's sake! Don't forget we're intellectuals." But it is just as intelligent to put aside one's mind, at least temporarily, and let oneself be carried away by the deep and menacing ground swells that also exist in a man, if he is a man.

A play interests me only if the plot is reduced to its simplest expression and if it serves as a pretext for the exploration of man. I am interested only if the author has set about expressing with his utmost sincerity, intensity, and depth some of the varied manifestations of the human soul, not if he has invented and constructed a mechanical plot.

If I were fond of someone—man or woman—who wanted to act on the stage, I would try above all to keep him or her from being sullied by acting in mediocre plays, let alone ignoble ones. When Mr. or Miss X dons the sock or buskin a few hours after having incarnated the inept creation of some movie-directing clown, he or she can try to act all they want, I will never be more than half convinced. I've been told that if you pour cheap wine into a jug that previously held only good wine, you'll ruin the taste of all good wine it might hold thereafter.

I am amazed that a man as sharply intelligent as Alfred Fabre-Luce can write me, speaking of *La Reine Morte*: "You don't end it at your strongest pitch." And yet, what does the final action of the young page Dino del Moro mean? Even beyond silence, there lies terminal solitude, between abandon and treachery. Consider the triumph of the flock: It kneels around Inès' body, and Dino del Moro joins it. When the page, that evil little angel, finally walks on tiptoe toward the flock, looking back for the last time at what he has betrayed and abandoned, we are, in my opinion, at the very height of emotional intensity. It reaches far beyond church bells, kneeling, or prayer. In any case, that is how I feel, and if the audience does not feel the same way, I must have expressed myself very badly at that point.

(Dino del Moro finally joins the flock just like a youngster standing near the entrance of a movie theatre who sees his three pals about to go in; he has already seen the movie but he ends up by going with them because he is afraid of being different.)

Actresses have a tendency to add to the beginning of your sentences: They add "Ah!" or "Oh!" and even sometimes "But" or "Well." They are afraid of clarity. They tend to surround your text with the same vagueness with which "woman" likes to surround her personality because she is repulsed by the reality of things. She tends to look for leaning posts outside your text if she cannot find them within it, just as "woman" looks for leaning posts in her life, and if reality affords her none, she will invent them.

A bad audience upsets an actor. This actor in turn upsets the others. The play is thrown off course and cracks like an ice floe splitting apart. Later, one sees the actors' faces full of embarrassment and disappointment when the audience does not applaud to their satisfaction. They are clever at hiding behind the feelings of others, but not at hiding their own.

People have understood the depth of *La Reine Morte* and

often study the play with a great deal of earnestness, sub-
tlety, and intelligence. The series of the *Jeunes Filles* (*The
Young Girls*) is just as profound but this has not been understood (in France) because these novels vexed the public.
Isn't it a real pity that the interest a work deserves can be
denied it because it piques the reader?

La Reine Morte is a dagger with a black and gold inlaid
handle. *Fils de Personne* (*No Man's Son*) a dagger with a
naked handle.

A young woman told me: "*La Reine Morte* represents the
triumph of love: The love of Inès for Pedro and for her son,
the love of the Infanta for Inès. Love is the only ultimate
object of concern. Ferrante had to kill love and put out its
light; his fate logically demanded it. However, he dies believing in love, no matter how hard he tries not to. And this
triumph of love is stressed once again by the final scene
where everyone surrounds Inès' body."

La Reine Morte is unwittingly a representation of present-
day political reality. The shadow of death never ceases to
pass over this play. All its characters live in fear. Ferrante
awaits his death in a perpetual state of fear. Inès lives under
the threat of death and Pedro is put in jail. The atmosphere
of the play—executions, national wars, civil wars, and even
famine—is also the atmosphere of the Europe of today. Those
who will read the play in future times will have to remember at how dramatic a moment it was written and performed.

I read, in black and white, the following statement:
"Psychological truth is the domain of the observer and the
thinker; conventional truth belongs to the playwright. The
theater is essentially the art of convention. It follows its own
laws, which are completely different from those of other
literary genres." This statement exemplifies what I refuse to
accept; and I hope my plays illustrate the falsehood of this
argument. Here is an example: According to this statement
it would seem that "the very essence of the theatre is to reveal everything." And that, no doubt, is why we will never
know Egas Coelho's secret.

I make each character say what he must say, given his
personality. That is why they write that *I contradict myself*.

When I read Shakespeare or Racine, I never ask myself
whether or not I am reading "theatre." I am seeking a deeper
knowledge of the human soul and its reactions, of pathetic
situations, and of those words which "bear at their peak a

strange light" (Victor Hugo); in brief, I search for something that will nourish both the heart and the mind. Without doubt, what is intrinsically "theatrical" about them interests me the least.

Sainte-Beuve found "three beautiful silences" in Greek and Roman literature: Ajax' silence in *The Odyssey*, Dido's in *The Aeneid*, and Euridyce's in *Antigone*. Corneille and Schiller do not know the power of silence, but Racine and Goethe do.

La Reine Morte and *Fils de Personne* end with silence.

Ferrante curses Inès' son but the curse skips over her son and falls on Gillou (in *Fils de Personne*). Inès' statement "I accept having to despise the whole world but I cannot despise my son. I think I could kill him if he did not meet my expectations" foreshadows the drama of Georges and Gillou.

All the principal characters *of La Reine Morte* refer to their religious faith at one time or another, which is natural, for religion then was everywhere. Since Inès and Pedro have rather weak personalities, I attributed to them a rather weak and inarticulate religious faith. They believe because they are surrounded by people who believe, but that is all. The Infanta, who is more intelligent or perhaps more educated, quotes the scriptures passionately, in and out of context. King Ferrante's Christianity is typical of one kind of medieval faith. He sometimes follows his good, sometimes his bad impulses and there is no indication that Christianity keeps him from following his evil ones. But he ceaselessly refers to Christianity. Whenever he is troubled, he invokes God, he calls on Him, he holds Him responsible. I have the following problem about him: In the eyes of the Catholic faith, who is better, the unbeliever, even the virtuous atheist, or the scoundrel who reacts like a Christian (becomes conscious of his sin, feels remorse, calls on God, does charitable works, etc.) once his passions are spent? Which of the two shall be saved, the just unbeliever, or the believing sinner?

There is another Christian aspect to his character. Ferrante, who continues to act when he no longer believes in the validity of those acts, reminds me of a remarkable Old Testament turn of mind; it evolved from the observation of life itself, and often from the observation of life's most trivial aspects, a philosophy that tended to prove the vanity of all that is real. The rantings of the prophets and the ravings of Ecclesiastes do not stem from the contemplation of the infinite, the "stratospheric" contemplation that we find in Hinduism. The Jew is more of an artist and plunges into observation of daily life; and yet his conclusions are nearly those of the Hindu. Both arrive at a belief in detachment, in the vanity of all actions, and they have the distinct feeling that a divine being makes worlds move with a touch of His fingertips. The infinitely small and the infinitely great are explored in turn, or at least are felt at one's sides like luminous borders, like the borders of the spectrum. The Hindu, however, delights in losing himself in those regions, whereas the Jew barely brushes by them and uses them as contrast to make life more vivid, even when he is proving its futility.

Ferrante is a witness to this Jewish tradition because he is halfway between the vulgar man who takes everything he does seriously and the totally spiritual man who refuses to act. He seeks to be of this world without being of it; to belong without total commitment; to play the game without trying to win. He does not refuse to act; rather, he seeks the power of restraint in action. His is the moving abandon of the swimmer, the free fall of the mountain climber using his rope.

An article is written to show that an actor is marvelous. When it is published, he is no longer marvelous.

The worse the actors become, the larger the audience. A bad actor attracts the public as tainted meat attracts flies.

When an author tears himself apart to offer his still bloodstained work to an indifferent or sardonic audience, how can he help thinking of Alexander the Conqueror, carried away by the waters of the Hydaspe and saying: "O Athenians! What does one have to do to deserve your praise?"

Translated by Danielle Haase-Dubosc

QUEEN AFTER DEATH

by HENRI DE MONTHERLANT

1942

QUEEN AFTER DEATH[1]

Translated by Jonathan Griffin

CHARACTERS

FERRANTE, *King of Portugal, aged 60*
PRINCE DON PEDRO, *his son, aged 26*
EGAS COELHO, *Prime Minister*
ALVAR GONÇALVES, *councillor*
DON CHRISTOVAL, *the Prince's former tutor, an old man*
THE GRAND ADMIRAL AND PRINCE OF THE SEA
DINO DEL MORO, *page to the King*
DON EDUARDO, *private secretary, an old man*
DON MANOEL OCAYO
THE INFANTE OF NAVARRE
CAPTAIN BATALHA
TWO OF THE KING'S PAGES
LIEUTENANT MARTINS
INES DE CASTRO, *aged 26*
THE INFANTA OF NAVARRE (*Doña Bianca*), *aged 17*
THREE LADIES-IN-WAITING TO THE INFANTA
OFFICERS, SOLDIERS, COURTIERS, *etc.*

In Portugal, in the past.

1 From *The Master of Santiago and Other Plays* by Henri de Montherlant, translated by Jonathan Griffin. Copyright, 1951 by Alfred A. Knopf, Inc. Reprinted by permission of the publisher.

ACT ONE

[*A hall in the royal palace at Montemor-o-Velho.*]

Scene 1

[KING FERRANTE, THE INFANTA, THE INFANTE, DON CHRIS-
TOVAL, THREE LADIES-IN-WAITING OF THE INFANTA, SEVERAL
GRANDEES.]

THE INFANTA. I cry out to you, I cry out to you, my lord! I
cry out to you, I cry out to God! I go about with a sword
plunged in my heart. Each time I move, it tears me.
FIRST LADY-IN-WAITING [*in a whisper, to the other* LADIES-
IN-WAITING]. Poor thing! Look! How it is hurting her!
SECOND LADY-IN-WAITING. She is utterly steeped in pride. And
it's her pride that that sword is piercing. Oh, how it's hurting her!
THIRD LADY-IN-WAITING. Ah, she is from Navarre!
THE INFANTA. You came, my lord, to my Navarre (God
protect it!) to converse with the King, my father, about
the affairs of your realms. You saw me, you spoke to me,
you believed that an alliance between our crowns, through
the instrument of the Prince your son, and of me, might
be made for the great benefit of those crowns and for that
of Christendom. You, the kings, decided between you upon
a journey to be made by me to Portugal, accompanied by
the Infante, my brother, not long after your return. We
come, we are received magnificently. The coldness of the
Prince toward me neither surprises nor saddens me. I had
been looking farther; beyond him, I saw the work to be
accomplished. Three days passed. This morning Don
Pedro, alone with me, makes a confession. He pleads that

[317]

he did not know your intentions till your return from Navarre, when it was too late to countermand our journey. He declares to me that his heart is bound forever to a lady of your country, Doña Ines de Castro, and that our union will not take place. I believe that if I had not restrained him he would have told me the tale of his love from end to end and in detail: such a mania have those afflicted by the amorous disturbance for believing themselves the object of admiration and envy of the whole world. So I am made to come, like a servant girl, to be told that I am disdained and to be flung back into the sea! My mouth dries up at the thought. My lord, do you know that in our country, in Navarre, people die of humiliation? Don Guzman Blanco, reprimanded by King Sancho, my grandfather, developed fever, took to his bed, and passed away within a month. Father Martorell, my father's confessor, when he was suspended, had an outbreak of boils all over his body and expired after three days. If I were not young and vigorous, my lord, after the affront I have received from the Prince I should be dead.

FIRST LADY-IN-WAITING. To die of wounded honor is certainly the death that befits our Infanta.

SECOND LADY-IN-WAITING. She is always crucified upon herself and she scatters about the blood that flows from her honor.

THIRD LADY-IN-WAITING. Ah, because she is of Navarre, our Infanta!

THE INFANTE OF NAVARRE. I have let the Infanta speak. Her wisdom is great, and her restraint. I shall only add that it is with us as with a bush from which someone wants brutally to tear off a leaf. He tears off a single leaf, but the whole tree shudders. In the same way, with the outrage done to the Infanta the whole of Navarre is shaken. Out of respect and true affection for Your Majesty, we prefer to limit ourselves to stupefaction, for fear of spilling over into fury.

FERRANTE. If I, the King, say to you that I understand your pain, and if by that your pain is not softened, you in your turn will have offended me. Your pain is mine: I cannot say more than that. When I arrived back from Navarre and announced to the Prince my intentions, I certainly saw in his countenance that to him it was a blow; but I thought this meant no more than reluctance at tying himself down and at entering a life of seriousness that is not to his taste. Doña Ines de Castro was not named. He hid his obstinacy from me. And it is at you that he flings it, with a discourtesy that overwhelms me.

THE INFANTA. It's not the woman that is insulted in me, it's the Infanta. Little I care about the Prince!

FERRANTE [to DON MANOEL OCAYO]. Don Manoel, go and warn the Prince, and bring him in when Their Royal Highnesses have left.

THE INFANTA. My lord, allow me to return now to my country. To my country, where I have never been insulted. Navarre is what I love. The east wind that brings me the snow mist of my country is sweeter to me than the fragrant wind of Portugal and its orange trees. The wind that comes from Navarre——

FERRANTE. Leave! Think of all we should be losing! All you would be losing!

THE INFANTA. Better lose than acquiesce.

FIRST LADY-IN-WAITING. The Infanta was not so fond of the Navarrese when she was in Navarre!

SECOND LADY-IN-WAITING. Nor of the cold, nor of the snow mist.

THIRD LADY-IN-WAITING. What a wonderful change in favor of our Navarre!

FERRANTE. Please, Infanta, stay a few days more. I am going to speak to the Prince. His folly may pass.

THE INFANTA. If God were willing to give me heaven itself, but wished to put it off till later, I should rather hurl myself into hell than have to wait on God's good pleasure.

FERRANTE. You like suffering, it seems to me.

THE INFANTA. I like a suffering that comes to me from myself. Besides, Navarre is a hard country. The bulls from our lands are, of all Spain, those that have the toughest hoofs, because they are always walking on rock. . . .

FERRANTE. Stay till the end of the festivities given in honor of Your Highness. If Don Pedro were irreducible, you would leave then, but all scandal would be avoided.

THE INFANTA. I shall not come to life again until our ships begin to move toward my country.

FERRANTE. Is it, then, too hard for you to control your face for a few days?

THE INFANTA. Too hard?

FIRST LADY-IN-WAITING. *Mira! Mira!* How she tosses her head, with the roughness of a bird of prey!

SECOND LADY-IN-WAITING. Oh, the proud little creature!

THIRD LADY-IN-WAITING. God be praised! She is of Navarre!

FERRANTE. Can you not constrain nature for a few days?

THE INFANTA. There is something that I could not do?

FERRANTE. To sustain for long the line of conduct that's most opposed to one's character: how tiring! But how honorable! You are as great as you are noble. Don Pedro is there: he is going to hear what I have to say. Perhaps this evening destiny will have changed course.—Live long years, my young princess! Your exaltation was like that of the wave raising its crest. By it you have raised us all.

THE INFANTA. Say rather that I should live eternally, to have the time to accomplish all the great things which are in me, and which, now as I speak, make me tremble.

FERRANTE. You will live, and you will live washed free of all stain. One thinks one is dying of humiliation and rage, and nothing is so transient as an insult.

THE INFANTA. If God wills, if God wills, I shall be healed by my great things. It is they will wash me free of all stain.

Scene 2

[THE KING, DON MANOEL OCAYO.]

FERRANTE. The Prince is there?

DON MANOEL OCAYO. He awaits Your Majesty's orders.

FERRANTE. Let him wait a little longer, till my anger has cooled down. I've turned pale, have I not? My heart, which in the thick of battles has never lost its royal rhythm, is ragged and palpitating like a cock when its throat is slit. And my soul has fallen into my boots.

DON MANOEL. The worst anger of a father against his son is more tender than the tenderest love of a son for his father.

FERRANTE. I'm ashamed. I do not wish my son to know the power he has over me, a power my worst enemy could not have. But good heavens! He is one of my acts, and all our acts master us, one day or another. Ah! why, why

did I beget him? And why am I forced to reckon with him,
why am I forced to suffer because of him, since I don't
love him?

DON MANOEL. Magnanimous Ferrante——

FERRANTE. There I must check you. I don't know why, each
time someone praises me, I smell my tomb.

DON MANOEL. Must my devotion then be silently——

FERRANTE. At the Day of Judgment there will be no sentence
against those who have kept silence. Bring in the Prince.
I never know what to say to him; but today I know.

Scene 3

[FERRANTE, PEDRO.]

FERRANTE. The Infanta has told me of the monstrous things
you have said to her. Now listen to me. I am tired of my
throne, of my court, of my people. But there is also someone of whom I am particularly tired, Pedro, it's you. For
just thirteen years I have been tired of you, Pedro. As a
baby, I confess, you scarcely held my attention. Then, from
five to thirteen years old, I loved you tenderly. The Queen,
your mother, had died, very young. Your elder brother
was on the way to dullness, and to holy orders. You alone
were left to me. Thirteen was the year of your great
glory; you had at thirteen a grace, a gentleness, a delicacy,
an intelligence that you have never recovered since; it was
the last, marvelous ray of the setting sun; only one knows
that, within twelve hours, the sun will reappear, whereas
the genius of childhood, when it goes out, has gone forever. They always say that the butterfly comes from a
worm; with man it's the butterfly that turns into a worm.
At fourteen it was all over, you had gone out; you had
become mediocre and coarse. Before then, God forgive me,
I used sometimes to be almost jealous of your tutor; jealous
at seeing you take seriously the things said to you by that
old fool Don Christoval, more so than the things I said to
you myself. I used to think, too: "Because of the business
of the State, I shall be forced to lose my child: I haven't
time to devote myself to him." From the moment you
were fourteen, I was delighted for your tutor to relieve

me of you. I no longer looked for you, I avoided you. You
are now twenty-six: for thirteen years I have had nothing
more to say to you.

PEDRO. Father——

FERRANTE. "Father": all through my youth that word made
me tremble. It seemed to me—apart from any idea of
political expediency—that to have a son must be something tremendous. . . . But why don't you look at me?
Your eyes shift unceasingly to hide from me all there is
in you that does not love me.

PEDRO. They shift to hide from you the pain you are causing
me. You know very well that I love you. But what you
blame in me is my not having your character. Is it my
fault if I am not you? Never, in how many years, never have
you taken an interest in what interests me. You have not
even pretended. Yes, once—when you had your attack of
recurring fever and thought you were going to die; while I
was saying something to you by your bedside, you asked
me: "And the wolves, are they giving you good sport?" For
my passion then was wolf hunting. Yes, once only, when
you were reduced to utter weakness and despair by illness,
did you speak of me of what I like.

FERRANTE. You think that what I blame in you is your not
being like me. It is not altogether so. I blame you for not
breathing the air of the heights at which I breathe. One
can be indulgent toward the mediocrity one sees fore-
shadowed in a child. Not for that which spreads out in a
man.

PEDRO. You used to talk to me with interest, with gravity,
with kindness, at an age when I couldn't understand you.
And at the age when I could have, you never again talked
to me like that—to me, whom in the public proclamations
you call "my well-beloved son"!

FERRANTE. Because you could not understand me at that
age either. My words seemed to pass through you as
through a phantom, to die out in God knows what world:
the game had long been up. You are empty of everything,
and, above all, of yourself. You are little, and you reduce
everything to your stature. I have always noticed how you
abased the motives of my undertakings: how you believed that I was doing from greed what I was doing for
the good of the realm; how you believed that I was doing

from personal ambition what I was doing for the glory of God. From time to time you would throw at my head your fidelity. But I looked at your actions, and they were always pitiable.

PEDRO. Father, if I have behaved badly to you, I ask you to pardon me.

FERRANTE. I pardon you. But what a vain thing pardon is! What's done is done, and what's not done is not done, irremediably. And besides, I've done so much pardoning, all my life long! There's nothing so worn out for me as pardoning. Others take pleasure in pardoning; not I. Anyhow, this time the matter is one in which you can repair a great deal of the harm. I shall not hark back to your incredible conduct, in refusing for years to adopt the spirit and point of view that befit your position; in evading the issue every time I spoke to you of a marriage that is necessary to the throne; in continuing, these last days, to conceal from me your determination, only to reveal it brutally to the Infanta, at the risk of an explosion of the worst sort, with unheard-of lack of decorum. I hardly know Ines de Castro. She is of good birth, though a natural child. She is well spoken of, and I wish her no ill. But she must not put me out. A king may put himself out, but does not let himself be put out.

PEDRO. What do you mean to do against her?

FERRANTE. I shall be gentle with you. Because it is the best way, in my opinion, to get what I want. I could exile Doña Ines, or forbid you to see her again. I shall not do so. Since the Moors have brought to our country something of their own customs and even at the court it is now established usage that a man may have a regular mistress as well as his legitimate wife, marry the Infanta, and do not deny yourself the pleasure of meeting Ines, with suitable discretion. The Infanta, well warned, will not object, especially since in Navarre concubinage is formally authorized by law. She will have the kingdom, and the kingdom is well worth this little vexation. And she doesn't love you, any more than you love her, which is the best condition for making your union a happy one for the State, and even a happy one quite simply. You understand? I *want* you to marry the Infanta. She is the son I should have had. She is only seventeen, and already her virile spirit is capable of supplying the defects of yours. In your view, the State is always going along nicely when it gives you license to do whatever you want; governing is hateful to you. The Infanta—— In short, I love her. She did daze me a little with the cries of her pride, when she was dancing before me the dance of honor (by my faith, she hardly touched the ground). But she is sudden, profound, singular. And that energy full of innocence—— Her face is like those faces of adolescent genii one sees carved on breastplates, crying eternally with wide-open mouth their vexed cry. It's she, yes, it's she that is needed at the head of this realm. And think of the strength it means for us: Portugal, Navarre, and Aragon gripping Castile as in a vise! Yes, I am passionately set upon this marriage. When everything so clearly converges to make a thing good, there must be no mistake about it: God is behind it. I am the King, and to contradict me is to contradict God. But to contradict me in this affair is to contradict Him twice over.

PEDRO. Live partly with the Infanta and partly with Ines. . . . Live torn between obligation and affection. . . .

FERRANTE. I do not see it in terms of being torn, but of a sensible sharing.

PEDRO. I have not your facility for being double. I owe myself to her whom I love and who loves me, and I do not owe myself to her by halves.

FERRANTE. So there exists only your pleasure in the world?

PEDRO. My pleasure? My love.

FERRANTE. Unfortunately they are the same.

PEDRO. There is another reason why I cannot marry the Infanta.

FERRANTE. What reason?

PEDRO. . . . In any case no, even if I could, I will not sacrifice us—myself and a being whom I love—to duties whose importance I do see, but to which I have the right to prefer others. For there is private life, and it too is important, and it too has its duties. A woman, a child, the business of forming them, making them happy, helping them to come through this ordeal of life with a joy they would not have had without you, isn't that, too, important?

FERRANTE. Strange words, among which God and the kingdom are conspicuously absent, though you are Christian and will tomorrow be king.

PEDRO. Christian, yes; the destiny of one being matters as much as the destiny of a million beings; a soul is worth a kingdom.

FERRANTE. What a lot of ideas to justify a vice!

PEDRO. A vice!

FERRANTE. You have a mistress and can't bear the sight of another. Thereupon the whole world must arrange itself so as to prove you right.

PEDRO. I have perhaps forty years to live. I do not propose to be mad. I do not propose to render them, of my own free will, unhappy, when they need not be so.

FERRANTE. There you are at last utterly sincere! It's you all this is about. And your happiness! Your happiness! . . . Are you a woman?

PEDRO. Leave the throne to my cousin Bragança. He relishes such morsels. Let 'em be given to those who like 'em. Not to one who abhors them.

FERRANTE. That's enough absurdities. In you are my succession and my memory. Even if you do not want them. Even if you are not worthy of them. Give the matter more thought. The Infanta, who is so attentive to what is due to her, has nevertheless, after a first heated movement, agreed to dissemble. She will remain here during the festivities organized in honor of her brother and her. You have therefore five days to decide. In five days' time you will tell me if you are marrying the Infanta. If not——

PEDRO. If not?

FERRANTE. Pedro, I am going to remind you of an incident from your childhood. You were eleven or twelve years old. I had given you, for the New Year, a marvelous tiny astrolabe, the work of the good craftsman Estevan, who used to begin every piece of work with prayer and purification. That toy had not been in your hands for more than an hour or two when you appear, your face all to pieces, as if on the point of tears. "What's the matter?" At first you won't say any thing; I press you; finally you confess: you have broken the astrolabe. I say all the things that such an act of folly deserves, for the object was a real masterpiece. For a long while you let me storm. And suddenly your face clears, you look at me with eyes full of malice, and you say to me: "It isn't true. The astrolabe is quite all right." I am nonplussed; "But in that case, why?"

And you, with an innocent smile: "Sire, I love it when you are angry. . . ."

PEDRO. It was to see——

FERRANTE. To see what?

PEDRO. To see what you would say.

FERRANTE. Well, my dear son—and this is the point to which I was leading—if at twelve you were so insensitive to my anger, I swear to you by the blood of Christ that at twenty-six it shall make you tremble.

PEDRO. Ah! You are not kind, Father!

FERRANTE. Yes, I am kind when I want to be. I tell you, sometimes my heart comes into my mouth from kindness. Look, I have had the experience, when I have just tricked somebody marvelously, of finding myself sorry for him, seeing him so tricked, and of wanting to do something for him. . . .

PEDRO. To leave him a little of what doesn't matter to you, having despoiled him well and truly of what does matter.

FERRANTE. Exactly.

PEDRO. And if you punish me, will you spare Ines?

FERRANTE. Once more, I do not blame you and Ines for your liaison. It was known to me: I had nothing against it. I blame you—you—for not being willing to marry the Infanta: that is all. There, I've finished what I had to say to you. You may withdraw.

PEDRO. Father, after such grave words am I to withdraw without your embrace?

FERRANTE. Let us embrace if you wish. But these kisses between parents and children, these kisses which make one wonder why one receives them and why one gives them——

PEDRO [*who had advanced toward his father, drawing back*]. In that case, no use.

FERRANTE [*suddenly hard*]. You are right: no use.

Scene 4

[*In the house of* INES, *at Mondego, not far from Montemor-o-Velho. A room giving on a garden.*]

[PEDRO, INES.]

PEDRO. Judge me severely: I didn't dare confess to him either that we were married or that this marriage was going to bear its fruit in you. His anger paralyzed me.

INES. Since we cannot be unbound, even if we wished to be, the Pope being at present so stiffened against your father, since therefore it is useless for the King to insist on your marriage with the Infanta, go back and see him again, Pedro, and tell him all. Better that he should see that he is checked by a fact against which he can do nothing than that he should believe he is checked by obstinacy of yours. Better his anger today than tomorrow.

PEDRO. It will be terrible. It will envelop us like a flame.

INES. I believe I shall find it easier to bear than our present uncertainty. Strange as it may appear, it seems to me that when it bursts, there will be something in me that will cry: "Land!"

PEDRO. He will separate us.

INES. Isn't it as if we were so already? And I like to think, yes, I like to think he'll not separate us for long. For when he sees that he is facing something done and irremediable, then there'll only be one way out: to persuade him to recognize our union. And why should you not succeed? If the King is so anxious for you to marry the Infanta, it's because he sees in her a woman of government, whereas you are so little that sort of man. Learn to govern, my friend, accept the peril and the boredom of it, doing it from now on for love of me, and perhaps the King will in his turn accept that the future queen should be only a simple woman, whose sufficient reason for living is to make you happy. But for God's sake, when you are laying siege to him, find a way of convincing him that to be a queen is to me a cup of bitterness, and that I have only been willing to drink it for the sake of drinking it mouth to mouth with you. I believe I should die of humiliation if he took it into his head to think me ambitious, when my whole dream would be to spend my life withdrawn in the nook of tenderness, lost and forgotten in the depths of this garden.

PEDRO. You are right, I shall speak to him like that. We are in the hand of destiny like a bird in a man's hand. Sometimes it forgets us, it looks elsewhere, and we breathe. And suddenly it remembers us, and it tightens its grasp a little, it throttles us. And again it relaxes the embrace—if it has not throttled us once for all. The embrace will relax, Ines. And I should like to think, I too, that we shall spend many hours yet withdrawn in this garden, and that we shall chatter away there as we have done so often, sitting by the edge of the basin, with the fountain that sometimes sent us drops, and sometimes sent us none, according to the wind. And I breathed in dust of water. And I reflected that you were making of me what every being makes of the one who desires and loves him: you were making me into that basin continually overflowing. And a song as sweet as sadness came now and then from the road, the song of the stonebreakers, it too coming and ceasing, like the water's dust, according to the wind's caprice.

INES. That sweetness mingled with sadness is certainly the taste of our love. You have given me nothing but joys; none the less, always, when I thought of you, if I had wanted I could have started to cry. For two years, hanging over us, this menace, this feeling of black rain ceaselessly ready to fall and yet not falling. The destiny one feels piling up in silence. How many times, in our house, with you, I have imagined to myself the time when these hours would belong to the past. I was regretting them at the very moment I was living them. And they were doubly dear to me, because they were present and I could enjoy them; and, already, because I could no longer enjoy them. Look, I am like that old Captain Orosco, who had fought for seven years, here and in Africa, with a lion's bravery, and then, when he was put on the retiring list, told me: "I'm very pleased! I'd had enough of risking my life every day." With the same simplicity I'll say to you: I've had enough of being every day afraid. Of finding again every morning this fear, on awaking, like a thing left on the table the evening before. Fear, always fear! Fear that makes your hands go cold. . . .

PEDRO. It's true, those gentle, cold hands of yours. . . . But consider the way the whole world lives under the empire of fear. My father has passed his life in feeling fear: fear of losing his crown, fear of being betrayed, fear of being murdered. He knows his crimes better than we know them, and knows that each one of them creates the threat of a reprisal. I've many a time seen his face at the moment when he had just scored a point against an adversary; what was on that face then was never an expression of triumph, it was an expression of fear: fear of the counterstroke. Wild beasts, too, are dominated by fear. And look at the motes in this ray of sunlight: I've only to advance my hand a little here, at the bottom of the ray, and up there, at the other end, and they go mad, mad with fear.

INES. Often, at sunset, I am invaded by a sort of anguish. For instance, when I see the shopkeepers closing their shutters. A lance-stroke pierces me: "At this very moment something frightful is being decided against me. . . ." Or else (how silly it is!) it's at night, when I'm undressing, at the moment when I unbind my hair.

PEDRO. Do you know that each time you move your head, you send me the fragrance of your hair? And that fragrance is never quite the same? One time impregnated with air and sunshine, and smelling of flame; at another cold and smelling of cut grass. O dear head, so well shaped for my hands! Ines, dear woman, my love with the name "woman," Ines of the clear face, clearer than the words that lull it, you who are the bond uniting me to all beings; yes, all beings attached to you, and to you alone, as fruits are attached to the tree. . . . And today I do not only love you: I admire you. I find you braver than I.

INES. By dint of worrying without anything happening, one becomes almost calm on the day when the bolt falls. Besides, today I feel as if I were supported by our child. He carried on a ferocious struggle inside me, and I—I'd be ashamed if I were not as strong as he is, to save him by saving us. When you came the first time, two years ago, I had no power of resistance in front of you. A single cruel word from you, and I'd have fallen, yes, fallen to the ground. I cannot defend myself. But to defend him I feel I have all forms of courage. Even to telling myself that to bring him into the world easily would be a diminution. Even to telling myself that the fact of his being formed in tribulation is somehow happy. You I found already created, and later you created me. He, this thing that is being fashioned every moment, this material and immaterial thing that makes you live in the feeling of a perpetual miracle, is made by that into my wealth, Pedro! Pedro! yes, in a way I think you yourself could never—— But I'm mad, am I not? No, what I give him is merely not taken from

you, but in giving it to him, I give it to you. I hold you,
I clasp you to me, and it's him. His neck has not quite
the same fragrance as yours, he smells of child. . . . And
his breath is that of the doe fed upon violets. And his
little hands are warmer than yours. And his arms are
around my neck as water is, in summer, when you dive
into it and it closes over your shoulders, all full of sunshine.
And he makes about my neck a sweet humming, like doves
cooing. Adored child, thanks to whom I shall get more
power of loving!

PEDRO. You think of him, and, in the middle of all our
miseries, there you are as if surrounded with a mist of
happiness.

INES. That happiness on whose summit I can still for a moment stay motionless. . . . What is it? Why leave me in this
sudden way? You shouldn't have taken me in your arms if
it was to let me go like that.

PEDRO. Horsemen are drawing up at the end of the garden.

INES. Here at last is the moment I have always dreaded.

PEDRO. It's he!

INES. Moment so like that I expected.

PEDRO. Withdraw. I shall tell him everything, as you advised
me. You were right. This a sign: destiny has come to meet
us.

INES. Perhaps, for years, I shall have to live on this minute I
have just lived. I knew it, but not well enough.

A SERVANT [entering]. Sire, the King!

PEDRO. I am his servant.

THE SERVANT. It is Doña Ines de Castro that His Majesty
wishes to see. And he wishes to see her alone.

PEDRO. It is well. Ines, may God inspire you!

INES. I pass my hand over your face, as the blind do, to
carry it with me twice over.

Scene 5

[FERRANTE, INES.]

FERRANTE. So here you are, then, Doña Ines, before me.
Your renown had predisposed me in your favor. Your expression, your bearing, even your way of dressing, everything confirms that you are well bred. And so I have no

doubt that you will find in yourself the qualities to raise
you to the height of the circumstances in which you have
placed us.

INES. I am Your Majesty's servant.

FERRANTE. I am glad that you are partly Portuguese,
through your mother, while your father was a nobleman
from one of the oldest families of Galicia. You were brought
up at Santiago de Compostela, were you not, at the court
of the Duke of Peñafiel? And you came here, two years
ago, to accompany your aged uncle, the Count of Castro,
whom I summoned to my side. By ill luck, he returned to
God, too soon for all of us. And especially for you, I think.
For you were left alone at the Mondego. The situation was
a rather strange one for a young girl. Perhaps one should
be sorry that I did not know you better. I saw you hardly
ever at the court or not at all.

INES. Having no intrigue to carry on there, I should not have
felt at ease. I think I should have asked myself without
ceasing: "But what am I doing here?" And they say that
at the court whoever is at a loss is always in the wrong.

FERRANTE. The court is a place of darkness. In it you would
have been a little light.

INES. And besides, I should have had sometimes to hide
things from Your Majesty. And I should not have been
able.

FERRANTE. Lying is, for my grandees, second nature. Just as
they prefer getting by threats what they could get by per-
suasion, getting by fraud what they could get by straight-
forwardness, so they prefer getting by hypocrisy what
would easily be theirs through frankness: that's the ordinary spirit of courts. And you yourself, come, come! you
would very quickly have got a taste for it. Besides, not to
lie to others is less important than not to lie to oneself.

INES [smiling]. If I lied, I should soon become tied up in my
lies. Perhaps that's all that stops me.

FERRANTE. I wanted to make you smile. When one is in
doubt whether an unknown person is dangerous or not,
one has only to watch that person smile: his smile is an
indication, even if not an infallible guide. Yours completes
the revelation of what you are. Well, Doña Ines, I was
joking: always be truthful with me; you will have no need
to regret it. And be truthful, first of all, in speaking to me
of my son.

INES. The day I first knew him is like the day I was born. That day my heart was taken away and there was put in its place a human face. It was during the throne feast, in the gardens of Montemor. I had gone a little apart, to breathe the fragrance of the wet earth. The Prince came up to me. One could no longer hear any sound of the festivities, no longer anything except the little cries of birds changing branches. He told me that as soon as he had heard my voice, he had started to love me. That made me sad. I saw him again several times, in the countryside around Mondego. He was always full of reserve, and I, I was always sad. At length I said to him: "Let me simply place my mouth against your face, and I shall be healed eternally." He let me do so, and he placed his mouth upon mine. Later his face was not enough for me, and I desired his breast and his arms.

FERRANTE. All that is long ago?

INES. Two years come the 13th of August. For two years we have been living in the same dream. Wherever he is, I turn toward him as the serpent always turns its head in the direction of its enchanter. Other women dream of what they have not; I dream of what I have. And not a single time have I wished anything not to his profit. And not a day have I missed saying to him within myself: "May God bless the happiness you have given me!"

FERRANTE. These sentiments will facilitate my task: I am at home everywhere where there is gravity. And it would be a sin to try to diminish your image of the Prince, even though, in my view, it is a little embellished. In my view, the Prince is—how shall I put it? The Prince is not very deep. A sin, also, to tell you too much about the way I conceive what men and women call love—going into dark houses to the depths of alcoves sadder than themselves, to mingle there in silence like the shadows. No, let's leave that and come to the heart of my anxiety. I am not asking you to break with Don Pedro. I am asking you to use your power over him to make him accept a marriage on which the fate of the realm depends. That may be hard for you, but it is necessary. I have no need to set out for you the reasons for it: the Prince's marriage is an event for which, during two years, you had ample leisure to prepare yourself.

INES. Alas, my lord, you are asking of me the impossible.

FERRANTE. Doña Ines, I am ready to give to human emotions the share that is due to them. But not more. Do not
force me to argue the State's case all over again for your
benefit—it would be boring for you. [*Leading her to the
window.*] Look: the road, the cart with its mule, the olive-
carriers—it's I that maintain all that. I have my crown, I
have my land, I have this people which God has entrusted
to me, I have hundreds and hundreds of thousands of
bodies and souls. I am like a great tree that has to give
shade to hundreds of thousands of beings. And all that requires that this marriage, which serves my policy marvelously, be made. Don Pedro has given a brutal no, and
he has been mad enough to say it to the Infanta herself.
But that is only a first impulse, on which I wish him to go
back. It is for you to help him to do so. You have no
call to resent his sentiments for the Infanta: between them
there is no question of love. And you will be fulfilling the
wishes of your King, who is declining toward the tomb and
needs his affairs to be in order. Do it, then, on pain of my
displeasure, and remembering that any obedience yielded
to me magnifies the person who yields it.

INES. My lord, if I would I could not put asunder what God
has joined together.

FERRANTE. I don't understand.

INES. Nearly a year ago, in great secret at Bragança, the
Bishop of Guarda——

FERRANTE. What?

INES. —united us, the Prince and me——

FERRANTE. Ah, terrible! Terrible! Married! And to a bastard
girl! Criminal folly and irreparable harm, for never will
the Pope annul this marriage: on the contrary, he will
exult in seeing me at his mercy. Marriage? You had the
bed: wasn't it enough? Why marry?

INES. Well—to be more happy.

FERRANTE. More happy! Happiness again, like the other! It's
an obsession! Do I worry about being happy? If your answer had even been: to come clear of sin. And for a year
my son has been hiding that from me. For a month he has
known my intentions about the Infanta, and he has said
nothing. And it's to you he leaves it to face my anger, like
those miserable tribes that in battle make their women
march in front to protect them!

INES. He was afraid of that anger of yours.

FERRANTE. He knew perfectly well that one day he would have to endure it, but he preferred putting it off to the morrow, and he's no less a coward than a cheat and a fool. He's no longer a child, but he has kept the deceitfulness of children. Unless—unless he was counting on my death. I understand now why he argues against all marriage. I die, and at once you are queen! Ah, I was perfectly right when I thought that a father, when he lies down to sleep, should always slide a dagger under his pillow to defend himself against his son. Thirteen years of being strangers to each other, then thirteen years of being enemies: there's your paternity. [Calling.] Don Felix! Have Don Christoval brought in, with three officers. Madame, you are not the one to blame, go back to your apartments; no harm will be done to you. Don Felix, escort Doña Ines de Castro and see she does not meet the Prince.

INES. But Don Pedro? Oh, my lord, be merciful to him!

FERRANTE. Enough!

INES. God! it is as if a blade were cutting away from me my child.

Scene 6

[FERRANTE, DON CHRISTOVAL, THREE OFFICERS of the palace guard.]

FERRANTE. Don Christoval, I am entrusting to you a mission that you will find painful. With these three good men, you will arrest at once the individual whom I have for son. You will take him to Santarem Castle, and you will detain him there until I have indicated who is to guard him.

DON CHRISTOVAL. My lord! Not me! Somebody other than me!

FERRANTE. Oh yes, you, and nobody but you. That hurts you? Well, the time has come for people to begin to be hurt a little around me.

DON CHRISTOVAL. Him whom I've brought up——

FERRANTE. And nicely brought up, with a vengeance! A worthy pupil! And a worthy son!

DON CHRISTOVAL. I call the living God to witness that Don Pedro reveres you and loves you.

FERRANTE. If he despised me, if he had my effigy painted on the soles of his shoes to trample me when he walks, or if he loved me so much that he was ready to give his life for me, that would still be indifferent to me. Pedro is married to Doña Ines.

DON CHRISTOVAL. Alas! After what he said to me!

FERRANTE. What did he say to you?

DON CHRISTOVAL. That he would never make a marriage like that. Already he knew he was being laughed at a little for having as mistress—only as mistress—a natural child. One day when I mentioned this tactfully, he said to me: "Never again speak to me of this."

FERRANTE. That is him all over. Go, go, to prison! To prison for mediocrity! [*He goes out.*]

Scene 7

[PEDRO, DON CHRISTOVAL, *the* OFFICERS.]

PEDRO [*coming in*]. The King has gone?—But what's this? Ah! I see!

DON CHRISTOVAL. In the King's name, Prince, I arrest you. [*Going onto one knee.*] Don Pedro, forgive me.

PEDRO. Rise, Don Christoval. The day will come quickly enough when I shall have to see men on their knees before me.

DON CHRISTOVAL. I shall not rise until you have given me your blessing.

PEDRO. I give it you. And Ines?

DON CHRISTOVAL. Free.

PEDRO. I wish to be sure of that. I wish to see her. For a moment only.

DON CHRISTOVAL. Sire, you shall not leave here!

PEDRO. Wretched old man! You dare! Ah, you have it at last, your hour of glory!

DON CHRISTOVAL. Kill me, and then I'll no longer have to dare.

PEDRO. I fear the worst for Ines.

DON CHRISTOVAL. I repeat she is free, free!

PEDRO. And tomorrow? Ah, I have been too bold. I ought to have put Ines in safety a year ago: there are three hundred convents in Portugal where she would have found asylum, even against the King. But one would think oneself cowardly for taking precautions. Ines is in danger because I was not afraid. Dear child, how guilty I am toward you, for not having managed to protect you better. You were leaning on me, and I have failed you!

DON CHRISTOVAL. There is always gain in having courage.

PEDRO. Don Christoval, it is waste of time shoving your nose up against reality, you persist in your optimistic commonplaces: they make you drunk. You were a tutor. You thought that that was the food to give to poor young people, although they have already all too much of a tendency to love commonplaces. And you go on. One sometimes gains by being courageous. And sometimes one loses. That is what you should say. But that's too simple. That's too true. You are a tutor and moralizer: you aren't made for the simple and true. And you will never perceive how serious it is to preach courage, above all to young people. [*Holding out his sword.*] Come, disarm me. It's time for me to leave a world where I shall be an object of contempt. And among my countrymen, of course: the fact that the Moors took me prisoner wasn't interesting. It's curious, men of real value always end by getting arrested. Even in history one can hardly imagine a great man who doesn't find himself at some moment before a judge and before a jailer; it's part of the character. And those of them who haven't gone through prison look in a way like deserters. Gentlemen, what you are really is a guard of honor, for in my father's prison I shall join the flower of the kingdom. But tell me, isn't there one among you who has been put in prison by the Portuguese? What, not one? Ah, you, Lieutenant Martins! Prisoner! And for what?

THE LIEUTENANT. Oh, Prince, for something very modest: for debt.

PEDRO. Whether it's for debt, or for robbery, or for rape, or for murder, anyone who has been made prisoner by his own people is from now on my brother. Lieutenant Martins, I shall remember you. And now, guard of honor forward, to prison! Or rather no, better say: forward, to the other side of prison! [*They go out.*]

ACT TWO

Scene 1

[*The King's working-room in the palace.*]

[FERRANTE, EGAS COELHO, ALVAR GONÇALVES, DON EDUARDO *seated at a large table.*]

FERRANTE. Here is the dispatch for the Catalonian Cortes.

ALVAR GONÇALVES [*after reading it*]. It seems to me that in it Don Eduardo rather exaggerates the poverty of the kingdom. [*He passes the paper on to* EGAS COELHO.]

FERRANTE. On a directive from me. What is the point? To get something. And to complain is one of the ways of getting something. Pity brings in wonderful returns.

EGAS COELHO. May I venture an observation? Since in this letter we are using methods that are legitimate as between princes but would between individuals be considered horrible treachery, I should like Your Majesty to make mention in it of our honor.

FERRANTE. You are right. It is when the thing is not there that one should put in the word. Don Eduardo, you will begin this letter again and you will introduce the word "honor." Once only. Twice, nobody will take it seriously.

ALVAR GONÇALVES. We are all lost in admiration of Don Eduardo's phrase about last year's wheat harvest. Under Don Eduardo's pen an untruth becomes a real intellectual treat.

DON EDUARDO. Lying by itself is not enough. One must lie efficiently. One must also lie elegantly. Alas, what obligations are laid upon poor mortals! One has to live and move in bad faith like a fish in water.

FERRANTE. One should not live and move in bad faith like a

[337]

fish in water, but like an eagle in the sky. And now, gentlemen, I am going to tell you some news that will surprise you: I have decided to negotiate with the King of Aragon.

EGAS COELHO. After all that you have said! Your doubts! Your apprehensions!

FERRANTE. What I have said never counts. The only thing that counts is what I write. Even that, of course, is a manner of speaking. Alas, at that game there is no beating Ferdinand of Aragon. I don't know at what point his villainy will manage to slide into our agreement and turn it against me, but I know it will get there. I look in vain for the chink in the armor, but I am sure that it exists, and that Aragon will find it.

EGAS COELHO. In that case, don't sign! Let's examine it again.

ALVAR GONÇALVES. We have already been four months examining it.

FERRANTE. Since I had to give in to him, at least I've kept him waiting.

EGAS COELHO. Sire, I beg of you: having such fears, do not sign!

FERRANTE. I am aware of a great mistake; nevertheless I am irresistibly impelled to make it. I see the abyss, and I seek it.

ALVAR GONÇALVES. After those words shall we still be indiscreet enough to offer advice to Your Majesty?

FERRANTE. I command it.

ALVAR GONÇALVES. On no matter what subject?

FERRANTE. I see: you mean Doña Ines. Not only may you speak to me of that, but I invite your suggestions and your views.

EGAS COELHO. There are two guilty parties: the Bishop of Guarda and Doña Ines.

FERRANTE. And Don Pedro. I do not like your being afraid to name him.

EGAS COELHO. The Bishop is in prison: if all goes well, we shall have his head. The Prince, your son, is under guard. Doña Ines is free.

FERRANTE. Doña Ines is the least guilty. There would be nothing against her without Don Pedro and without the Bishop.

EGAS COELHO. Obviously there would be nothing against them without Doña Ines. Your Majesty asks us for our views. In our soul and conscience we form the wish that Doña Ines may no longer have the power to be in future a cause of trouble to the realm.

FERRANTE. That she be imprisoned? Exiled?

EGAS COELHO. That she pass without delay from the King's justice to the justice of God.

FERRANTE. What! Put her to death! What an incredible excess! If I kill someone for having loved my son, what then should I do to someone who had hated him? She has returned love for love, and she has done so with my consent. Love rewarded by death! That would be great injustice.

EGAS COELHO. Injustice consists in not inflicting a deserved punishment.

ALVAR GONÇALVES. And public offenses do not allow of pardon.

FERRANTE. The Prince and Ines are equally guilty. But Ines alone would be killed!

ALVAR GONÇALVES. Tacitus writes: "Both were guilty. Cumanus alone was executed, and order reigned once more."

FERRANTE. Is it not frightful cruelty to kill someone who has done no wrong?

ALVAR GONÇALVES. No wrong! She has been the occasion of wrong.

EGAS COELHO. When a decision of this kind does not arise from a movement of anger but from the counsel of reason, it is not an act of cruelty, but an act of justice.

FERRANTE. Oh, the impossible position into which reason and justice have got!

EGAS COELHO. Besides, even if there were injustice in this case, God's creation is a heap of innumerable injustices. Should the society of men have the infernal arrogance to claim to be more perfect?

FERRANTE. I am ready to put Doña Ines into a monastery.

EGAS COELHO. From which the Prince, imprisoned or not, will have her kidnapped within three months.

FERRANTE. I can exile her.

EGAS COELHO. Wherever she is, she will be a center of sedition. The Prince will group around her all your enemies. They will wait for your death, or perhaps hasten it, because your death is all that is needed for Ines to become queen. No: all or nothing. Either pardon with its mad consequences, or death.

ALVAR GONÇALVES. Not to mention that—monastery or exile

—people would think Your Majesty had been afraid of shedding blood. And that would fit in badly with the idea people ought to have of a king.

FERRANTE. If I were the sort to boast of the blood I've shed, I should recall that I have shed enough, in war and otherwise.

EGAS COELHO. Blood shed in war does not count.

FERRANTE. I said: and otherwise. It seems to me that, in my reign, executions have not been lacking.

EGAS COELHO. People will say that, this time, you had the courage to kill a minister of God, but not a woman, simply because she is a woman.

FERRANTE. Doesn't nature revolt at the idea of taking life from her who gives it? And Doña Ines, besides, is a very pleasant woman.

ALVAR GONÇALVES. Any number of women are pleasant.

EGAS COELHO. More than one monarch has sacrificed his own child—that is to say, the most pleasant thing he had in the world—for the good of the State, and Your Majesty would hesitate to sacrifice a foreign woman, a bastard who has turned your son aside from all he owes to his people and to God! But the question is on a higher plane still. Hundreds of thousands of men from this country have died to prevent the Moors from setting foot in Portugal. And you would be stopped by the death of one human being!

FERRANTE. Ah, there's no proportion!

EGAS COELHO. No, you are right, there is no proportion! And it's always the men that are killed, never the women: that is not just. What is more, when their crime is equal before the law, a woman is not put to death: that is not just. A woman, by treachery, delivers up the army: she is imprisoned for life, and adapting herself little by little, because it is part of nature that everything hard relaxes, she comes in time to draw from this a life not devoid of all amenities. But a man, for the same crime, is cut down at a blow. If Doña Ines said to you: "Why are you putting me to death?" Your Majesty could reply: "Why should I not put you to death?"

FERRANTE. I cannot believe that posterity will reproach me for not having put to death a woman who is more or less innocent.

EGAS COELHO. Posterity would call that an act of clemency,

if it took its place in a series of energetic acts. As things stand, it will call it a weakness.

FERRANTE. What are you insinuating?

EGAS COELHO. I am not insinuating, I am speaking openly, covered by my loyalty. Your Majesty, at present, not only is in reality weak on certain issues, but on others is obliged to feign weakness, the better to deceive your antagonists. Hence, in part rightly, in part wrongly, the country appears weak, and this situation is destined to last for a long time yet.

ALVAR GONÇALVES. I would add that the habit of feigning weakness can easily lead to real weakness. When one has begun swallowing some insults, even though from policy, one ends by swallowing them all. One has got used to it: the fiber is loosened.

FERRANTE. It is, all the same, the greatest proof of strength—accepting disdain while knowing one does not deserve it. But what is all this? Do I really appear so weak?

EGAS COELHO. Look at the facts: it can't be denied that on all hands Portugal is in retreat.

FERRANTE. O humiliated Infanta, I am more like you than you think!

EGAS COELHO. And that faith in the Crown is compromised here and there.

FERRANTE. My daughter in the horror of bitterness.

EGAS COELHO. One gesture pulls you out of this abasement. You strike terror and respect into the realm. The rumor of it swells and crosses the sea. The desert is amazed by it.

FERRANTE. And I raise up against me my son, forever. Between him and me I destroy all possibility of remission, of reconciliation or any forgiveness, irrevocably.

EGAS COELHO. No. With Ines alive and banished, the Prince would rebel because he would be sustained by hope. Once she is dead, he who is unwilling to give himself the trouble of governing will not give himself, either, the trouble of a revolt with no object but vengeance. All will pass away together, love and grievance. What is frightening about the death of a beloved person is not the death, it's the way one gets over it.

FERRANTE [aside]. O God, never forgive him, for he knows what he is doing.

DON EDUARDO. And if I may be allowed to venture a modest

opinion, I will say that, if Your Majesty is afraid of a sensation, it would be much to Your Majesty's advantage to
have Doña Ines at liberty but have her given some food
that would not agree with her.

FERRANTE. Alas, we are a long way here from the kingdom
of God.

EGAS COELHO. Which has, in fact, nothing to do with our
subject.

FERRANTE. That was simply a passing sigh which escaped me.

EGAS COELHO. A single act, my lord, will deliver you from
all sighs.

FERRANTE. To be sure. The tragedy of acts. An act is nothing
at the moment. It's an object you throw into the river. But
it follows the course of the river, it is still there, in the distance, right in the distance, always there; it passes through
countryside after countryside; you come on it again when
you were no longer thinking of it, and where you least
expected it. Is it fair, this interminable existence of acts?
I think not. But so it is.

EGAS COELHO. That's all wrong, my lord. The death of Doña
Ines, which torments you now, is what will set you free.
In this instance the woman is like a chicken; kill her and
she feeds you. Acts don't last as much as one thinks. What
a lot of your acts, after having fulfilled their expected object, have dried up, have lost their poison, are hencefor-
ward as harmless as a dead serpent that the ants are
nibbling!

ALVAR GONÇALVES. Besides, after a certain age it no longer
pays to do things by means of slow intrigue: one might not
see the end. Hurrah for a prompt act, which one can savor
fully.

EGAS COELHO. And is it not senseless, the way men are content to sigh, to suffer, to be bound hand and foot by an
inextricable situation, merely because one human being
is alive, when it would be enough to suppress that being
for the whole to be untied, while millions of beings are
dying, whose death is useless, or even deplorable? You
kill, and the sky clears. Truly, it is stupefying that so many
human beings continue to obstruct the world by their
existence when a murder is a thing relatively so easy and
free of danger.

FERRANTE. If that is how it is, that ease is a form of weak-

ness, a weakness that in the present case would have to be
added to the others that you believe you see in me. It is
weakness to do what is quickest, most brutal, what demands the least expenditure of the individual. For instance,
there are gallants who would rather force a kiss from an
unknown woman, at the risk of a slap in the face, than
speak to her: they are taken for strong fellows and are
really cowards. However that may be, I am glad that
you have spoken to me so openly. I shall reflect upon all
this. [*He rises.*]

EGAS COELHO. May God assist Your Majesty and guide your
heart.

[*All rise.*]

FERRANTE [*calling*]. Ho there! A page! [*Aside, to the page*
DINO DEL MORO, *who has come in.*] Go and summon Doña
Ines de Castro and let her wait in the audience chamber.
[*To* EGAS COELHO.] You, stay a moment.

[*The others go out.*]

Scene 2

[FERRANTE, EGAS COELHO.]

FERRANTE. Why do you want to kill Doña Ines?

EGAS COELHO. But—for all the reasons we have just told Your
Majesty.

FERRANTE. No, there is another. You are too keen on this
business. You put too much edge into it. Why do you want
to kill Doña Ines?

EGAS COELHO. May my mouth be filled with earth if I have
spoken with anything in view but an increase in Your
Majesty's glory!

FERRANTE. That's enough honey: I want to reign over men
who stand up, not over men who are prostrate. And besides, the honey that is offered to me always has on it a
bee to sting me. Why do you want to kill Doña Ines? You
have a secret. I want to see what you are, after seeing what
you display.

EGAS COELHO. My lord, what can I say more than——

FERRANTE. There is a secret! There is a secret! A man of

your age doesn't demand the death of a young and beautiful and gentle woman without some secret. Doña Ines has
rebuffed you? You are handsome, though, you too. Elegance, ease, you've only too much of all that. You are
undulating like a flame, like one of those wicked flames one
sees wandering over rotting pools, and they go out when
one tries to touch them.

EGAS COELHO. Let Your Majesty inquire of his spies if I have
seen Doña Ines more than three times in my life, and if I
care about her.

FERRANTE. Well then?—it's not a secret directed against me,
is it?—I want to know what you are hiding. I give chase to
you and cannot track you down. Look me in the eyes.

EGAS COELHO. I am looking you in the eyes, and my face is
clear.

FERRANTE. Yes, you are looking me in the eyes, but do you
think I can't see you clenching your fists, from your tense
effort to stop your eyes from shifting? And your face is
clear. But do you think I don't know what there can be
behind a clear face?

EGAS COELHO. Will Your Majesty give me his hand to kiss?

FERRANTE. Let us kiss the hand we cannot cut off.

EGAS COELHO. Great King, our head and our father——

FERRANTE. I'll have your tongue burned out if you go on
fawning on me. The wash of the waves brings down in the
end the walls it has fawned on too much. One of my
grandees, who came to the court late in life, told me that
on the day when he discovered hypocrisy he grew ten
years younger, so good it was. It is true?

EGAS COELHO. I don't know.

FERRANTE. Ah! it is good, isn't it?—being a knave. You feel
alive. Don't you?

[*Gesture meaning: "I don't know," from* EGAS.]

There is in you something that escapes me, and this irritates me. I like a man to be disarmed before me as a
dead man would be. There is in you some ignoble motive,
and I want to pierce it. Of course, I like people to have
a little mud in them. It cements. In Africa whole cities
are built only of mud: it makes them hold together. I
could not get on for long with anyone altogether limpid.
And besides, every vice that the King approves is a virtue.

But when there is an ignoble motive, even if I do not blame it, I want to know it. It belongs to me. I want to know yours.

EGAS COELHO. I was born to punish.

FERRANTE. There's something else.

EGAS COELHO. What Your Majesty believes, I too will believe, since it cannot be mistaken.

FERRANTE. Stand up! Man, stand up! One spends all the time making you rise to your feet. You are all the time on your knees, like the camels of the Moors, which kneel at the gates of each city. Ah, when I look at this people of dulled adorers, I sometimes say to myself that respect is a horrible sentiment. Come, speak. Why do you want to kill Doña Ines de Castro?

EGAS COELHO. If Your Majesty drives me so, I shall say anything that comes into my head: is that what Your Majesty wants? I repeat, I have spoken.

FERRANTE. That is all? [*Silence.*] Well? [*Silence.*] One day you will be old. You'll relax. Your secrets will come out in spite of you. They'll come out through that mouth of yours sometimes, too loose and sometimes too set, through those too mobile eyes of yours, always flying to right and left to look for something or to hide something. [*Silence.*] You fawn on me and trick me at the same time: the two together is too much. [*Silence.*] I know that in everything you have your motives and look only to them, rather than my service, and that they are ignoble motives, but I place confidence in you all the same. That is strange, but there are only strange things throughout the world. And so much the better, for I like things to be strange. Or rather I know very well why I like you: because you have managed to capture my confidence without deserving it, and I like clever people. I place confidence in you, yes, except on this point. I shall not kill Ines de Castro. [*Silence.*] You heard me? I shall not kill Doña Ines.—— You may go out through my private room. You will take from there my sentence against the Bishop of Guarda. You want someone to die? You have the Bishop. Glut yourself on him. [*Calling.*] Pages! [*To the pages, pointing at the council table.*] Take away that table. It gets on my nerves. [*Aside.*] O kingdom of God, toward which I drag, I drag, like the ship dragging at its anchors! O kingdom of God!

[FERRANTE *goes out in the direction of his private room with* EGAS COELHO. *Left alone, the pages busy themselves with removing the table.*

FIRST PAGE [*sitting down at the table and clowning*]. We, by the grace of God, sublime monarch, taratata, taratata . . .

SECOND PAGE [*likewise*]. May His Most Grandiose Majesty be pleased to agree that taratata taratata . . .

THIRD PAGE (DINO DEL MORO) [*likewise, making the sign of the cross*]. *Dominus vobiscum adjutorium nostrum* . . . taratata taratata . . .

FERRANTE [*having come back alone and seen them*]. So our proverb is true: "The little boys play behind the altar." You can't, then, stay one moment without being up to some folly?

FIRST PAGE. No, may Your Majesty forgive us, we can't.

FERRANTE. What! You can't!

FIRST PAGE. God made us like that.

FERRANTE. All right! Then, if God—— No doubt one must consider it good.

[*The pages remove the table.*]

At any rate, don't upset the inkstand: God does not insist on that.

FIRST PAGE. And what would happen if we did upset the inkstand?

FERRANTE [*watching the table*]. Will you look what you're doing!

FIRST PAGE. Would we be hanged? [*With farcial gestures.*] Oh, we're going to be hanged! Ekk! Ekk!

FERRANTE. My poor children, you are even stupider than the monkeys, and of them too much good is spoken. Bring in Doña Ines de Castro.

Scene 3

[FERRANTE, INES.]

FERRANTE. Praise God, Doña Ines: my pages have not upset the inkstand over your dress—over your lovely dress. You heard them, how they laugh: a day of their life goes by and they don't know it. They have no more fear of me than my son had at their age. They annoy me sometimes by their frankness, but when they are men—that is to say, hypocrites—I shall miss the period of their frankness. Their function here is not what people think: it is to cure me of my grandees. I have just been in council with two of those. The Moors say that the man who has many servants around him has many devils around him. I would say as much of ministers. They are there, living off my aged strength as an ivy plant lives off the trunk of a gnarled tree. Rogues who will live to bury me! My Prime Minister is a wonderful devil. He has played several tricks even on me, but with infinite art. Oh, what art! For its sake I've forgiven him. Only, on whom can one lean? On my enemies' enemies? They too are my enemies. Only the idiots manage to serve and to be devoted: the only ones who are devoted to me are incapables. Matters of weight dealt with by frivolous people, opinions asked for with the firm intention of not following them, meetings for information at which nobody knows anything, discussions adjourned without reaching any conclusions because it is time to go and sup, decisions taken at random to save someone's idiotic self-esteem, indignation that is just but is expressed by men quite as corrupt as those who have made them indignant—there you have what, for thirty-five years, I have seen in government.

INES. If that is how it is, my lord, it is surely not peculiar to our country.

FERRANTE. No. Thank God, one says to oneself that it must be the same over the way. That's what makes one able to go on. And ruling is like charity: when one has begun, one must go on. But it is hard, sometimes. [*Pointing to the window.*] Look at this spring. How like it is to last year's! Isn't it enough to make one die of boredom? And God created that! He is indeed humble.

INES. It is always the same thing, and yet it seems to me as if it were always the first time. And there are also acts that are always the same, and yet each time one performs them it's as if God were descending upon the earth.

FERRANTE. For me, everything is repetition, refrain, ritornello. I spend my days beginning again what I've done already, and beginning it again less well. I've been governing for thirty-five years: it's far too long. My luck has

grown old. I'm tired of my kingdom. I'm tired of my acts
of justice, and tired of my good deeds; I've had enough of
giving pleasure to people who do not matter. The things in
which I've succeeded, the things in which I've failed, all
have for me today the same taste. And men, too, seem to
me far too much alike. All those faces together make up
for me now only one face, with shadowy eyes, watching
me curiously. One after the other, things are deserting me;
they are going out, like those candles one extinguishes
one by one, at regular intervals on Holy Thursday at the
midnight service, to symbolize the successive desertions of
the friends of Christ. And soon, at the hour of death, the
contentment of saying to oneself, thinking of each of
them: "There's something else I don't regret."

INES. "Soon!" But Your Majesty has long years of life to
come.

FERRANTE. No. Soon my soul will have reached the extreme
of its flight, like a great eagle hungry for depth and light.
In an instant I shall appear before my God. I shall know
at last all things. . . .

INES. Sire, if it is your privy council that has put into Your
Majesty's head these funereal thoughts, I should like to
throw myself on my knees to thank God for never having
mixed me up with those men.

FERRANTE. Do you know what they want? A policy of intimi-
dation against Don Pedro and against you. The Infanta,
alas, goes away tomorrow. She will be leaving me alone,
the prey—in the rooms buffeted on all sides by her genius
—to my remorse at not having been able to keep that falcon
here because of you and your sentimentality. And yet I
do not blame you. The Infanta is an inspired and feverish
young woman: she was cradled on a brazen buckler; you,
one would say you were born of a smile. . . . But it is not
written that she is escaping me forever. The marriage of
Don Pedro with the Infanta could take place in a few
weeks or a few months if the Pope agreed to grant the
annulment, and if Don Pedro consented. And my grandees
would like me to gain this consent by letting fly against the
Prince and against you. If they dared—which of course
they do not—they would ask me for your head. They are
hot at my heels like dogs after a bull. I resist; then they
accuse me of being faint-hearted. As though by chance,

the Dominican who preached yesterday evening in my
chapel gave a sermon on firmness! It is true that there's
nothing I esteem so much in a man as moderation in the
exercise of any sort of power. It is sometimes less admirable to use one's power than to restrain oneself from
using it. Added to which the sensation of a power one
doesn't use is certainly one of the most exquisite in the
world. But all that is taken for weakness, and one has to
put up with being disdained unjustly, and that is of all
things in the world the most painful to endure.

INES. Sire, severe as the punishment inflicted on Don
Pedro seems to me, I understand better now that it could
be more so, and I thank you for your kindness.

FERRANTE. No gratitude! Stay natural. And besides, I beg of
you, don't talk to me of my kindness. Sometimes there
passes over my spirit a breeze of kindness, but it is always short-lived. I am not kind, get that into your head.
I am like the rest of them: at times, even I see a serpent
darting its brilliant head out from me. It is not from kindness that I am not punishing the Prince more harshly, it's
from reason; because an ass has made a misstep, should
one cut off its leg? It is not from kindness that I'm doing
nothing to you. Some people think gallantry forbids that
we should punish women. That is not at all my view: if a
man and a woman have committed an equal crime, their
punishment should be identical. For example, a woman be-
trays the army: she is imprisoned for life, and this allows
her still some amenities. But a man, for the same crime,
pays with his head. That isn't just.

INES. In that case, Sire, I ought to be put in prison like Don
Pedro. And it's true that feeling myself free, when he is
captive——

FERRANTE. Oh, you'll be there one day, in prison, you too.
And prison is so becoming to women! Once there, they
stop painting, get thin, wear decent clothes at last, together with a languid paleness that sets them off to great
advantage. Yes, if I treat you gently, it's not from kindness, it's above all from policy. Understand my situation. I
have to obtain two things. First, that the Pope annul your
marriage. At Rome everything's for sale, granted; but the
Pope is in a passion against me, and he is like the rest of
men: he puts his passions before his interests. In spite of

everything, naturally, I shall seek to negotiate. Next, I have got to bring Don Pedro to agree to marry the Infanta, if Rome annuls. Can you help me?

INES. Oh, Sire, how hard that is for me! So much tenderness offered up before God, only to be——

FERRANTE. Don't talk to me of tenderness. Long ago those emotions ceased to interest me. Be reasonable; you have everything to gain by it. Go and see Pedro, and try to persuade him.

INES. See him?

FERRANTE. Yes, I authorize you.

INES. Ah, Sire, thank you! What joy you are giving me! What joy you are giving me!

FERRANTE. Moderate yourself. One should never rejoice so quickly.

INES. When? Tomorrow? My whole life is opening again, like the tail of a peacock unfolding.

FERRANTE. Tomorrow. At the gates of Santarem Castle. Guards will be there at a distance.

INES. May I not enter the castle and stay a moment alone with him?

FERRANTE. No. Outside. And guards within sight. Ask him if he is prepared to engage himself solemnly to marry the Infanta, should Rome give the dispensation, and if so, I'll relax my severity altogether. I regret to have to make conditions. The necessities of the kingdom have forced me to hold to this language.

INES. But do you not want to see him?

FERRANTE. Face to face with him, my patience would ooze away through all my pores. Besides, he and I live in different worlds. His presence bores me and weighs on me. Oh, do not imagine it is bitter, losing affection. On the contrary, you have no idea how good it is to feel one no longer loves. I don't know which is better: to break away, or to have someone break away from you.

INES. To break away from one's child!

FERRANTE. Yes, yes, why not? You will experience it one day with Pedro, you too. Our loves are like those immense armies which yesterday covered the plain. Today one looks for them: they have vanished.

INES. Not ours.

FERRANTE. Most affections are only habits or duties that people have not the courage to break.

INES. For one's son!

FERRANTE. What do I care for the bond of blood! There is
only one bond, the bond one has with the people one
esteems or loves. God knows I did love my son, but there
comes a moment when one must make an end with what
one loves. One ought to be able to break abruptly with
one's children, as one does with one's mistresses.

INES. But you love him still, after all!

FERRANTE. He doesn't deserve it.

INES. Oh, if one's to start calculating what human beings
deserve!

FERRANTE. Everything I have done for him comes home to
roost in my heart. Let's say I love him enough to be sorry
that I don't love him more. He makes me ashamed of myself—of having at one time believed in my love for him
and of not being capable of keeping that love. Go now,
Doña Ines. When you have seen Don Pedro you will come
and see me again. You will tell me if he is very sad, if he
is really feeling the edge of the punishment I am applying
to him. Unless you tell me that he consents, and in that
case you would be bringing me an immense joy. Bring it
me: I have great need of it. Good-by.

Scene 4

[*Outside the gates of Santarem Castle. It is out in the country.*]

[INES, PEDRO.]

INES [*throwing herself into his arms*]. Don't speak! Don't
speak! Let me drink of you. I was so thirsty. My God,
sustain me in this supreme happiness! It seems to me as if
from now on I shall never again be able to taste any happiness that is not near to madness. . . .

PEDRO. Ines, if you——

INES. Don't speak, I said! This moment which perhaps will
never come again. After it I can bear anything. Only let
this moment not be taken away from me. A moment, a little
moment more, let me rest on the man's shoulder, the place
where one does not die. [*Pause.*] Is it your heart beating
so hard, or mine?

PEDRO. Ours.

INES. I'd like to give my life for you. You are laughing! How can you laugh?

PEDRO. To see you so in love. You threw yourself on me like the wolf on the lamb!

INES. And to think I stayed for an hour stretched on my bed before coming here, to be mistress of myself when you appeared! What days I have just lived through! Your name spoken in my solitude, spoken in my dreams. Nailed there as by an arrow. And I kept looking at the sky and I kept crying: "Ah, a little less blue sky, and the body of the man I love!" I kept getting up to go to the fountain (that water, so cool, my only support all through the day), or else to pick a flower and bring it back into my room, to keep me company. And now I've found you again. And I've found again the smell of your clothes. . . . When I saw you my heart burst. Ah, let me drink of you again. Let me hold you in my mouth as the fierce birds do when they possess each other rolling in the dust.

PEDRO. Those soldiers always edging nearer——

INES. All right! Let them shoot with their blunderbusses! For I'd gladly die, I and the life I'm carrying in me, yes, I'd gladly die if death was going to fix me forever in a moment such as this. No, you cannot know what these four days have been. There's a brave and almost defiant way of receiving the first onslaught of fate. And then, little by little, it wears you down. It's on the third day that one should see a person who's been stricken. After three days I began to be bathed in sweat at night, and to realize that in those three days I had got thinner. And when I was in the presence of your father, I was as weak as you had been. You hadn't dared to tell him of our marriage. I didn't dare tell him of our child. And I don't know how I managed to say nothing of that, seeing how much I love talking about him.

PEDRO. How is that famous little boy?

INES. In the daytime he doesn't worry me too much. It's at night. . . . He is in the warm place of my heart, and I should like to make myself warmer still to give him better shelter. Sometimes he moves, hardly at all, like a boat in calm water, then suddenly a sharper movement hurts me a little. In the great silence I wait again for his small sign:

we are accomplices. He knocks timidly; and then I feel myself melting with tenderness, because all of a sudden I had thought he was dead, he is so fragile. I wish he would never cease moving, to spare me those anguished moments when I imagine he will never move again. And yet it is those moments that make possible the divine joy of finding him again alive.

PEDRO. May the hard world on which he is going to disembark not treat him as enemy; he is enemy to no one. May the deep earth welcome him with gentleness; he knows nothing yet of its terrible secrets. But tell me, how is it the King let you come to see me?

INES. He wishes—but I do not wish it!

PEDRO. What?

INES. That I should get your promise to marry the Infanta if the Pope grants the annulment. But I don't wish that, I wish you still to be mine alone. Do you love me?

PEDRO. I love you as the sun loves the sand. I love you, and also I love loving you.

INES. So you missed me?

PEDRO. Oh, foolish woman! Let us be serious. Did my father treat you gently?

INES. Very gently. He spoke to me with an extreme lack of reserve. He was bitter because there are always people urging him against us, and also because he is weary of the throne. All those great deserted halls one passes through to get to him, how well they call to mind the loneliness there must be in power! And how much more loudly a man's inner lamentation must resound there—it must ring like steps on the stone floors! He asked me to look carefully and see if you seemed sad, but I have a feeling that when he's harsh, he is forcing himself and that by nature he's benevolent and generous.

PEDRO. He has, all the same, done horrible acts.

INES. No doubt there were reasons.

PEDRO. Oh, there are always reasons. But to try to portray the King is like trying to carve a statue out of sea water.

INES. He also said some bad things about you. But when people say bad things about you to me, it gives me no pain. On the contrary, it's as if because of it I love you more, as if because of it you belong more to me alone. No, it's not of him that I'm afraid. Our whole fate depends on him, and only on him. And yet the fear I feel is a confused fear, and one that doesn't come from him in particular.

PEDRO. What dread is there which that sad heart of yours will never have harbored? What, even now, in my arms!

INES. I'm thinking of the moment when I shall be leaving you.

PEDRO. Ines, always in the past or future! Always busy looking at me as if it were the last time. Hello, what's this? Our guards are moving. . . .

INES. Truly, you think of nothing but them! If you really loved me you would not see them.

PEDRO. You heard? A sound of horses on the road.

INES. Ah, that's enough! That's enough! So two people cannot embrace without there being men who rise up and say to them: "No"? I shall not move.

PEDRO. The soldiers are returning in our direction. . . .

INES. Wait, my death, wait. Let me first have my fill. I shall not move. Even if it were God Himself appearing in this bush.

PEDRO. The Infanta!

INES. She! Here! Doubtless urged on by the King, she is coming, before leaving, to ask you herself for that promise. She's coming to tear you from me. Don't speak to her. Go back into the castle and refuse to receive her. Besides, if necessary I'll bar her passage.

[*The soldiers surround the* PRINCE *and take him back into the castle.*]

Scene 5

[INES, THE INFANTA.]

THE INFANTA [*into the wings, to her attendants*]. Stay some way off, please, and wait for me. [*To* INES.] Doña Ines de Castro?

INES [*with claws out*]. Your Highness!

THE INFANTA. You think I've come to see the Prince. Not at all, it's you I'm looking for. You saw the King yesterday?

INES. Yes, Princess.

THE INFANTA. What impression did he make on you?

[*A vague, prudent gesture from* INES.]

Well, I am going to tell you. Your necklace of medals has pressed upon your neck and has left a red mark. That is the place where you will be beheaded.

INES. God!

THE INFANTA. Princes put lions on their coats of arms, on their oriflammes. And then one day they find one in their heart. Did you see the green pallor of his face? Like someone who has forgotten to get buried. And with all that, the heavy eyes that lions have. The King has the dying sickness: well, it's at the end of the bullfight that the bull is wickedest. Oh, I'm not saying the King has the clear intention of having you killed. He is as men are: weak, variable, and not very sure of what he wants. But a dangerous thought like a blade has been slid into his mind, and he has not repelled it as violently as he should have.

INES. How do you know?

THE INFANTA. One of the pages has talked.

INES. One of the pages!

THE INFANTA. One of my people took care of the pages on duty yesterday at the door during the council, or rather during a small meeting between the King, Alvar Gonçalves, and Egas Coelho. Two of the pages knew nothing, or wouldn't say anything. The third, the youngest, had listened, and listened well.

INES. The youngest! The one who's so handsome!

THE INFANTA. A young demon is always handsome.

INES. And he talked? But—from thoughtlessness, I suppose?

THE INFANTA. No, from passion.

INES. How horrible!

THE INFANTA. You mean: what blessed good fortune! So, Egas Coelho and Alvar Gonçalves demanded your death. The King could have cut them short, with an energetic no. But they argued interminably. "Like lawyers," the page said. At the end the King said: "I will think it over." Afterward he remained alone with Egas Coelho, but the page had gone to look for you.

INES. "I will think it over." . . . That is not a sentence of death. . . . The King, in all this business, has treated me with such openness——

THE INFANTA. My father says of King Ferrante that he plays with his perfidy as a baby plays with its foot.

INES. "I will think it over." . . . Perhaps he wanted to give himself elbowroom.

THE INFANTA. Doña Ines, Doña Ines, I know the world and its ways.

INES. Oh, yes, you know them. To think that in three days you, a foreigner, and so young, find out such secrets. I could have lived for years in the palace without knowing what was being said about me.

THE INFANTA. I was brought up to rule.

INES. And Don Pedro—did the King speak of him?

THE INFANTA. According to the page, Ferrante did not speak about his son. And now, Doña Ines, I must tell you: I leave tomorrow, profiting by the fact that the winds are favorable. Look: a cloud in the shape of a wing! It's flying toward Navarre. And fleecy clouds: they are seeking pasture toward my Navarre, which is always astir with flocks. Yes, tomorrow at this time, God willing, I shall be cleaving the shadowy sea: with what vehemence the waves will rebel before my ship's bow, only to abase themselves amazed, as if they knew who I am! My Navarre! I desire so much to see it again that I am almost afraid of what I shall see when I get there. Well, I invite you to come with me. You will be a member of my house. You will not be in safety as long as you are in Portugal. But from the moment I take you under my mantle, the King will not dare to touch you: offend me a second time, never! Only, you must decide at once, and leave your Mondego just as it is. I know, people prefer dying to dropping their affairs, or to taking the trouble to put them in order promptly. But you must see what is important to you, whether it's the Mondego or to be alive. So follow me to Navarre and wait. Either the King will die, and you will return and reign. Or the King will destroy his son——

INES. Oh!

THE INFANTA. Forgive me!

INES. But who can have made you believe——

INFANTA. I do not believe that Ferrante has any such thought today. But today and tomorrow are no sons of the same mother, and less than ever so in the shadow of the King. He is by nature uncertain, and his art consists in making his uncertainty pass for policy. He plays a situation as if he were playing a fish; he does it out of hesitation and inconsistency, but manages to disguise this dallying play as profound calculation. He affirms both of two contradictory things, at once spontaneously, because he is irresolute, and systematically, to cover up his trail. He makes dangerous mixtures of irreconcilable elements; and so nobody knows what he thinks, but it's because he thinks nothing definite, except, sometimes, about his immediate interest. How long will he believe it is in his immediate interest to spare Don Pedro and you?

INES. I am overwhelmed. But do at least realize that I am grateful. . . . That it should be you!

THE INFANTA. There are two forms of glory: divine glory, which consists in God's being satisfied with you, and human glory, which consists in being satisfied with yourself. By saving you I win both glories. And especially the second, for nature would, if anything, command me to hate you. But I attach little importance to nature.

INES. True, madame, for in your place——

THE INFANTA. You forget yourself, Doña Ines. Nobody can put herself in my place.

INES. Forgive me, Infanta. It is true, your rank——

THE INFANTA. Where I am, there is no rank. Doña Ines, I let you off your politenesses: you are not very happy at them. But what of that? You are charming as you are. Let me tell you that I have never been jealous of you. I was not even curious to know you, so indifferent is Don Pedro to me. People kept telling me: "She is beautiful," but I thought: "I am great. And the beautiful can never equal the great." Then they told me: "She is full of gentleness for everyone," and those words pleased me. I translated them into my language as: she is the friend of all the gentle things of the earth. They gave me this instance: that, for years, you let your hair be done in the worst possible way by your hairdresser in order not to give him pain by dismissing him.

[INES *puts her hand up to her hair.*]

No, no, your hair is not so bad. You have your hair done by the hands of Charity; it is marvelous.

INES. It's because my hair sometimes needs to be given a rest. So for a whole day I wear it in a chignon. Only afterward it won't come straight. . . .

THE INFANTA. Your hair is very nice, I assure you; stop worrying about it. Finally, I heard that for twenty-four

years you had lived in Spain: after that I was no longer
astonished at your merit. Also that you were a natural
child: and that pleased me. And so I wanted to see you,
and I gave orders to one of my ladies-in-waiting, the
Marchioness of Tordesillas, to place herself near you at
Mass, at Santa Clara, and not to leave you, so that I
might recognize you. But as those ladies got up and
changed places on the slightest occasion, the better to exchange their gossip, that and the uniformity of their clothes
and the darkness of the church made me in the end lose
sight of you. So I had the Marchioness recalled, and in-
structed her to tear your cloak a little——

INES. What, Your Highness, it was you!

THE INFANTA. It was. The opening the tear made was at
your neck. I followed you by that little pale patch moving
in the half-light. I looked at you for a long while, Doña
Ines. And I saw that Don Pedro was right to love you.

INES. If you knew him better, you would know that I am a
thousand times more right to love him.

THE INFANTA. I believe you, to please you. And do you know
whom I shall find, at my return, on her knees? The
Marchioness of Tordesillas, I'm sure, praying that our
meeting may have turned out to your good. Come, Doña
Ines, grant the good Marchioness's prayers. Tell me that
you'll accompany me into Navarre.

INES. No, Princess, I cannot.

THE INFANTA. Why?

INES. When the bird of noble breed is captured, it doesn't
resist. You spoke of a cloud in the shape of a wing. If I
had a wing, it would not be for flying away, but for pro-
tecting.

THE INFANTA. I know, being noble is dearly paid for. But you
are not "captured." You may have only one night before
you: at least you have it.

INES. No! No! I cannot exist anywhere but at his side! In
whatever state, however wretched, provided I don't leave
him. And, if necessary, to die with him or for him.

THE INFANTA. There is no human being worth dying for.

INES. A man one loves!

THE INFANTA. I have not yet come to understand how one
can love a man. Those whom I have come near I have seen,
almost all, coarse, and all cowardly. Cowardice: that's the
word that's brought into my mind irresistibly by men.

INES. Have you never, then, been in love, Infanta?

THE INFANTA. Never, by the grace of God.

INES. But you must have been loved?

THE INFANTA. If a man had been so ridiculous as to love me, I should have paid so little attention to it that I should have no recollection of it. [*With bluntness and candor.*] You hear the sparrows? They are singing my praises. Oh, don't think me proud: I have no pride, not an ounce. But to love being praised, one doesn't need to think oneself worthy of it. Now, Ines, come with me! I offer you your life. The breath of kings is fiery. It will consume you.

INES. It consumes what will be consumed anyway. I was not made to struggle, but to love. As a little child, when the formation of my breasts was not yet visible, I was already full of love for my dolls; and there was always one of them I called the Lover, and the other the Beloved. And already, if my bosom had been opened up, love would have flowed from it, like that sort of milk which flows from certain plants when you break their stems. To love —I don't know how to do anything else. Look at that waterfall: it doesn't struggle, it follows its course. One must let the waters fall.

THE INFANTA. The cascade does not fall: it hurls itself headlong. It also works mills. Water is guided in channels. The oar beats it, the prow cuts it. Everywhere I see it suffer violence. Oh, how soft you are!

INES. It's when the fruit is rather soft that it receives right into its heart all the rays of Creation.

THE INFANTA. Please don't sing me the praises of softness: you wound me personally. Come to Spain instead: there you will recover vigor. Don't try to deny it: I know that Spain is not much liked here. Portugal is a woman stretched out by the side of Spain; but Spain, which stays none the less apart and burns alone and is mad, prevents Portugal from sleeping. If I had married Don Pedro, I should have been the man: I should have prevented him from sleeping.

INES. Highness, since the King, you say, cannot but do what you ask, I beg of you, before you go, obtain pardon for Don Pedro!

THE INFANTA. It is not Don Pedro, it's you I want to save. Come to Pampeluna. Pampeluna is like the inner courtyard of a citadel, shut in between high mountains; and around it there is my soul, going from height to height,

watching, and not allowing. . . . The King's hand will be
powerless to reach you, over those mountains. Come to
Pampeluna, even if my court has no attractions for you.
The sensation of being in security would give some charm to
any place, and you will recover your soul with your security.

INES. He is my soul.

THE INFANTA. You are soft, and at the same time too courageous.

INES. Don't tell me I have courage: I should lose it at once.

THE INFANTA. There, where your breasts rise, in the down
between your breasts, one of your eyelashes has fallen. It
lies there like the feather of a swallow wounded in flight;
it moves a little, one would think it was alive. The swallow
is wounded, Doña Ines. How many times more will it
fly if it does not find shelter? One day it will no longer be
there to announce the spring, one day there will be no
more spring for it on earth. Give me ground for believing
I can still find the words to convince you. To think that
you will have eluded me! And I, to be the Infanta of
Navarre and fail to convince! And fail to convince the
person to whom one wishes so much good! How is it that
the good you wish a person does not shine out on your
face and does not pass into the tone of your voice, so that
there could be no mistaking it? But no, on the contrary,
it's perhaps my face that frightens you. Perhaps new faces
frighten you? Or is it perhaps that mine is covered with
sweat? Or have I perhaps said too much? When one wants
to convince, and when one has passed the point where it
was still possible, all that one says in addition merely
makes one suspect and hardens the person one wants to
convince. You must be thinking: "Why is she so keen on
it? Mustn't there be a trap?" . . . O door, door! What word
is there to open you? I'll stop, for my mouth is dried up.
[*Pause.*] I see, you are looking at the foam at the corners
of my mouth. It comes from my mouth's dryness, and
from the burning glare of that road, which was pale like a
lion. All the inside of me is dried up as if I had had driven
down my throat, to the hilt, the fiery sword of the nocturnal angel; you know, when the voices from the wall
cried yet again: "Sennacherib!" Ah, the senselessness of it,
that a violent desire should not suffice to shake down from

the tree the thing one desires. For the last time, Ines: are you coming with me?

INES. Princess, do not blame me: I can't.

THE INFANTA. Very well, so be it! You have let pass the moment when I loved you. Now you annoy me. Why should your life matter to me, when it does not matter to you?

INES. I, madame, I annoy you?

THE INFANTA. You disappoint me. Well, go and die, Doña Ines. Go and die quickly, as quickly as possible now. Let your face not have the time to imprint itself in me. Let it be washed away, and may I be able to forget it—washed away like a stain of blood on the flagstones, which is washed away with water. I should have liked the whole of my stay in Portugal to vanish like a bad dream, but that is no longer possible, because of you. You alone are poisoning the sweet honey of my forgetfulness, as it is written of the fly in the ointment in our Holy Scriptures. Go, Doña Ines, God be with you. Is it not fine that, whatever happens, and even if one has sinned, one can always say to oneself: "God be with me"? Look up at the heavens, where He is who will protect you.

INES. God will protect me if I am worthy of it. But why look up at the heavens? Looking up at the heavens always brings me back to the earth, for it is on earth that I have experienced those divine things that I know. Our passions are the Lord's angels.

THE INFANTA. Then, my dear, if you will not look up at the heavens, turn right away in the direction of hell. Try to win the page, who belongs to hell, and to find out through him the King's intentions. His name is Dino del Moro. He is Andalusian. The Andalusians are not reliable. He will betray anything one wishes.

INES. I think I should never have the heart to tempt a child into betraying.

THE INFANTA. Even if your life and the life of Don Pedro are at stake?

INES. Pedro! . . . But, all the same, a child! A child—like what, one day, a son of mine might be. . . .

THE INFANTA. Very well, Doña Ines, be sublime, then, since that is decidedly what attracts you. Sublime by refusing to leave. Sublime by refusing to tempt into betrayal. All right, take your fill of being sublime, and die of it. Good-by.

[INES *bows, takes the* INFANTA'S *hand, and is about to kiss it. The* INFANTA'S *jeweled bracelet comes undone and falls to the ground.* INES *picks it up and holds it out to her.*]

Keep it, Ines. In our country a princess of the royal blood may accept nothing that is not offered to her by someone of her house. This bracelet which clasps so badly will remain to you as a symbol of our own failure to clasp.

INES. If it is a symbol, there are things so much purer than the diamond——

THE INFANTA. That's true. [*She throws the bracelet to the ground and crushes it with her heel. A pause.*] Embrace me.

[*They embrace.*]

God keep you! [*Left alone, gazing at the waterfall in the distance.*] One must let the waters fall. . . .

ACT THREE

Scene 1

[A hall in the royal palace. It is almost in darkness. Only the part near the hearth, on which a fire is burning, is lit by a few clusters of candles.]

[FERRANTE, INES, *later* A PAGE.]

FERRANTE. The smells that rise from the sea have a savor less bitter than the smell breathed out by the heart of a man of sixty. I don't know why men of that age pretend that they're going to live forever. I don't deceive myself. Soon death will be pressing his black helmet well down over my head. Indeed, I've been dying for a long time; it's simply a question of finishing it off.

INES. Always, my lord, always that somber presentiment!

FERRANTE. I have my visitations. At night above all: night is mother of all things, and even of appalling gleams. At the deepest hour of night, deep as the deepest place in the hollow of a wave, as I lie there in the dust of pride. My hands are paralyzed and cold as if in death; a long moment is needed, when I wake, before the blood comes back to them and they unstiffen. I lie there in the position of those recumbent stone figures on tombs, but without having, like them, to warm me, my feet on a greyhound or on a little pageboy. At those moments, often, my heart stops beating. . . . When it starts again, I am quite surprised to find myself alive—and a little bit put out.

INES. But your doctors——

FERRANTE. I speak of my illness to nobody, and the world believes I'm going to live a thousand years. Besides, doctors—— It is a sin to want to change the time that God

[363]

has chosen. All the same, you are perhaps right, and one can lay it down as a general axiom that it is better to be assassinated by one's doctor than by one's son. [*Pause.*] Last night—perhaps because of an extreme sadness that came upon me yesterday—I dreamed that I was in the death agony. No physical suffering, and absolutely lucidity. There was surely someone present, for I was pointing out to him that I was getting weaker moment by moment. And, moment by moment, reddish marblings kept appearing on my skin. I kept writing on my skin, and it was so rotted that in places the pen burst it.

INES. And what did you write?

FERRANTE. I kept writing: "Much better and much worse. . . ." For I have been better and worse than the world can know. Then dawn showed through the curtains and the casements of my room, and those long lines of whiteness seemed to be great funeral candles surrounding me. Every night, or nearly, abysses like that open for me. Then, at those hours, I see. . . . I see all that I have done and undone, I, King of Portugal, conqueror of the Moors, victor of the Indies, terror of rebels, Ferrante the Magnanimous, miserable sinner. And I see that of all I have done and undone, during more than a quarter of a century, nothing will remain, for it will all be overturned, and perhaps very quickly, by the hazarding hands of time; nothing will remain but a portrait, among a dozen others, in the Armeria at Coimbra, the portrait of a man of whom the people who will come after will be unable to cite a single act, and about whom all they will think, as they look at that portrait, will be: "That one has a longer nose than the others."

INES. My lord, the glory of great men is like shadows: it lengthens as they set.

FERRANTE. Ah, don't talk of my glory. If you knew how far away from myself I am. And the fetid breath of admiration. . . . And besides, I am not a king of glory, I am a king of sorrow. On the standard of Portugal I have increased the number of the signs that represent the wounds of Christ. It is a king of sorrow that brings you that great belling of a stag in the forest. But I don't have to withdraw, before dying, into forests or onto a mountain, for I am my own forest and my own mountain. My network of souls is the undergrowth of the forest, and I have had, being king, to make of my own thinking a high place and a mountain.

A PAGE [*entering*]. Sire, Don Alvar Gonçalves insists that Your Majesty deign to receive him at once.

FERRANTE. I have to see him tomorrow morning. . . .

THE PAGE. He says his message is extremely urgent.

FERRANTE. Tell him that I'll see him tomorrow.

[THE PAGE *goes out.*]

[*To* INES.] But perhaps you would have liked to make the acquaintance of a man who is asking me to have you assassinated.

INES. Sire!

FERRANTE. To see your faces, the two of you, would, one must admit, have been diverting. [*To the* PAGE, *who has just come back.*] Again!

THE PAGE. A note from Don Alvar.

FERRANTE [*having read it, with changed face*]. Terrible! Terrible! Terrible! Have Don Alvar brought to my private room. I'll join him there. [*To* INES.] Doña Ines, wait for me here for a moment. [*To the* PAGE.] After that you will make up the fire. It's going out. [*He goes, in the direction of his private room.*]

Scene 2

[INES, DINO DEL MORO.]

INES [*aside*]. So the page told the truth: they want my death.

[*The* PAGE *comes in again, accompanied by* DINO DEL MORO. *They set about poking the fire.*]

God! It's he! If I could get him alone! Speak to him—win him—know, from now on, through him——

[*Dumb show. The first* PAGE *goes out for a moment.* INES *draws near to* DINO. *The first* PAGE *comes back. At last he goes.*]

[*Embarrassed.*] I know your name is Dino del Moro.

DINO DEL MORO. At your service, my lady. Although—that's
only a nickname. My father is Fernando de Calla Fuente,
Marquis of Duero. He is Governor of the Genil province.
But they call him Fernando del Moro because, when he
found out that his steward, a Moor who had abjured, was
going on with the pagan practices, he stabbed him with
his own hand. My father has the strength of two horses.

INES. Bravo! Was it long ago that you left Andalusia?

DINO DEL MORO. A year. You don't know the Genil? It's the
biggest river in Europe. They say its source is in paradise.

INES. Like the rivers of Navarre, I suppose. And—doesn't
it depress you, living separated from your parents?

DINO DEL MORO. Oh, no!

INES. What a cry from the heart! Someone's been speaking
to me about you, Dino del Moro.

DINO DEL MORO. Ah, the Infanta!

INES. So—you listen at the King's keyhole?

DINO DEL MORO. I wasn't listening, my lady. A few words I
caught in passing——

INES. No, no, you were listening. Your whole face proclaims
it. Oh, if you could only see it! You're just as physically
incapable of hiding the confession in your face as you are
of lifting up a chest in your arms. [*Aside.*] How can I
ask him? I don't know what to say to him. . . . [*Aloud.*]
So you are aware that there are men here who wish me
evil, great evil. It is very important for me——

[*Loud voices are heard, coming from the* KING'S *private
room.*]

DINO DEL MORO. Sh! The King! Say something to me, anything.

INES [*in a loud, affected voice, and pointing at a sprig of
jasmine the page is wearing in a buttonhole of his doublet*].
That jasmine, page—— The other day, too, you were wearing a carnation. So you like flowers so much?

DINO DEL MORO. When I was small, my mother liked me always to wear a flower.

INES. When you were small! . . . And those gold and silver
threads twined in your hair——

DINO DEL MORO. That too was my mother—she used to twine
them like this for me when I was small. She used to say it
was to bring me luck.

INES. But now, so far away from your mother——

DINO DEL MORO. Now I put them there myself.

INES [*aside*]. How strange he is! [*To* DINO.] Your
mother—— [*Aside*.] This conspiracy with this child—And
his mother. . . . No, it's impossible! I can't. [*To* DINO.]
Dino del Moro, why do you listen at your King's keyhole?
That's work for valets, not for the son of Fernando del
Moro.

DINO DEL MORO. The King isn't fond of me. Why should I
be fond of him?

INES. He isn't fond of you?

DINO DEL MORO. He never stops laughing at me. Yes, all the
time! About my hair, about my accent. He can't say a
word to me without laughing at me.

INES. If he makes fun of you, it is because he is fond of you,
don't you see? The cat always leaves his mark on his
friend.

DINO DEL MORO. At night—because I'm the best dancer of
all the pages—I'm the one who leaps up and catches the
fireflies and I bring them to him in the hollow of my hand.
Well, he isn't a bit grateful.

INES. That's certainly a most important charge you've got
against him. But is the King, then, so fond of fireflies?

DINO DEL MORO. He says they are like him: by turns dark
and luminous, luminous and dark. I—when he told me
they were like him, I told him they were nasty creatures.

INES. If you say disagreeable things to the King, don't be
surprised if he's a little annoyed with you. But even if he
were annoyed with you, that would be no reason for cheat-
ing him.

DINO DEL MORO. Everybody cheats him here.

INES. That's just why *you* mustn't do so. If you don't like
serving him, ask your parents to call you home, on some
pretext or other. Don't stay with someone who puts trust
in you, only to betray him. You who are so small! How
old are you?

DINO DEL MORO. Thirteen.

INES. Thirteen, you say. Then you must be twelve, for you
have to pretend to be big. Twelve! You're a little man, already with your full power of doing evil. No, don't go on
like that. I tell you as your mother would. [*Tidying his
hair*.] The gold threads in your hair mustn't be there

simply to bring you luck, they should also remind you that you must be pure like them.

DINO DEL MORO. But, my lady, wasn't I very useful to you when I repeated to the Infanta's messenger——

INES. That's true! That's true! And yet—don't go on!

DINO DEL MORO. The King! [*He rushes out.*]

Scene 3

[FERRANTE, ALVAR GONÇALVES, INES.]

FERRANTE. Putting up with things! Always putting up with things! Oh, that wears one out. To be without cease in the hands of other men! To have reigned nearly thirty-five years, and still bound hand and foot.—— Doña Ines, Don Alvar Gonçalves who often enlightens me with his counsels. But perhaps you know him already?

ALVAR GONÇALVES. If I had met Doña Ines, I could not have forgotten it.

INES. And I, Don Alvar, if I have met you, I have forgotten it. But rest assured that I shall not forget this meeting.

ALVAR GONÇALVES. I beg you, madame, to keep me in your good graces.

INES. For just as long as you keep me in yours.

FERRANTE [*to* ALVAR]. Come back and see me tomorrow morning. But with no illusions. For there is nothing to be done, nothing, nothing!

Scene 4

[FERRANTE, INES.]

FERRANTE. If you have remained free, if Don Pedro has been allowed back to his apartments in the palace and only kept under house arrest, that was because I thought I held the Bishop of Guarda. And now he's escaping me. The Nuncio sends me word by Don Alvar that the Pope would take it as an outrage if I let myself go against the Bishop. According to him, the Bishop, in joining you to Don Pedro, was only obeying the Prince, as was his duty; above all, he is covered by ecclesiastical immunity. Not only must I spare the Bishop, but the Nuncio even desires that he be set at liberty. It is of little consequence to me now that Don Pedro, so you tell me, has again put off promising to marry the Infanta if the Pope were to grant the annulment. The Pope will not grant it: at present that is certain. I am like a lion that's fallen into a trap. I can bite, leap, roar—in vain. You are bound to Don Pedro, and this bond can be broken only by the Pope's dying and being succeeded by someone differently disposed toward me. Oh, I am tired of this situation. I wish it would take some other form. Normally I find that great affairs are settled easily and quickly, while the small ones are interminably drawn out with a thousand hitches. This one is great and full of hitches. And I am tired of you, of the fact that you exist. Tired of wishing you well, tired of wishing to save you. Ah, why do you exist? The infuriating obstacle that human beings are! A river, a mountain, one understands, one accepts. But a poor soft thing of flesh and nerves, that stands up one can't think how—— Well, everything I have done is destroyed. I have been scooping with a sieve. And, true enough, why should what I've done go on existing, since I have long ceased to exist? The bow of my intelligence has come unstrung. I look at what I have written, and ask: "Who wrote that?" I think of what I had understood, and I've ceased to understand it. And what I have learned I have forgotten. I am dying and it seems to me that all remains to be done, that I am at the same point where I was at twenty. My hands are open, everything has fled me. I've been playing the flute for the love of God?

INES. Isn't that our common fate?

FERRANTE. Happy the man who has given little and has taken back what he has given. Happy the man whose children do not bear his name.

INES. Happy the man who heard those words and over whom they flow without affecting him!

FERRANTE. I have flowed away like the wind of the desert, which begins by chasing before it waves of sand like a cavalry charge and ends by being diluted and exhausted: nothing is left of it. Such are the deep thoughts that King Ferrante imparts to you, thoughts of which, deep as they are, he does not guarantee the originality. For I heard one day, as I was passing down a passage near a kitchen, a spoiler of sauces proclaiming with emphatic gestures: "The final somersault, they'll all have to come to it, yes, all! The King like the rest of them!" And I thought it right that at the end of my philosophy I should find a kitchen varlet. We were coming together even sooner than he said.

Scene 5

[*The same*, THE GRAND ADMIRAL AND THE PRINCE OF THE SEA, EGAS COELHO, TWO OTHERS, VARIOUS LORDS.]

THE PRINCE OF THE SEA. My lord, the gravity of the thing obliges me to force a way through your guards. An odious insult has been offered to Your Majesty, and its reparation requires immediate orders. A party of Moors has landed at Tavira, massacred some of the harbor people, and crucified the captain who hurled some men against them, by the side of a dog's crucified carcass. They have re-embarked almost without loss. The insolence of those wretches calls for exemplary punishment. They keep their enterprises for Your Majesty alone. Do you think they'd have dared attack a port belonging to Andalusia or Valencia? Never!

FERRANTE. There was nobody, then, guarding the sea along the south coast?

THE PRINCE. As the result of a most grave negligence, the fleet commanded by Don Lourenço Payva was at that moment all cruising north of Cape St. Vincent.

FERRANTE. Yes, that's the way, there are always certain hours during which a realm is without defense: a hole, you need only go in. And in the same way there are always certain hours when a man is so weak, morally and physically—quite astonished to be still standing—that a little push and you would make him fall over. Luckily, it is rare for the enemy to smell out those hours. Ah, if he knew!

THE PRINCE. It's above all at those hours that it's important to look determined. I request an implacable punishment for Lourenço Payva.

FERRANTE. What punishment?

THE PRINCE. In normal times I should have requested a heavy term of prison. At this moment I request death.

FERRANTE. Why be more severe at this moment?

THE PRINCE. Because at this moment we have need of guilty men.

FERRANTE. I have observed that putting to death is nearly always done too soon. A day or two later and the person put to death wasn't any longer so guilty. How many assassinations are misunderstandings!

EGAS COELHO. In that case, Sire, one would never again put anyone to death!

FERRANTE. Isn't Payva an old and faithful servant?

EGAS COELHO. Sire, I was expecting your royal anger, and I am dumfounded——

FERRANTE. When one grows old, fits of anger turn into fits of sadness.

EGAS COELHO. Or of pity. And to arrive at pity one has only to let oneself slide, but to arrive at firmness one has to raise oneself up. Well, one should always be raising oneself up.

THE PRINCE. Is the King the man to forgive an insult?

FERRANTE. Yes, when forgiveness is to his advantage. No doubt that is not the case here. The fate of Don Lourenço shall be considered. Let it be brought up again.

THE PRINCE. So then that man has a chance of going scot-free! Sire, let's make an end: allow me to go and seek death in Africa, that death from which traitors are spared. Dead, I shall no longer witness their impunity.

FERRANTE. Don't flare up so.

EGAS COELHO [under his breath, to the LORDS]. Ines's face is calm. I don't like these conversations she has with the King. She comes out from them fortified. Let us stay in the shadows for a while and listen to what they say.

FERRANTE. Very well! Let Don Lourenço be brought before my privy justice. I shall not be lenient.

EGAS COELHO. O King, you are yourself again!

THE PRINCE. And shall we not set on foot, at once, something against the Moors?

FERRANTE. That I shall consider later. [Heavily.] I have made enough decisions for today. [Aside.] War. . . . Men who don't deserve to live. And ideas that don't deserve to be died for.

Scene 6

[FERRANTE, INES. *At the back in the shadows,* EGAS COELHO *and the* LORDS, *later* MORE PEOPLE.]

INES. Are you going to have him put to death?

FERRANTE. I am inclining that way. There are those who say that an old man should be severe, because he hasn't much time. And again, that cruelty is the only pleasure left to an old man, that for him it takes the place of love. In my view, that is going too far. But I could easily believe that one of the best guarantees of long life lies in being insensitive and implacable; there you have a buckler against death.

INES. If you were really so wicked, you wouldn't say so.

FERRANTE [*ironically*]. I see you have a profound knowledge of the human soul.

INES. But if Lourenço Payva were only half guilty, what remorse you would be laying up for yourself!

FERRANTE. Remorse dies, like everything else. And in some cases the remembrance of it is balm. But perhaps the whole of this business will blow over like smoke. For do you know what I think? That it has been invented, lock, stock, and barrel, or at any rate appreciably magnified.

INES. Invented?

FERRANTE. The idea is to humiliate me, on top of the humiliation I had from the Nuncio—all too well founded, that one. "The Moors would never dare make a landing in Andalusia or in the kingdom of Valencia." It is reckoned that, being wounded, I shall want to wound; then, having played the mouse once, to avenge myself I shall play the tomcat next time. And tomcat against whom? Against Pedro and you. But their childish calculations have not come off. I can see too clearly through their machinations.

INES. You are generous toward us, my lord.—— So if it's made up, Lourenço Payva will not be executed?

FERRANTE. Upon my soul, it might be a good opportunity.

INES. A good opportunity! But execute him? Why?

FERRANTE. The Grand Admiral said it: we have need of guilty men at this moment. Well, Lourenço Payva is certainly guilty of something. Everyone is guilty of something. All those who are at liberty owe me more than they realize. So do all those who are alive. But from time to time I must say no and let fly, more or less at a venture: simply to regain control. Yes, one must go on sacrificing the lives of human beings, even when one has stopped taking their guilt seriously, just like that empty suit of armor in the legend, which was drawn up against the wall and used to hit on the head anyone passing under its iron gauntlet. Or again I'm thinking of that story of our King Enrique IV of Castile, to whom a certain Sultan was bound to give up the city of Trujillo, which he was occupying, at the King's death. And so the King's men, fearing that the Sultan would decide to defend the city if he heard the news of the death, set up the King's corpse on a throne, lower the lights in the hall—heavens, yes, just as in this hall now—and the Sultan's envoys give up the keys of the city to the dead King. I too have withdrawn myself and my whole soul from my appearance of royalty; but this appearance still receives the honors like the corpse of King Enrique or even still deals death, and deals death almost at a venture, like the empty suit of armor.

EGAS COELHO [*aside*]. The King's delirious. That sorceress is bewitching him. His awakening will be terrible. He'll drive into the silence from which there's no return those who have surprised his secret. He'll have the sorceress put to death. Me too, if he finds me here. [*He makes his escape.*]

INES. Can one put someone to death for a thing one doesn't believe?

FERRANTE. Of course, that is regular. And even die for a thing one doesn't believe. People die for causes in which they don't believe, just as they die for passions they don't feel, and for persons they don't love. The Moors I saw in Africa worshipped stones and springs. But let 'em be told that Islam was menaced, and they would arise and go and perish in battle for a religion that was not theirs. In our country, during the rebels' war, there were so many corpses heaped up all along the Mondego road that from here you couldn't see a horseman passing down the road. Well, the greater part of those men had been civilians, and the rebels had killed them simply because they lived on land where the loyal troops still held out; they were supposed to have loyalist convictions because they lived on one side

of the river; if they had lived on the other side, it would
have been my soldiers that would have fired on them, as
rebels.

INES. How can the King have so deserted his own colors, the
King who a few days ago led me to the window and said
to me: "It's I who uphold all that. Behold the people with
whom I have a treaty"?

FERRANTE. Ines, this night is full of prodigies. I feel that in
it I am going beyond myself, that in it I am taking up my
largest measure, the measure I shall have in my tomb,
and that this night is made for me to say in it things
that are frightening in their purity. When I said to you:
"There is my people . . ." I wasn't lying, but I was saying
words of habit, in which I had believed once, in which I
no longer believed altogether at the moment when I was
saying them. I was like an old hen laying empty eggshells.

INES. My lord!

FERRANTE. Do not be surprised. I like to confess to women.
It's a taste I have.

THE PRINCE OF THE SEA. Let's not stay here! [He makes his
escape.]

FERRANTE. I have also to try to make people believe that I
still feel something, when in fact I no longer feel anything.
The world no longer does more than brush against me.
And that is just, for I perceive that all my life I have
done no more than brush against the world.

INES. You no longer feel anything!

FERRANTE. There are the words one says and the acts one
performs, without believing in them. There are the errors
one commits, knowing they are errors. And there is even
the obsession with what one doesn't desire.

ONE OF THE LORDS. It's the drunkenness of Noah! [He makes
his escape.]

[During the following dialogue, up to the departure of the
shade of the INFANTA, shades appear in the darkness at the
back of the room, listen for a moment, then disappear with
horrified gestures.]

FERRANTE. Just now I lamented in front of you like a beast;
I cried out like the wind. Do you think that that can possibly fit in with faith in the kingly function? To play the
king, one needs faith, courage, and strength. Courage I

have. Strength God gives me. But faith neither God nor I can give me. I'm prisoner of what I have been. One of the Infanta's ladies-in-waiting was saying in my presence that the Infanta was always crucified upon herself. I too, in a different sense, am crucified upon myself, upon duties that for me no longer have reality. I'm no longer inside my armor of iron. But where am I?

INES. Certainly, I understand you, Sire, for duties of State they're beyond me! So is the future of Christendom! Christendom is within us. But why, then, do you hold against Don Pedro an indifference that is your own also?

FERRANTE. I have reached the age of indifference. Pedro has not. What's one to do with one's life if one doesn't busy oneself with those sorts of things?

INES. Love. I should like to bury myself in the deepest retreat of mutual and lawful love, as in a tomb, and then let all cease, let all cease.—— But if you no longer believe in the affairs of the kingdom, there are the acts that a king can do for his people and that are simply from man to man. There is in your kingdom that great poverty, that disease of hunger which is continually in need of healing. At Lisbon, on the quay where one lands, I've seen the captains of your army, my lord. They were standing up, their backs to the wall, they had their hands joined as if in prayer, and they were following with their eyes those who were landing, without moving and without saying anything. And their hands were in fact joined for a prayer, for they were asking for alms. These were your war leaders, Sire, and they had not had their pay. And I, if I'd been the King, I should have wanted to go and unknot their hands myself and say to them: "Never more shall you feel hunger." And since that day it has seemed to me that, from now on, it is all very well for me to eat and to eat my fill, I shall always be hungry as long as they are not satisfied.

FERRANTE. People are glad enough to ask the heads of states for charity. People ought also to have a little charity for them. When one thinks of the temptations of absolute power, resistance to them calls for respect. As for your captains, if I were younger I should say that there was a disease to heal, far worse than their bodies' danger, and that is the disease of their immortal soul, which without cease hungers after sin. But at my age one had lost the taste for looking after other people. Nothing's left today but an immense: "What does it matter to me!" which for me covers the world. . . . I should like now to look after nobody but myself, at so few days' distance from appearing before God: to stop lying to others and lying to myself, and to deserve at last the respect that is given to me, after having for so long usurped it.

THE SHADE OF THE INFANTA [*at the back of the hall*]. Ines!

INES. Who is calling me?

THE SHADE. Someone who wishes you well. Leave this hall immediately. Stop listening to the King. He is throwing into you his despairing secrets, as into a tomb. Later he will slide back upon you the tombstone that you may never speak.

INES. I shall not leave the person who has said to me: "I am a king of sorrow." At that moment he was not lying. And I am not afraid of him.

THE SHADE. How you do woo your death! How you will have wooed it! Ines, Ines, remember: kings have lions in their hearts. . . . Remember: the mark of the necklace on your neck. . . .

INES. Oh, now I recognize you!

THE SHADE. You have never recognized me. Ines, Ines, as soon as I was out at sea, I found the words I ought to have used to convince you. Already all full of the open spaces, already my soul was beating back against the wind toward you. And a few moments from now, when it'll be too late, I shall find what I should have been saying to you now. Ah! it is frightful not to know how to convince.

INES. She repeats forever the same cry, like the Malurus bird, at the fall of evening, above the melancholy of the lakes.

THE SHADE. Ines, for the last time, get away from here.——— No? You will not? Very well! You too, in your turn, shall fail to convince. [*It disappears.*]

FERRANTE [*his back turned to the shades*]. Do they imagine I don't hear them as they whisper and make their escape? They say that I'm delirious because I tell the truth. And they believe they are escaping out of fear of my reprisals, where they are escaping out of fear and horror of the truth. The noise of the truth alarms them like a leper's rattle.

INES. O my King, I shall not desert you because you tell the

truth, but on the contrary I too shall tell you at last the
whole truth, which I have kept back a little till now. O my
king, since this night is full of great things, let me at last
confess it: a child of your blood is forming in me.

FERRANTE. A child! Another child! So the thing will never
have an end!

INES. And what does it matter to you if he troubles your
plans, since you have just cried aloud that you no longer
believe in the kingly function! This is where we are going
to see if you were really being truthful.

FERRANTE. Another spring to begin all over again, and to
begin again less well!

INES. I, who so much love being loved, shall myself have
created a human being, and it will depend entirely on me
whether I can win his love! How I long to give him an
idea of his mother that will keep him safe from everything
all his life! One will have to be even stricter toward oneself, to guard oneself from every baseness, to live upright,
firm, clear and pure, so that a human being may later
retain of one the fairest possible image, tenderly and without any reproach. He is a revised version, or rather a
second creation, of me; in making him I am making myself anew. I carry him in me and he carries me. I melt
into him. I pour into his mould my wealth. I desire with
passion that he may be like me in what is best of me.

FERRANTE. And the reproach he will bring against you is
precisely that: that you wanted him to take after you.
Come, I know all that.

INES. If he does not think as I do, he will be a stranger to
me, he who is me. No, no. He is the dream of my blood.
My blood cannot deceive me.

FERRANTE. The dream. . . . You say better than you know.
You are simply dreaming.

INES. Is it mere dream, this flesh that I have created out of
mine? Oh, it is heady and immense.

FERRANTE. Really one would think you were the first woman
to give birth.

INES. I believe every woman who is having a child for the
first time is in fact the first woman to give birth.

FERRANTE. I dislike naïveté. I hate vice and crime. But if I
have to choose between them and naïveté, I believe I
prefer vice and crime.

INES. It's as if I can see him, five or six years from now.

Look, he's just passed us, running along the terrace.
Running, but at the same time his head is turned toward
us. My little boy.

FERRANTE. One day, as he passes, he will no longer turn his
head. But who told you it was a boy? The Astrologer?

INES. I want it too much to be so.

FERRANTE. I understand that a second Pedro must really be
an intoxicating prospect.

INES. Yes, intoxicating. We shall call him Dionis. My little
boy with the improbable eyelashes, handsome and coarse
at the same time, as boys are. Asking to be fought with,
to be danced with, not letting himself be touched. An
excess of pleasure makes him sigh. And if he isn't handsome, I'll love him even more, to console him and to ask
his forgiveness for having wished him other than he is.

FERRANTE. I have known all that. How he used to kiss, that
little one! We called him Pedrito (but sometimes, if he was
asleep and someone whispered him his name, he would
say in his sleep: "Pedrito? Who's that?") His incomprehensible affection! If I teased him, if I made fun of him,
if I scolded him, he used to answer everything by throwing
himself on me and embracing me. And he used to look
at me long, close to, with an astonished expression. . . .

INES. Already!

FERRANTE. At first I was embarrassed. Later I accepted it. I
accepted his knowing what I am like. He used to get on
my nerves a little when he used to romp with me. But
when he no longer did that—— For he has become a man
—that is to say, the caricature of what he was. You too
will see the self-undoing of what was your child. To the
point where no more of him is left in you than there is
left of that sheet of paper on which for the first time,
when five years old, mine wrote his Christian name, that
sheet of paper which I preserved for years and finally tore
up and threw to the wind.

INES. But one day, perhaps, if you had kept it, you would
have wept on seeing it again.

FERRANTE. No, neither their delicate words nor their delicate ways save human beings at the hour of the great
settlings of accounts.

INES. I consent to being obliged to despise the whole world,
but not my son. I think I should be capable of killing
him if he did not answer to what I expect of him.

FERRANTE. Then kill him as soon as he comes out of you. Give him to the pigs to eat. For as surely as through him you are not rapt in dreams, you will through him be rapt in nightmare.

INES. Sire, it is sinful of you to curse this child, who is of your own blood.

FERRANTE. I like discouraging. And I do not like the future.

INES. The child who is going to be born has already his past.

FERRANTE. Nightmare for you. Nightmare for him too. One day people will tear him to pieces, people will speak ill of him. . . . Oh, I know all that.

INES. Is it possible for people to speak ill of my child?

FERRANTE. People will detest him——

INES. People will detest him, him who never asked to be born!

FERRANTE. He will suffer, he will weep——

INES. You have the art of finding the words that are made for destroying hope!—— How hold back his tears, take them upon me, make them flow in me? I can bear everything: I can suffer in his place, weep in his place. But he! Oh, how I wish my love had the power to put into his life an everlasting smile! Already, though, they're attacking it, this love of mine. They disapprove of me, they give me advice, they claim to be better mothers than I am. And here are you, Sire—not content with that!—upon this love of mine you have just cast anathema. Whereas it seemed to me sometimes that if men knew how much I love my child, perhaps that would be enough to make hatred dry up forever in their hearts. For I, ever since I've been carrying him in me, I've felt in myself a wonderful power of tenderness toward mankind. And he is the defense of that deep region of my being from which there springs all that I can give to creation and to God's creatures. His purity defends mine. His candor safeguards mine against those who would destroy it. You know against whom, my lord.

FERRANTE. His purity is only a moment of him, it is not himself. Women are always saying: "Why bring up a child to be killed in war!" But there is something still worse: to bring up a child that he may live and degrade himself in living. And you, Ines, you seem to have staked a singular amount on his living. Have you looked at yourself in a mirror? You are indeed fresh, for someone menaced by great suffering. You too are part of all those things that want to go on, to go on. . . . You too, like me, are ill: your illness is hope. You deserve that God should send you a terrible trial, ruin, once for all, that mad candor of yours, so that once at least you might see things as they are.

INES. My lord, it's no good, believe me, reminding me of all the things that threaten me. Whatever they may seem to be sometimes, I never forget them.

FERRANTE [aside]. I believe I love in her the pain I give her. [Aloud.] I am not threatening you, but I get impatient at seeing you start out afresh, all sails set, upon the inexhaustible and infinite sea of hope. Other people's faith depresses me. It takes children to believe like you in the void, without being depressing. Hope! Lourenço Payva too, at this moment, is full of hopes. And yet he's going to die, a sacrifice to the good of the State.

INES. Is it then decided?

FERRANTE. Yes, a moment ago it was decided.

INES. Die! And for the State! Your Majesty can still talk of the State!

FERRANTE. And why not? Ah! I see, you are thinking of how I said I did not believe in the State. I did say that, in fact. But I said also that I wished to act as if I did believe in it. Sometimes you forget, sometimes you remember too well, Doña Ines. I advise you not to remember too well the things I said during that sort of crisis of sincerity when those rascals were making their escape so as not to hear me.

INES. Perhaps I should have made my escape too.

FERRANTE. It's the fate of men who constrain themselves excessively that a day comes when nature snaps; they burst forth then and pour forth all at once what they have held back for years. From which it follows that, all in all, it's useless to be discreet.

INES. Sire, since Your Majesty from now on knows of the existence of my child——

FERRANTE. That's enough about that child. You've displayed your vitals before me, and you've gone looking for mine, which is tactless. You've made use of your future child to

stir my past child. You've thought it clever to make your
maternity known to me at this moment, and you have been
the reverse of clever.

INES. So Your Majesty is reproaching me with not having
been clever!

FERRANTE. Yes, I'm reproaching you with that.

INES. I have not "Thought it clever." I have talked to you
of your grandson at a moment when you were suffering,
when you were weak, not to profit from that weakness,
but because then you were telling the truth. I wanted also
to tell you the truth, and to give you back trust for trust. I
put trust in human nature in you, just as I have put trust
in it all my life. Let me have trust in you, Sire. Would
it not be a fine thing to be able to say to you: "O King
like a hand upon my forehead—" You never put trust in
man, you?

FERRANTE. I sometimes put trust in his fear.

INES. I've never been able to believe that man, save some
rare exceptions, could render misdeeds for generosity. You
are perhaps astonished, Sire, that I am not afraid of you.
But, at those times when one is doubtful of a person,
when one is tempted to be afraid of him—at those times
when people were putting me on my guard against you—I
kept saying to myself: "No, the father of the man I love,
to whom I've never wished or done anything but good,
will not do anything against me." And besides, if one
must be punished simply for having trusted too much, well,
it can't be helped: one is punished by men, but one isn't
before God. There, Sire, that's why I am not and cannot
be very much afraid of you, although I've long been
vaguely afraid *of something*.

FERRANTE. I see that you are very conscious of your generosity, and that you expect a reward for it. But enough
of that. Out of all you have said to me, I retain the fact
that you believe you have surprised me at a moment of
weakness. What a joy it doubtless is being able to tell yourself, as women do: "King though he is, he's just a poor
man like the others!" What a triumph for you! But I am
not weak, Doña Ines. It's a great mistake you are making,
you and one or two others. Now I must ask you to withdraw. For a good hour you've been circling around me,
like a butterfly around a flame. All women, I've noticed,

are obstinate circlers around the thing that's destined to
burn them.

INES. Are you going to burn me, Sire? Little as I am worth,
there are two human beings who have need of me. It's for
their sake that I must live.——— And besides, for my sake
too, oh yes, for my own sake!——— But—your face has
changed; you look ill at ease. . . .

FERRANTE. Excuse me, being alone with good people always
makes me rather awkward. Come, let's break off there,
and you go home to the Mondego reassured.

INES. Yes, you would never kill me before I'd embraced him
once more.

FERRANTE. My only fear for you is of the bandits on the
road, at this hour. Is your escort numerous?

INES. Four only.

FERRANTE. And armed?

INES. Barely. But the night is light and free of ambushes.
Look. It will be fine tomorrow: the sky is full of stars.

FERRANTE. All those worlds which have not had the Redemption. . . . Do you see the ladder?

INES. The ladder?

FERRANTE. The ladder that goes right up into the heavens.

INES. Jacob's ladder, you mean?

FERRANTE. No, not at all: the ladder from hell to heaven. I,
all my life I've done nothing but make that climb; all the
time going up and coming down, between hell and heaven.
For, with all my sins, I've none the less lived enveloped by
the hand of God. Another strange thing.

INES. Oh! There's a star that has gone out.

FERRANTE. It will light up again elsewhere.

Scene 7

[FERRANTE, *then* A GUARD, *then* CAPTAIN BATALHA.]

FERRANTE. Why am I killing her? There is doubtless a reason, but I cannot pick it out. Not only will Pedro not
marry the Infanta, but I am arming him against me, irre-
deemably. I'm adding yet another danger to this horrible
mantle of dangers which I drag about on me and after me,
always heavier, always more loaded, and I load myself at
will, and under its weight one day——— Ah! death, which

puts at last out of reach—— Why am I killing her? Useless action, fatal action. But my will is driving me before its wind, and I'm committing the error, knowing that it is one. Well, at least, let me get rid of this action straight-away. Remorse is better than prolonged hesitation. [*Calling.*] Page!—— Oh no! Not a page. Guard!

[*Enter* A GUARD.]

Call me Captain Batalha. [*Alone.*] The more I measure the injustice and atrocity of what I'm doing, the more deeply I plunge into it, because it gives me the more pleasure.

[*Enter* THE CAPTAIN.]

Captain, Doña Ines de Castro is leaving here and making for the Mondego, with four men of her own, ill armed. Take some men, catch up with her, and strike. It's cruel, but it's necessary. And take care not to bungle your business. People have all sorts of tricks for not dying. And do the thing at one blow. There are people it's wrong to kill at one blow—it's too quick. Her at one blow. On my soul, I want her not to suffer.

THE CAPTAIN. I've just seen the lady go past. From the look of her, she was a long way from imagining——

FERRANTE. I had reassured her forever.

THE CAPTAIN. Should I take with me a confessor?

FERRANTE. No point. Her soul is as smooth as her face.

[*The* CAPTAIN *makes to go.*]

Captain, take men who are reliable.

THE CAPTAIN [*pointing to his sword*]. This is reliable.

FERRANTE. Nothing can be too reliable when killing's to be done. Bring back the body and put it in the palace oratory. Painful as it may be, I shall have to see it myself. A person's never dead until one's seen the body dead with one's own eyes, and until one's touched it. Alas, I know all about that.

[*Exit* THE CAPTAIN.]

There would still be time for me to give a counter-order. But could I? What invisible gag is it stopping me from giving the shout that would save her? [*He goes and looks out of the window.*] It will be fine tomorrow: the sky is full of stars. . . . There would still be time.—— Still. Multitudes of acts, for year after year, are born of a single act, of a single instant. Why?—— Still. When she was looking out at the stars, her eyes were like calm lakes. . . . And to think people believe I'm weak! [*With sudden tenseness.*] Oh!—— Now it is too late. I have given her eternal life, and I—I shall be able to breathe.—— Guards! Bring lights! Tell everyone you can find in the palace to come in. Here, what are you waiting for? Lights! Lights! Nothing here has happened in the dark. Come in, gentlemen, come in!

Scene 8

[FERRANTE, PALACE PEOPLE, *of every condition,* EGAS COELHO *among them.*]

FERRANTE. Gentlemen, Doña Ines de Castro is no more. She informed me of the approaching birth of a bastard of the Prince. I have had her executed to preserve the purity of the succession to the throne and to end the trouble and the scandal she was causing in my realm. That is my final and weighty justice. Such a decision is not taken without pain. Beyond this unfortunate woman I have my kingdom, I have my people, I have my souls; I have the burden God has entrusted to me, and I have the contract I made with my peoples, when I consented to be king. A king is like a huge tree which must cast shade. . . . [*He passes his hand over his forehead and staggers.*] Oh! I think the saber of God has passed above my head. . . .

[*A seat is brought, and he is made to sit.*]

EGAS COELHO. My King!—— Quick, get a doctor!

FERRANTE. I've finished lying.

EGAS COELHO. Don't die, for heaven's sake! [*Aside.*] If Pedro's King, I'm lost.

FERRANTE. Now I'm no longer asking you for your secret. Mine is enough for me. I'm leaving you in peace.

EGAS COELHO. You're leaving me in hell. But no, you're not going to die, are you?

FERRANTE. In a moment I shall be dead, and my son's paw will have come down on you.

EGAS COELHO. Ines is perhaps not dead. A note, scribble a note. . . . I'll try and catch up with them on the road.

FERRANTE. She is dead. God has told me. And you, you're dead too.

EGAS COELHO. No! No! It's not possible!

FERRANTE. They'll tear your heart out of your breast and show it to you.

EGAS COELHO. No! No! No!

FERRANTE. Before breathing your last you shall see your own heart.

EGAS COELHO [*haggard*]. Who has told you?

FERRANTE. God has told me.

EGAS COELHO. Don't push me to despair.

FERRANTE. You don't know yet that at a pinch I can give way to someone who doesn't beseech me; never to one who beseeches me.

EGAS COELHO. Live! You must live!

FERRANTE. Draw away from me, Egas. Your breath's in my face. And I don't like it.

EGAS COELHO. Then let me escape. Live a little while! Only a little while! Long enough for me to escape. . . . [*To all present.*] Loving flesh and blood, my companions, you who will go on living, isn't there one of you that wants me to remain alive? [*Silence.*] So there's no one who wants me to live? [*Silence.*]

FERRANTE [*taking him by the wrist*]. Gentlemen, I do not know how the future will judge the execution of Doña Ines. Perhaps as a good thing, perhaps as a bad. However that may be, here is the man who, before everyone else, inspired it. See that he answers for it before the King my son.

[*Some of those present surround* EGAS COELHO.]

O my God! In this respite which is left me, before the saber passes again and strikes me down, make it cut this appalling knot of contradictions within me, so that, at least for one instant before ceasing to be, I may at last know what I am. [*He pulls* DINO DEL MORO *to him and holds him clasped against him.*] May the innocence of this child serve me for safeguard when I am about to appear before my Judge.—— Have no fear, and stay close to me, whatever happens—even if I die. . . . God shall requite you for it, God shall requite you for it, my little brother.

—— Much better and much worse.—— When I revive——
Oh, the saber! The saber!—— My God, have mercy on
me! [*He falls in a heap.*]

[*Extreme confusion. Various voices. The King is dead!——
Let's go and set Don Pedro free!—— Long live King Pedro!
Scuffles. Some of the grandees are stopped from going out.
No, you shan't go out!—— Shut the door of the King's private
room!—— Find the key to the desk!—— Someone arrest
Alvar Gonçalves! In the midst of this tumult* INES, *dead, is
brought in on a litter. The tumult at once dies down. In
silence all leave on one side the corpse of the* KING *where it
sprawls on the ground and mass together on the other side of
the stage around the litter, kneeling on one knee, with the
exception of* DINO DEL MORO, *who, after a gesture of hesitation, has knelt down near the* KING. *At this moment there
appears* DON PEDRO; *he throws himself upon the litter, sobbing. At the extreme right the corpse of* KING FERRANTE
sprawls, with nobody near it except the Andalusian PAGE-
BOY *kneeling by its side. The* PAGEBOY *steals a look, several
times, in the direction of the group of people in prayer. At
last he rises and goes over, he too, to kneel among them.
The dead body of the* KING *lies there alone.*]

EUGENE IONESCO

1912–

EUGÈNE IONESCO like so may of the writers in that movement which has come to be known as the "Theatre of the Absurd," is deeply committed to finding a metaphor for universal modern man that is viable in the theatre. He is looking for a metaphor that is symbolic of the inalienable part of every man—that irreducible part of each of us which exists after all the differences have been stripped away, and which is beyond and beneath all that is social, political, economic, religious, and ideological. In short, Ionesco is searching for a metaphor of man left face to face with himself. For this reason his theatre, at least not until his most recent plays, is not a social theatre. It is, rather, a theatre that reveals man detached from the machinery of society—man with no function, man with no historical situation. It is a theatre that shows man defined by his solitude and estrangement, not by his participation.

In all his plays Ionesco goes deep into the immediate experience of the metaphysical absurd by isolating and objectifying it. (Ionesco has defined the absurd as "that which has no purpose, or goal, or objective.") No magic, no divinity with impenetrable ways, is held responsible for man's condition; there are no sociological or psychological explanations. Ionesco quite simply communicates the bewildering paradox of man's life and the complete absurdity of the mechanism of his being. Ionesco's theatre is the image of a world where everything is equally important and, by the same token, unimportant.

But to express this kind of image of the world requires a new dramatic form. Ionesco makes it quite clear that he wants a theatre "which progresses not through a predetermined subject and plot, but through an increasingly intense and revealing series of emotional states." As a result, he has created a form of drama which might best be called contextual. His drama is a drama of situation alone, a drama in which the situation has been inflated to replace the plot.

The purpose of his plays is not to represent an action, but to reveal a condition.

It is still too soon to tell where Ionesco's "anti-theatre" will finally come to rest, but it is already clear that Ionesco has done the modern theatre a great service by experimenting with new forms and with nonverbal techniques. He has broken down many of Naturalism's restrictions and, in so doing, has opened up the theatre so that it is now receptive to many new forms of experimentation.

THE TRAGEDY OF LANGUAGE[1]

In 1948, before writing my first play, *The Bald Soprano*,
I did not want to become a playwright. My only ambition
was to learn English. Learning English does not necessarily
lead to writing plays. In fact it was because I failed to learn
English that I became a dramatist. Nor did I write these
plays as a kind of revenge for my failure, although *The Bald
Soprano* has been called a satire on the English middle-
classes. If I had tried and failed to learn Italian, Russian or
Turkish, it would have been quite as easy to say that the play
resulting from these vain efforts was a satire on Italian, Russian or Turkish society. I feel I should make myself clear.
This is what happened: Nine or ten years ago, in order to
learn English, I bought an English–French Conversation
Manual for Beginners. I set to work. I conscientiously copied
out phrases from my manual in order to learn them by heart.
Then I found, reading them over attentively, that I was
learning not English but some very surprising truths: that
there are seven days in the week, for example, which I happened to know before; or that the floor is below us, the
ceiling above us, another thing that I may well have known
before but had never thought seriously about or had forgotten, and suddenly it seemed to me as stupefying as it was in-
disputably true. I suppose I must have a fairly philosophical
turn of mind to have noticed that these were not just simple
English phrases with their French translation which I was
copying into my exercise book, but in fact fundamental
truths and profound statements.

For all that, I had not yet reached the point of giving
English up. And a good thing too, for after these universal

[1] From *Notes and Counter Notes: Writings on the Theatre*, by Eugène
Ionesco, Translated from the French by Donald Watson, Copyright ©
1964 by Grove Press, Inc., Published by Grove Press, Inc.

truths the author of my manual passed on from the general to the particular; and in order to do so, he expressed himself, doubtless inspired by the Platonic method, in the form of dialogue. In the third lesson two characters were brought together and I still cannot tell whether they were real or invented: Mr. and Mrs. Smith, an English couple. To my great surprise Mrs. Smith informed her husband that they had several children, that they lived in the outskirts of London, that their name was Smith, that Mr. Smith worked in an office, that they had a maid called Mary, who was English too, that for twenty years they had known some friends called Martin, and that their home was a castle because "An Englishman's home is his castle."

Of course, I imagine Mr. Smith must have been somewhat aware of all this; but you can never be sure, some people are so absent-minded; besides, it is good to remind our fellows of things they may be in danger of forgetting or take too much for granted. Apart from these particular eternal truths, there were other temporal truths which became clear: for example, that the Smiths had just dined and that, according to the clock, it was nine o'clock in the evening, English time.

Allow me to draw your attention to the nature of Mrs. Smith's assertions, which are perfectly irrefutable truisms; and also to the positively Cartesian approach of the author of my English Manual, for it was his superlatively systematic pursuit of the truth which was so remarkable. In the fifth lesson the Martins, the Smiths' friends, arrived; the conversation was taken up by all four and more complex truths were built upon these elementary axioms: "The country is more peaceful than big cities," some maintained; "Yes, but cities are more highly populated and there are more shops," replied the others, which is equally true and proves, moreover, that contrasting truths can quite well coexist.

It was at that moment that I saw the light. I no longer wanted merely to improve my knowledge of the English language. If I had persisted in enlarging my English vocabulary, in learning words, simply in order to translate into another language what I could just as well say in French, without paying any attention to the matter contained in these words, in what they reveal, this would have meant falling into the sin of formalism, which those who nowadays direct our thinking so rightly condemn. I had become more ambitious:

I wanted to communicate to my contemporaries the essential truths of which the manual of English–French conversation had made me aware. On the other hand the dialogue between the Smiths, the Martins, the Smiths and the Martins, was genuinely dramatic, for drama *is* dialogue. So what I had to produce was a play. Therefore I wrote *The Bald Soprano*, which is thus a specifically didactic work for the theatre. And why is this work called *The Bald Soprano* and not *English Made Easy*, which I first thought of calling it, or *The English Hour*, which is the title that occurred to me a little later? It would take too long to explain in full: one of the reasons why *The Bald Soprano* received this title is that no prima donna, with or without hair, appears in the play. This detail should suffice. A whole section of the play is made by stringing together phrases taken from my English Manual; the Smiths and the Martins in the Manual are the Smiths and the Martins in my play, they are the same people, utter the same maxims, and perform the same actions or the same "inactions." In any "didactic drama," it is not our business to be original, to say what we think ourselves: that would be a serious crime against objective truth; we have only, humbly, to pass on the knowledge which has itself been passed to us, the ideas we have been given. How could I have allowed myself to make the slightest change to words expressing in such an edifying manner the ultimate truth? As it was genuinely didactic, my play must on no account be original or demonstrate my own talent!

. . . However, the text of *The Bald Soprano* only started off as a lesson (and a plagiarism). An extraordinary phenomenon took place, I know not how: before my very eyes the text underwent a subtle transformation, against my will. After a time, those inspired yet simple sentences which I had so painstakingly copied into my schoolboy's exercise book, detached themselves from the pages on which they had been written, changed places all by themselves, became garbled and corrupted. Although I had copied them down so carefully, so correctly, one after the other, the lines of dialogue in the manual had got out of hand. It happened to dependable and undeniable truths such as "the floor is below us, the ceiling above us." An affirmation, as categorical as it is sound, such as: the seven days of the week are Monday, Tuesday, Wednesday, Thursday, Friday, Saturday, Sunday, so deteriorated that Mr. Smith, my hero, informed us that the week was composed of three days, which were: Tuesday, Thursday and Tuesday. My characters, my worthy bourgeois, the Martins, husband and wife, were stricken with amnesia: although seeing each other and speaking to each other every day, they no longer recognized each other. Other alarming things happened: the Smiths told us of the death of a certain Bobby Watson, impossible to identify, because they also told us that three-quarters of the inhabitants of the town, men, women, children, cats and ideologists were all called Bobby Watson. Finally a fifth and unexpected character turned up to cause more trouble between the peaceable couples: the Captain of the Fire Brigade. And he told stories which seemed to be about a young bull that gave birth to an enormous heifer, a mouse that begot a mountain; then the fireman went off so as not to miss a fire that had been foreseen three days before, noted in his diary and due to break out at the other side of the town, while the Smiths and the Martins took up their conversation again. Unfortunately the wise and elementary truths they exchanged, when strung together, had gone mad, the language had become disjointed, the characters distorted; words, now absurd, had been emptied of their content and it all ended with a quarrel the cause of which it was impossible to discover, for my heroes and heroines hurled into one another's faces not lines of dialogue, not even scraps of sentences, not words, but syllables or consonants or vowels! . . .

. . . For me, what had happened was a kind of collapse of reality. The words had turned into sounding shells devoid of meaning; the characters too, of course, had been emptied of psychology and the world appeared to me in an unearthly, perhaps its true, light, beyond understanding and governed by arbitary laws.

While writing this play (for it had become a kind of play or antiplay, that is to say a real parody of a play, a comedy of comedies), I had felt genuinely uneasy, sick and dizzy. Every now and then I had to stop working and, wondering what devil could be forcing me on to write, I would go and lie down on the sofa, afraid I might see it sinking into the abyss; and myself with it. When I had finished, I was nevertheless very proud of it. I imagined I had written something like the *tragedy of language!* . . . When it was acted, I was almost surprised to hear the laughter of the audience, who took it all (and still take it) quite happily, considering it a comedy all right, even a sort of joke. A few avoided this mistake (Jean Pouillon for example) and recognized a certain malaise. Others realized that I was poking fun at the theatre of Bernstein and his actors: Nicolas Bataille's cast had already realized this, when they had tried to act the play (especially during the first performances) as if it were a melodrama.

Later, serious critics and scholars analyzed the work and interpreted it solely as a criticism of bourgeois society and a parody of boulevard theatre. I have just said that I accept this interpretation too: but to my mind there is no question of it being a satire of a petit bourgeois mentality that belongs to any particular society. It is above all about a kind of universal petite bourgeoisie, the petit bourgeois being a man of fixed ideas and slogans, a ubiquitous conformist: this conformism is, of course, revealed by the *mechanical language*. The text of *The Bald Soprano*, or the Manual for Learning English (or Russian or Portuguese), consisting as it did of ready-made expressions and the most threadbare clichés, revealed to me all that is automatic in the language and behavior of people: "talking for the sake of talking," talking because there is nothing personal to say, the absence of any life within, the mechanical routine of everyday life, man sunk in his social background, no longer able to distinguish himself from it. The Smiths and the Martins no longer know how to talk because they no longer know how to think, they no longer know how to think because they are no longer capable of being moved, they have no passions, they no longer know how to be, they can become anyone or anything, for as they are no longer themselves, in an impersonal world, they can only be someone else, they are interchangeable: Martin can change places with Smith and vice versa, no one would notice the difference. A tragic character does not change, he breaks up; he is himself, he is *real*. Comic characters are people who do not exist.

(The start of a talk given to the French Institute in Italy, 1958.)

Translated by Donald Watson

IMPROVISATION

or

THE SHEPHERD'S CHAMELEON

by EUGENE IONESCO

1956

IMPROVISATION[1]
or
THE SHEPHERD'S CHAMELEON

Translated by Donald Watson

CHARACTERS

BARTHOLOMEUS I
BARTHOLOMEUS II
BARTHOLOMEUS III
MARIE
IONESCO

[1] *Improvisation* or *The Shepherd's Chameleon*, by Eugène Ionesco, is from *The Killer and Other Plays* by Eugène Ionesco, Translated by Donald Watson, Published by Grove Press, Inc., Copyright © by John Calder (Publishers) Ltd., 1960.

[IONESCO *is asleep, his head on the table, surrounded with books and manuscripts. A ballpoint pencil is sticking out of one hand. A bell rings.* IONESCO *snores. It rings again and then there is the sound of beating on the door and cries of: "Ionesco! Ionesco!" Finally* IONESCO *jumps and rubs his eyes.*]

MAN'S VOICE. Ionesco! Are you there?

IONESCO. Yes . . . Just a second! . . . What's the matter now? [*Smoothing his untidy hair* IONESCO *goes to the door and opens it.* BARTHOLOMEUS I *appears, in a scholar's gown.*][2]

BART I. Morning, Ionesco.

IONESCO. Morning, Bartholomeus.

BART I. Glad I've found you in! I damned nearly went away and I'd have been very angry, specially as you haven't a phone . . . What on earth were you doing?

IONESCO. I was working, working . . . I was writing!

BART I. The new play? Is it ready? I'm waiting for it.

IONESCO [*sitting in his armchair and motioning* BARTHOLO-MEUS *to a chair*]. Sit down. [BARTHOLOMEUS *sits.*] Well, I'm working on it, you know. I've got right down to it. I feel quite overworked. It's coming along, but it's not easy. It's got to be perfect, hasn't it? No repetition, no dull passages . . . So you see I'm tightening, tightening it up . . .

BART I. You *have* finished it, then? . . . The first draft, let's see that . . .

IONESCO. But I tell you I'm still tightening the dialogue . . .

BART I. Do I understand you're tightening the dialogue before you've finished the play? I suppose that's *one* way of writing.

IONESCO. It's *my* way.

BART I. Now listen, have you finished the play or haven't you?

2 In the French production the gowns worn by the three Bartholomeus were the scholars' gowns of Molière's time. [Tr.]

IONESCO [*hunting among his papers on the table*]. Yes . . . well no, you see . . . not exactly. It's here, of course, but I can't read it to you in its present state . . . so long as it's not . . .

BART I. . . . finished . . . polished off! . . .

IONESCO. No, no . . . not polished off . . . polished, perfect! It's not the same thing at all.

BART I. Pity. We're going to miss a good chance. I've had a very interesting offer. A theatre that's dead keen on having one of your plays. The directors want it at once. They've asked me to take the job on and produce it according to the latest dramatic theories. Theories worthy of a people's theatre in this ultra-scientific age we live in. They'll bear all the costs, publicity and so on, providing the cast's limited to four or five and it won't cost too much to mount . . .

IONESCO. Tell them to be patient for a day or two. I promise I'll have tightened it all up by then . . . though, it's true, the season *is* getting on . . .

BART I. So long as the *play* is, we can still fix it up . . .

IONESCO. Which theatre is it?

BART I. A new theatre, with a scientific director and a young company of scientific actors who want to launch out with *you*. You'll get scientific treatment. The auditorium's not too big, seats for twenty-five and standing room for four . . . It's for a people's audience, but a select one.

IONESCO. Not too bad. If only we could fill it every evening!

BART I. Half fill it, even, and I'd be satisfied . . . Anyway, they want to start at once.

IONESCO. That'd be fine, if only the play was absolutely ready . . .

BART I. But you say it's practically all written!

IONESCO. Yes . . . yes . . . it is *practically* all written!

BART I. What's it all about? What's it called?

IONESCO [*embarrassed and rather conceited*]. Er . . . what's it about? . . . You want to know what it's about? . . . And what it's called? . . . Er . . . you know I never know how to talk about my plays . . . It's all in the dialogue, in the acting, in the stage effects, it's very visual, as usual . . . With me there's always first some image, some line or other which sets off the creative mechanism. And then I just let my own characters carry me along, I never know exactly where I'm going . . . For me every play is an adventure, a quest, the discovery of a universe that's suddenly revealed, and there's no one more surprised than I am to find that it exists . . .

BART I. We know all about that! Empirical stuff. You've explained it all before, dozens of times, in your previews, your articles and your interviews, about your creative mechanism, as you call it, though I don't like the word: "creative." "Mechanism" is all right though. I like that.

IONESCO [*naively*]. That's true, I *have* talked about my, sorry, creative mechanism before. You've a good memory!

BART I. Tell me more about your new play. What was it this time, the initial image that set off the process of construction . . .

IONESCO. Well . . . er. Well . . . er . . . It's rather complicated, you know . . . That's a really sticky question! . . . Oh well, here goes! The title of my new play is: *The Shepherd's Chameleon*.

BART I. Why *The Shepherd's Chameleon*?

IONESCO. It's the crucial scene of the play, the motive force. Once, in a large country town, in the middle of the street, during the summer, I saw a young shepherd, about three o'clock in the afternoon, who was embracing a chameleon . . . It was such a touching scene I decided to turn it into a tragic farce.

BART I. That's feasible scientifically.

IONESCO. It'll only be the starting point. I don't know yet whether you'll really see the shepherd embracing the chameleon on the stage, or whether I'll simply call the scene to mind . . . Whether it'll just be an invisible background . . . drama once removed . . . In fact, I think it will only have to serve as a pretext . . .

BART I. Pity. The scene somehow seemed to me to illustrate the reconciliation of the Self with the Other.

IONESCO. You see, this time I'm going to put myself in the play!

BART I. That's all you ever do.

IONESCO. It won't be the last time, then.

BART I. Well, which are you to be, the shepherd or the chameleon?

IONESCO. Oh, no, definitely not the chameleon. *I* don't change color every day . . . I'm not always being towed along by the latest fashion, like . . . but I'd rather not say who . . .

BART I. So you must be the shepherd then?

IONESCO. Not the shepherd either! I told you this was only a pretext, a starting point . . . In fact I put myself in the play to start off a discussion on the theatre, to reveal my own ideas . . .

BART I. As you're not a scholar, you've no right to have ideas . . . That's where I come in.

IONESCO. Let's say my experiences, then . . .

BART I. Scientific experiment's the only experience that's valid.

IONESCO. . . . Well then . . . my beliefs . . .

BART I. Possible. But they're only provisional, we'll rectify them for you. Go on with your precarious exposition . . .

IONESCO [*after a second's pause*]. Thank you. You can say I *am* the shepherd if you like, and the theatre's the chameleon. Because *I've* embraced a theatrical career, and the theatre, of course, *changes,* for the theatre is life. It's changeable like life . . . The chameleon's life too!

BART I. I note the formula, which is almost a thought.

IONESCO. So I'll talk about the theatre, about dramatic criticism and the public . . .

BART I. You need to be more of a sociologist for that!

IONESCO. . . . and the new drama, the essential character of which lies in its newness . . . I'll present my own points of view.

BART I [*sweeping gesture*]. Points of view with no optical instrument!

IONESCO. . . . It'll be an improvisation.

BART I. Read me what you've written so far, anyway.

IONESCO [*pretending to hold back*]. It's not quite ready. I told you . . . the dialogue's not tightened up . . . Still, I could read you a short extract . . .

BART I. I'm listening to you. I'm here to pass judgment on you. And put you right.

IONESCO [*scratching his head*]. I always find it rather embarrassing, you know, to read out what I've written. My own text makes me sick . . .

BART I. Autocriticism does honor to the writer, dishonor to the critic.

IONESCO. All right, I'll read it to you anyhow, so you won't have come for nothing.

[BART I *settles himself down comfortably.*]

This is how the play starts. Scene One. Ionesco is asleep, his head on the table, surrounded with books and manuscripts. A ballpoint pencil is sticking out of one hand. A bell rings. Ionesco snores. Then there is the sound of beating on the door and cries of: "Ionesco! Ionesco!" Finally Ionesco jumps and rubs his eyes. Voice from outside the door: "Ionesco! Are you there?" Ionesco: "Yes . . . Just a second! . . . What's the matter now? . . ." Smoothing his untidy hair [*With these words* IONESCO *makes the gesture.*] Ionesco goes to the door and opens it; Bartholomeus appears. Bartholomeus: "Glad I've found you in! I damned nearly went away, and I'd have been very angry, specially as you haven't a phone. What on earth were you doing?" Ionesco: "I was working, working, I was writing! . . ." Bartholomeus: "The new play? Is it ready? I'm waiting for it! . . ." Ionesco, sitting in his armchair and motioning Bartholomeus to a chair: "Sit down!"

[*While reading his play* IONESCO *sits down in his armchair as before. At this moment the bell is really heard to ring, followed by a beating on the door.*]

ANOTHER MAN'S VOICE. Ionesco! Are you there?

[BART I, *who has been nodding his head in approbation during the reading, glances over to the door where the Voice comes from.*]

IONESCO. Yes, just a second. What's the matter now? [*Smoothing his untidy hair,* IONESCO *goes to the door and opens it.* BARTHOLOMEUS II *appears.*]

BART II. Morning, Ionesco.

IONESCO. Morning, Bartholomeus.

BART II [*to* BART I]. Well, Battholomeus, how are you?

BART I [*to* BART II]. Well, Bartholomeus, how are you?

BART II. Glad I've found you in! I damned nearly went away, and I'd have been very angry, specially as you haven't a phone . . . What on earth were you doing?

IONESCO. I was working, working, I was writing . . . Sit down! [*He indicates a chair to* BART II *and sits down himself.*

There is more knocking on the door and a third man's voice.]

THIRD MAN'S VOICE. Ionesco! Ionesco! Are you there?

IONESCO. Yes, just a second! What's the matter now? [IONESCO *stands up, smooths his hair, makes for the door and opens it.* BARTHOLOMEUS III *appears, in a scholar's gown, like the other two.*]

BART III. Morning, Ionesco.

IONESCO. Morning, Bartholomeus.

BART III [*to* BART II]. Well, Bartholomeus, how are you?

BART II [*to* BART III]. Well, Bartholomeus, how are you?

BART I [*to* BART III]. Well, Bartholomeus, how are you?

BART III [*to* BART I]. Well, Bartholomeus, how are you? [*To* IONESCO.] Glad I've found you in! I damned nearly went away, and I'd have been very angry, specially as you haven't a phone . . . What on earth were you doing?

[*The pace of the actors' delivery should increase.*]

IONESCO. I was working . . . working . . . I was writing!

BART III. The new play? Is it ready? I'm waiting for it.

IONESCO [*sitting down and indicating a chair to* BART III]. Sit down. [BART III *sits down by the others, all three in a row.*] Well, I'm working on it, you know. I've got right down to it. It's coming along, but it's not easy. It's got to be perfect, no repetition, no dull passages. I'm always being accused of going round in circles in my plays . . . so I'm tightening, tightening it up . . .

BART III. You can read us at least the beginning.

BART II. [*echo*]. At least the beginning . . .

BART I [*echo*]. . . . least the beginning . . .

IONESCO [*reading*]. "Ionesco is asleep, his head on the table, surrounded with books and manuscripts. The doorbell rings. Ionesco snores. It rings again. Ionesco goes on snoring. Then there is a knocking at the door . . ."

[*Suddenly there is a real knocking at the door.*]

IONESCO. Yes, just a second! . . . What's the matter now? [*Smoothing his untidy hair,* IONESCO *starts making for the door.*]

BART III. Sounds quite interesting . . . but let's hear the rest . . .

BART II [*to* IONESCO]. It's very unexpected.

[Fresh knocking at the door.]

BART I *[to the other two]*. That's because you weren't here from the start. I know this play a bit better. *[To* IONESCO.*]* It's a vicious circle.

IONESCO. A vicious circle can have its virtues too!

BART I. So long as you get out of it in time.

IONESCO. Oh, yes, that's true . . . so long as you get out of it.

BART II. And there's only one way to get out of it, and that's the right way. *[To* BART I.*]* Isn't it, Dr Bartholomeus? *[Then, to* BART III.*]* Isn't it, Dr Bartholomeus?

BART III. Perhaps.

BART II *[to* IONESCO*]*. You can only get out of a vicious circle by enclosing yourself in it. So don't go and open the door or the vicious circle will close in more . . . on you.

BART I. We've seen it happen before.

BART II. Yes, we've seen it happen before.

IONESCO. I don't understand.

BART III. I don't understand, there's an expression I do understand . . . or at least it's one I *use*.

BART II *[to* IONESCO*]*. It's easy to see *you*'re not a scholar!

[Gesture of commiseration from the three BARTHOLOMEUS.*]*

BART I *[to* IONESCO*]*. We'll explain it all to you. Now.

BART II. Well now.

BART III. Let's see.

BART I. Instead of the expression "get out of," say "get away from," which means "alienate yourself," and then you'll understand. For example, you can only alienate yourself from a vicious circle by not escaping from it; whereas you can only escape from it by staying inside. What is inside is experienced from the outside, and what is outside is experienced from the inside. For the more alienated you are . . .

BART II. . . . the more involved you are . . .

BART I. . . . and the more involved you are . . .

BART II. . . . the more alienated you are. It's the electrical shock of alienation, or the Y effect.

BART III *[aside]*. Pure philosophistry! They're both philosophisters!

BART II *[to* BART I*]*. We understand each other, Maître

Bartholomeus. [*To* BART III.] We understand each other, Maître Bartholomeus, although there are still some little points of disagreement . . .

[*The three* BARTHOLOMEUS *bow to one another*.]

BART I [*to* IONESCO]. That is to say, one is inside when one is outside, outside when one is inside, or popularly speaking, I mean . . .

BART II. Scientifically . . .

BART III. Quite simply.

BART I. . . . and dialectically speaking, it's called: The Being-In-on-the-Outside-and-Out-on-the-Inside. [*To the other two* BARTHOLOMEUS.] It's also the Being of not-Being and the Not-Being of Being in the Know . . . [*To* IONESCO.] Have you thought about this question?

IONESCO. Er . . . a little . . . vaguely . . . I haven't exactly gone into it . . .

BART II [*to Bart* I]. Authors aren't here to think, they're here to write what they're told.

IONESCO. I beg your pardon, but I . . . I find you're expressing yourself in a very contradictory way. I'm all for contradiction, everything is nothing but contradiction, and yet any systematic exposition ought not to . . . should it . . . in words, confuse opposites . . .

BART I. I can see you don't know . . .

BART II [*to* BART III]. He doesn't appear to know it . . .

BART III [*to* BART II]. Doesn't know it at all!

BART I [*to* BART II *and* BART III]. Be quiet! [To IONESCO.] So you don't know that opposites are identical? Here's an example. When I say that something is truly true, that means that it's falsely false . . .

BART II. Or just the reverse: if something is falsely false, it's also truly true . . .

IONESCO. I'd never have thought of that. Oh, how clever you are!

BART I. Yet, on the other hand, you can say that the more truly false something is, the more falsely true it is. And the less truly false it is, the less falsely true. To sum up: the false true is the true false, or the true true is the false false. And so opposites cancel out, *quod erat demonstrandum*.

IONESCO. In such a case, I'm sorry, it seems to me that the

false is not the true, the true is not the false, and opposites exclude each other.

BART II. What cheek! He thinks ... [*To* BART I *and* BART III.] ... He thinks like a pig!

IONESCO [*speechless, after a short pause*]. Ah yes, yes ... I see ...

BART II. What do you see?

IONESCO. I see ... I'm beginning to see ... er ... what you mean ... I can see a few shadows ...

BART III. He's beginning to see the light ...

BART II. Do you think his mind's going to thaw?

IONESCO. What, I'm muddling it up ... what's true is true and what's false is false ...

BART I. Horror! Tautologies! Nothing but tautologies! And every tautology is the expression of wrong thinking!

BART II. It's obviously inconceivable to identify something with itself.

BART III [*to* BART I]. Don't get so worked up. It's not his fault if he doesn't understand. He's an intellectual. A man of the theatre ought to be stupid!

BART II. He hasn't got a people's mind, by that I mean scientific.

BART I [*to* BART II *and* BART III]. His mentality's prehistoric, pithecanthropic, he's the "missing link" ... [*In a whisper.*] I even suspect him of being a bit of a Platonist.

BART III. Oh ... how ghastly! A Platonist ... what animal's that?

BART II [*whispering in* BART I's *ear*]. I don't think so. I've still got some faith in him, in spite of everything ...

BART I. Well, *I* haven't got much ... These prolific poets and playwrights who deliver the goods like hens laying eggs ... You can't trust them, can't trust them ...

BART III [*aside*]. A Platonist? ... Oh yes, it's a kind of platypus!

BART II. But we have to make use of them!

[*The three* BARTHOLOMEUS *whisper in each other's ears.*]

IONESCO. I'd like to know what I'm being accused of!

BART III [*severely*]. Laying eggs!

IONESCO. I'll try not to lay any more ...

BART III. You'd better not!

BART I [*after a confabulation with* BART II, *to* IONESCO]. Now
listen, Ionesco. Bartholomeus [*Pointing to him.*] Bartholomeus [*Pointing to* BART II.] and I, we all wish you the
best . . . and we want to do something for you.

IONESCO. Thanks very much . . .

BART II. We want to teach you.

IONESCO. But I went to school.

BART II [*to* BART I]. That's just what we were afraid of.

BART I [*to* IONESCO]. All the knowledge and science you
picked up there was false . . .

IONESCO. I was very bad at science.

BART III. Well, at least that's something in his favor. [*To the
two* BARTHOLOMEUS.] His mind's a blank on that score . . .

BART II [*to* BART III]. So long as he learnt something else,
something else.

IONESCO. I was made to read the works of Aeschylus,
Sophocles and Euripides . . .

BART I. Outdated, outdated, all that! It's dead . . . of no value
at all . . .

IONESCO. And then . . . and then . . . Shakespeare!

BART III. He's not a *French* writer. The others may be, but
he's a Russian.

BART II [*to* BART I]. We don't blame him for being foreign.

BART III. But I do, I blame him for it [*Aside.*] I think he was
Polish after all.

BART II [*to* BART III]. My dear Maître Bartholomeus, you've
every right to blame him, you're a critic . . . [*Visibly ill at
ease,* IONESCO *mops his brow.*] You can be full of blame,
for everything, that's your mission in life.

BART III [*to* BART II]. It's yours too, my dear Bartholomeus.
[*To* BART I.] And yours, my dear Bartholomeus.

BART I [*to* BART II *and* BART III]. And yours . . . and
yours . . .

BART II [*to* BART III *and* BART I]. And yours . . . and
yours . . .

[*Bows all round.*]

IONESCO. I studied a little Molière too.

BART II. Dreadful, dreadful mistake!

BART I [*to* BART II]. Molière? Do you know?

BART II [*to* BART I]. An author who wrote about Affected
and Learned Ladies . . .

BART I [*to* BART II]. If he praised Affected and Learned Ladies he belongs to the Age of Science! He's one of us!

BART II [*to* BART I]. You're mistaken, my dear Bartholomeus, on the contrary, he held them up to ridicule.

BART I [*horrified, to* IONESCO]. Disgraceful! Poor man, are those your authors? That explains why you've the mentality of the lower middle class.

BART III. He hasn't been accepted by the commercial theatre yet. That makes him dangerous. [*He points his index finger at* IONESCO.] And so are you.

IONESCO. Yes . . . I see . . . I'm sorry.

BART II [*also pointing his finger at* IONESCO]. He's a bad writer.

BART I [*doing the same*]. A reactionary!

BART III [*as before*]. Ah yes, I remember, he got his inspiration from foreigners, from the Italians.

BART II [*as before*]. With a bad influence!

IONESCO [*very timidly*]. As Molière still amuses, I thought he was of universal, of eternal interest.

BART II. Blasphemy!

BART I. Only the ephemeral is of lasting value.

IONESCO [*backing to the right before the pointed fingers of the Doctors*]. . . . Like the provisional . . . of course . . . yes, yes . . .

BART II. If these plays still seem to you to have some value, your deluded senses have led you astray.

BART I. All it means is that Molière failed to express the social *gestus* of his age.

BART III [*to* IONESCO]. You hear what these gentlemen are saying?

IONESCO [*with a supreme effort*]. It's true. I prefer Shakespeare.

BART III [*aside*]. He's not Polish. I must look him up in Larousse. [*He looks in the* Petit Larousse.]

BART I [*to* IONESCO]. What do you find so wonderful about this writer?

IONESCO [*to* BART I]. I find Shakespeare's very, very . . .

BART III [*shutting the dictionary*]. Yes, Larousse says he's Polish.

BART II [*to* IONESCO]. What do you find he is?

IONESCO. I found that Shakespeare is . . . poetic!

BART I [*perplexed*]. Poetic?

BART II. Poetic, poetic?

IONESCO [*timidly*]. Poetic.

BART III. Poetic, poetic, poetic?

IONESCO. Yes, by that I mean that there's poetry in it . . .

BART III. Jargon! Another piece of jargon.

BART I. But what *is* this poetry?

BART III [*to* BART I *and* BART II]. Good Lord . . . Poetry! . . . [*Pursing his lips in scorn.*]

BART II [*to* BART III]. Be quiet! No poetry, please. [*To* BART I.] Poetry's an enemy of our science!

BART I [*to* IONESCO]. You're steeped in false knowledge.

BART III. He only likes wild and extravagant nonsense.

BART I [*to* BART II *and* BART III, *indicating* IONESCO]. His mind hasn't been properly trained . . .

BART II. It's been warped.

BART III. We must straighten it out.

BART II. If we can. [*To* BART III.] But not, my dear Bartholomeus, in the direction you want it to take. We disagree on several points, as you very well know.

BART I. We'll straighten it first. And once we've got it straight we'll argue about the direction it's got to take.

[*Short, inaudible confabulation between the three* BARTHOLOMEUS.]

BART III. That's right. We must take the most urgent things first.

BART II [*to* IONESCO]. Can you hear what we say?

IONESCO [*with a start*]. Yes, yes . . . yes . . . of course . . . I'm not deaf.

BART I [*to* IONESCO]. Wer'e going to ask you a few questions . . .

IONESCO. A few questions?

BART II [*to* IONESCO]. To find out what you know . . .

IONESCO. What I know . . .

BART III [*to* IONESCO]. Straighten your warped knowledge.

IONESCO. Warped, yes . . .

BART I [*to* IONESCO]. Clear up all the confusion in your mind . . .

IONESCO. All the confusion in my mind . . .

BART I [*to* IONESCO]. First of all, do you know what the theatre is?

IONESCO. Er, the theatre is theatre.

BART II [*to* IONESCO]. Quite wrong.

BART I [*to* IONESCO]. Wrong . . . the theatre is a manifestation of theatricality.

BART III [*to Bart* I *and* BART II]. But does he know what theatricality is?

BART I [*to* BART II *and* BART III]. We'll soon find out. [*To* IONESCO.] Define theatricality.

IONESCO. Theatricality . . . theatricality . . . is what is theatrical . . .

BART I. I was afraid of that . . .

BART II. So was I.

BART III. So was I.

BART I. I was afraid his thinking was tainted. [*To* IONESCO.] You're out of your mind, theatricality is what is anti-theatrical.

BART III [*to* BART I]. I don't quite agree with you there. I believe, my dear Bartholomeus, that theatricality may be . . . it's not because *he* said it, [*He points to a collapsed* IONESCO.] *he* doesn't know what he's saying, he got it right because he misunderstood . . . What is theatrical is theatrical . . .

BART I. Give an example.

IONESCO. Yes, an example!

BART II [*to* IONESCO]. Keep out of this, can't you!

BART III. I can't find an example that springs to mind, but I'm right . . . All that matters is that I'm always right!

BART II [*conciliatory, to* BART I]. Perhaps one kind of thing that's theatrical is theatrical, while another isn't . . . it's all a question of knowing which kind . . .

BART I. But no . . . but no . . . [*To* IONESCO.] It's not your turn to speak!

IONESCO. I'm not saying a word.

BART II [*to* IONESCO]. There you are, you see, you *are* . . .

BART I [*to* IONESCO]. But no . . . [*To* BART II.] You're wrong, my dear Bartholomeus. Phenomenologically speaking theatricality is never theatrical.

BART II. Sorry, sorry, but *theatre* is theatrical . . .

IONESCO [*timidly raising one finger*]. I wonder if . . . I could . . .

BART I [*to* IONESCO]. Quiet. [*To* BART III.] You're thinking tautologically! The theatrical resides in the anti-theatrical and vice versa . . . vice versa . . . vice versa . . .

BART II. Veecee-verso . . . Veecee-verso . . . Veecee-verso!

BART III. Veecee-verso? Oh not veecee-verso, it's versa-vircee.

BART I. I say vircee-versa.

BART III. I maintain it's versa-vircee!

BART I. Vircee-verso!

BART III. You can't frighten me: versa-vircee.

BART II [*to the other* BARTHOLOMEUS]. Don't argue in front of him . . . It weakens our academic doctoral authority . . . [*Indicating* IONESCO.] Don't forget, don't forget we must first straighten him out, then train him straight.

IONESCO [*who has recovered some of his courage*]. Gentlemen, perhaps the theatre is, quite simply, drama, action, action at a given time and place . . .

BART II [*to* BART III *and* BART I]. You see! He's already taken advantage of us, because of our quarrels.

BART I [*to* IONESCO]. What do you know about it?

IONESCO. I believe it . . . and then Aristotle said it.

BART III. A Levantine!

BART I. Aristotle, Aristotle! What's Aristotle got to do with it?

BART II. To start with, he wasn't the first who said it.

BART I [*to* IONESCO]. Do you know who said it long before Aristotle? Long before!

BART II. Oh yes . . . long, long before Aristotle!

IONESCO. I don't know . . .

BART I. Adamov, Monsieur.

IONESCO. Really? . . . He said it before . . . before Aristotle?

BART II. Certainly!

BART III. Yes, that's true, he said it first.

BART II. All Aristotle did was say the same thing in different words.

BART I. Only Adamov has realized his mistake since then!

BART II. And so must Aristotle.

BART I. The theatre, Monsieur, is a lesson about some instructive happening, an event of educational value . . . We must raise the level of the public . . .

BART III. We must lower it.

BART I. No, maintain it!

BART II. They should come to the theatre to learn!

BART I. Not laugh!

BART III. Or cry!

BART I. Or forget!

BART II. Or forget themselves!

BART I. Or for exaltation!

BART II. Or for sublimation!

BART I. Or self-identification!

BART III. A playwright should be a schoolteacher . . .

BART II. That's who we train, we critics and scholars: Schoolteachers.

BART III. It's the schoolteacher should train the playwright!

BART I. The public shouldn't enjoy themselves at the theatre!

BART II. Those who enjoy themselves will be punished!

BART III. After all, there's a sensible way of finding entertainment.

BART I. Learning is part of entertainment.

BART III. But the theatre's where you have a good time.

BART II. Boredom is entertainment.

BART III. It's theatre when it's not la-di-da.

BART I. Our kind of entertainment's become an anachronism! We haven't as yet discovered the appropriate recreation for our time.

BART III. I don't belong to my time . . . what's it matter, let's be zany . . .

BART I. You're right there . . . it's amazing how limited the public is in the way it expresses its feelings . . .

BART II. Their reactions show little variation.

BART I. I've drawn up a list. And I've noticed the public shows its approval by means of applause.

IONESCO. I've noticed that too.

BART III. That's what theatre is, when you shout: Bravo!

BART II. Or catcall . . .

BART I. Or whistle . . .

IONESCO. It hasn't happened at my plays yet!

BART II. Or stamp their feet.

BART I. Very unusual.

IONESCO [aside]. What else do they want them to do! Hiccup, belch, click their tongues, whoop like Red Indians or break their wind?

BART I. The public's reactions are really very elementary.

BART II. Monotonous, stereotyped . . .

BART III. The public's too intelligent!

BART II. The public's too stupid!

BART I. Why do they clap their hands, then?

BART II. The Latins called it *plaudere*.

BART I. The Greeks used the ver*b* *Krotein*.

BART II. But why do they tap their feet?

IONESCO [*aside*]. No one will ever know.

BART I. Is it because a lively emotion provokes irregular motion?

IONESCO [*aside*]. I've never asked myself that question.

BART I [*to* BART III]. It must be due to the theatre's social past.

IONESCO [*aside*]. That must be it.

BART I. If we can't get the public to bring intelligent variation to the expression of their feelings, they'd better stop having any! From now on the public will have to observe the maximum restraint . . .

BART II. The theatre will be a night school.

BART III. For the dull and the backward!

BART II. A compulsory course.

BART I. With medals and rewards.

BART III. And hot steam baths for their health!

BART I. And a system of punishment.

[IONESCO, *alarmed, is turning his head rapidly from one Doctor to the next, faster and faster.*]

BART II. The theatre's a lesson in things.

BART I. In the scientific theatre the program sellers will be prefects.

BART II. Or junior teachers to invigilate at rehearsals.

BART III. No objection to that!

BART II. The director will be the vice-principal.

BART I. No more intervals!

BART II. Just a ten minute break for recreation!

BART III. Objection to that!

BART II. If any playgoer fails to understand . . .

BART I. Or wants to leave the room . . .

BART III. All I say is . . .

BART I. He must raise his hand . . .

BART II. And ask permission to go . . .

BART III. . . . that I don't understand a word . . .

BART I. Every playgoer will be expected to come and see the same play several times and learn it off by heart . . .

BART II. To understand it properly and each time study a different scene! From a different point of view!

BART III. . . . never understood a word!

BART I. Concentrate on a different actor!

BART II. Attain the ultimate interpretation of the work in question . . .

BART I. Which would be the sum of a whole line of successive and contradictory interpretations . . .

BART II. . . . and so reach a final understanding, which should be simple, multifarious and unique!

BART I. Theatregoers will take notes and be classed in order of merit at the end of the year . . .

BART III. The last shall be first.

BART II. The lazy shall be failed . . .

BART III. The loafers rewarded!

BART I. We'll organize holiday shows and summer festivals.

BART II. When the non-scientific public will come back and see the same play again.

BART I. Until they get it into their thick heads and we make scientists of donkeys!

BART III [*to* IONESCO, *who has retreated, terrified, into a corner*]. You're keeping very quiet?

IONESCO. I . . . I . . . I . . . It's because you . . .

BART II. Be quiet!

BART III. Say something!

BART I *and* II [*to* IONESCO]. Speak . . .

BART III [*to* IONESCO]. Be quiet!

IONESCO. I . . . I . . .

BART II. Don't you agree with us?

IONESCO [*as before*]. Oh . . . no . . .

BART I. What, no?

IONESCO. I mean . . . yes . . . yes . . .

BART III. Yes what? Have you got reservations?

IONESCO [*as before*]. I mean, yes . . . yes . . . yes . . .

BART II. What does Yes mean?

IONESCO [*with a great effort*]. I agree . . . yes . . . all right . . . I agree to your . . . enlightening me . . . there's nothing I want more . . .

BART I [*to* BART II]. He's making confession of his own ignorance.

BART II [*to* IONESCO]. You admit your mistakes?

IONESCO [*with an effort*]. Why yes, Gentlemen . . . yes . . .

my ignorance, my mistakes . . . I'm very sorry . . . please forgive me . . . all I ask is to be taught what's right . . . [*He beats his chest*]. *Mea culpa! Mea maxima culpa!*

BART III [*to* BART I *and* II]. Is this sincere?

IONESCO [*with warmth and conviction*]. Oh yes . . . I swear it is! . . .

BART II. No sinner but should find mercy.

IONESCO [*overcome*]. Oh thank you . . . thank you . . . How good you are, Gentlemen!

BART I [*to* BART II]. Don't give way to the temptation of goodness! We'll soon see if he's really sincere.

IONESCO. Oh yes, I am sincere.

BART III. Let him prove it, then, by his works.

BART I. Not by his works.

BART II. His works don't count.

BART I. It's only his theories that count.

BART II. What one *thinks* of one's work.

BART I. For the work in itself . . .

BART II. Doesn't exist . . .

BART I. Except in what one says about it . . .

BART III. In the interpretation you're willing to give it . . .

BART II. That you impose on the work . . .

BART I. That you impose on the public.

IONESCO. Very well, Gentlemen, very well, Gentlemen, I agree with what you say . . . I tell you again I'll do as you say and I'll prove it to you.

BART II [*to* BART I *and* BART III]. But we've still got to decide what we mean by sincerity!

BART I. Which is not what one usually thinks it is!

BART II. What one takes empirically . . .

BART I. Unscientifically . . .

BART III. Foolishly . . .

BART II. . . . to be sincerity . . . For sincerity, in fact, is its opposite!

BART III. Not always, perhaps!

BART II. More often than not!

BART I [*to* BART III *and* BART II]. *Always,* Gentlemen! . . . Always, for to be sincere, you have to be insincere!

BART II [*to* BART III]. The only real sincerity . . .

BART I [*to* BART III]. . . . . is when you're double-faced . . .

BART II [*to* BART III]. And ambiguous.

BART III [*to* BART I *and* BART II]. Gentlemen . . . allow me, on
   this point . . .
BART I [*interrupting* BART III]. But it's perfectly clear.
BART III. It seems obscure to me.
BART II. It's clear-obscure.
BART I. I. I'm sorry, it's clear obscurity . . .
BART III. Forgive me, but clear obscurity is not clear-obscure.
BART II. You're mistaken . . .

[*While the three Doctors are quarreling,* IONESCO *withdraws
slightly, apparently hoping to be forgotten. Then he tries to
escape on tiptoe to the door.*]

BART I. Gentlemen, I maintain that obscurity is clear, just as
   a lie is truth . . .
BART II. You mean, just as truth is a lie!
BART III. Not quite to the same extent!
BART II. Yes, exactly the same!
BART III. Not quite.
BART I. Oh yes.
BART II. My dear Bartholomeus . . .
BART III. No . . .
BART I. Yes.
BART III. No.
BART I. Yes . . .
BART II. Yes and no.
BART III. No.
BART I. Yes.
BART II. No and yes.
BART III. No.
BART II. My dear Bartholomeus, there's a subtle distinction
   there . . .
BART I. I don't hold with distinctions . . .
BART III. Neither do I.
BART II [*to* BART I]. You know perfectly well I quite agree
   with you about general principles . . . But on this particular
   point . . .
BART I. To hell with particular points: mystification is
   demystification, confession is dissimulation, trust is abuse
   . . . abuse of trust.
BART II. That's really profound!
BART III [*to* BART I]. I'd say it was just the opposite.

BART I. Rubbish! . . . According to you, I suppose dissimulation is confession.

BART III. Obviously!

BART I [*to* BART III]. You're floundering.

BART III. No, I'm not!

BART II. Gentlemen, Gentlemen . . .

BART I. Yes you are . . .

BART II. Gentlemen, Gentlemen . . . *please,* don't start that again. We mustn't set a bad example. United we stand against the foe!

BART I [*holding his hand out to* BART III]. United we stand against the foe!

BART II. United we stand against the foe!

BART III. Very well, united we stand against the foe.

[*All three stand in a solemn group, giving a triple handshake; then, a moment later, they look at the place where* IONESCO *was and is no more.*]

Where *is* the foe?

BART I. Where *is* the foe?

BART II. Where *is* the foe? [*Catching sight of* IONESCO *near the door.*] Traitor!

BART III. Traitor!

BART I. So you wanted to escape, you were running away?

BART III [*to* BART I *and* BART II]. Shame on him! He deserves hanging!

IONESCO. Oh no . . . really I don't . . .

BART I [*to* IONESCO]. What does this mean, then?

BART III [*to* IONESCO]. Why are you over by the door?

IONESCO. It just happened, I swear, it happened quite by chance . . .

BART III [*to* IONESCO]. You can't deny you left your chair . . .

IONESCO. No, I can't deny that.

BART II [*to* IONESCO]. Well?

BART III [*to* IONESCO]. Defend yourself . . .

IONESCO [*stammering*]. I was only going away to find it easier to stay, it was just an escape, or rather an unjust escape, to prevent me from leaving . . . [*With greater assurance.*] Yes, I was going away the better to stay . . .

BART III [*to* BART I *and* BART II]. What do you make of it?

BART II [*to* BART I *and* BART III]. What he says seems sensible enough, it's true the more you stay the more you go away . . .

BART I [to BART II and BART III]. And the more you go away the more you stay, it's all in line.

BART II. He sounds dishonest to me, that is to say, dialectically, honest . . .

BART III. Isn't he trying to pull the wool over our eyes?

BART I [to BART III]. He's too stupid for that.

BART II. He wouldn't dare. [To IONESCO.] Anyhow don't you move again without our permission! [To BART III and BART I.] We'll be on the safe side.

[An old woman's voice behind the door calls out: Ionesco! Monsieur Ionesco!]

IONESCO. Gentlemen, Gentlemen, please, I must open the door, she's been there a long time!

BART III. Who is it then? Some uninvited guest!

IONESCO. It's the woman next door who does my house-work.

BART II. Ionesco, don't move . . . sit down . . . be quick about it . . .

BART III. You've already been told twice before: I shan't say it a third time.

BART II. Do you realize you've got everything to learn from us?

[Knocking at the door, then you hear: What on earth's the matter with him! IONESCO throws worried glances at the door, he'd like to open it.]

IONESCO. I admit that! Everything, my dear Maîtres, every-thing . . .

BART II. All about theatricality?

IONESCO. Yes.

BART I. All about costumology?

IONESCO. All about costu . . . what?

BART I [to BART II]. Poor devil! He doesn't know what cos-tumology is! [To IONESCO.] You'll learn!

IONESCO. I'll learn . . .

BART II. All about historicization and decorology . . .

IONESCO. I'll do the best I can!

BART III. You must also know about the psychology of the audience, about audienco-psychology! Up to now you've been writing plays without thinking about them . . .

IONESCO. I'll think about them from now on, I'll think about them day and night!

BART I. Promise?

IONESCO. Promise, I swear!

BART III. I shan't say it a third time.

IONESCO [*scared*]. Oh no . . . There's no need, really there isn't!

BART I. We'll give you the basic elements of this new science. The theory first, the practice later.

BART III. Just listen to us for now and take notes!

IONESCO. Yes . . . yes . . . I'll take some notes.

[*Sitting at his study table, he searches among his numerous exercise books, with difficulty finds a blank page and fever-ishly settles himself down, pencil in hand; meanwhile the Doctors are talking among themselves.*]

BART III. What shall we start with?

BART II [*to* BART I]. Start, dear colleague, if you like, your-self, with costumology . . .

BART I [*to* BART II]. Start, dear colleague, yourself, with theatricology . . .

BART I *and* BART II [*to* BART III]. Start, if you like, yourself, with audienco-psychology . . .

BART III [*to* BART I *and* BART II]. After you, Gentlemen . . . Make a . . . methodical start.

[*Knocking at the door.*]

WOMAN'S VOICE. Monsieur! Ah! . . . He's locked himself in . . . What's he doing? I haven't the time to . . .

[IONESCO *is worried, makes a gesture toward the door, opens his mouth, but dares not open the door.*]

BART I [*to* BART II]. After you . . .

BART II [*to* BART I]. I'll do no such thing . . .

BART III. Neither shall I . . . I'd never forgive myself.

BART II [*to* BART I]. It would be lacking in courtesy . . .

[*Knocking at the door. The woman's voice*: Hey! You there, inside!]

BART I [*to* BART II]. I should be wanting in manners . . .
BART II [*to* BART III]. After you . . .
BART III [*to* BART I]. You can't really mean it . . .
BART I [*to* BART II]. Neither can you . . . After you . . .

[*Then suddenly, turning to face* IONESCO, *who is gazing at the door, looking more and more worried, the three* BARTHOLO-MEUS *all together and at precisely the same moment rush into the following.*]

BART I.   ⎫   Every playwright's ABC of theatricology . . .
BART II.   ⎬   Every playwright's ABC of costumology . . .
BART III.   ⎭   Every playwright's ABC of audiencology . . .
ALL THREE. . . . . decorology!
IONESCO [*alarmed*]. Gentlemen, Gentlemen . . .
BART I [*to* BART II *and* BART III]. So sorry!
BART II [*to* BART I *and* BART III]. So sorry!
BART III [*to* BART I *and* BART II]. So sorry!
IONESCO. Please don't apologize!

[*Then, suddenly as before, while* BART I *and* BART III *fall over each other in exchanging compliments and apologies behind* BART II*'s back, the latter, standing alone to face* IONESCO, *addresses him in a loud voice.*]

BART II. Monsieur. [IONESCO *stands up.*] Sit down. [IONESCO *sits down again. To the two* BARTHOLOMEUS, *who have not stopped being silently polite to each other.*] Be quiet, Gentlemen.

[BART I *and* BART III *take up a position on each side of* BART II *and slightly to the rear, showing true doctoral deference.*]

[*To* IONESCO.] You're seriously ill, my dear chap . . .

[*The other two* BARTHOLOMEUS *gravely nod approval.*]

IONESCO [*very frightened*]. Why, what's the matter with me?
BART II. Don't interrupt! Even if you are no longer ignorant of your own ignorance, you still seem to ignore the fact that an ignorant man is seriously ill . . .
IONESCO [*relieved*]. Oh . . . so it's not so bad as I thought! I feared the worst!
BART III [*to* BART I]. What ignorance!
BART I [*to* BART III]. A really sick man!

BART II [*to* BART I *and* BART III]. *I'm* doing the talking. That's
what we agreed. [*To* IONESCO.] The disease of the ignorant man is ignorance. As you are an ignorant man, you're
suffering from ignorance. And I'll prove it to you! [*With
great satisfaction to the other two* BARTHOLOMEUS.] I'll
prove it to him. [*To* IONESCO.] Do you know why plays are
written?

IONESCO. I don't know how to answer that. Let me think.

BART II [*to* IONESCO]. My dear chap, plays are written to be
performed, to be seen and heard by the public in a play-
house, like this one for example . . .

BART I. Well said, my dear Bartholomeus, well said, a very
profound thought . . .

IONESCO [*quite lost*]. I don't know whether . . . whether it's
profound, but it's certainly correct. Why, even I, in my
ignorance, I thought *I* knew that.

BART II. But that's not all. A theatrical performance brings
the theatre into being. A text is made to be spoken, and
who, do you think, should speak it? . . . Actors, my dear
fellow, actors. To put the idea succinctly, you might say
that performance is the breath of life to the theatre!

IONESCO. True. Yes, that's very true.

BART I [*to* IONESCO, *severely*]. It isn't true, it's more than
true, it's erudite, it's scientific!

BART III. Plays are made to be performed before an audience!

BART II. You can't say it too often: there's no theatre without
an audience!

BART I. And no theatre without a stage, or at least without
boards!

BART II. No stage without decor, no admission without ticket,
no box office without attendant, male or female . . .

BART III. No stage without actor.

VOICE [*from outside the door*]. Now look here, Monsieur
Ionesco, I've been here for an hour and I've got other
things to do. [*To someone else outside.*] I think they're
having a fight in there, perhaps they'll hurt him, should
I call the police?

IONESCO [*directing his words to the door*]. I'm coming,
Marie, I'll open the door . . . don't call the police . . . [*To
the three Doctors.*] Gentlemen, I'm very sorry, my room's
got to be tidied up a bit, you can see the state it's in, the
cleaner's waiting . . .

BART I. Don't worry your head about that!

IONESCO. It's so dirty.

BART II. That's not important!

MARIE'S VOICE [*from behind the door*]. If you don't open up, I'll call the concierge to break the door down.

IONESCO [*directing his voice to the door*]. I'm coming . . . I'm coming . . . [*To the Doctors.*] Gentlemen, Doctors, dear Maîtres, you've just said, haven't you, so wisely and so brilliantly explained that there's no theatre without an audience . . . then why not let Marie in . . . [*He makes for the door.*]

BART I [*to* IONESCO]. One second, wait until I give the order.

IONESCO [*to the door*]. Just a minute, I'm waiting for the order.

[*The Doctors whisper together, with much gesticulation, in conference.* IONESCO *is like a cat on hot bricks.*]

BART II. I think he'd better open it.

BART I. She might have the whole district up in arms.

BART III. We don't want any trouble with the police . . .

BART I [*to* IONESCO]. Go and open it, then . . . [IONESCO *starts moving.*] Wait, just a minute! . . . We can't let the audience in just like that. We've got to arrange the set, historicize it.

BART II. Let's arrange the set.

BART I. Open the treatise of the great Dr. Bertholus.

IONESCO [*shouting to the door*]. Be patient, Marie, just a little longer, they're getting the set ready.

MARIE. What's that?

IONESCO. The set. It won't be long!

[*Meanwhile the Doctors have consulted Bertholus' book and are fetching and arranging the props.*]

IONESCO [*to the Doctors*]. Hurry up. Gentlemen . . . please hurry up!

BART I [*reading from the treatise*]. It is essential to put up a sign to indicate the action . . .

[*At the front of one side of the stage* BART III *puts up a sign which reads*: A PLAYWRIGHT'S EDUCATION. IONESCO *goes up to it to read what is written and makes a gesture of despair.*]

[*Reading.*] . . . to summarize it and draw the public's attention to the fundamental epic attitude enshrined in each tableau . . .

[*At the opposite side of the stage* BART II *places another sign, on which is written:* STYLISED REALISM. IONESCO *crosses over to read once more what is written and makes the same gesture of despair.*]

[*His nose in the treatise.*] . . . To make it clear that the place is not a real one . . .

[BART II *abruptly sweeps all the books and papers from the table and hangs up a sign which reads:* FALSE TABLE. *Same reaction from* IONESCO.]

IONESCO. My manuscripts!! [*He tears at his hair.*]
BART I [*his nose still in the treatise*]. . . . that it makes no claim at all to represent a real place . . .

[*At the back of the stage* BART II *puts up a larger sign on which is written:* FALSE PLACE. *Same reaction from* IONESCO *who, his back to the audience, raises his arms in the air.*]

[*To* IONESCO.] Keep still, can't you, what's wrong with you? Instead of running wild like that, you'd far better help us with the props, which characterize the historical situation we're expected to pass judgment on.

[*Meanwhile, on an old armchair and on one of the chairs* BART I *and* BART II *place two signs which read:* FAKE.]

BART III [*aside*]. Fake is the concrete convention!
BART II [*aside*]. Fake is the abstract convention!
IONESCO [*to* BART I]. Yes, all right . . . all right . . . [*He runs wildly from one to the other.*]
BART I [*reading*]. Above all one must historicize.

[BART II *and* BART III *pull down a picture hanging on the back wall in order to put signs up in its place.* BART II'*s sign reads:* BRECHT TIME, BART III'*s sign reads:* BERNSTEIN TIME.]

BART II [*to* BART III]. Oh no, you've got the wrong period . . .
BART III [*to* BART II]. You've got the wrong period . . .
BART II [*to* BART III]. I'm very sorry but . . .

BART III [*to* BART II]. You're quite mistaken . . .

BART I [*interrupting his work and turning round*]. That's enough . . . come on now . . . Can't you agree?

BART III. I'm for Bernstein!

BART II. I'm for Brecht!

[*In their excitement the three* BARTHOLOMEUS *upset the furniture and other objects, while* IONESCO *tries despairingly and in vain to put everything back in place.*]

BART I. Gentlemen, Gentlemen . . .

BART III. Bernstein is great! I'll have no one but Bernstein! . . .

BART II. Brecht is the only god for me. I am his prophet!

[BART II *and* BART III *each brandishes his sign.*]

BART II *and* BART III. Brecht, Bernstein, Bernstein, Brecht!!!

[BART I *takes another sign, on which the words:* THE B CENTURY *are written in enormous letters. He fixes it in the middle.*]

BART I. There you are!

[BART II *and* BART III *go and fix their signs in place, one in each opposite corner of the stage.*]

IONESCO [*looking at the sign: The B Century*]. It's all the same to me.

BART I [*to* BART II *and* BART III]. That should settle the argument . . . Critics must stand together.

IONESCO. I like it better when they quarrel!

[BART II *and* BART III *contemplate the sign: The B Century.*]

BART II [*pointing to the sign*]. B, that definitely means Brecht.

BART III. B, that definitely means Bernstein.

BART I [*to the other two*]. You're both right . . .

BART II [*to* BART III]. What did I tell you?

MARIE'S VOICE. Well, what's up now? I'm waiting . . .

BART III [*to* BART II]. What did I tell you?

IONESCO. Do you think this time I could open the door?

BART I [*to* BART II]. Between ourselves, it means the century of Brecht, not Bernstein . . . [*To* BART III.] Between ourselves, it means Bernstein, an improved version, modernized and alienated . . .

BART III [*to* BART I]. What do you mean by that?

BART I [*to* BART III]. It's Bernstein just the same, still Bernstein, don't worry . . . [*He winks at* BART II.]

IONESCO. May I open the door? . . .

[*The three* BARTHOLOMEUS *turn together to face* IONESCO *again.*]

BART I. Yes, but you can't go like that . . .

BART II. Not like that . . .

BART III. Not in the state you're in . . .

IONESCO. What state am I in?

[*The three* BARTHOLOMEUS *inspect* IONESCO *from head to foot. They exchange looks, wagging their chins.*]

MARIE'S VOICE. There are limits, you know. [*Banging on the door.*]

BART I [*to* BART II]. Look . . . look at the way he's dressed . . .

BART II. It's incredible!

BART III. Such a mess!

IONESCO. But what's the matter with me then?

BART I. Ionesco, do you know why we wear costume?

[*The three Doctors show their costumes.*]

IONESCO. Why you're wearing costume?

BART I. Because, after all, actors and actresses can't go naked onto the stage.

IONESCO. Yes, I half thought . . .

BART III [*aside*]. And yet even nudity is a costume, say, at the Folies-Bergères!

BART II [*to* IONESCO]. If doctors of medicine care for the body's ailments, and priests the ailments of the soul, and theatricologists the ailments of the theatre, costumologists have a special care of the ailments of costume: they are costumological doctors. [BART II *and* BART III *sound* IONESCO's *clothes.*]

BART II. Everything is clothed . . .

IONESCO [*who struggles while* BART II *and* BART III *twist him round about*]. Gentlemen . . . Gentlemen . . .

BART III. Everything is clothed. The trees . . .

BART I. The animals, with their fur.

BART II. . . . The earth, with its crust . . .

BART I. The stars . . . fire, water and wind . . .

IONESCO. I don't understand.

BART I. We children of the scientific age, one day we'll learn how to distinguish the form of fire from its content.

BART III. The form of wind . . .

BART II. . . . from the content of wind . . .

BART I. The form of water . . .

BART II. . . . from the content of water . . .

BART I. The very walnut is clothed in its shell, which protects it and alienates . . .

BART III [*to* IONESCO]. Be a walnut!

BART II. We'll be nutologists . . .

BART I. Everything, everything is clothed! Costumology in fact is a veritable cosmology . . .

MARIE [*outside*]. What do you take me for?

BART II. . . . for by restricting the word, you widen the notion . . .

BART I. Costumology is also a moral science: costume must not be egocentric.

BART II. We know the whole pathology of costume.

BART III. Your costume is seriously ill . . . It's got to be cured . . .

IONESCO. It's true . . . it is a little worn . . . and moth-eaten . . . I admit.

BART III [*smiling at* IONESCO's *naïveté*]. *That's* not what we mean . . .

BART II. Your costume ought to be costumic, and if it isn't it's in that sense that it's ill!

BART I. You're not dressed like an author of our time . . . [*To* BART II *and* BART III.] Let's dress him!

BART II *and* BART III. Yes, yes, let's dress him!

BART I. A man is nothing without his clothes. Is a naked man really clothed? I dare maintain he is *not*.

[BART II *and* BART III *have been removing from the startled* IONESCO *his jacket, tie and shoes, which they promptly put back exactly as before.* BART II *and* BART III *perform this task while* BART I *perorates.*]

Clothing is an investiture . . .

IONESCO. I can see it's an investment.

BART III. It's also a little investition.

BART I. There are, as you've seen, a few simple little rules for telling whether a costume is ill or well . . . Yours is suffering from hypertrophy of the historical function . . . It's veridical . . .

BART II. And it shouldn't be . . .

BART I. Your costume is just an alibi. It's shirking its responsibility!

IONESCO. I've always dressed like this!

BART I. It's an end in itself.

BART II. It's no connection with your plays . . . or it's got too much.

BART I. It ought to be, without being, the costume of an author of our time . . .

BART II. It ought to be a sign.

BART III. Costume has its systematical side.

BART I. Your costume is suffering from faulty nutrition . . .

BART II. It's over-nourished . . .

BART III. It's under-nourished . . .

BART II. After all, it doesn't have to be destitute!

BART I. At least, it isn't beautiful! It's not suffering from any aesthetic disease . . .

BART II. Your costume must undergo a careful and exhaustive course of treatment.

[*An attempt is made to lower* IONESCO's *trousers. He protests*].

IONESCO. Gentlemen . . . it's not decent . . .

BART I. Your costume ought to tear at the heart!

IONESCO. Don't tear it . . . I haven't got another . . . It really is the only one . . .

[*Another pair of trousers is put on over* IONESCO's *pair*.]

BART I. And now for the system of signs, put his badges on . . .

[BART II *puts a sign on* IONESCO, *who is at this moment with his back to the audience. On it is the word:* POET.]

IONESCO [*sniveling*]. Please, Gentlemen, please. I don't feel I want to write any more at all!

BART III. Be quiet!

BART I. You were a free agent when you committed yourself.

[BART II *puts over his chest another sign, which is not yet visible.* BART III *puts a dunce's cap on his head.*]

BART I [*to* IONESCO]. You'll never escape again now . . .

[*They turn* IONESCO *round to face the audience. The word* SCIENTIST *is written on the sign over his chest.* IONESCO *grows more and more tearful.*]

BART II [*to the other two*]. We've made something of him, anyhow.

BART I. Now he belongs to us. We've historicized his costume!

[IONESCO *drops down at his table in the same position he had at the start. They raise him up, he falls forward, they raise him up again.*]

BART II. Not completely yet . . .

BART III. He's coming along, anyway!

BART II. We've still got to teach him to write!

BART III. In the way we want.

BART I. In the state he's in, it's plain sailing . . .

BART III. It'll be a piece of cake!

BART I [*to* IONESCO]. Now you're presentable, you can let the audience in.

IONESCO [*at the door, which is still being thumped, in a pitiful voice*]. I'm ready, Marie, I'm coming.

BART I [*looking round him with satisfaction*]. It's a regular laboratory!

BART II. We've done a good job of work.

BART III. We're not doctors for nothing.

[*The Woman's voice is still heard behind the door: Monsieur, Monsieur Ionesco!*]

BART I [*to* IONESCO]. Open it.

BART II [*to* IONESCO]. We'll let you.

BART III [*to* IONESCO]. Open it.

MARIE'S VOICE. Are you still there?

IONESCO [*pitiful as ever*]. Yes . . . just a second . . . What's the matter now? [*He stands up and takes a step to the door.*]

BART I [*to* IONESCO]. Be careful now, when you go and open it, to play the scene according to the theory of alienation.

BART III. I shan't tell you a fourth time.

IONESCO [*in the same tone as before*]. How do I do it? . . .

BART II. Without any self-identification. You've always made the mistake of being yourself.

IONESCO. Who else could I possibly be?

BART II. Alienate yourself.

IONESCO [*almost blubbering*]. But how do I do it?

BART III. It's perfectly simple . . .

BART I. Watch yourself acting . . . Be Ionesco not being Ionesco!

BART II. Look at yourself with one eye, listen to yourself with the other!

IONESCO. I can't . . . I can't . . .

BART I. Why don't you squint, then, squint! . . .

[IONESCO *squints.*]

BART III. That's the idea. [*To* BART I.] Well done, Bartholomeus!

BART II [*to* BART I]. Well done, Bartholomeus!

BART I [*to* IONESCO]. Now move to the door . . .

[IONESCO *says no more. He moves to the door like a sleepwalker.*]

BART III [*to* BART I]. Not like that!

BART I [*to* IONESCO]. Move forward one step! . . .

BART II [*to* IONESCO]. While you move two back! . . .

BART I. One step forward!

[IONESCO *moves.*]

BART II. Two steps back! . . .

[IONESCO *moves.*]

BART III. I shan't tell you a fifth time!

BART I. One step forward . . .

BART II. Two steps back . . .

BART III. That's it.

BART II. That's it . . . He's alienated himself! He's done it!

[IONESCO *should arrive right back at the opposite side to the door.*]

BART I [*to* IONESCO]. Now . . . dance . . .

BART II. . . . sing . . . talk . . .

IONESCO [*gambols about on the same spot and brays*]. Hee . . . haw . . . hee . . . haw . . . hee . . . haw . . .

BART I. Write!

IONESCO. Hee . . . haw . . .

BART II. Write harder!!

IONESCO. Hee . . . haw . . .

BART II. And scientifically!!!

IONESCO [*modulating his braying*]. Hee . . . haw . . . hee . . . haw . . .

BART I, II *and* III [*together*]. Write! Write!! Write!!! Write!!!!

IONESCO. Hee . . . haw . . . hee . . . haw . . . hee . . . haw . . .

BART I, II, III *and* IONESCO [*together*]. Hee! Haw! Hee! Haw! Hee! Haw!

MARIE'S VOICE. They're going to kill him! I'll break the door down!

[*Meanwhile the three* BARTHOLOMEUS *have donned dunce's caps too. While the four characters on the stage go on braying and gamboling about, the door flies open or falls in with a crash.* MARIE *comes in, broom in hand.*]

MARIE. What's all this about? A circus act?

BART I. Stop! . . . Here's the audience!

[*Stillness falls. The three* BARTHOLOMEUS *may or may not remove their dunce's caps, but* IONESCO *in any case keeps his.*]

MARIE. Well, so that's what you call your "set"? You've set everything upside down! How can I start cleaning your room now? . . . Monsieur Ionesco's untidy enough at the best of times, he didn't need you to help him! What have you got the poor man in this state for? And what are you doing, Messieurs, dressed up like that?

BART I. Madame, we'll explain everything . . .

MARIE [*pointing to the signs*]. You can start by clearing all that away!

BART II. Don't touch them, whatever you do!

MARIE [*threateningly*]. And why shouldn't I?

BART III. It's for you . . . we've been working for you, for the general public!

MARIE [*pointing to* IONESCO]. This isn't our carnival time! [*She moves to* IONESCO.]

BART III. Don't go near him or I'll bite!

MARIE. I'm not afraid of you! Just you try, you little mongrel! [*She turns on* BART III, *broom at the ready*.]

BART III [*recoiling*]. It was only a manner of speaking!

IONESCO [*to* MARIE]. Let me keep my distance . . . fifteen feet away from the audience.

MARIE [*to* IONESCO]. They've been having you on a piece of string! And you've let them get away with it . . . [*She goes up to* IONESCO *and turns him this way and that*.] A dunce's cap! . . . Poet . . . Scientist . . . You don't think that's clever, do you? They're making a fool of you!

IONESCO. Marie, you don't understand, these Gentlemen have given me a costumical costume and signalectical signs . . . These Gentlemen are learned doctors . . .

MARIE. Doctors? What sort of illness do *they* cure?

IONESCO. Yes, doctors . . . theatricologists, costumologists . . . they cure costume diseases . . . My costume was very ill!

MARIE. That's a funny thing to cure! Why didn't you send it to the cleaner's?

IONESCO. They're quite right, Marie, you don't understand, they're very clever scientists . . .

BART II. Listen to us, Madame!

MARIE. Just a minute! . . . [*She goes up to* IONESCO *and starts removing his signs and accoutrements*.] *To* IONESCO, *who is resisting*.] Come along, come on now . . . Let me put you back straight . . .

BART I. Madame, Madame . . . You really don't understand . . .

IONESCO [*to* MARIE]. They cure the theatre's ailments too.

MARIE. They ought to cure themselves . . .

IONESCO. They're great psychologists and sociologists!

BART II [*to* MARIE]. You hear what he says! He's saying it himself!

MARIE. That's because you've got him all tied up, he's lost his mind!

BART III [*to* MARIE, *who is removing the props*]. Leave them alone, can't you!

MARIE. I'll say I will! You needn't think *I'll* take any notice of you! . . . You'd better look out, if *I* lose my temper!

[*She lifts her broom and swings it round. The Doctors take refuge in the corners of the stage.*]

IONESCO [*intervening*]. Don't you hurt my doctors!

[MARIE *makes for the Doctors with her broom, after turning her sleeves up for action. The Doctors try to protect themselves from the blows to come.*]

BART II [*to* MARIE]. Wait at least until we've explained . . .

MARIE. Explained what?

IONESCO. Marie, I know now what function costume has . . . [*Reciting.*] In the theatre costume should link the content of the play to its externality.

MARIE. So you wrote a play which had an ordinary fireman in it . . .[3]

BART III [*reacting, shocked*]. An ordinary fireman?

IONESCO [*to* BART III]. Any reference to any character, living or dead, in one of my plays is purely coincidental.

MARIE [*to* IONESCO]. An ordinary fireman, yes, and on his head you put a fireman's helmet, a helmet, mind, and not a bride's veil . . . And so you really linked the content of your play with its externality! . . .

BART II [*who has recovered some of his assurance*]. Yes, you wrote in prose and never knew it!

IONESCO. That's what they're here to teach me!

MARIE. Oh, I'm sorry, Monsieur, but you really are ill! [*She slaps* IONESCO *twice in the face.*]

IONESCO. Where am I?

MARIE. You were hypnotized. That'll wake you up.

[*Dazed,* IONESCO *looks about him, pinches himself, takes off his dunce's cap etc.*]

[*To* IONESCO] They've got nothing to teach you! . . . These wretched doctors have no business giving you advice, it's they who ought to take lessons in drama.

IONESCO [*to* MARIE]. You really think so?

MARIE [*to* IONESCO]. I should say . . . of course they ought . . . You're a great big baby!

BART I [*indignantly*]. What's that? What's that? And what about theatricology?

[3] A reference to the character of the Fireman in Ionesco's *La Cantatrice Chauve*. The word for Fireman also provides a pun, which has been lost in translation. [Tr.]

MARIE [*pushing the Doctors towards the door*]. We couldn't care less. [*Quite ferociously following her attack right up to the door.*] You can get rid of all that rubbish!

BART II. And what about audienco-psycho-sociology!

MARIE. Scram!

BART III. Do you know who I am?

MARIE. Vamoose!

BART II. And decorology!

IONESCO [*rather frightened*]. Marie . . . Marie . . . Go easy . . . They'll tear me to pieces in their columns . . .

MARIE [*still pushing the three Doctors out and bundling more props into their arms*]. Don't be afraid of them, pack of good-for-nothings! [*To the Doctors.*] And take this away with you too . . .

BART I [*at the door*]. And the science of sciences, costumology?

BART II [*to* BART I, *recoiling back to the door with the others*]. Oh no, not costumology, costumitude!

BART I [*to* BART II]. What do you mean by that?

BART II. I'm a costumitudist, I study the essence of costume.

BART I. No such thing as the essence of costume! Costume's created by costumology . . .

BART II. It's exactly the opposite!

BART I. So you're an essentialist, then!

BART II. So you're a phenomenalist!

[BART I *and* BART II *come to blows.*]

BART III [*to* BART I *and* BART II]. It's all your fault! Filiburstering philosophisters! Snooty snobs!

BART I [*to* BART III]. Snob yourself!

BART II [*to* BART III]. Commercial hack!

BART III. A snob . . . I may be . . . but I'm a well-bred snob! . . .

BART II [*to* BART III]. Philistine!

BART I [*to* BART III]. You're a silly sot!

BART III. And proud of it!

BART II [*to* BART III]. Boar!

BART I [*to* BART III]. Pig!

BART III [*to* BART II]. Swine!

BART I [*to* BART II *and* BART III]. Hogsheads![4]

---

[4] The sequence in the original is "Calf! Cow! Pig! Brood!" a famous sequence from La Fontaine's fable *La Laitière et le pot au lait*. [Tr.]

IONESCO. Gentlemen, *please!*

EACH BART *to the* OTHER TWO. Phoneys! Phoneys! Phoneys!

MARIE [*to the Doctors*]. Go and fight outside!

IONESCO. Marie, a little less violence!

MARIE [*to* IONESCO]. But I tell you they're nothing to be afraid of! [*To the Doctors.*] Out! out! out!

IONESCO. Gentlemen, don't get too excited . . . don't get so angry!

[*The Doctors go out,* MARIE *pushing them. From the wings can be heard cries of:* "Costumology, costumitude, theatricology, psycho-audiencology . . . cology . . . cology."* IONESCO, *who is not exactly calm, stops suddenly next to the door. Then, while you can still hear* "cology . . . cology . . . cology . . .,"* he turns round, cups his hand to his ear and listens to the noise dying away. He walks quietly to the table, sits down with assurance and looks again toward the door.*]

Right! Come on now! . . . That's enough! The play is over . . . Back on stage!

[*The muffled sounds from the wings stop abruptly. Then, one by one, the three* BARTHOLOMEUS *come on and line up at the back of the stage behind* IONESCO, *who stands up and says:*]

Ladies and Gentlemen . . .

MARIE [*who now comes on with a glass and a jug of water*]. Just a minute . . . I expect you're thirsty . . . [*She pours some water into the glass.* IONESCO *picks it up and drinks it.*]

IONESCO. Thank you, Marie . . . [*Then, to the audience.*] Ladies and Gentlemen . . . [*He takes a paper from his pocket and puts on his spectacles.*] Ladies and Gentlemen, the text you have just heard was very largely taken from the writings of the doctors with me here. If you have been bored, I can hardly be held responsible; if you have been amused, I can claim no credit. The weaker lines and the obvious dramatic tricks are my own. Bartholomeus [*Pointing to* BART I.] is a pedant. Bartholomeus [*Pointing to* BART II.] is also a pedant. [*He hesitates.*] Bartholomeus [*Pointing to* BART III.] is an unpedantic fool. I blame these doctors for discovering elementary truths and dressing them up in exaggerated language so that these elementary truths appear to have gone mad. These truths, however, like all truths, even elementary ones, are open to argument. They become dangerous when they take on the appearance of infallible dogma, and when in their name scholars and critics claim to reject other truths and govern artistic creation even to the point of tyranny. The critic should describe, and not prescribe. Our learned doctors, as Marie has just told you, have everything to learn and nothing to teach, for the creative artist himself is the only reliable witness of his times, he discovers them in himself, it is he alone, mysteriously and in perfect freedom, who can express his day and age. Constraint and control—the history of literature is there to prove it—falsify this evidence and distort it by pushing it [*Gesture to the right.*] in one direction [*Gesture to the left.*] or the other. I distrust the truisms [*Gesture to the right.*] of one side as much [*Gesture to the left.*] as of the other. If however we admit that the critic clearly has the right to exercise his judgment, he should only judge a work on its own terms, according to the laws that govern artistic expression, the mythological structure of each work, and so penetrate each new universe afresh: we don't bring chemistry into music, we don't judge biology according to the criteria of painting or architecture, and astronomy is kept apart from political economy and sociology; if Anabaptists, for example, want to find in a play the illustration of their Anabaptist beliefs, they are free to do so; but when they claim that their Anabaptist faith overrides all and try to convert us, then I oppose them. For my part I believe sincerely in the poverty of the poor, I deplore it, but it is true and can serve as material for the theatre; I also believe in the grave cares and anxieties that may beset the rich; but in my case it is neither from the wretchedness of the poor nor the unhappiness of the rich that I draw the substance of my drama. For me, the theatre is the projection onto the stage of the world within: it is in my dreams, my anguish, my dark desires, my inner contradictions that I reserve the right to find the stuff of my plays. As I am not alone in the world, as each one of us, in the depths of his being, is at the same time everyone else, my dreams and desires, my anguish and my obsessions do not belong to myself alone; they are a part of the heritage of my ancestors, a very ancient deposit to which all mankind may lay claim. It is this which, surpassing the superficial diversity of men, brings them together and constitutes our deepest fellowship, a universal language.

[MARIE *takes one of the Doctor's gowns and moves nearer* IONESCO, *who is sounding more and more pedantic.*]

It is these hidden desires, these dreams, these secret conflicts which are the source of all our actions and of the reality of history. [IONESCO *is working himself up into an almost aggressive state, very solemn and very ridiculous, accelerating his delivery.*] You see, Ladies and Gentlemen, I believe the language of modern music and painting, as well as the language of physics and higher mathematics and the very essence of history itself are well in advance of the language of the philosophers, who, far behind, painfully struggle to keep up . . . Scholars are always behind the times, because, as we are told by the eminent Bavarian Steiffenbach and his American disciple Johnson . . .

[MARIE, *who has come right up to* IONESCO *during the last sentence, suddenly throws the gown over his shoulders.*]

But . . . what are you doing, Marie, what are you doing?
BART I. Are you by any chance taking yourself seriously, Ionesco?
IONESCO. Taking myself seriously? No . . . yes . . . I mean no . . .
BART III. It's your turn now to turn academic!
BART I. To be or not to be a doctor, you know, it's the same thing!
BART II. You hate us to give you lessons and now *you* want to give *us* one . . .
BART I. You've fallen into your own trap.
IONESCO. Oh . . . this is all very upsetting.
MARIE. One swallow doesn't make a summer.
IONESCO. I'm sorry, I won't do it again, this is the exception . . .
MARIE. Not the rule!

THE WRITERS AND THEIR PLAYS

HENRY BECQUE—1837–1899 (publication dates) *L'Enfant Prodigue*, 1868; *Michel Pauper*, 1871; *Les Honnêtes Femmes*, 1880; *Madeleine*, 1896; *The Departure*, 1897; *An Execution*, 1897; *The Crows*, or *The Vultures*, 1912; *A Quiet Game*, 1913; *The Merry-Go-Round*, 1913; *The Parisian Woman*, 1913. Opera: *Sardanapale* (with Victorian Joncières), 1867.

JEAN GIRAUDOUX—1882–1944 (completion dates, except as noted) *Siegfried*, 1928; *Amphitryon 38*, 1929; *Judith*, 1931; *The Enchanted*, 1933; *Tessa*, 1934; *End of Siegfried*, 1934; *The Trojan War Will Not Take Place (Tiger at the Gates)*, 1935; *Supplement to Cook's Voyage*, 1937; *Electra*, 1937; *The Improvisation of Paris*, 193*; *Song of Songs*, 1938; *Ondine*, 1939; *The Apollo of Bellac*, 1942; *Sodom and Gomorrha*, 1943; *The Madwoman of Chaillot*, 1945 (production date); *Duel of Angels*, 1953 (production date).

JEAN ANOUILH—1910– (completion dates) *Humulus the Dumb*, 1929; *Mandarine*, 1929; *Attila the Magnificent*, 1930; *Hermine*, 1931; *Jezabel*, 1932; *Thieves' Carnival*, 1932; *The Savage*, 1934; *There Was a Prisoner*, 1934; *The Small Happiness*, 1935; *Traveler Without Baggage*, 1936; *The Rendezvous at Senlis*, 1937; *Léocadia*, 1939; *Eurydice (Legend of Lovers)*, 1941; *Antigone*, 1942; *Romeo and Jeanette*, 1945; *Medea*, 1946; *Ring Round the Moon*, 1947; *Ardèle*, 1948; *Episode in an Author's Life*, 1948; *The School for Fathers*, 1949; *The Rehearsal*, 1950; *Colombe*, 1950; *Waltz of the Toreadors*, 1951; *The Lark*, 1952; *Ornifle*, or *The Current of Air*, 1954; *Poor Bitos*, or *The Dinner of Heads*, 1956; *The Fighting Cock*, 1958; *Becket*, 1958; *La Petite Molière*, 1959; *The Grotto*, 1961.

MICHEL DE GHELDERODE—1898–1962 (publication dates) *Piet Bouteille*, 1918; *La Mort Regarde à la Fenêtre*, 1918; *Le Repas des Fauves; The Old Men*, 1919; *Le Cavalier Bizarre*, 1920; *A Night of Pity*, 1921; *Le Mystère de la Passion de Notre Seigneur Jésus-Christ*, 1925; *oude Piet*, 1925; *The Death of Dr. Faust*, 1925; *Three Actors and Their Drama*, 1926; *The Public Life of Pantagleize*, 1926; *Escurial*, 1927; *Christopher Columbus*, 1927; *Images de la Vie Saint François D'Assise*, 1927; *Venus*, 1927; *The Women at the Tomb*, 1928; *Don Juan*, 1928; *La Transfiguration dans le*

Cirque, 1928; *Barabbas*, 1928; *Chronicles of Hell*, 1929; *La Tentation de Saint Antoine*, 1929; *The Slaughter of the Innocents*, 1929; *Pantagleize*, 1929; *The Actor Makes His Exit*, 1930; *Masques Ostendais*, 1930; *Le Ménage de Caroline*, 1930; *Le Club des Menteurs*, 1930; *Duveloor, ou La Farce du Diable Vieux*, 1931; *Red Magic*, 1931; *Le Sommeil de la Raison*, 1931; *Le Voleur d'Etoiles*, 1931; *Prosper de Troyer*, 1931; *Arc-en-ciel, Féerie*, 1933; *Le Siège d'Ostende*, 1933; *The Blind Men*, 1933; *Le Soleil se Couche*, 1933; *La Balade du Grand Macabre*, 1934; *Lord Halewyn*, 1934; *D'un Diable qui prêcha Merveilles*, 1934; *Miss Jairus*, 1934; *Adrian et Jusemina*, 1934; *Godelieve*, 1934; *Hop, Signor!*, 1935; *La Pie sur le Gibet*, 1935; *La Farce des Ténébreux*, 1936; *The School of Buffoons*, 1937; *Jeudi Saint*, 1943; *Le Singulier Trépas de Messire Ulenspiegel*, 1951; *Le Perroquet de Charles-Quint*, 1951; *La Folie d'Hugo van der Goes*, 1952; *La Farce de La Mort qui Faillit Trépasser*, 1952; *Marie la Misérable*, 1952.

HENRI DE MONTHERLANT—(1896–   ) *L'Exil*, 1929; *Queen After Death*, 1942; *No Man's Son*, 1943; *Un Incompris*, 1943; *Malatesta*, 1946; *The Master of Santiago*, 1947; *Pasiphae*, 1949; *Tomorrow the Dawn*, 1949; *Celles Qu'on Prend Dans Ses Bras*, 1950; *La Ville Dont La Prince Est Un Enfant*, 1951; *Port-Royal*, 1954; *Brocéliande*, 1956; *Don Juan*, 1958.

IONESCO, EUGENE—1912– (completion dates, except as noted) *The Bald Soprano*, 1948; *The Lesson*, 1950; *Jack, or Submission*, 1950; *The Chairs*, 1951; *The Motor Show*, 1951 (production date); *The Future Is in Eggs*, or *It Takes All Sorts to Make a World*, 1951; *Victims of Duty*, 1952; *Amédée*, or *How to Get Rid of It*, 1953; *The New Tenant*, 1953; *Les Grands Chaleurs* (based on a play by Caragiale), 1953 (production); *The Maid to Marry*, 1953 (production); *The Leader*, 1953 (production); *Le connaissez-vous*, 1953 (production); *La Nièce-Épousé*, 1953 (production); *Le rhume Onirique*, 1953 (production); *The Picture*, 1955 (production); *Improvisation*, or *The Shepherd's Chameleon*, 1955; *Impromptu pour la Duchesse de Windsor*, 1957; *The Killer*, 1957; *Rhinoceros*, 1958; *Foursome*, 1959; *The Pedestrian in the Air*, 1962; *Bedlam Galore, for Two or More*, 1962; *The King Dies*, 1963.

SELECTED BIBLIOGRAPHY

GENERAL
CHIARI, JOSEPH *The Contemporary French Theatre*, New York, 1959.

FOWLIE, WALLACE *Dionysus in Paris, a Guide to French Contemporary Theatre*, New York, 1959.

GROSSVOGEL, DAVID *The Self-Conscious Stage in Modern French Drama*, New York, 1958.

GUICHARNAUD, JACQUES *Modern French Theatre: from Giraudoux to Beckett*, New Haven, 1961.

PRONKO, LEONARD *Avant-Garde: The Experimental Theatre in France*, Berkeley, 1962.

PUCCIANI, ORESTE *The French Theatre Since 1930*, Boston, 1954.

WELLWARTH, GEORGE *The Theatre of Protest and Paradox*, New York, 1964.

HENRY BECQUE
BENTLEY, ERIC, *The Playwright As Thinker*, New York, 1943, revised, 1955.

HUNEKER, JAMES *Iconoclasts*, London, 1905.

WAXMAN, S. M. *Antoine and the Théâtre Libre*, Boston, 1926.

MICHEL DE GHELDERODE
FRANCIS, JEAN *Michel de Ghelderode*, Brussels, 1949.

GHELDERODE, MICHEL DE "The Ostend Interviews," *Tulane Drama Review*, Volume III, No. 3, 1959. "To Directors and Actors: Letters 1948–1959," *Tulane Drama Review*, Volume IX, No. 4, 1965.

HERZ, MICHELINE "Tragedy, Poetry and the Burlesque in Ghelderode's Theatre," *Yale French Studies* (No. 29), 1962.

LILAR, SUZANNE *The Belgian Theatre Since 1890*, New York, 1950.

Tulane Drama Review, Ghelderode Issue, Vol. VIII, No. 1, 1963.

JEAN GIRAUDOUX
INSKIP, DONALD, *Jean Giraudoux, The Making of a Dramatist*, London, 1958.

LeSage, Laurent *Jean Giraudoux, His Life and His Works,* University Park, Pa., 1959.

Tulane Drama Review, Giraudoux Issue, Vol. III, No. 4, 1959.

JEAN ANOUILH

Champigny, Robert "Theatre in a Mirror: Anouilh," *Yale French Studies,* No. 14, 1955.

Marsh, E. O. *Jean Anouilh: Poet of Pierrot and Pantaloon,* London, 1953.

Nelson, Robert *Play Within a Play,* New Haven, 1958.

Pronko, Leonard *The World of Jean Anouilh,* Berkeley, 1961.

HENRI DE MONTHERLANT

Hobson, Harold *The French Theatre of Today,* London, 1953.

Laprade, Jacques *Le Théâtre de Montherlant,* Paris, 1950.

Montherlant, Henri de *The Master of Santiago and Four Other Plays,* trans. with an Introduction by Jonathan Griffin, New York, 1951.

EUGENE IONESCO

Coe, Richard *Eugène Ionesco,* New York, 1961.

Corrigan, Robert W. *The Theatre in the 20th Century,* New York, 1962.

Esslin, Martin *The Theatre of the Absurd,* Garden City, 1961.

Ionesco, Eugene *Notes and Counter Notes,* New York, 1964.

Tulane Drama Review Ionesco—Genet Issue, Vol. VII, No. 3, 1963.